The West Wind Blows

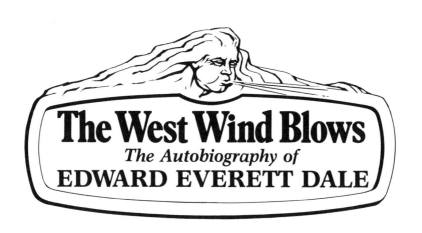

The West Wind Blows
The Autobiography of
EDWARD EVERETT DALE

Edited and With an Introduction by
Arrell Morgan Gibson

Oklahoma Historical Society
Oklahoma City
1984

To the memory
of
my father and mother

Library of Congress Catalog No.: 84-060270

Dale, Edward Everett
The West Wind Blows
  1. Dale, Edward Everett—Biography. I. Title.
ISBN 0-941498-40-9

Contents

Introduction

by Arrell Morgan Gibson[1]

When I see a prairie Schooner
  With the tongue a-pointing west
What a mighty nameless longing
  Always swells and fills my breast.
For it's headed toward a country
  I shall always love the best
Toward a land of stars and sunshine
  Toward the prairies of the West.[2]

Edward Everett Dale divided his life story into two parts, his intention being to publish a two-volume autobiography, the first volume dealing with his boyhood on the North Texas Cross Timbers frontier, the second volume to depict growing to manhood in Old Greer County, relating his experiences as a cowboy, homesteader, and pioneer school-master on the Oklahoma Territory frontier, and his later professional life. Dale completed the manuscript for the first volume in 1965 and published it the following year under the title *The Cross Timbers: Memories of a North Texas Boyhood.* He chose to title this second volume of his autobiography *The West Wind Blows.* Dale was still active as a writer and lecturer in his nineties; he was composing the closing comments on his incomparable life experiences when he died in 1972 at the age of 93.[3]

The first volume of Dale's autobiography is out-of-print, and the reader without benefit of access to it necessarily requires some knowledge of Dale's origins in order to couple with the second volume of his life story. It begins with his family's move from the hardscrabble North Texas farm to Old Greer County, where the Dales switched from farming to ranching, and continues his life narrative to 1972, the year of his death.[4]

Both volumes fairly throb with human motion. Dale acknowledged that it was a "family trait of restless feet itching to scratch strange gravel." His great-grandfather was a Maryland sea captain; his son, and Dale's grandfather, migrated from Maryland to Kentucky where John Dale, Edward Everett's father, was born. Thence the Dales followed Daniel Boone into Missouri. John Dale grew to manhood on the Missouri frontier. During the California gold rush he ventured to the Pacific to seek his fortune, driving an ox team across the plains, mountains, and deserts to the lodes of the Sacramento. Returning to Missouri with a comfortable stake he settled on the Nebraska frontier for a time, then moved to Texas, taking a farm in the lower Cross Timbers of Tarrant County. John Dale lived the stern doctrine of the Primitive Old School Hardshell Baptist Church which braced him for the hardships and challenges of pioneering.[5]

Edward Everett Dale was born in 1879 on this north Texas farm. By the time he was five years old Edward labored at his father's side clearing brush to open more cultivable land and working the fields of cotton and corn. The youth's knowledge of the frontier was twofold—his personal exposure and experience in the pioneer milieu; and from the lore imparted by his father, which extended back to the time of Andrew Jackson. His father's role in the drama of expansion of American settlement from Kentucky to Missouri, the trek to California, then into Nebraska, and on to Texas provided Dale a genuine genetic and cultural connection with this epic and also a model—Edward Everett Dale, as he admits in the second volume of his autobiography, was no less peripatetic than his forebears.

The force of the pioneer family in Dale's experience included a frontier mother who listened attentively to the prattle of her young son and who taught him to read at the age of four. Her tender devotion imparted to Dale an awe for pioneer womanhood which he romanticized in *Prairie Schooner* verse. She died when Dale was five, leaving him to the care of a brother, George, five years his senior.

George was young Dale's interpreter of the universe, the source of all wisdom, patiently answering the many questions raised by the very curious little brother. Dale acknowledged his debt to George, recalling in the autobiography's second volume that his brother was his "guide, philosopher and friend. . . . Always to me he was fountainhead of all wisdom, and everything he told me was accepted as Gospel truth."

Until the age of thirteen, Dale commented that he had not had "any schooling to amount to anything," probably in attendance no more than twelve months altogether. Most of the years of his early youth Dale worked in the fields of the Cross Timbers farm. In the second volume of his autobiography he explains why the school term began in late November and lasted only a few months. "As in many other parts of the South at this time cotton picking had a distinct priority over education. There was ample reason for this. Few local school districts had enough money for more than a three to five month-term of school. To begin it in September when the cotton-picking season was just opening and let the children remain idle during the latter part of the winter and early spring did not make sense" to Cross Timbers farm parents.

Dale attended school briefly at the age of eight, and advanced to the fourth then, in a few weeks, to the fifth-grade reader group. For the most part he had to content himself with reading the Bible, his father's church paper *Signs of the Times, Pilgrims Progress*, Longfellow's *Poems*, and *The Farm and Fireside*.

Dale recalled in *Memories of a North Texas Boyhood* that at an early age he became aware of a special sense of being, in which he included George. He explained, "I began to feel that George and I were not quite like the other boys of the neighborhood. This did not mean a feeling that we were better or worse than other kids of the community but only that we were *different*. Just how or why we were different never occurred to us, but it seems clear to me now that because we both read a good deal we lived, to some extent, in a make-believe world, into which few of our boyhood friends could enter."[6]

The Cross Timbers in the 1880s was a zone of blending cultures as people from the Deep South, Middle Border, and a few from the East settled the country. Even as a youngster Dale was sensitized to the interactive processes at work here, and he was able to recapitulate them in the autobiography's first volume as swatches of childhood flashbacks, depicting the cultural cross-fertilization occurring on this agricultural frontier. Certainly these flavored his adult life and surface in various forms in the autobiography's second volume.

Young Dale was fascinated by visits in homes of members of the Hardshell Baptist Church, centering on women quilting, patching worn clothing, and sewing garments, while their "tongues often moved faster than their fingers as they discussed the local news and gossip." Superstitions and taboos, powerful individual and group behavior determinants, were rich grist for the folklorist's mill. Dale reported the injunction against killing frogs in a pond, for such an act would cause cows using the water to give bloody milk. The pain of an infant at tooth-cutting time was eased by the mother tying a mole's foot around the baby's neck. And old men in the community often carried potatoes in their pockets to ward off rheumatism.[7]

The Puritan values of Cross Timbers society hallowed certain female parts and functions and banned them as subjects of public discussion. A "woman did not break her leg but a 'lower limb.'" Dale commented that with "floor-length skirts and the use of the term 'limb' it almost seemed that it was social error for a woman to admit that she had legs. . . . To refer to an unmarried woman's future children was a grave social error. . . . Such words as 'belly,' 'boar,' and 'pregnant' were never used in mixed company." When a woman was pregnant the euphemism "in a family way" was used to describe her state.[8]

Indelibly impressed in Dale's recollection was the compassion of Cross Timbers society—one instance of an ancient blind woman left alone by the untimely death of her son he reported. Rather than see her committed to the county poorhouse, the members of the local Primitive Baptist Church agreed to keep her in their homes as long as she lived. She resided with the Dales for two months.[9]

The workings of Cross Timbers nester culture exposed Dale to extra-legal practices which he later revealed to his mentor at Harvard, Frederick Jackson Turner, confirming for the eminent frontier historian that which to him had been theory as an inevitable American pioneer response. Dale observed neighbors substituting simple arbitration for "going to the law" to settle disputes over land, property boundaries, or stock ownership. His father was called upon several times to assist in this process. The two parties to the dispute, Dale explained, beforehand agreed to settle that matter by private arbitration. The local arbitration panel consisted of three men, each party to the dispute appointing one man, and these two choosing a third. The extra-legal frontier tribunal investigated the matter in dispute, heard the evidence, and rendered a decision which both parties had agreed to accept as final.

Young Dale moved easily and enthusiastically from the agrarian routines of the Cross Timbers farm to ranching on the prairie-plains. The tone of the second volume of his autobiography rings with the relief at this change in lifestyle. He quickly learned the technique of handling range cattle and horses, helping his father on the Greer County ranch and riding as cowboy for neighboring ranchmen. Also Dale explains that occasionally he worked as a trail driver, moving herds from north Texas ranches to new ranges in the Cherokee Outlet near Woodward in Oklahoma Territory.

He gloried in the free life of the cowboy. Later in essays on life in the prairie-plains environment, he stressed the easier existence in the region, both for ranchmen and the intruding nesters, permitting a more *simpatico* lifestyle than was possible in the Cross Timbers. People in this new land had more leisure than had been the case for the early settlement frontiers in the East. He found the prairie-plains a more permissive region, its mores permitting dancing, card-playing, and other forms of frontier entertainment which were banned in the Puritan-Primitive Baptist culture of the Cross Timbers.

Dale explains that the pioneer on the prairie-plains had more leisure because of environmental conditions which to a large degree determined the economic enterprises conducted there. Stockmen had considerable leisure because their industry required during the year only short periods of intensive labor and close attention at roundups, and in winter feeding made necessary by occasional blizzards. Otherwise the herds required only casual attention, the rich grasslands and mild climate making it possible for the animals to shift for themselves. This allowed ranching families much more time for visiting, dancing, and other recreation.

Dale noted that the intruding nester also had more leisure on the thick grass-carpeted prairie-plains. He had no forests to clear and was liberated from his eternal contest with the ubiquitous sprouts, which each planting season had to be grubbed from the soil after the trees had been removed. Also the one-crop emphasis of the agrarian frontier extension into the prairie plains in cotton and wheat production required only intensive seasonal attention, permitting the nester during certain periods of the year time for other activities which had not been the case in the multi-activity, self-sufficient agrarian frontier of the East.

From the leisure available to the pioneer in the prairie plains environment Dale drew the opportunity to continue his education, and the description of his first contact with adult education, found in the second volume of his autobiography, brings to light another frontier institution—the Camp School.

As 1900 approached his life story indicates that Dale's frontier seasoning was nearly completed. A combination of incidents led him to a teaching career in the prairie-plains pioneer schools, which ironically began as a means and became in a sense, an end, in that this was the beginning of a formal two-step process for him to transmit his legacy of frontier experience. He and his brother George were eager to become independent ranchmen on a partnership basis. Beginning with the small tract they had inherited from their father and a few cows, they leased additional range and attempted to stock their expanded pastures with cattle purchased by money borrowed from a local livestock commission company. Dale decided to prepare himself to teach school, his salary to grubstake their ranching enterprise.

He explains that for about two months he attended the school at Navajoe, a settlement in Greer County serving the nesters, ranchmen, and Indian trade from the nearby Kiowa-Comanche Indian Reservation. Then he applied for and passed the territorial examination, receiving a certificate stating that he had completed the equivalent of eighth grade school work. Next he enrolled in a four-week county normal institute for teachers at Cloud Chief, a village situated to the north in the Cheyenne-Arapaho country, a vast tract recently opened to homesteaders. The institute was held in the village schoolhouse. On enrollment day Dale recalled that teacher candidates rode in from all directions, extra clothing and a few books in a sack tied on behind each saddle. At the end of the four-week term Dale submitted to the territorial examination. Dale said the county superintendent who graded the examinations for certification "tempered justice with mercy" and he passed, and received a certificate stating that he was qualified to teach in the schools of Oklahoma Territory. His first school was at Clabber Flat near Navajoe on a contract calling for a three-month term at twenty-five dollars a month. He enrolled fifty-eight pupils, ages six to twenty, with one student twenty-four. At the time for added income Dale recalled that he held a commission as deputy sheriff.

Dale reported that teaching to build a grubstake for expanding their ranching operations was to no avail. In 1900 he and his brother went broke in the ranching business, wiped out by limited pasture, a harsh, killing winter, flooded cattle markets, and low beef prices. They sold their land, cattle, most of the horses, household and even personal effects to settle their debt with the livestock commission company. Dale lamented that while the brother partners had "paid the last dollar" of their debts, they faced a "grim and bleak future."

The autobiography's second volume discloses that Dale had one last experience in pioneering before his frontier legacy was completed. In 1901 he and George homesteaded in the Kiowa-Comanche country. They selected a 160-acre claim on Otter Creek. Dale's recollection of their search and ecstatic discovery of the homestead was a reiteration of the pioneer's land lust lyric which had sounded time and again since the 1790s. He recounted, it was situated in "a lovely valley about a mile and a half wide and extending approximately the same distance north to where Otter Creek emerged from a deep canyon in the mountains. The valley was open to the south but was hemmed in by low mountains on the east and west. We turned east, and crossed the crystal clear stream flowing over a colorful mosaic of many colored pebbles." It was the "loveliest valley we had ever seen. It was level as a floor and covered with grass reaching to our stirrups." He added, "As we looked to the north we were fairly dazzled by the prospects before us. Clearly this was it!"

Dale returned to teaching to earn a stake to develop the Otter Creek homestead. His role as schoolmaster on the Oklahoma Territory frontier included teaching at Red Fork, Duke, Headrick, Roosevelt, and Blair. In 1905 he relates his beginnings in higher education by enrolling at the Territorial Normal School at Edmond to strengthen his teaching credentials. Attending full time in 1908, he graduated the next year with a two-year associate degree. Formal education had disturbed his pioneer moorings and quickened his desire for further study. When he announced his plan to enroll at the University of Oklahoma in Norman, cowboy friends are reported to have expressed their doubts that this was the best step for him to take, pointing out that when he graduated he would be well past thirty. Dale is supposed to have answered them with a simple but compelling logic that he expected to live past thirty-one anyhow, and the really important question was whether he wished to reach that age with a bachelor's degree. His educational record thereafter is well-known. He enrolled at the University of Oklahoma in 1909 and graduated two years later with a Bachelor of Arts degree in history. Thereupon he applied for admission to Harvard University for graduate study and received the Austin Teacher's Scholorship. At Harvard he fell under the spell of Frederick Jackson Turner, who according to Dale "opened . . . a new Heaven and a new earth in the field of American History." He completed the Master of Arts and Ph.D. degrees at Harvard and received successive appointments to the University of Oklahoma faculty in the Department of History as instructor, and assistant, associate, and professor, chairman of the department, and later George Lynn Cross Research Professor.

Sharpened by academic study and Turner's influence, Dale proceeded vigorously to the formal dissemination of his frontier experience heritage. His writings consist of eighteen books, sixty essays and articles, and six volumes which he edited. Many of his writings are braced with scholarly research, but all of them are seasoned with his frontier heritage. Of Dale's books, *The Range Cattle Industry* (1930), *Cow Country* (1942), *Indians of the Southwest* (1949), and *Frontier Ways* (1959) loom the strongest. The essays which dominate his bibliography are "Old Navajoe," "Two Mississippi Valley Frontiers," "The Speech of the Pioneers," and "Cow Country in Transition."

Dale's value to Western historiography is less that of a stern scholar producing new knowledge from intensive research, and more that of a participant in much of the drama of frontier development, sharing his experiences with a vicarious reading public. His best, most engaging, compelling, and significant writings were derived from his legacy of frontier experience. This does not mean that Dale did not himself engage in serious research and expect the same from his students. The important thing about Dale is that he did not need to do research to write important books and essays, but simply to share what he already had experienced. Dale must be regarded less a hard-nosed professional historian and more of a romantic interpreter of the frontier milieu. He was never the bitter, carping cynic, but always the enduring optimist, a living witness, a vibrant participant to what he interpreted, taught, and wrote about. If Dale requires a professional identity, he could be classed as a social historian, more interested in people than presidents.

Edward Everett Dale was a bridge, a sparkling spirit and genuine link connecting the simplistic frontier past and the complex technological present. With splendid poise, disarming innocence, and sensitive response he provided exciting, living connective tissue between these two eras through a long and distinguished career as teacher and writer. This volume of his autobiography, with the already published volume one, provides future reading generations an illuminating vista on the incomparable life story of a truly uncommon man.

> So when from the ties that bind me
>   I at last shall break away.
> Leave each sordid task behind me,
>   As I surely shall someday.
> When I choose a craft for cruising
>   Love or fortune as my quest,
> It will be a prairie schooner
>   With the tongue a-pointing west.[10]

Endnotes

[1] Portions of this essay are adapted from Arrell Morgan Gibson, *Frontier Historian: The Life and Work of Edward Everett Dale* (Norman, 1975).

[2] Edward Everett Dale, *The Prairie Schooner and Other Poems* (Guthrie, 1939), p. 14.

[3] Edward Everett Dale, *The Cross Timbers: Memories of a North Texas Boyhood* (Austin, 1966).

[4] At that time, 1892, Greer County was a part of northwest Texas, but in 1896 the U.S. Supreme Court assigned it to the emerging Oklahoma Territory.

[5] Interview with Edward Everett Dale, Norman, Oklahoma, December 5, 1969.

[6] Dale, *Cross Timbers*, p. 46.

[7] *Ibid.*, pp. 144-145.

[8] *Ibid.*, p. 157.

[9] *Ibid.*, p. 156.

[10] Dale, *Prairie Schooner*, p. 14.

Preface

In 1913 it was my good fortune to be awarded a $250 Austin Teachers' Scholarship by Harvard University. Naturally this pleased me a great deal, but since at that time I had never been outside Texas and Oklahoma except for a brief visit to relatives in Nebraska, it seemed wise to try to get a little information about this strange region which was to be my home for the next year. Accordingly I called upon one of my former professors who had been born and bred in New England.

"You will like Boston and Boston people, Dale," he said when he had heard my story, "And they will like you." Then after a moment's hesitation he added, "Oh, not right at first perhaps but just as soon as you get used to the ice and they get used to the wind you'll like one another fine."

Probably my friend was only joking or it might be that any ice among the people of Greater Boston was melted by the warm wind of the West. At any rate I never found it during the total of three and a half years that it was my privilege to live among Boston people, but found only courtesy, kindness, and generous hospitality.

It is true that my best efforts were directed toward conforming, in some degree, to their customs and pattern of society and curbing the exuberance acquired by many years of life on the plains of the West. Now, over half a century later, and some 2000 miles removed from the glories that are New England, it is possible to write as a Westerner thinks and feels.

It must be confessed that I have written largely from my own recollections. As a student and teacher of history, however, I fully realize that "memory may be the most plausible and convincing of liars." Such being the case, old letters, family papers, diaries, pictures, account books, and other materials have been used to verify dates and some details of events. To persons who have helped to supply these, to my former secretary who typed the manuscript, and to my wife Rosalie whose encouragement and help have been of inestimable value, I express my sincere thanks and deep appreciation.

Whether or not my life story is worth writing or reading may be questionable, yet my memory reaches back over by far the most eventful nine decades of a century that the world has ever seen. Within my own life span have come greater changes to people than any period of a thousand years prior to my birth.

My own contributions to these changes or to the world-shaking events of the past seventy-five years have been negligible. Even in the settlement and development of my own homeland, the American West, my part has been a minor one. Thousands of other lads have migrated to the almost unpeopled Western plains, "grown up with the country," and learned to love the land because they "had been children together."

Perhaps this alone is some justification for telling this story of my life, for it is not my story alone. It is that of many thousands of others who helped win to civilization a raw, untamed land when the wooing was difficult and sometimes dangerous and most of whom now sleep in its bosom. Largely speaking it is the story of social and economic evolution in the American West, because society is made up of individuals. When a million individuals of a region have passed from a crude and primitive pattern to one of high standard of living, a new social order has emerged.

Anyone who expects to find accounts of thrilling adventures and hair-raising experiences in this book will be disappointed. Yet, the words of a little rhyme occur to me. It deals with an old man's recital to a friend of the happy life of a couple whom he had known since their wedding forty years before. When the friend walked away apparently disappointed, the narrator concluded:

> Well now he seemed a little bored
> And I reckon that I was wrong
> To tell him such a commonplace yarn
> Of two such commonplace lives
> But we can't all get drunk and gamble and fight
> And run off with other men's wives.

The West Wind Blows

Pioneer Forbears

Without entering into the age-old controversy of the relative importance of heredity and environment, it seems clear to me that my life has been considerably affected by the fact that my immediate ancestors were restless pioneers. My great grandfather was a sea captain who grew to manhood on the eastern shore of Maryland. My knowledge of him is very slight, but he was apparently engaged in trade with the West Indies but may have made an occasional voyage to the East Indies.

My grandfather left Maryland as a young man and migrated in the wake of Daniel Boone to Kentucky. He died long before I was born, but family tradition pictures him as a man slightly above medium height but of enormous strength and vigor who made seven trips down the Ohio and Mississippi rivers with flatboats loaded with flour and bacon for the New Orleans market.

Perhaps grandfather had what has been called by the late Professor Channing "a constructive memory," but many colorful stories have been told me of his adventures as he walked back across the Indian country to Kentucky with the gold received from the sale of cargo and flatboat in a money belt around his waist next to the skin. Even one such jaunt would hardly be called a pleasant little "Sabbath day's journey," but the very thought of seven such treks is appalling.

Of my grandfather's own family I know little, for most Westerners seem to have more interest in the ancestors of their livestock than in their own. I know, moreover, that he had four sons of whom my father was the third, and that there was a daughter, Elizabeth, commonly known as "Aunt Lib." It was never my privilege to see her or any of these uncles except Uncle Isaac, two years younger than my father. Uncle Ike was a salty old character—a frontiersman born and bred who once told me that he had lived for a time "with old man Cody," uncle of Buffalo Bill, who was then "just a little shirttail kid runnin' around the yard of the Kansas Prairie home."

About 1833, when my father was three years old, grandfather decided that Kentucky was no longer any place for an up-and-coming man. The game in the woods had been killed off, and most of the best land had been gobbled up by well-to-do Easterners who demanded eight or ten dollars an acre for it, farm hands wanted up to a dollar a day for their work, and the country had become so thickly settled that from your front door you could see the smoke of three or four chimneys. Missouri must be a wonderful place to live, so once more following the example of Daniel Boone, he sold his farm, gathered up his family and four Negro slaves, and headed west for Missouri.

The family settled on a tract a little northwest of Richmond, the county seat of Ray County. Here my father grew to manhood and from here he started westward in 1850 for the California gold fields, walking all the way beside the ox team pulling his covered wagon. Upon reaching one of the newer mining districts, he took a claim and set to work panning gold. In this he was not too successful but said later that he never washed out less than five dollars worth of gold a day, which was not bad, even in a land where the price of food and every other commodity was extremely high. When his claim played out after about a year, he was determined, like many others who had braved the hardships of the journey across the plains, to return home by ship.

From San Franciso he sailed to Panama and walked halfway across the Isthmus to the upper waters of the Chagras River where Negro boatmen took him down that stream to the sea. Here he boarded a ship for New Orleans and from that city went by steamboat up the Mississippi and Missouri rivers to Lexington. From that historic

Missouri town it was only a few miles walk to his father's home near Richmond.

Back among his own people again with money in his pocket, Father soon married Louise Colley, bought a farm, and established a home of his own. Children came along with astonishing rapidity; Louise Colley bore my father six sons and four daughters; a son and a daughter died in childhood. In 1858, following the discovery of gold in Colorado, he again drove his covered wagon westward to this new El Dorado. He took a claim near Denver but found no gold, and in a few months he returned home.

The four years of the Civil War were hard ones for the people of Northwest Missouri. Bands of guerrillas, bush-whackers, and thieves and outlaws roamed the countryside stealing, robbing, and murdering peaceful citizens. Among them were Quantrill, Frank and Jesse James, and "Bloody Bill Anderson." As a small boy I was often regaled with stories of these troublous times, including one to the effect that when Bill Anderson was killed, he had the scalp of one of my cousins tied to his saddle horn.

Although my father did not believe in slavery, his urgent need for more help on the farm prompted him to buy a young Negro field hand just before the outbreak of the war. He remained completely loyal to the Union, however, and while he did not serve in the Northern Army, he became a member of the Home Guards, who were furnished arms by the Union government and sought to preserve order in this border region.

For some years after Appomattox he continued to live on this Missouri farm, during which time Louisa died. After about two years he married Louisa's younger sister, Mattie Count Colley, who was to become my mother five years after the birth of her first child, my brother George.

In the early 1870s his fast growing family, the rising prices of land, and above all, his own restless spirit, led him to remove to Nebraska. The journey seemed short to a man who had walked all the way to California. The Missouri farm was sold, the tools and household goods were loaded into covered wagons, and two older sons were detailed to drive the cattle. His younger brother Isaac, my Uncle Ike, had already visited Nebraska and Kansas, and he and his family, a son and two daughters, formed part of the little caravan migrating to the western prairies.

The two families settled on Rock Creek about sixteen miles northeast of present Lincoln, filing on lands under the homestead laws of the United States. However, settlers were so numerous that my father was able to secure only eighty acres of choice land instead of the usual homestead of 160 acres. He energetically set to work to improve his property by building a house and barn, breaking sod, and planting an orchard and vineyard.

For four or five years the two brothers and their families were very happy working from dawn to dusk widening and fencing their fields, erecting more farm buildings, and growing crops. Then when the harsh years of pioneering seemed over and they could live comfortably, Texas beckoned, a land free from bitter Nebraska winds and deep snows. The climate was mild, land said to be fertile and cheap, and reportedly free of grasshopper plagues. Moreover, it was a new country as yet undeveloped.

The farms were sold, the wagons again loaded with the families and all movable property and accompanied by one or two of the neighbor boys eager for adventure, the long journey across Kansas and Indian Territory to Texas was begun. Uncle Ike's wife had died leaving him with a son and two daughters, one of them old enough to keep house for him.

The Texas migration was begun very early in the autumn. Weather was pleasant and game was plentiful, especially in the Indian Territory. Stories have been told me of how the older boys shot turkeys, squirrels, and quail to add to the food supply and the smaller fry picked up pecans and gathered wild plums and grapes. Also there was a fiddler in the party and every night after supper the young people danced by the light of the campfire.

The journey ended at Eagle Ford near Dallas. Here they erected tents and camped for the winter, the men and older boys working at various jobs they might find, and using their wagons and teams in freighting goods or hauling lumber and other building material.

6

My father's older children were by this time young men and women, and Henry, his eldest son, had acquired a farm in Nebraska so he did not accompany the rest of the family to Texas. When winter was over the second son, Frank and his chum, who had been a member of the migrating party, decided each to buy a horse and saddle and return to enter the University of Nebraska. About this time the sweetheart of the oldest daughter, Fannie, came down from Nebraska, married her, and took her back to his home in the Rock Creek community. This divided the family into two branches, one in Texas and the other in Nebraska. In addition, my father's older brother, Moses, had remained in Missouri and reared a large family.

During the winter my father had been looking about for a farm which he might buy, but land was higher than he had expected. As a result, shortly before his two older children left for Nebraska, he rented for three years a fairly large blackland prairie farm in the northern part of Tarrant County some twenty miles southwest of Denton. It was improved with a comfortable frame house and fields enclosed by hedge fences. It was in this house that I was born on February 8, 1879.

Little as I know of my paternal ancestors, my knowledge of my mother's people is far less. I only know that they were Virginians named Colley and that Grandfather Colley migrated from Virginia to Northwest Missouri with his family and settled in the same community as Grandfather Dale. Apparently he also was of the restless, adventurous type because he started for California to seek gold, probably in 1849. Grandfather Colley was never to see this land of his dreams for he died on the trail and was buried at that monument to so many of the Argonauts, Independence Rock.

His death left his widow to carry on the Missouri farm with the help of the children, a grownup daughter, two teen-age boys, and a younger daughter ten years of age.

It has not been my privilege ever to see any of my mother's people, but old family stories have given me the impression that her brothers, John and Jim, were inveterate readers.

Also, in their younger days they devoted much time to hunting, fishing, courting the neighborhood girls, and playing the fiddle while weeds grew in the corn. Whether my itching feet, always eager to scratch strange gravel, are an inheritance from these pioneer forbears is only a guess. At any rate my background has been such as to occasion little surprise when my wife says that ever since our marriage I have dragged her about over the world like an old mother cat drags little kittens!

Chapter

II

Home on the Range

The story of the ten years of my life as a boy in the Texas Cross Timbers has been told with some detail in a book published in July, 1966, by the University of Texas Press. These years from the age of three to thirteen were the formative period of my life. Here, under the guidance and discipline of a somewhat stern and puritanical father, were developed in me those fundamental principles of living which have remained with me ever since.[1]

Here, too, I acquired certain skills that have proved of great value. These included not only the ability to cook but to do every phase of housework as well as of farm labor. In addition I learned to ride, swim, fish, hunt, and to take care of myself at all times and in virtually any situation.

Perhaps even more important, I had learned to curb my blazing temper, to share with others my scanty possessions, and always to be respectful of my elders and to all women. Up to this time, my interest in girls was quite negligible, but it was my belief that all of them were just a little lower than the angels. This feeling still lingers to some degree, but it must be confessed that over forty years of teaching in a co-educational university have at times brought grave doubts as to the complete validity of any such assumption!

In 1889 my father decided to leave the Tarrant County farm and remove to Greer County, Texas. Several of my

---

[1] Edward Everett Dale, *The Cross Timbers: Memories of a North Texas Boyhood* (Austin: University of Texas Press, 1966).

Picnic party at the Navajoe Mountains, southwestern Oklahoma. (Courtesy Western History Collections, University of Oklahoma Library)

brothers and sisters had taken claims there, and because I had visited them as a small boy, I was somewhat acquainted with the region where we were to settle.

We had all felt some regret at leaving the old home but looked forward eagerly to the one on the Western plains. Sadly we gave the cats to the neighbors, but our old dog, Turk, could go west with us, trotting along beneath the wagon. The old musket had become totally useless and the Kentucky rifle had been traded to a neighbor, but just before we left my father bought me a second-hand single-barrel twelve-gauge shotgun.

The trip westward was made without incident, and within about a week we reached Vernon, Texas. We stopped there for the night at the Davis Wagon Yard[2] and had just finished supper when we were surprised by the arrival of Uncle Ike who had driven down for a load of supplies for the stores at Navajoe.[3]

We remained there the following day in order to buy our winter's supply of groceries and clothing, and then, with Uncle Ike accompanying us, continued on the last lap of our journey.

Since we had started very early every morning of our trip and did not camp until nearly sundown, there had been little opportunity to use my gun. After leaving Vernon, however, a bit of sheer good luck enabled me to impress the whole party with my ability as a marksman. Soon after we had crossed the South Fork of Red River, a small flock of prairie chickens flew across the road and alighted in the tall grass about a hundred yards away.

I slipped a shell in the gun and approached them with the stealthy tread of an Indian. As they rose in flight I threw the old Zulu to shoulder, pointed it in their general direction and

---

[2] The wagon yard, commonly found in each southwestern settlement, provided overnight comfort for travelers and teams including grain, hay, and water for stock, and cooking facilities with firewood. The larger yards often maintained a crude bunkhouse with beds much like motels today, although most travelers slept in their wagons.

[3] See Edward Everett Dale, "Old Navajoe," *The Chronicles of Oklahoma*, XXIV (Summer, 1946), pp. 128-145.

pulled the trigger. To my great surprise two of them fell. Uncle Ike stood up in his wagon and yelled at the top of his voice:

"Hooray! If he didn't kill two of 'em a-flying' I'm a liar and so I am!"

For the moment my reputation as a wing shot was made, but unfortunately it did not last long.

We had fried prairie chickens for supper that night and early the next afternoon reached our new home. Uncle Ike continued on to his farm some nine miles farther north while we unloaded the wagon, moved in, and set up housekeeping.

Great changes had been wrought on this claim since I had last seen it several years before. The old dugout had been filled up and Henry had built an unpainted lumber room connecting with the half-dugout where Jay and I had bached the winter of 1888-89. After his marriage, Henry had added another larger room to this which was painted white and had a lightning rod on the roof. As a result, we had three rooms extending east and west. From the white painted east room one descended two steps to the middle room and from that about four steps to the half-dugout. As a result we were far in advance of our time for we had a fashionable "split-level house!"

The village of Navajoe had grown very little, but Mattie's husband, Herbert Acers, had built them a new three-room house about a hundred yards west of the store and had turned part of the former living quarters into a room for the storage of surplus stock such as flour, barrels of syrup, and other bulky commodities. They now had another little girl called Hazel, but their business was fast going on the rocks.

Herbert, who was a born gambler, began to neglect the store to devote his time to playing monte or poker with the Indians. Most of the nearby reservation had been leased to ranchmen for grazing, and upon receiving their "grass money" bands of Indians would come to Navajoe, pitch their tipis at the edge of town, and spend a few days and nights gambling with the three or four professional card sharks of the village and any others who happened to feel lucky. In less than a year Herbert's tendency to gamble and chase women was to result not only in the collapse of his and Mattie's business but of their marriage as well.[4]

There was no one at our new home when we reached it, but John and Ava lived half a mile away in a big sod house which they had built on their claim joining my father's on the west.[5] Henry's wife and small daughter were with Virgie's parents, who lived six or seven miles west of us, while he and Jay were in the Cheyenne country on Henry's claim busily engaged in improving it. A few more settlers had moved in during the past two years but not many and there were large areas of vacant land all about us.[6]

After a day or two of visiting Mattie and John and Ava, my father's characteristic energy foced him to start work improving the farm. The orchard trees which Henry had planted had grown surprisingly fast and promised an abundance of fruit the following year. A couple of good sized fields had been plowed and planted in kaffir corn which had been cut and stacked in one of the lots. The only buildings on the claim, other than the house, were some hay-covered sheds and a cellar that had been built near the half-dugout kitchen.

Most of the 160-acre tract, however, was covered with tall bunch grass and the fences were poor and needed repair. In addition, more sheds and lots were needed and my father who had spent a fair share of his time for the past ten years in felling trees now was eager to plant them as soon as spring came. Also, he purchased two milk cows and four pigs.

---

[4] This is the Kiowa-Comanche reservation, situated across the North Fork of Red River to the northeast and adjacent to Old Greer County.
[5] The prairie-plains sod house was used for pioneer shelter in regions of scarce timber. It was constructed of blocks of thick, heavily-rooted grassland, sliced from the surface with a sod plow, cut into blocks generally twelve inches by eighteen inches, three to four inches thick, and placed like large, flat bricks to form the house wall. The sod house roof generally was made of laced sapling limbs covered with several inches of clayey soil.
[6] The Cheyenne country refers to the Cheyenne-Arapaho reservation situated on the northern edge of the Kiowa-Comanche reservation. Until it was opened to homesteaders in 1892, most of it was under lease to cattlemen.

George helped father with this work, and I did my bit including part of the cooking and housework, but a large share of my time was given to ranging the prairies and fields with my gun in search of game. A family lived on the claim joining ours on the east, another on the south, and a third on the one joining John's claim on the south. All of these had planted fields of corn, kaffir corn, and milo maize, some of which had been cut and shocked. Every evening flocks of prairie chickens flew in from the tall grass to feed in these fields.

This gave me a golden opportunity to display my marksmanship, but I soon discovered that my feat of bringing down two birds from a small flock at one shot had been only sheer luck. Nevertheless, I visited these fields nearly every evening, and tramped through the tall grass by day banging away every time one or more prairie chickens rose but discovered that my ability as a wing shot had been vastly overestimated. Even so, by expending much powder and shot, I was able to make considerable contributions to the family larder.

A couple of weeks after our arrival Henry drove down to get a wagon load of his furniture and asked me to go back with him to his claim in the Cheyenne country where he had left Jay to bach alone.[7] When we reached the sandy hills near the North Fork of Red River, I got out of the wagon with my gun to examine some likely looking cover for quail. In a small plum thicket some fifty yards from the road I found a large covey and fired into it killing four.

We forded the river at the old crossing of the Western Cattle Trail and camped for the night in a grove of mesquite trees. After supper of fried quail, bread, jam, and coffee, we spread our blankets on the soft buffalo grass and slept warm and snug though the night was a bit cool. The following morning we were up at dawn, and I prepared breakfast while Henry fed and harnessed the horses.[8]

---

[7] "Bach" is derivative of bachelor, a colloquialism for living alone.
[8] Western Cattle Trail is the Dodge City or Great Western Cattle Trail, a stock highway running from Fort Worth northwesterly to Doan's Crossing on Red River then across Oklahoma to the western Kansas cow towns, primarily Dodge City.

Once on the road again we soon passed out of the mesquite trees onto a level prairie where we saw a good many longhorned steers, for we were on that part of the Kiowa-Comanche Reservation leased to the Muleshoe Cattle Company. We caught sight of a few coyotes from time to time and after ten or twelve miles went through a gate onto the Bar-LO range. Late in the afternoon we crossed the north line of the reservation into the Cheyenne country where we saw an occasional house though most of the area was as yet unsettled. About a mile from the border we passed a small store and post office known as Combs. The proprietor's home was nearby and those of a couple of other settlers. About two miles farther on we reached our destination.

Henry had built a big sod house near the south edge of his claim some 200 yards from the creek which was bordered by trees. This house had a dirt floor and a big fireplace at the north end, a cookstove in the southwest corner, a long dining table along the central part of the west wall, and a few benches, chairs, and stools. There was an open cupboard near the stove and beds along the east wall.

Jay had taken in James and Black, two ranchers who had several hundred head of cattle grazing on the unfenced public lands nearby. They ate and slept in the house and had killed a beef a day or so before our coming so we had an ample supply of fresh meat. In addition a Mr. Giles, who had a sod house on his claim joining Henry's on the east, ate with us so there were six of us in the house every night with Jay doing the cooking, although I soon joined in to help him.

It was truly a man's world in which I found myself, but this was nothing new to me. Naturally there was a great deal of rough "man talk" but again this was nothing new and my two weeks spent there were most enjoyable. My days were largely spent in hunting but every evening after supper we assembled around the open fire and I listened eagerly to the talk and stories of the men. Jay, who next to George was my favorite brother, was the life of the party but the others made their contributions and helped much in promoting my education and increasing, if not exactly enriching, my vocabulary.

After a few days Henry and Giles took me on a trip into the rougher country farther north to get a couple of wagon loads of timbers for erecting other sod buildings. They took the beds off their wagons, and with bedrolls and chuck box strapped to the "running gears" we headed north. There was not even the semblance of a trail, but we jolted over the rough prairie following a tiny stream called Spring Creek which cut across a corner of Henry's claim. Near its head we came to a grove of trees where two men on horseback were engaged in netting quail. It was a misty day and the birds, reluctant to fly, could easily be driven into the open end of the V-shaped nets terminating in a small covered pen.

Not to interfere with their work we went around them and some miles farther on came to a broad canyon with a small stream flowing down its center. The canyon floor was covered with trees including hackberry, elm, ash, coffee bean, and walnut. This seemed a good place to cut timbers so after some search we located a gentle slope by which it was easy to get the wagons down to the floor of the canyon where we made camp.[9]

The next morning Giles and Henry set to work cutting and trimming small trees, usually coffee bean which was light but durable wood. After washing the breakfast dishes I started hunting. We had seen several deer that afternoon but always at some distance which they promptly increased when they saw us. Also we had seen many prairie chickens and one or two wild turkeys. Trails made by deer were abundant and their tracks were all about so my great hope was to bag one.

Instead of taking Henry's Winchester, however, I put a couple of shells loaded with buckshot in one pocket and in another a dozen with smaller shot for turkeys, prairie chickens, and quail. Not taking the Winchester was a mistake. I had not gone far until a small deer appeared on the open ground 100 yards away. He was too far away, but I

---

[9] Coffee bean tree, attains height of 80 to 100 feet, leaves oval-shaped and sharply pointed, one to three inches long; greenish white flowers appear in May or June, and the fruits mature in late summer, flat green to brown pods four inches long each containing several seeds.

slipped in a buckshot shell and took a shot at him, but he merely trotted away over the ridge bordering the canyon, apparently not much alarmed by the report of the gun.

Considerably crestfallen by my lack of success, I returned to camp and helped the men all afternoon. When we quit work about sundown, Henry and I began cooking supper while Giles took the Winchester and, telling us not to wait supper for him, strolled off down the canyon. We were finishing our meal when we heard a couple of shots followed by two or three more. Then we heard Giles yelling so Henry mounted a horse bareback and soon returned with the hunter and a two-year-old buck, which we promptly dressed and hung in a nearby tree. The next morning we loaded the poles and deer on the wagons and reached home a little before night.

A week later Henry and I returned to my home and my hunting of prairie chickens and quail, and working to improve the farm, were resumed. Jay came down to spend Christmas and soon after asked me to join him on an expedition to poison wolves. The cattlemen who were pasturing herds on the Indian reservation were having much trouble with coyotes and the big "lobos," the Spanish word for wolf, which everyone corrupted into "loafers." These killed calves and even yearlings.

Accompanied by Speed Smith, one of Jay's neighbor boys who was about twenty-one years old, we packed the wagon with a camping outfit and crossed the river at Trail Crossing into the Indian country. Our technique was to split the carcass of a rabbit, tie it by a piece of rope to the rear of the wagon and drag it across the prairie stopping every 50 or 100 yards to lay our baits. These were small pieces of beef liver split nearly half in two with strychnine inserted in the split and edges squeezed together so the animal would swallow it without getting the bitter taste of the poison.

We killed three coyotes the first night and the second, while camped at the foot of a small mountain, got two more as well as two large "bob cats" or catamounts. Speed had been a cowhand in the Texas Panhandle the previous year and, like Mr. Daugherty of our cotton-picking days some years before, knew only one song which he sang continuously morning, noon and night.

> I'll sell my horse and sell my saddle
> And I'll bid farewell to the long horned cattle
> And it's ti yi yoopy yoopy ti yi yay
> And it's ti yi yoopy yoopy yay.
> There's a stray in the herd and the boss says kill it
> And we'll all sop gravy out o' one big skillet
> And it's ti yi yoopy yoopy ti yi yay
> And it's ti yi yoopy yoopy yay.
> We jumped in th' wagon and we fetched one yell
> And th' goose neck broke and th' leaders went to
> hell
> And it's ti yi yoopy yoopy ti yi yay
> And it's ti yi yoopy yoopy yay.[10]

Speed sang it so much that we finally voted, two to one, to fine any fellow who started to sing this "ti yi yoopy song" twenty-five cents, which was the price of a bottle of strychnine.

I went with Jay on some other "wolfing trips" on one of which we got six coyotes in a single night. The skins sold for only about fifty cents each but that was important money in our community. Poisoning wild animals seems horrible to me now but one who has seen the remains of a calf or yearling hamstrung by two or three wolves and the helpless animal half devoured while still alive did not feel too much sympathy for the victim of a heavy dose of poison which killed almost as quickly as a bolt of lightning.

By this time my impression gained four years earlier that this was a land of abundant leisure had been fully confirmed. My father was evidently chafed a bit because of this, and he also missed his church and the former association with his Old-School Baptist brethren. As spring approached, however, the necessity of planting crops gave him the opportunity to devote his energy to farm work. This

---

[10] A parody on the cowboy classic "Strawberry Roan."

also took some time from my hunting, but as there was no closed season for game and no bag limits, I still ranged the surrounding region with my gun when not called upon to plow and plant or set out slips of cottonwood about the borders of the fields.

In addition to planting sorghum cane, and the non-saccharine sorghums, kaffir corn, and milo maize, which were just coming into this country from Africa, my father decided to plant a small patch of cotton. This had been our chief "money crop" on the Cross Timbers farm, but our Greer County neighbors asserted that he was wasting his time as it would never mature on these Western plains. They were wrong, of course, for this county now produces more cotton than any other in Oklahoma. We also put out a great many sweet potato slips for father was determined to have something to sell that fall, even if the price of farm products was almost unbelievably low.

The year of 1893 went by on wings bringing some changes to the Dale clan. In September, 1893, the great Cherokee Outlet of over six million acres in northern Oklahoma was opened to settlement by a run in which an estimated 100,000 persons took part. A little before this the creditors of Herbert Acers sent a receiver to take over his business. This left Herbert free and footloose so he left to join the ranks of the gambling fraternity which flocked to the new towns of the Outlet. Of his later movements we learned little, but he never returned to his family.[11]

During the summer I had made some trips to Henry's place in the Cheyenne country to which he had brought his wife and baby girl as soon as the new home was made ready for them. Yet I was usually at home helping to maintain our new bachelor's hall, working a bit on the farm, and doing some fishing and hunting on the reservation. In November we picked probably the first bale of cotton ever grown in what was then Greer County, Texas. Father and I hauled it

---

[11] Cherokee Outlet, often confused with Cherokee Strip, a 6 million-acre tract west of 96 degrees extending to 100 degrees, flanked on the north by 37 degrees and on the south by 36 degrees 30 minutes, and assigned to the Cherokee Nation by the Treaty of 1828.

the forty-five miles to Vernon where the nearest cotton gin was located. It brought $4.85 a hundred pounds which gave us less than twenty-five dollars for growing and picking the bale of cotton and spending four days on the trip to market. Clearly farming in this region was not a remunerative occupation and there seemed some reason for the leisurely life of its few widely scattered inhabitants.

Growing Up
With The Country

Early in February, 1894, came my fifteenth birthday, and the next few years were my "salad days." In the Cross Timbers expression, used in referring to a teenage girl, I was "between grass and hay." Boyhood days and ways were very slowly being replaced by some of the attitudes and responsibilites of a man, although some might be found ready to assert that I've never yet quite made the grade!

Herbert's store was sold by his creditors to George Blalock who had taken a claim adjoining Navajoe on the south and built his home near its north line only two or three hundred yards from his new place of business. The druggist, W. H. H. Cranford, secured the post office and built an addition to his store to house it. He also removed the drugs to one side of his store and installed a stock of dry goods and clothing on the other side.

Mattie and her two little girls spent the winter of 1893-94 in her home but at the suggestion of Jay and Henry, she took a homestead in the Cheyenne country joining that of Henry on the west. To this the two brothers removed her Navajoe house and set it down on the prairie about two hundred yards west of the sod house home of Henry and his family.[1]

While Mattie had only a common school education, she was quite a good musician and owned a "Chicago Cottage Organ." Jay, who still had his claim about a mile farther

---

[1] The nester shack, a frame structure generally twelve feet by fourteen feet, boxed and covered with tar paper, could easily be jacked up, fitted with running gear, and drawn to a new location.

down the creek, had been living with Henry and Virgie but now removed to Mattie's home to look after her and the two children. Just how they were able to live seems to me now something of a mystery, but Jay had been elected county commissioner, an office which required little time and provided a small salary. It helped and, with milk cows, pigs, and a garden, they managed to get along.

The white house of three big rooms was by far the most commodious residence in the community and soon became something of a social center. It was seventy-five miles to the nearest railroad point and the area was thinly peopled, mostly by small ranchmen since to haul farm products that distance was virtually impossible. In consequence everyone had ample time for social diversions, which were usually square dances, and Mattie's home became a favorite place for such affairs.

As this was essentially a man's country, every dance was attended by numerous "stags" and comparatively few girls and women. Music was furnished by an old fiddler named Van Horn, while Mattie would "second" on the organ. Such a dance might last all night with supper served at midnight. Cowhands would gladly ride fifteen or twenty miles to attend. Some man would be appointed bookkeeper to list the names of all male dancers, who usually paid twenty-five to fifty cents for the privilege of dancing. This money was divided between the two musicians, but if supper was served the fee for every man was a dollar.

It was my privilege at fifteen to attend one of these dances at Mattie's home. Henry and Virgie served a midnight supper at their home, and the last set was danced after sunrise. While I did not dance, sitting up all night to watch those who did left me almost a wreck by daylight! As there were so many men, the few girls must have danced almost every set, and after a hasty breakfast mounted their horses and rode in a side-saddle ten to twenty miles to their homes. Surely if "men were men" in that region, women must have been women too!

Mattie's home was large enough to run two sets of four couples each. As there were often twenty or thirty men, Van

Horn and Mattie might have ten or twelve dollars to divide between them for their evening's work, which was important money at that time. By playing for a couple of dances at different homes in the community every week, they derived quite a little income.

Most of these affairs were conducted with great decorum. Girls would usually refuse to dance with a man if his breath smelled of liquor. More important, to come to dance half drunk was regarded as a personal affront to the host and hostess at whose home it was held. Upon one occasion when a drunken cowhand appeared at a dance held at Mattie's house, Jay with his Winchester under his arm promptly waited upon the offender and the man who accompanied him, and demanded that they betake themselves elsewhere "immediately if not sooner." The sober one offered his apologies, and in two minutes they were both mounted and on their way.

While I made many visits to my relatives in the Cheyenne country during the next couple of years, most of my time was spent at home with Father and George. Although there was not much work to be done that promised any financial return, my father could usually find something to keep us all busy. Such tasks included improving the place and putting out sweet potatoes, which we hauled to Vernon and sold for fifty cents a bushel. We also grew a little corn, made a big garden, and there were always such chores as cooking and "keeping house," feeding and caring for the livestock, milking cows, and running errands.

Much of my spare time, however, was still given to hunting. Prairie chickens could be sold at Vernon for twenty-five cents each and quail for ten or eleven cents. As a result I spent most of one or two winters in hunting for the market. Hunting was never for sport but for food, and one who had subsisted for days upon a diet consisting largely of bread, butter, blackeyed peas, fat bacon, and "sorghum molasses" found a mess of fried quail or stewed prairie chicken and dumplings a most welcome change. In addition, any surplus game that was sold provided a little cash.

Money was almost unbelievably scarce. The ranchmen

had money, of course, and so did the cowhands to whom they paid twenty to forty dollars a month. Most of the settlers, however, seldom had more than a few coins in the pockets of their faded jeans and many never had as much as fifteen dollars all at one time during an entire year. Prices were extremely low, but this meant nothing to the man who had no money at all and no means of getting any. With flour selling as low as a dollar to a dollar and a half a hundred pounds, frying chickens at fifteen cents each, and beef at five or six cents a pound, it is not surprising that a dinner consisting of baked chicken, two or three vegetables, pie and coffee could be had at almost any hotel or restaurant for twenty-five cents.

Clothing and other commodities were equally cheap. A pair of work pants could be bought for seventy-five cents, "Sunday shoes" for two dollars, a good suit of clothes for ten or eleven dollars, and the best in stock for fifteen. We sold peaches from our orchard at fifteen cents a bushel, and I was twenty years old before discovering that there were any watermelons other than the nickel and dime sizes, or that eggs were sold at over ten cents a dozen. Under such conditions the only ways in which a settler might get any money was by selling a little feed to some ranchman or loading his family into a covered wagon in the fall and going to Texas or the Chickasaw Nation to pick cotton for a couple of months.

Some twenty years later my teacher at Harvard, Frederick Jackson Turner, asserted that persons who left their homes in the wooded areas of the East to settle lands in the Prairie West felt their horizons broadened by this new environment. Whether or not this is true it is certain that our migration from the Texas Cross Timbers to the level plains of Greer County soon gave us a different conception of distance. In our old home in East Texas we seldom knew anyone who lived over three or four miles away, and it is doubtful if my father made the sixteen-mile trip to Fort Worth more than once every two or three years.

Here on our prairie claim it was very different. We might visit relatives in the Cheyenne country, thirty-five miles to the north, every month or so and make some half-a-dozen trips to Vernon, forty-five miles to the south, in a single year. When my father, who had been ordained a minister, at last located a small community of Old School Baptists about fifteen miles west of our home, he frequently visited it. Much later he discovered another about twenty-five miles northwest of Henry's claim in the Cheyenne country. This church had preaching once a month, so in good weather father would sometimes ride on horseback the sixty miles to this neighborhood and would occasionally preach either the morning or the evening sermon. Usually my trips to Vernon with father were uneventful enough. They were made to sell a bale of cotton or load of sweet potatoes, which we often peddled out to residents of the town, or sometimes only to buy provisions and articles of clothing. We camped on the prairie the first night, reached town before noon the following day, and after transacting our business, drove far enough back on the return journey to reach home the third day. On one or two occasions when it was necessary to spend the night in Vernon, we always stayed in the wagon yard which cost only fifteen cents for stalls for the horses and the privilege of cooking and sleeping in the camp house.

One trip which I made with Ava, John's wife, however, lasted a full week. John was teaching school thirty miles away that year and Ava and her eight-month-old baby were living all alone in their sodhouse home. She wanted to go to Vernon and asked me to go with her. We camped beside a little schoolhouse the first night and when it began to rain went inside to sleep on pallets spread down on the floor.

The sun was shining when we awoke the next morning and while the Red River was a bit muddy we were able to cross it without difficulty and reached Vernon safely. It rained heavily the next night, and on our return when we reached Doan's Crossing we found the river a raging torrent over a half a mile wide. Fortunately, Ava had a friend living near Doan's Crossing with whom we stayed three or four days with Ava and the baby sleeping inside the house and I in the wagon. The river seemed fordable by this time, so we drove into the muddy water only to get stuck in the quicksand some forty yards from the opposite shore.

I unhooked one of the horses, carried the baby out, deposited him on the wet sand, and returned for his mother. I then rode up the road in search of help and found a kindly farmer who brought his mule team and pulled us out. We then resumed our journey and about sundown reached a small dugout home beside the road. The family, consisting of an elderly man, his wife, and two grown daughters, earnestly urged us to stop and spend the night with them as it was beginning to rain.

They had only two beds but made down a pallet for Ava and the baby on the hard-beaten dirt floor in one corner of the room while I slept in the wagon beneath its canvas cover. Unfortunately it rained hard most of the night, and the dugout roof leaked in several places. Ava's bed was in the driest corner and she and her baby did not get very wet, but when I came in the next morning the formerly hard-beaten dirt floor was mud a couple of inches deep. The two girls were busily engaged in getting breakfast, walking about barefoot with the soft mud squishing up between their toes at every step.

After a breakfast consisting of only large hot biscuits, butter, and milk, we hitched up the team and headed for home reaching it about noon. The trip of forty-five miles and back had taken a week, but time was of little importance in this prairie land in the last decade of the nineteenth century, and such experiences were only part of my "growing up."

It seemed that I never had much in common with most of the boys about Navajoe, but on the claim adjoining ours on the east lived Jim Ferris with his wife and nine children. Ferris had moved to Greer County from near Austin, Texas. He was a man of considerable education and was a son of W. A. Ferris, who accompanied John C. Fremont on some of his western explorations. Jim was a professional peace officer who had been a Texas Ranger, secret service operative, and was currently deputy sheriff.[2]

---

[2] John C. Fremont, called the Pathfinder for his several explorations during the first half of the nineteenth century, across the American West, several of them ending on the Pacific Coast.

His second son Warren, about my own age, became my closest friend and companion. His father had been an inveterate hunter when he was not chasing cattle thieves and bandits along the Rio Grande. He told me that one year he had killed 104 deer. He was by far the best rifle and pistol shot I have ever known, which is saying more than it sounds like. I have seen him put two shots through a badger's head at seventy-five yards with a .45-caliber Colt's revolver, and hit a spot the size of a dollar five times in succession with a .38 Colt's army pistol at a distance of sixty feet.

Warren was a "chip off the old block." We hunted together on every possible occasion and usually brought in plenty of game, for he carried his father's big ten-gauge Winchester shotgun which would reach out much farther than my single barrel twelve-gauge. His father was so accustomed to hunting big game that he scorned joining us in hunting birds and squirrels, but two or three times he took us on expeditions into the Indian reservation in search of deer, bear, and antelope.[3]

This was contrary to federal law, as was taking wood from Indian lands, but everyone did it, even ministers of the gospel. On one such trip Jim killed an antelope at some 300 yards with his .38-caliber Marlin rifle, while on another we narrowly escaped an encounter with the Indian police. The three of us were deep in the mountains several miles from the border of the reservation and had just stopped the wagon on the bank of a little creek when a long-haired Indian in the uniform of the reservation police rode by on the opposite side of the stream.

We had seen plenty of both deer and bear sign but had no relish for being arrested and lodged in the agency jail at Anadarko some forty miles distant. We accordingly made a hasty departure and after a three-mile drive made a fireless camp in the head of a little canyon. Jim climbed a nearby mountain and located the encampment of apparently a dozen or more Indian police. By this time it was growing dark so we ate a bit of cold supper and spent an uneasy

---

[3] The adjacent Kiowa-Comanche reservation.

night. At dawn we headed for home and crossed the river into Greer County safely.

While it seemed too bad to have such a promising hunt interrupted, I was very glad to have escaped without incident. Jim Ferris was dangerous. As soon as the lone Indian police appeared, Jim buckled on his big Colt .45 and told Warren and me that if some Indians came for us that night accompanied by a white man we would submit to arrest, but if only a couple of Indian police appeared he would kill them both rather than go with them. Knowing him and his corrugated past, I had no doubt but that he meant exactly what he said.

How Ferris was able to feed his wife and nine kids was hard to understand, but he had milk cows and chickens, kept a few pigs, and raised enormous quantities of sweet potatoes, beans, and other vegetables. His scanty income as deputy sheriff provided enough money to buy flour, sugar, and seventy or eighty pounds of Arbuckle coffee which the family consumed every year. I ate with them often, and there was always ample food but a great shortage of tableware. Some of the kids always had tin plates and cups and a single knife, fork, or spoon, but never all three.

Jim had a sorghum mill and made sorghum every summer. I helped in this for two seasons and learned every phase of the business. To make fifty gallons a day it was necessary to get up at four in the morning and start a fire under the evaporator, which was operated by two persons to handle skimmers and rakes. One of the girls usually fed the cane between the steel rollers of the mill. On one occasion Jim's second daughter, Allie, got her hand caught in the mill. This might have proved a serious accident, but fortunately the dejected-looking old horse that furnished the power to turn the mill was always listening for the word "whoa," and when Allie yelled at the top of her voice he stopped so quickly that she lost only part of one finger!

I was at the Ferris home one day chatting with the oldest daughter, Mattie. She told me that her dad had left very early that morning in search of a nineteen-year-old boy who had shot his former employer through the shoulder with a

Winchester rifle the night before and fled on foot toward the Indian reservation.

A few minutes later Jim rode up and hobbled into the house to tell us that he had overtaken the boy who had shot him through the leg at a distance of 200 yards and then ran into a small thicket near the bank of the river. Jim, who was armed only with his shotgun, had left a cowhand to watch the thicket and follow the lad at a safe distance if he left it. He had then hurried home to have his wound dressed and collect a posse.

The bullet had gone through the fleshy part of the thigh, missing the bone. Mattie, shaken and white-faced, tore strips from an old sheet for bandages. With my help the wound was cleaned, bound tightly, and Jim rode into Navajoe. It was Saturday afternoon and the entire population of the community, masculine, feminine, and canine, seemed to be in town. Every man and boy who owned or could borrow any kind of shooting iron mounted a horse and followed Jim. The kid was still in the thicket where he had scooped out a sort of rifle pit. For two or three hours there was a loud exchange of gunfire, barely missing some of the besiegers, but with his ammunition about gone he at last surrendered and was brought in and locked in jail.

A week later Ferris received a purse of thirty-five dollars made up for him by the people of the county seat town of Mangum. Jim probably had never had that much money at one time in the past two years. Nevertheless, he promptly returned it with a brief note of thanks to which he added that his wound was fast healing and had cost him only twenty-five cents for a bar of Castile soap and a bottle of turpentine. Of such hardy and independent fiber were most of these prairie pioneers made. J. M. Ferris, who was known on the Rio Grande border as "Mexico Jim," was one of the kindest men it has ever been my privilege to know, and I shall always cherish his memory.

The young chap who shot Jim Ferris had apparently merely been attempting to imitate a group of outlaws who had been operating in this region for the past year. They were Red Buck Weightman, Joe Beckham, Hill Loftis, and a young chap known as "The Kid," who was apparently Weightman's partner. For some two years they ranged this region robbing stores, stealing horses, and killing settlers. At last Beckham and Red Buck were killed and the other two disappeared, it was rumored to Mexico.

About 1895 my father traded for sixty head of cattle. While we had always been a little better off financially than most of the settlers of the community, this transaction improved our economic situation considerably by making us small livestock owners. About this time my sister Mattie, who had secured a divorce a year or more after the desertion of her husband, was married to Albert S. Woods, whom she had met on one of her frequent visits to friends in Cordell.

Woods was a cowman who for a couple of years had been ranching on Boggy Creek some twelve or fifteen miles north of that little town. Since there was ample range on the public lands about Mattie's home, he promptly moved all of his cattle down there and made her house the headquarters of the Rail-W Ranch. Jay had married a few months earlier than Mattie. He still owned his claim but except for a small sodhouse had put no improvements on it. After Mattie's marriage he sold it to Woods and built himself a little home on one corner of Henry's land.

All of us liked Mattie's husband, Al Woods, a tall, stalwart Kentuckian, who had come west several years before and had been ranching in the Indian Territory before removing his herd to the Cheyenne country. My father had given most of the cattle acquired in exchange for the Texas farm to George. Once Woods had established his headquarters at Mattie's home he proposed that we drive George's cattle up there, as he had ample range, and he and his cowboys would look after them. It seemed a good idea, so George and I, with the help of one cowhand, drove the little herd of D-Slash cattle to the Woods ranch and put them on the range with his Rail-W steers.

This was in the summer of 1896, a year of great importance to the widely scattered settlers of Greer County. In March, 1896, the United States Supreme Court in the case of the *U.S. v. Texas* held that the South Fork of Red River was the main stream and therefore Greer County was not a part of Texas. A few weeks later a special act of Congress attached Greer County to Oklahoma Territory, which had been created by Congress in 1890. Thus by judicial and legislative action people residing in a region some ninety miles long and seventy miles wide were transferred from the jurisdiction of Texas to that of the Territory of Oklahoma.[4]

The results were far-reaching to the people most concerned. All land in Greer County not reserved for education or some other purpose became part of the public domain of the United States and so subject to homestead entry. Since some persons had fenced and improved more than the 160 acres, the standard homestead size, a special act of Congress provided that anyone in actual possession of more than that amount of land might purchase an additional 160 acres for one dollar an acre payable in five equal annual installments.

The United States land office was established at the county seat town of Mangum, and my father promptly filed a homestead entry on his claim. Since he already had an eighty-acre homestead in Nebraska, however, he was forced to buy eighty acres of the claim at one dollar an acre. My brother Tom, who was living on a rented farm in Texas, also came to Greer County and homesteaded the 160 acres joining father's farm on the north. On this he built a small house only a quarter of a mile from ours to which he removed his family. In the early autumn, after crops had been harvested, he brought his cattle to the new home and settled down as our nearest neighbor.

We were all delighted to have Tom and Lucy so near us. They had married when I was only two years old so I had literally grown up with them. Tom was as solid and substantial as the Rock of Gibraltar, and Lucy a more or less happy-go-lucky person always fond of having young people

---

[4] The State of Texas had claimed this triangle of land, bounded by the North Fork of Red River on the northeast, the 100th meridian on the west, and Red River on the south, on the basis of army surveys and mapping during the 1850s when the North Fork of Red River was determined to be Red River's main channel. The Oklahoma Organic Act, 1890, provided for the absorption of Greer County into Oklahoma Territory.

about her. In addition she was a wonderful cook, and if her housekeeping left something to be desired, it did not matter either to her or her family. For some years after their marriage they had no children, but at the time of their removal to Greer County had three and eventually two more.

It seems amazing that their sandy land claim cornering with the Navajoe townsite had not been occupied before 1896, but most persons thought that the soil was too sandy to produce crops. J. M. Ferris had paid $250 for his 160-acre claim with a three-room house, a well, and straw-covered sheds, fenced fields, and pastures. A 160-acre claim with only a board shack or small dugout was frequently abandoned or traded for a pony, cow, or horse and saddle if it had a small fenced field or pasture. We could not foresee that at the time of World War I Tom's farm would produce 100 bales of cotton which sold at $200 a bale yielding $20,000. Truly, "if foresight were as good as hindsight, we might all be rich."

Schooling
and an "Inside Job"

The transfer of Greer County from Texas to Oklahoma Territory not only made a radical change in the land system but in many other things. The county officers elected under the laws of Texas were out, and new ones were appointed by the governor of Oklahoma to serve until their successors were elected early in the following November. In addition, the schools came under the jurisdiction of the Territory of Oklahoma.

This left most teachers in an unfortunate position. While teaching under the laws of Texas, their salaries had been paid by warrants drawn on either the treasurer of that state or of Greer County, Texas. Often there were not sufficient funds to pay these immediately, and teachers had to hold them two or three months before they could be cashed. Once Greer County became part of Oklahoma Territory, Texas refused to pay these outstanding warrants. This left many teachers in sore financial straits, and they began to petition the Texas Legislature to provide funds for the payment of what they felt was a just debt.

After Greer County became a part of Oklahoma Territory the question of land titles had been settled, and the citizens of school districts could vote bonds for the construction of schoolhouses. The Navajoe community promptly voted bonds for a two-room building at the west edge of town to replace the little board shack which had hitherto served as their schoolhouse. It was completed before the end of summer and John was chosen principal and his wife, Ava, as his assistant to teach youngsters in the so-called "little room."

When George and I returned from delivering his cattle to the Woods's ranch we began to plan to attend John's school. Up to that time my total formal schooling had amounted to little over twelve months. There had been two or three brief terms at Keller, Texas, and about as many at Navajoe in the small box-like structure which served as a school building. Three sessions at Navajoe had been taught by two maiden ladies of uncertain age whose qualifications and appearance both left much to be desired. I had read a great deal, of course, including history and good literature, together with quite a bit of trash.

Before the opening of school in the late autumn of 1896, Warren Ferris and I spent the month of August attending a peculiar type of "camp school" of speech and singing held in a grove near Granite by T. E. Jones, a fairly prominent teacher of the county. Granite is a small town about twenty-five miles northwest of the site of Navajoe at the south side of a mountain. A mile farther north at the foot of this mountain there is a large, beautiful grove and a gushing spring of pure, cold water.

Jones was an old bachelor with the appearance and manner of a top sergeant. Unlike most teachers of the region he was not a claim holder and part-time farmer but taught school in winter and singing and elocution in the summer. He was also an ardent prohibitionist and very much a promoter.

This particular summer he planned a four weeks' school of this type to be held in the grove near Granite to be concluded by a three-day picnic. At this his students would entertain the crowd with temperance orations for which silver, gold, and one "grand gold" medal were to be awarded to the students in each class who made the best showing. Between the contests they would regale the audience with songs.

Granite businessmen cooperated fully in the enterprise. They provided lumber to build a large platform and seats and the school board promised to lend the school organ. It was also agreed that Jones should sell concessions for a merry-go-round, cold drink stands, doll racks, a shooting gallery, and vendors of peanuts and popcorn in order to provide funds to buy the medals and for other expenses. His own payment for his work was derived from the enrollment fees of three dollars from each student.

Warren and I fully enjoyed the four weeks of this school. Mrs. Abbott, who was a close friend of the Ferris family, erected a large tent near the spring and provided board and lodging for four or five girls from the Navajoe community including a couple of ten-year-olds. Warren and I slept in her covered wagon which was parked about 200 yards away near the south end of the grove. We took our meals with her, however, and as I recall, paid six dollars each for a month's board. The food was plain and course, consisting largely of beans, cornbread, dried fruits, and sorghum, but it was wholesome.

On the first morning of school, some fifty students assembled at the platform. Most of them lived in the community, but a number came from homes forty or fifty miles away. These boarded either in town or at some nearby farm home, as did Jones himself. He had a number of books of temperance speeches issued by the W.C.T.U. and other prohibition organizations. From these each of us selected a fifteen or twenty minute oration and set to work to memorize it and practice its delivery.

Our teacher worked hard at his job but so did we. Every morning at 7:30 when his trumpet sounded, "Assembly," we all raced to the platform. After fifteen to twenty minutes of calisthenics or "setting-up exercises," song books were distributed and we sang about half an hour. Not all the songs related to temperance but some did of which the following first stanza of one is a good example:

Somewhere tonight in a cold, dreary world
Wanders a boy I cherish so,
Treading the dark and unbidden road
Leading to misery, pain, and woe.
Once he was pure as the saints in white,
Noble and manly, my joy and delight,
Facing a future so happy and bright,
But now, Oh my God, he's a drunkard tonight.

The students had been divided into classes according to ages as far as possible, and the teacher helped to choose orations that were best fitted to the student's age. These classes were the younger girls, younger boys, older girls, and older boys. After the period of exercises and singing, the teacher retained one class at the platform where each member delivered his speech and received suggestions and criticisms from the instructor. The rest of the students scattered to various parts of the grove, each finding some secluded spot in the shade to memorize his speech and practice delivering it.

Jones evidently believed that "practice makes perfect." Every student when not engaged in group singing or receiving instruction as to voice, enunciation, emphasis, and gesture, devoted hours every day practicing delivery of the chosen oration. Any stranger who happened to be passing by must surely have felt that he had discovered a new Forest of Arden where there were "tongues in the trees ... and sermons in stones," for most of us had chosen a nook "remote from public haunt" to practice delivering our speeches.[1]

I thoroughly enjoyed those four weeks and learned a great deal about public speaking. The three-day picnic was also an enjoyable affair. Virtually everyone in the community attended it as well as many persons from a considerable distance. Some drove forty or fifty miles to camp in the grove for the entire three days. Everyone seemed to like both the singing and the speaking contests a great deal, though some of the so-called orations must have been pretty bad. Yet the delivery of them was usually quite as good as the content of the speech, if not better. One, given by a girl who was awarded the grand gold medal, was typical of all the others, so its first two paragraphs are given here.

> Recently a vast procession of laboring men marched through the streets of Chicago behind a

---

[1] Forest of Arden, a wooded tract in Warwickshire, England, setting of Shakespeare's *As You Like It*.

banner on which was written: "Our children cry for bread!" My friends, that inscription was true. In these cities of America there are thousands of children, the offspring of honest laborers, who cry for bread. I have lived in three of the largest cities of the United States and have seen half-fed and half-clothed children by the thousands. I have seen hundreds of nursing mothers shivering with cold and wasting away for the lack of nutritious food. The explanation of this destitution lies in a number of well-known facts, but the *main* fact is that fourteen hundred million dollars worth of grain grown in these United State is destroyed every year by the men who make and sell liquor.

Think of it, my philanthropic friends! Think of it, you who profess to love your brother man! Think of it you who believe in and practice pure and undefiled religion! America's children, America's women cry for bread, and yet fourteen hundred million dollars worth of grain is destroyed and worse than destroyed every year! Stop your distilleries and breweries! Let the bounteous harvest with which God annually blesses our land flow into legitimate channels, and while the world stands it shall never again be said of the children of American laborers that they cry for bread!

The "flow into legitimate channels" was always accompanied by a rippling motion made by the hand of an extended right arm as we had been carefully coached on gesture. The audience listened with rapt attention to this and similar tripe, but it is doubtful if our efforts had the slightest effect upon the consumption of liquor. Moreover, none of us could foresee a time when the United States would be paying millions of dollars daily for the storage of surplus grain.

Warren and I both won medals in these contests and at the conclusion of the picnic left for home feeling that our four weeks' training in speech had been well spent. As to the educational value of what we had learned about singing, we were far less enthusiastic.

The Navajoe school opened fairly late in the autumn as the term lasted for only six months. Warren and I both enrolled, and George attended for some three months before withdrawing to work for Al Woods as a cowhand. Woods had bought 1,000 head of two-year-old steers at Bowie, Texas, in September. He was to receive them on the first of October and George helped drive them to the Woods ranch. He then entered school, but a few months later Woods found himself short of help and asked George to come and work for him. The pay was fifteen dollars a month and George accepted gladly because he could also look after his own cattle that were ranging with those of Woods.

My brother John was an excellent teacher in spite of his easy-going nature and tendency to live in the clouds rather than on the Mother Earth of the latter part of the nineteenth century. He had taught in various parts of the county with so much success that several older girls and boys who had been his pupils in other schools came to Navajoe and secured board and lodging in order to continue their schooling with him.

The long benches of the little box schoolhouse had been discarded in favor of double desks, and John had no objection to older boys and girls sitting together if they were studying the same subjects. Probably he reasoned that both would be inspired to study harder by the immediate proximity of one of the opposite sex, which seems a bit doubtful. Most of the older students were earnest, conscientious young people in their late teens, although none of them had advanced as far as what we today call the eighth grade.

In a region of abundant leisure and few recreational facilities, every school became something of a social center. Visitors often appeared on Friday afternoons to attend the spelling matches or a program of recitations so often provided at that time. With John's help we soon organized a literary and debating society which met every other Friday evening. At every meeting the room was packed by a people starved for entertainment and not too particular as to the quality of that offered.

Recitations included such old-time favorites as *Curfew Must Not Ring Tonight, Spartacus to the Gladiators, The Lips That Touch Liquor Can Never Touch Mine*, and *The Face on the Barroom Floor*. The small fry from the "little room" offered contributions ranging from *Twinkle Little Star* or *The Boy Stood on the Burning Deck* to *The Widder Spriggins' Daughter, Little Orphan Annie*, and many more. One-act plays, commonly called "Dialogues," were also presented. These were usually of humorous nature as *The Train to Mauro* and *Arabella's Poor Relations*, but the subjects for debates always dealt with current affairs, historical themes, or moral and philosophical questions.

As winter drew to a close, Cranford, who operated the drug, dry goods, and clothing store, as well as the post office, asked me to work for him. He explained that my duties would be to take charge of the post office and when not busy with the mail to act as clerk selling goods. For my services he offered the munificent salary of ten dollars a month and board, provided I would sleep in the big room above the store used for the storage of surplus stock, including a dozen coffins of assorted sizes!

My father assured me that this "would beat farming" which was an interesting commentary upon the profits of growing crops in Greer County at this time. I therefore promptly withdrew from school and began work at my first "inside job." In fact I had never before worked for a fixed wage for anyone unless picking cotton could be so designated.

Cranford was a slightly corpulent individual who was always neatly dressed and demanded that everything about the store be kept immaculate. He had married "Miss Anna," my former school teacher, who had been kind enough to lend me so many books a few years earlier. She had formerly helped in the store but had suffered a slight stroke a few weeks before which is probably why Cranford employed me. In fact she was not able to do all of her housework at home so her husband soon brought a girl from Fort Worth to help her.

One reason why Cranford employed me was that his fear of being robbed amounted almost to an obsession. On my first day of work he gave me a .38-caliber Colt's army revolver and told me to buckle it on at four every afternoon, wear it when I went to his home for supper, and sleep with it under my pillow at night. Like most lads of my age I was glad to swagger about with a gun on my hip but was such a sound sleeper that burglars could probably have broken in at night and looted the store without waking me.

Cranford had some reason for fearing robbers and burglars. Members of the outlaw gang previously mentioned were robbing stores, stealing horses, and engaging in various other forms of crime in western Oklahoma. They usually struck any business establishment just before sundown, so that it would be dark before an adequate posse could be organized for pursuit. Riding out of town in one direction, they would double back or shift to another as soon as darkness had fallen and might be forty miles away by daylight.

There was no bank nearer than Vernon, Texas, nearly fifty miles away, and the post office had the only safe in Navajoe. It often held a considerable amount of money derived not only from several days' receipts, but also from the cash paid by cowboys and ranchmen for postal money orders when they sent their wages home, ordered merchandise, or paid debts by mail. Fearful as he was of a holdup, my employer was almost equally afraid of burglary and sometimes talked of setting a "booby trap" with his .45 caliber Colt's pistol in such fashion that anyone going behind the counter at night would shoot himself in the legs.

Delighted as I had been to begin my work with Cranford, within three or four months I began to realize that operating a post office and selling merchandise was no job for me. The work was not hard, the meals served at his home were excellent, and I did not mind sleeping with the coffins in the storeroom. Up to this time, however, my work had always been outside, and my chief duties had been breaking land, plowing, cultivating, and harvesting crops, and riding after cattle. In consequence, I chafed at working all day indoors.

Even more important, it seemed to me that there was nothing creative about post-marking letters, putting up and delivering the mail, and selling and wrapping merchandise. To me one who planted, cultivated, and harvested a few bales of cotton and several hundred bushels of corn had accomplished something, and the same was true of growing beef or pork. I even felt that teaching children to read, write, spell, and do problems in arithmetic was creative work, but what I was doing was not.

Cranford lived only for business, but his insistence that everything about the store be kept clean, neat, and orderly added much to my education in the broadest sense of that term. Unfortunately he was completely devoid of a sense of humor, took no part in the social or civic life of the village, and was cordially disliked by virtually everyone in the community. Yet he was always very kind to me, and I had for him a certain measure of liking and respect although he was not a person to inspire affection. Early in the autumn I asked him to get someone else for the job and he hired a local girl whose only duty was to take care of the post office.

A few months later Cranford's wife died and shortly thereafter the new administration in Washington got around to replacing him as postmaster by the appointment of about the only Republican in the community. He accordingly sold his home, store building, and stock of drygoods and clothing, and removed his drugs and medicines to Cloud Chief, the county seat of Washita County. Here he established a drugstore and built a small house. He then went to Fort Worth, married the girl who had been his housekeeper, and brought her back to preside over his new home.[2]

In August before I quit my job with Cranford, Al Woods had shipped to Kansas City the thousand steers he had bought the previous October and sold them for a net profit of over $10,000. By this time settlers had homesteaded most of the public land in that area, and Woods realized that he must find a new location if he expected to continue ranching.

---

[2] Cloud Chief, first county seat for Washita County, later situated at Cordell.

He accordingly rode up to Woodward, a little town on the Rock Island Railroad. Woodward at that time had about 1,000 people. It was in the western part of the Cherokee Outlet, opened to settlement in 1893, but because of the rough, sandy nature of the land, almost no settlers had taken homesteads there. As a result it was still largely a region of ranchmen who pastured their herds on the public domain.

The region seemed to offer excellent possibilities for ranching, so Woods bought 160 acres of land adjoining the townsite, built an addition to the house on it, and leased a fenced pasture of 10,240 acres four miles south of town. He then returned home, and began to make plans to sell his land there, and move his family and remaining cattle to the new location.

This meant that George must bring his own cattle home, and he asked me to help him. This I was only too glad to do for my work in the store had ended only a couple of weeks before. Just at this time a herd of 800 Texas Coast steers was passing on the trail near Navajoe on its way north, and one of the owners rode into town to look for a new hand to replace one who had quit that day.

As the herd would pass within fifteen or twenty miles of the Woods ranch, I agreed to help him for two or three days so I took my two horses and joined this drive. The outfit had a Negro cook, but the food that he turned out proved so bad that one of the two owners took over the cooking and let the Negro ride. The boss put him and me on as night guards for the last shift which began at two a.m. and ended at daylight.

It was then about the first of November and a cold norther blew in bringing a light snow. I rode with these men about three days, and on the last night I was with them, we bedded the herd down at the foot of a small mountain. When the colored boy and I rode out at two o'clock in the morning, we decided that these steers would not go up the side of the mountain so we built a fire in a sheltered spot behind some huge boulders and took turns in riding the half circle at the edge of the sleeping herd and sitting by the fire.

42

Soon after daylight two men rode out to relieve us, and we had breakfast and changed horses. After the cattle had grazed for an hour, we drifted them along toward the north. The drive was then continued until nearly sundown with only a brief rest stop at noon. After supper and the herd had been "put to bed," I changed horses and leading my spare mount, started for the Woods home. It was about eleven when I reached my destination, a very tired and sleepy youth, for twenty-one hours largely in the saddle, except short stops for meals, will tire any lad and make him feel that a bed is the most desirable thing in the world!

The following day we rounded up George's cattle, put them in a well-fenced pasture, and the next morning started the little herd on the thirty-five-mile drive home. The trip was made in less than three days without difficulty. By renting some grassland from the neighbors, we had ample pasturage for them and had cut and stacked feed for the winter. As our fences were good, the cattle would need little attention, so George and I both decided to go to school.

John had been made principal of the high school at Mangum, the county seat town, and Ava remained at home, so the Navajoe school board had employed the irrepressible T. E. Jones as head of the school for the 1897-98 term. He had not taught the preceding year but had spent most of the winter in Washington, D.C. Soon after the close of the school of speech at Granite it became evident that Texas had ignored the petitions of the teachers to pay their warrants. In desperation, these teachers contributed funds to send Jones to the national capital where he spent the winter urging a congressional appropriation for their payment.

School had been in session only a couple of weeks when George and I enrolled soon after the first of November. We realized at once that Jones had a method of operating a school in direct contrast to that of our brother John. He interfered little with his assistant's technique of dealing with the small children in her room but ruled his own students with an iron hand. Gone were the days when older boys and girls sat side by side at a double desk to study their lessons. Jones seated all the boys on one side of the room and the girls on the other, and demanded that they occupy separate playgrounds during recess and the noon hour.

Moreover, with the full support of the school board, he issued a decree that no student could attend any evening party, social, singing, or other affair at any time including weekends, and one who did so would be instantly expelled from school. This was bitter medicine for the older boys and girls in school. Without the attendance of students there were not enough persons to make it worthwhile to hold a party. Social life for the "younger set" of the Navajoe community came to an abrupt halt. No doubt some young cowhand could have been found who would gladly have hung Jones to the nearest tree.

Perhaps this rule was not without merit, for deprived of any social life in the evenings, sheer boredom caused us to spend them in study. As some compensation, however, Jones harked back to his Washington experience and organized a "mock Congress" to meet every Friday evening in his schoolroom. Its membership included most of the teen-age boys, one or two members of the board, several businessmen of the town, and a few farmers who had formerly participated in debates.

Jones acted as Speaker of the House and each member chose the state or territory which he wished to represent, the territorial delegate being given the right to vote. A chief clerk, reading clerk, and sergeant-at-arms were elected, and small boys were chosen as pages. I represented the Territory of Alaska and succeeded in getting an appropriation to build a railroad across my territory to be owned and operated by the federal government.

Populism was still rife in the region, and the liberals introduced bills providing for government ownership of railroads, farm relief, free coinage of silver, national prohibition, internal improvements, a bounty on prairie dog scalps, and a host of other subjects. Amendments were freely offered making radical changes in the proposed legislation such as to kill a bill by striking out the enacting clause. We "moved the previous question," demanded a

44

"call of the house," and moved to "excuse the absentees." Debates were frequently hot, and eloquent speeches were made for or against a measure. All of this taught us much of parliamentary law and procedure and added to our experience in public speaking.

A couple of months before school was to close our teacher urged that one of the most mature young women and I should take the examination for an eighth grade, or common school, diploma. The questions for such examinations were made up by the Territorial Board of Education consisting of the presidents of the Territorial University, the A. and M. College, the Normal School, one county superintendent of schools, and one city superintendent. All of these were appointed by the governor. These questions in nine common school subjects, were sent to the various county superintendents and transmitted by him to the head of any school in the county who might request them.

The young woman and I were both a bit fearful of tackling examinations prepared by such an august group of educators, but Jones assured us that we could pass them. He added that if we did we each would receive a diploma signed by the Territorial Superintendent of Schools, the President of the Board of Education, the County Superintendent, the president of the local school board, and himself. He further asserted that if successful on this examination we could pass one for a teacher's certificate.

Reassured by our teacher's confidence, and the reward which success would bring, this young woman and I set to work manfully, and "womanfully," to review the subjects on which we were to be examined. Our hard work was not in vain. When the questions arrived we spent two harrowing days writing on them, and they were mailed to the county superintendent to be forwarded to the Territorial Board of Education which graded them. A few weeks later we received our diplomas. Mine is before me as this is written. It measures nearly twenty by sixteen inches and has, in addition to the promised signatures, a picture of the University, the A. and M. College, the Normal, and a typical rural school.

The so-called "institutions of higher learning" each had at this time only one brick building, and the picture of the rural school shows a frame structure with four windows on each side. Since then it has been my privilege to receive four other diplomas. All are from a college or university, but none except my Ph.D. diploma from Harvard had brought me as great a thrill as did this one.[3]

Under the laws of Oklahoma Territory, any county superintendent of schools was authorized to hold a four weeks' county institute, commonly called a "county normal," every summer. This was designed to give "refresher" courses to teachers and also to provide instruction in the common school branches for prospective teachers. At its close an examination for teacher's certificates was held. The county superintendent had a small fund to employ a conductor for such an institute who must hold a "conductor's certificate," issued by the Territorial Board of Education, and this fund was supplemented by a small tuition fee paid by each person enrolled.

My brother, John, by this time had graduated from the normal school at Edmond, which gave him a life certificate to teach in any school in Oklahoma Territory. He also had received a conductor's certificate and had accepted an invitation to conduct a four-weeks' teachers' institute for Washita County, at the county seat town of Cloud Chief. It was to be held during the following August, and he urged me to attend.

The idea appealed to me for, although I had no thought at this time of making teaching my life work, it seemed that it might be interesting to teach three of four terms and use my savings to buy calves. This would help me to achieve my real ambition which was to join George in establishing a successful ranching business. Money was scarce, but I sold an old horse given me by father and made ready to accompany John and Ava to Cloud Chief.

---

[3] The Territorial University, presently University of Oklahoma, at Norman; Territorial A and M College, presently Oklahoma State University, at Stillwater; and Territorial Normal School, later Central State Teachers' College, then Central State College, and presently Central State University, at Edmond.

As normal was to open on Monday we drove to Henry's on Friday. The following day Jay put his saddle in the wagon and accompanied us to our destination which we reached in the late afternoon. The town was very small, but had two little hotels and two saloons, the Elk and the Two Brothers. In addition, there were the courthouse, jail, Cranford's drug store, three or four general stores, a two-room school building, and a small restaurant. John and Ava secured room and board at the Central Hotel while Jay and I spread our blankets on the prairie near John's wagon that had been parked near the edge of town.

Here we were joined by the county superintendent, G. W. Hunt, who brought his bedroll declaring that it was too hot to sleep inside. Hunt was an elderly Confederate veteran whose former home, south of Atlanta, had been burned by Sherman's army on its "march to the sea." He had been away at the time with Lee's army in Virginia, had participated in numerous battles, and bore the scars of six or seven wounds. As a result he was still an "unreconstructed rebel" of the most violent type.

The following day Jay started for home riding one horse and leading the other. I arranged to take my meals with a lady whose home was at the west edge of town not too far from the school building. She served good substantial meals at a long table in her half-dugout kitchen, which was reached by descending four or five steps from one of the two other rooms built above the ground. She had eight or nine other boarders including Superintendent Hunt, and each of us paid two dollars a week or slightly less than ten cents a meal!

I also visited my former employer, Cranford, who seemed delighted to see me. His wife was visiting her relatives in Fort Worth so he took his meals at one of the hotels and slept on the floor of the store at night, probably as a precaution against burglary. He asked me to join him which I was glad to do and brought over my slim bedroll. The floor seemed a bit hard at first, but I soon became accustomed to it and slept there every night for the entire four weeks. Cranford was apparently very glad to have me with him for he was quite lonely, and also I provided an extra gun in case of need. He had lost none of his fear of being robbed and was pleased to learn that I had with me the .38 Colt's revolver which he had sold me when my job with him had ended.

Most of the would-be students drifted in Sunday in order to find living quarters and be ready for classes Monday morning. Among them was George Auxier, a young chap about my own age, who had already taught two terms of school. He came on horseback with his extra clothing and a few books in a sack tied behind his saddle. He was accompanied by his younger brother whose small pony seemed hardly big enough to carry a husky lad and a thin roll of blankets. All this luggage was deposited on the prairie near John's wagon and about a hundred yards from my boarding place where George had also arranged to eat. With his "mission accomplished" the younger brother then started home with the horses.

George Auxier was a very attractive young man and we immediately became fast friends. He slept on the prairie near the wagon every night for the entire term of the normal, except one when a shower caused him to "take up his bed and walk" to the shelter of his landlady's kitchen. Unquestionably his blankets spread down on the thick mesquite grass made a far better bed than mine on the hard floor of Cranford's drug store.

After an early supper, George suggested that we call on a couple of his teacher friends who had planned to attend the normal and "stay at the courthouse." I gladly agreed for this seemed a most unusual place for lodgings. The court-house was a long, one-story wooden building not far from the center of town. The door was open so we went in and looked about for George's friends. They were not there but a couple of rolls of bedding and two or three well-filled bags suggested that they were not far away.

I viewed the interior of the courthouse with much interest. It consisted of a single huge room and along the walls were desks some fifteen feet apart each with a couple of chairs in front of it and a sign on the wall above with the words County Clerk, County Attorney, County Superintendent, etc., for the entire roster of county officials. The County Treasurer's desk was unique because it, and a steel safe beside it, were enclosed by a low railing. The central part of the room had a large desk near one end with rows of chairs in front of it. This was the meeting place of the district court. How the county officials transacted business when the court happened to be in session I shall never know. Perhaps they declared a week's holiday and all went fishing!

We found George's friends behind the courthouse frying bacon and boiling coffee over a small campfire. They were under a large brush arbor which had been erected for a revival meeting that had closed only a week or so before. We sat on the ground and visited with them while they ate their supper and washed the tin plates and cups. They said that they would live in their present quarters during the session and expected to be very comfortable there.

They added that each morning they would finish breakfast, stash away their bedrolls, and be gone to school long before the county officers arrived each morning, and would not be back until after five in the afternoon when these officials had gone home. They said the only possible complication was that travelers sometimes spent the night there and might have squalling children who would disturb their sleep. Surely the courthouse was in every sense a "public building!" We chatted with these men an hour or so and then headed for bed, George using the wagon as a landmark to locate his pallet on the prairie and I to spreading mine down on the floor of Cranford's drugstore.

When we reached the schoolhouse the next morning at seven we found some fifty teachers and prospective teachers assembled. Each of us was given a pamphlet containing twenty lessons in all subjects required for a teaching certificate. These numbered eleven for a third-grade certificate, and included the nine upon which I had been examined for an eighth-grade diploma plus composition and methods of teaching. For a second-grade certificate, civics was added and for a first-grade, physics and bookkeeping.

One could secure a third-grade certificate without any

teaching experience by making an average of 70 percent on all eleven subjects and not less than 50 percent in any one branch. The second grade required an average of 80 percent with not less than 60 percent in any subject, while the first required an average of 90 percent and no grade lower than 70 percent. Three months of teaching experience was required for a second-grade, and twelve months for a first-grade certificate. The third-grade certificate was valid for only one year, the second for two, and the first for three years.

We all worked very hard during the next four weeks. Classes met at seven each morning and continued until noon with only one brief intermission. We returned at two for an afternoon session of a couple of hours and then studied until supper time and during the evening. John taught most of the classes but had one of the more mature teachers assist him with two or three of them.

Yet, there was some time for recreation. A watermelon feast was held one afternoon and a debate one evening between a teacher, representing the normal, and a young lawyer. In addition, a picnic was held in a little grove beside a nearby creek. Most of our time was devoted to work, however, and since the teachers came from many states, and with a varied assortment of textbooks, there were numerous arguments in class. American history and grammar especially brought forth a wide variety of opinions.

The session came to a close all too soon, and the last two days were devoted to examinations for teachers' certificates. The questions, prepared by the Territorial Board of Education, had been sent to Superintendent Hunt, who opened them in the presence of the anxiously waiting candidates. They were quickly distributed, and for two intensely hot days we wrote at top speed. Perspiration rolled down every face and dropped on the penciled sheets, sometimes mingled with the tears of the more nervous young persons.

While I could receive only a third-grade certificate and George Auxier only a second-grade certificate, we both wrote on the fourteen subjects required for a first-grade certificate. As soon as the first papers were handed in Superintendent Hunt and his two appointees, who constituted the County Board of Education, began grading them. They worked as rapidly as possible and must have tempered justice with mercy for there were few failures. Probably they reasoned that teachers were scarce and not many of us would have any pupils who had gone beyond the fifth reader! At any rate George and I both came out with an overall grade of nearly 90 percent and none below 75 percent.

Jay came in with the team the following day and we drove to Henry's where we spent the night, and the next day John, Ava, and I reached Navajoe late in the afternoon. It was good to be home again, but the four weeks of intensive study and close association with teachers had taught me a great deal. Also I was quite proud of my certificate, and my high grades encouraged me and gave me more confidence. Unconsciously, perhaps, I had been inspired to seek further education. Upon leaving my last class at Cloud Chief, I little realized that, except for a four-week county normal, I would not enter a school room as a student for eight long and busy years.

Cowhand and Ranchman

My work as a cowboy and small ranchman might be said to have begun when my father traded for sixty head of high-grade cattle. These, added to the animals we already had, gave us a considerable herd. Feeling myself something of a cowboy was then considerably strengthened when my sister Mattie married Al Woods, a real cowman. Some of our neighbors with small children did not own a single cow. To these my father was glad to lend two or three cows only asking them not to "churn-dasher" the calves by refusing to allow them a fair share of their mother's milk.

Upon reaching home about the first of September, 1898, with my teacher's certificate in my pocket I was naturally eager to secure a school. Learning that the members of a school board down on the river six or seven miles away were looking for a teacher I rode down to see them. Because the children would be needed to pick cotton, which by this time had become an important crop in that area, school would not open until November but the Board quickly offered me the job for three months at twenty-five dollars a month.

Things seemed to be going well for father, George, and me. The cattle were fat, we had ample grass and feed for the winter, and I had a job which would give me the opportunity to prove my ability as a teacher and provide me with a little cash.

Then disaster struck and the following winter was to prove the most tragic period of my entire life. Around the middle of September George was stricken with typhoid fever. For over six weeks my father sat at his bedside almost day and night while I looked after the cattle, did most of the cooking and housework, and ran errands. Tom and Lucy and kindly neighbors came in to bring food and help in every possible way. Of course I had to resign the teaching position.

Then my father came down with the dread disease and the situation became infinitely worse. John and Ava were away teaching school and in desperation we called upon Jay and his wife Belle who were living on one corner of Henry's land. They came immediately but by that time I was also in bed with the malady. Jay and his wife took over the care of all of us in wonderful fashion with much help from Lucy, Tom, and neighbors. Medical attention was poor, for the one or two old doctors in the community had few qualifications for medical practice except imposing whiskers and a bedside manner.

Father grew steadily worse, and Mattie came down from Woodward and stayed with Tom and Lucy, for our house had only two rooms because a year or so before my father had given the material from the largest room to Henry who had moved it to his claim. Soon after Mattie's arrival, it became evident that Father had only a few days to live, so George and I were carried to beds in a farm wagon and taken to Tom's house where a room was set aside for us. Dave Davis, a former United States deputy marshal, was employed as our nurse and a message was sent by the mail carrier to Vernon to be wired to Frank and Fannie in Nebraska. They started at once but it was a long and roundabout trip from Nebraska and they and Henry did not arrive until just after our father's death.

I had never before seen Frank, for I was born some months after he had left Dallas, Texas, on his long horseback ride to Lincoln to enter the University of Nebraska. For the first time in many years all these brothers and sisters were together for John came from his school in Mangum to attend the funeral. Sad as was the occasion, they used the opportunity to visit with one another and recall episodes when they had been children together.

Within a week, however, Frank and Mattie left for home but to avoid the circuitous route by way of Vernon, and from there by train, a man was employed to drive them to Woodward where they could get a train for the rest of their journey. George and I were still in bed and would be for some time, so Fannie remained for a few weeks to help take care of us. Dave Davis then drove her to Woodward, and George and I were taken back to our own home where Jay and Belle again took charge of us until we were able to be on our feet once more.

Convalescence was a slow process for both of us. I had spent six weeks in bed and George about twelve so we were both very weak. In a couple of months, however, I was about back to normal but George never fully recovered from this harrowing illness which had brought him so close to death. Although he lived to be nearly seventy-five years of age his health had been badly broken, and he never again had the strength and vigor of his earlier days.

Our father had made no will but his older children all agreed that such property as he had should all go to George and me because it had been accumulated after they had left his home. This generous attitude enabled us to come into full ownership of the 160-acre farm, the cattle, and father's personal property.

We felt most grateful to Jay and his wife who had come to nurse us when we were in such desperate need, so when Jay remarked to us one day that he and Belle would move in the spring, we replied that George and I had talked the matter over and had decided to deed the north eighty acres of the farm including the house and other improvements, to him and retain only the south eighty of grassland for ourselves. To Tom we also gave four head of cattle to round out his little bunch of milk cows. This left us only our cattle and eighty acres of lands.

Mattie had been urging us to pay her a visit as soon as we felt well enough to make the trip but the latter part of the winter was very cold with much sleet and snow. This delayed our trip and when warm weather came, there was land to plow and feed to plant which kept us busy at home.

Then T. E. Jones, who had again taught the local school, decided to hold his annual summer school of speech, followed by a picnic, in a grove near Navajoe. It began early in July and I enrolled, got some more training in oratory, and won another medal.

When it was over, about the first of August, we loaded some grub, bedding, and other equipment into a light spring wagon and started on our long-delayed journey to Woodward. Our route took us past the familiar community on Trail Elk Creek but Henry no longer lived there. A few months before he had sold his claim and moved to Cordell which had succeeded Cloud Chief as the county seat town.

We camped the first night on the prairie a few miles beyond his former home, and the following day traveled over a rough, hilly region with some wide stretches of level prairie. We were surprised to find the region so little peopled. It had been opened to settlement in 1892 and all the land, except two school sections in every township, was subject to homestead entry. Yet we would drive for ten or fifteen miles without seeing a single house. There were no roads but only a dim trail which sometimes disappeared, and we jolted over the rough bunch grass of the prairie for miles before picking up another.[1]

We saw a good many cattle from time to time and our sleep the second night was considerably disturbed by them. We had camped on flat prairie a mile or so south of the Canadian River. It was a bright moonlit night and after supper we spread our blankets on the grass near the wagon and were soon asleep. A few hours later I awoke to find the moon blotted out by a big steer that was standing directly over my bed licking the frying pan in which we had cooked bacon for supper!

I yelled and he jumped away, fortunately missing me with his hoofs. Several other steers were about apparently looking for salt. I chased them away lashing any in reach

---

[1] Although the Cheyenne-Arapaho reservation was opened by a land run in 1892, homesteaders passed over much of its western claims and it was several years before the vacant tracts were claimed.

with the buggy whip. The noise woke George, of course, and while we were both soon asleep again it was not long until the cattle were back. From then until daylight one or the other of us was up almost every hour chasing these pesky steers out of camp with the whip.

Fortunately, nothing disturbed our slumbers the third night and in the late afternoon of the fourth day we rolled into Woodward. Mattie, Al, and the little girls gave us a cordial welcome, as did Mrs. Bates, the housekeeper, who apparently had heard all about us many times over from Mattie and the two small daughters. Rance Rolfe, who had been Al Woods's foreman or "top hand" for several years, was also there and seemed happy to see us again.

Woodward was at this time strictly a cow town and a shipping point for cattle from an enormous area. Its population could not have been much over 1,000 but it had twelve saloons, a large general merchandise store, two or three smaller ones, a bank, and the Cattle King Hotel. Also, there was another hotel, a saddle shop, restaurant, barber shop, and a few other business establishments. All of these were south of the railway tracks. To the north of them there was nothing but a large dance hall and the tents and shacks occupied by women of the underworld.[2]

All about the town lay a great ranching region. There were almost no homesteaders and not many houses in the country for a number of the cowmen lived in Woodward. Woods had a small camp house by a spring in his pasture four or five miles south of town. Here he had stationed a cowboy to ride the fences and look after the some thousand head of cattle. A few miles farther out he had recently leased another pasture six miles square which had another shack occupied by a single cowhand. This pasture was not fully stocked but Woods was planning to put more steers there as soon as he could buy them at a fair price. Rance, as top hand, supervised the work of the other men and sometimes spent a

---

[2] For the character of Woodward, Oklahoma Territory, at this time see Arrell Morgan Gibson, "History of Woodward County," *Guide to Alabaster Cavern and Woodward County*, Oklahoma Geological Survey Guide Book XV (1969), pp. 25-38.

night or two at one of the camps, although he usually ate with the Woods family and slept in a small room a few yards from the main house.

While we had planned to spend only a week in Woodward, our visit was extended to over two weeks. George accompanied Woods, Mattie, and her younger daughter on a brief trip by train to Kansas City. Not interested in such a journey I spent the four or five days while they were gone playing croquet with the older niece, reading some of Mattie's newer books, and riding out to the pasture with Rance to look over cattle, fences, and pasturage.

As the time approached for us to return home our brother-in-law suggested that if we would like to buy some more cattle, it would be easy to secure a loan for that purpose from one of the livestock commission companies. There were many of these in Kansas City with which Woods had been doing business for years, and some of them kept a representative in Woodward.[3]

We talked it over and the idea seemed a good one to both of us. We had planted a great deal of feed and seemed to have ample pasturage. Also, we recalled that a year or so earlier Woods had made a net profit of over $10,000 in about nine months on a investment of $18,000 paid for 1,000 head of two-year-old steers. Moreover, the appeal to "get into the bigger time" as ranchmen was irresistible.

As a result we signed a note for a few thousand dollars payable in eight months to the Globe Live Stock Commission Company. The interest was 8 percent annually and we gave as collateral the cattle we already owned and those to be purchased with the money. In addition, company agents assured us that there would be no difficulty in renewing the loan if it became due before the cattle were ready for market.

Looking backward this venture was a foolish one, but this is hindsight judgement. Settlers were pouring into western

---

[3] Livestock commission companies in Chicago, St. Louis, Kansas City, Omaha, and Denver were special lending agencies designed to provide ready capital for western ranchmen, the loan contracts calling for the herd or portion thereof as collateral for the capital advance on the transaction.

Oklahoma to take and fence homesteads, thereby rapidly reducing the area available for grazing. Cowmen whose ranges were already fully stocked soon found themselves forced to ship some of their cattle to market. Many of these animals were thin and prices steadily declined.

This lay in the future, and George and I drove home in high spirits certain that we were well on the road to a successful career as young ranchers. The trip was made without incident and we immediately began to look about for young steers that could be bought at a reasonable price. We wanted "long yearlings," about sixteen to eighteen months old, that we could market as feeders in about a year.

They were not easy to find, but in a few weeks we bought 100 head from a ranchman some twenty miles west of Navajoe and a few small bunches from others nearby. These purchases exhausted our funds and we set to work cutting and hauling sorghum cane and kaffir corn which we stacked in fenced lots near the house. By late October this had been done and for the next few months we needed only to keep up the fences, look after the cattle, and haul and distribute feed to them in bad weather.

At this time I received a letter from Al Woods which was in the nature of an S. O. S. He wrote that he had recently bought 2,000 head of three-year-old steers and was shipping them to Oklahoma City to be fed three or four months until they could be marketed as fat cattle. He would have to send two men down there to feed them. This left him in sore need of more help. He would have to be away a great deal himself, which was most unfortunate for Mattie was not well and Rance and a couple of more men would be busy caring for his other cattle in the two pastures. Would I come and stay at the home place and look after things there? He would pay me cowhand wages.

The fact that Mattie was unwell made George and me decide that we could not refuse Al's request. George declared that he could easily manage our affairs at home as the pasture was well-fenced and about all he would have to do during the winter months would be to haul feed to the cattle in bad weather. Relieved by this assurance, I put a few extra clothes in a sack, tied it behind my saddle, and mounted my little gray horse "Steve" for the long ride to Woodward.

Perhaps it would not be out of place to turn aside for a moment to pay a tribute to this little horse that was my closest four-footed friend for some fifteen years. He was foaled early in March, 1893, and Father promptly gave him to me. His mother was a small yellow mare that my father bought from the Indians for fourteen dollars a few years before. I named him "Steve" for Adlai Stevenson who had just been inaugurated as Vice-President of the United States. During his life "Steve" must have carried me a distance equal to that around the world.

He was at all times a gentleman in the best sense of the word. I could walk up to him in the pasture at any time, jump on his back, and guide him home by a slight pressure of my knees. Quite often when riding along the road I would overtake a wagon driven by a friend. To visit with him it was necessary only to hook the reins over the saddle horn and climb to the seat beside him. Like a faithful dog "Steve" would follow us.

On a journey when I must sleep on the prairie I did not need to stake "Steve" with my rope. He was turned loose and when morning came he would be within fifty yards. Sometimes I would wake in the middle of the night to find him standing by my bed. Apparently he was lonely and wanted to be sure that his master had not sneaked off and left him. When at last "Steve" died of old age, I mourned his passing as I would that of an old friend.

The trip to Woodward was made easily enough in only three days. I spent the first night at the home of a young couple living near the Washita River and the second with an old rancher whose rambling log and lumber home was near the Canadian. Woods and Mattie seemed delighted to see me as did Rance who had just ridden in from the larger pasture. The 2,000 steers were in feed pens in Oklahoma City under the care of Winters, one of Wood's best men. Art, a young cowhand, was in the camp at the smaller pasture, and Isom Lynch, cowhand and "bronc buster," was at the larger one. Clarence Evans, another cowhand, was at the Woods home but on my arrival he went to Oklahoma City to help Winters.

Isom had twenty-four miles of fence enclosing the big pasture to ride every day as well as 1,000 head of cattle to look after. This was too much for one man and Rance spent much time with him in the camp there. Woods had to make frequent trips to Kansas City and Oklahoma City so when Clarence left to join Winters the responsibility for taking care of the home place became largely mine.

For the next few months my duties were numerous and varied. To my regret there was not much riding to do, for although we had only a few cattle there they had to be fed and the fences kept in good condition. Mattie's health continued bad and I did most of the cooking. In addition, I hauled and distributed feed to the cattle, helped butcher hogs, milked two cows twice a day, ran errands to town, and frequently rode out to one of the pastures to deliver messages to the men there or to help them on some special job.

By the latter part of January it had become evident that Woods, in common with most other ranchmen of the Prairie West, was in serious trouble. The winter had been very cold, and the cattle in the big pasture were starving. Plainly most of them would not live until spring without feed, but almost none could be had in the Woodward area at any price. In desperation, Al arranged to get wheat pasture for them in Kansas, and ordered cars to ship them.

Rance and another cowhand or two were sent out to help drive them to the Woodward shipping yards. They were barely started when they ran headlong into a frightful snow and sleet storm. With true cowboy fidelity, they stuck to the job and while nearly frozen finally got them to town and in the Woods's 160-acre pasture joining it. By the time the boys were thawed a message was received that the railway tracks were blocked by snow, and the cars might not reach Woodward for nearly a week.

The next three or four days were tragic ones. Two or three wagonloads of feed were obtained from a farmer but this hardly made over a mouthful a day each for 1,000 famishing cattle. Five or six died every night and each morning fifteen or twenty more lying on the frozen, snow-covered ground had to be helped to their feet. All day long the heart-breaking sound of pitiful lowing by hunger-crazed animals rent the air.

At long last the cars came and the animals we believed would reach their destination alive were shipped to what we hoped would be "greener pastures." Some thirty or forty were left behind, for Woods was able to get a carload of cottonseed and a few wagonloads of hay. For the next few weeks it was one of my chief tasks to feed these poor creatures every morning after "tailing up" those unable to get on their feet without help. Fortunately, I was able to save all of them but for some it was a close squeak. The seven or eight hundred head of cattle in the smaller pasture south of town had not been shipped to Kansas. They were thin but the grass was better there than in the big pasture, and it seemed that they would pull through the winter.

Tragic as was Woods's situation on the western prairies it was even worse from a financial standpoint in Oklahoma City. He bought these steers for $32 a head, giving in payment his note for $64,000, using cattle purchased for that amount as collateral. By March they were fat and ready for shipment but prices had been steadily declining for months while the cost of cottonseed cake, their principal feed, consistently increased. Yet there seemed nothing to do but continue feeding them and hope for a better market.

It was a vain hope. Prices continued to decline and by early April Woods's funds were exhausted and he was forced to ship these steers to Kansas City. After deducting the cost of feed, transportation, interest, and wages paid, he found that he had sold them at a loss of $9 a head or a total of $18,000. Bitterly Al Woods realized that his long years as a cowman were ended. Once he had checked up his assets he made a trip to Kansas City and arranged to turn over all of his property, except his home, to his creditors. All cattle, horses, mules, chuck wagon, and land went and Al was left with only his two hands to earn a living for himself and family.

In the meantime I had received a letter from George enclosing a notice from the First National Bank of

Columbus, Kansas, that it had bought our note due the first of May and demanding payment at that date. Plainly I must hurry home. I showed the notice to Woods and asked for his advice. It came without hesitation. "Tell that banker to go to hell. Your cattle aren't ready to sell yet, and he can either renew the note for a few months or bring suit, and before the case is tried your steers will be fat enough for market."

Woods had not paid my wages for months and knowing his financial difficulties I had never had the heart to ask for them. He now gave me twenty-five dollars and I said goodbye to him and the family, mounted "Steve," and headed for home. It was a warm day late in April and the prairies, fast becoming a bright green, were a welcome sight after the horrors of the past winter.

The first night was spent at the big rambling house where I had stayed six months before on my trip to Woodward. We had beans, salt pork, sorghum, big blue biscuits, and coffee for supper. Any payment for my entertainment was politely refused. The second night I spent with a young Yankee couple who lived in a small two-story house that seemed likely to be blown over by the first high wind. They fed me porridge, poached eggs, "light bread," and tea for supper and insisted that thirty-five cents was ample for two meals and lodging. When I urged them to take a dollar they declared that any such amount would be ridiculous! As a result my total expense for the three days trip was forty-five cents, the additional dime going for cheese and crackers for the second day's lunch.

I reached home to find John and Ava away teaching school and George baching in their big sod house. Jay was working in a hardware store at Navajoe, for several new business houses had been established in the little town since I had left over six months before. Tom, the only real farmer among my brothers, was diligently engaged in planting cotton and adding to his farm improvements.

George seemed delighted to see me, but it was clear that our outlook was not promising. He had written to Globe Commission Company officials asking them to take up our note in exchange for a new one for four or five months to give us time to get our young steers in marketable condition. They replied courteously that conditions had changed and they could not do it. A letter to the Columbus, Kansas, bank that had bought the note brought the same response. "Cattle paper," formerly considered a gilt-edge investment, was plainly a drag on the market.

We could take Woods's advice and "tell the banker to go to hell," but the thought of a long drawnout lawsuit was abhorrent to us both, if it could possibly be avoided. Representatives of three or four livestock commission companies were stationed in Mangum, some thirty-five miles to the northwest, so I saddled old "Steve" and rode up there to interview them. We had not lost a single animal during the winter, and the spring calves dropped by the cows of our original little herd had added to the total number of our cattle.

I presented these facts to the agent of one of the commission companies and with some difficulty finally arranged for a loan sufficient to pay our note. The interest was 8 percent and it matured soon after the first of September. We believed that by that time the young steers would be ready for market and we fondly hoped for a substantial advance in prices.

Relieved as we were to get by this particular crisis, George and I found ourselves faced by other serious problems. We were short of grass. The neighbors, following my father's early example, had plowed a great deal of their pasture land and planted it in cotton. A small cotton gin had been established at Navajoe and three bales of lint cotton weighed less than one in seed. This reduced by two-thirds the cost of hauling the staple to the Vernon market, and ranchmen operating across the river on the Indian reservation gladly bought the cottonseed for cattle feed. Cotton prices had increased and the farmers often used the money obtained from its sale to buy a few milk cows and so needed their reduced pasturage themselves.

Worst of all we had no money to pay for the lease of additional grazing land even if it had been available. Our cattle were all mortgaged so we had no collateral for a loan.

Our friends would have been glad to lend us money, but few of them had any. Eventually, we were able to scrape together enough funds to lease for ninety days a comparatively small acreage of unfenced grass land on which we herded the cattle by day and returned them to our fenced pasture at night. We bached at John's sod house, for he and Ava were away all summer and needed someone there to feed the pigs and chickens.

It was a hot, dry summer, but the leased land had a creek across it and that, and the windmill in our own pasture, supplied plenty of water. We milked a couple of cows, and ate biscuits, butter, eggs, sorghum, and vegetables from the garden. Our days were largely spent in the saddle day-herding the steers. They were gaining in weight, but cattle prices continued to decline. About the first of September, with our note due in a few days we decided to ship the steers to the Kansas City market.

By this time a railroad had been built westward to Mangum. Northeast of Mangum on this railroad was the little town of Granite where I had formerly attended the School of Speech taught by Jones. This was our nearest shipping point so cars were ordered and we made ready for the three day's drive to Granite.

We had only four horses: "Steve," "Claybank," a big yellow horse that was George's favorite mount, a medium-sized mare called "Babe," and "Old Red," a big dark bay semi-outlaw that we rode only when abolutely necessary. We packed bankets, grub, and cooking utensils on Babe, rounded up steers, and headed them northwest for Granite. We had no money to hire help, so when the cattle were bedded down at dark, one of us had to stand guard until midnight and then wake the other to take over until daylight.

It was gruelling work. By the second night I was going to sleep in the saddle and would awake to find myself and horse halfway back to camp. The only way to stay awake was to dismount and stand by my horse. Then upon going to sleep and starting to fall, I would wake up. By the time we reached a wide stretch of open prairie just south of Granite, we were both virtually dead on our feet.

We held the cattle there all the next day to allow the steers to graze and recuperate and just before dark drove them in and loaded them on the cars. George was to go with them to Kansas City riding in the caboose. As soon as the train pulled out, I put "Claybank" in the livery stable and rode back to our so-called camp where we had left the other two horses staked near the bed rolls and cooking outfit. After the soundest night's sleep of my life, I mounted "Steve" and, leading "Babe" and "Red," started for home. I arrived about sundown and for the next three or four days waited anxiously for George's return. About midnight on the fourth day, he rode in on "Claybank." It was a warm moonlight night and I was sleeping on blankets spread down on the soft mesquite grass some thirty or forty yards in front of John's sod house, when I was awakened by his shaking my shoulder. He sat down on the edge of my pallet and told me the sad story. It was far worse than either of us had believed possible. He gave the average weight of the steers, the price per hundred, and the cost of transportation. I did a little mental arithmetic and wailed: "Why George, we can't pay out!"

"Yes we can," he replied, "I figured it all out on the train coming back. We can sell the cows and calves locally here. 'Babe' will bring a fair price and some farmer will pay us something for 'Ole Red.' By selling everything we have except 'Claybank,' 'Steve,' and our saddles we can just pay off everything and might even have a few dollars left."

George pulled off his boots and lay down beside me and we talked for an hour before he fell asleep. I lay awake until nearly daylight thinking but my thoughts led to only one conclusion. The firm of Dale Brothers was broke flatter than old Aunt Lucinda's chest.

My brother's figuring proved correct except for having "a few dollars left." After paying off our note, local obligations, and buying a month's supply of groceries, we listed our total assets. They consisted of eighty acres of raw prairie land, two horses and saddles, the little mare, 'Babe,' which we found we did not need to sell, an old wagon, and less than fifteen dollars in cash. It was virtually a clean sweep of all property, but we were happy that no one was hurt by our misfortune except ourselves.

My years as a cowboy and ranchman were over, but they had taught me many things that vitally affected my future. They had made me an ardent conservative in all business matters. Probably even more important, they had instilled in me a cowhand's philosophy of life or more correctly perhaps, his attitude toward life. Every man who has worked with cattle will understand what this means. George was later to have a few cows on his farm, but for over fifty years after the collapse of our ill-starred ranching venture, I never owned another critter "that parteth the hoof and cheweth the cud!"

The Great Land Lottery

In September, 1900, when George and I had paid the last dollar of our debts, we faced a grim and bleak future. We were broke and virtually homeless, but unlike the earlier years in Greer County temporary employment was readily available. The cotton fields were white as snow and the farmers eagerly sought pickers to help harvest the fleecy staple.

Neither of us had done much except ride horseback for the past two or three years but we had picked plenty of cotton in Texas and now turned to it again as the best means of earning a little money. I picked a few weeks for Wallace Bailey who lived about six miles west of Navajoe. He paid fifty cents a hundred pounds and board, and I'll never forget that at the end of the first day I was almost too tired to sleep when I lay down on the cot set up for me on Bailey's porch. Fortunately, Mrs. Bailey was an excellent cook and her roast chicken, fresh vegetables, and peach cobblers furnished some compensation for back-breaking toil.

In the meantime George had been picking for a neighbor on a farm adjoining that of John and Ava. They were away teaching so he bached in their big sod house in order to be near the field and was paid sixty-five cents a hundred. He could pick around 300 pounds a day while my limit was around 250. When Bailey and I with the help of his two youngsters had gone over his field, I rejoined George and by the middle of November we had finished that field and each of us had quite a few dollars.

About two weeks before we had finished this work the

local school board of a district about six miles northwest of Navajoe offered me the job of teaching their three-month term of school beginning late in November when most of the cotton would be harvested. Here, as in many other parts of the South at this time cotton picking had a distinct priority over education. There was ample reason for this. Few local school districts had enough money for more than a three- to five-month term of school. To begin it in September when the cotton-picking season was just beginning and let the children remain idle during the latter part of winter and early spring did not make sense.

The prospect of teaching school for a time was most attractive to me, and I gladly accepted the offer. My salary was to be thirty-five dollars a month, and Mr. Frazier, one of the Board members who lived only a quarter of a mile from the schoolhouse, offered me board and lodging. He suggested that seven dollars a month would be enough for this, but I insisted on paying eight which included pasturage and feed for "Steve."

My Washita County teaching certificate had expired and at any rate would not be valid in Greer County. This presented no complication, however, for the county super-intendent issued me a temporary permit which was good until the first quarterly examination for certification of teachers was held. Equipped with this I started my first term of school teaching late in November, 1900, little realizing that this was the beginning of what was to be my life's work.

Comparatively little need be given about my first experience in teaching which was brief and uneventful. The schoolhouse, commonly called Lone Oak, but often referred to as "Clabber Flat," was a frame structure about twenty by thirty feet in size. It was furnished with long benches, a teacher's desk and chair, and was heated by a wood-burning sheet iron stove. I enrolled fifty-eight pupils ranging in age from six to twenty years with one about twenty-four years old. Teaching everything from the alphabet through most of the common school subjects was hard work, but there were few disciplinary problems.

The Frazier home where I lived consisted of a large dugout

with a room about fourteen feet square just in front of it. This was turned over to their eighteen-year-old son Bob and me while Mr. and Mrs. Frazier and their fourteen-year-old daughter Emma slept in the dugout which was also the kitchen, dining room, and living quarters. The Fraziers were a lovely family and my stay with them proved most pleasant.

As Christmas drew near, I gave the pupils a "treat" of candy and apples and dismissed school for a week's holiday which, including weekends, amounted to about ten days. The previous Christmas, I had served as special police officer to help the deputy sheriff at Navajoe keep the drunks in order. Anticipating that he might again need some help, that official asked the county sheriff to issue me a deputy sheriff's commission. This he did, and I again buckled on a gun and spent the holiday period in Navajoe aiding the regular peace officers in curbing the activities of the more boisterous celebrants. Fortunately there were no serious incidents and when vacation ended, I again resumed teaching. I retained my deputy sheriff's commission for about a year and was occasionally called upon to arrest someone for a minor offense or to help chase down stock thieves.

Soon after Christmas an epidemic of smallpox swept through the Navajoe community. The disease was in a mild form, but the word "smallpox" was a frightening term. Three or four families in our school district including several of my pupils were stricken, and most parents became alarmed and kept their youngsters at home. When my enrollment dropped from fifty-eight to less than a dozen, I called on the members of the school board and suggested that we close school and hold any money left in the treasury to provide a longer term the following year. They agreed and my first experience in teaching closed at the end of two and a half months.

I returned to Jay's home where George had been living since the cotton-picking season was over. February and March were both cold months with much sleet and snow so none of us did much until warmer weather came. Then we helped Jay plant feed and cotton. Rumors were current that the nearby Kiowa-Comanche Indian reservation would be opened to settlement that summer and this caused great excitement in the Navajoe community as well as through Oklahoma Territory and Northern Texas.[1]

By this time virtually all good land in Greer County had been taken by homesteaders and Mattie wrote us that there was a family living on every quarter-section of her husband's former pasture of sixteen square miles south of Woodward. Moreover, a flood of settlers had also poured into the western part of the Cheyenne country to occupy the wide stretches of empty prairie land which George and I had crossed in returning from Woodward less than two years before.

By the spring of 1901 land was so much in demand that George and I sold our eighty acres of grass land for five dollars an acre to Bailey Brothers who operated a general merchandise store in Navajoe. Our primary reason for selling it was that George was in sore need of medical attention. He had sustained a slight injury to one leg when a horse fell with him and a varicose ulcer developed that steadily grew worse. I took him to a small hospital in Mangum and he returned much improved but the leg troubled him as long as he lived.

Rumors of the opening of the Kiowa-Comanche lands to settlement continued, but exactly what method would be employed no one knew. Some asserted that it would be by a lottery in order to avoid the mad scramble and disorder which had characterized the openings of the Cheyenne-Arapaho reservation and Cherokee Outlet in the early 1890s by so-called "runs." All of us in the Navajoe area, however, hoped that it would be opened by a run. Our knowledge of

---

[1] The opening of the Kiowa-Comanche reservation to settlement in 1901 by the lottery was the culmination of negotiations between federal agents, members of the Jerome or Cherokee Commission, and tribal leaders which extended through the 1890s. Before homestead claims could be established for non-Indians to apply for, federal agents were required to prepare tribal rolls and assign to each Indian (man, woman, and child) a landed estate or allotment (title generally held in trust by the federal government for twenty-one years) of 160 acres.

the western part of the reservation obtained by hunting and fishing there or hauling wood from it, all in contravention of federal law, would give us a distinct advantage in choosing the best land. In addition we had far more faith in our legs than in our luck!

The area to be opened included not only the Kiowa-Comanche reservation but also that of the Wichita and Caddo tribes which adjoined it on the north. The Indians were under the jurisdiction of the United States Indian Agency at Anadarko. Most of the lands of both reservations had been leased to cattlemen who had divided them into huge pastures enclosed by barbed wire fences. All leases provided that when they expired these fences and other improvements placed on the reservation by the ranchmen should become Indian tribal property.

As early as 1892 Indian leaders of the two reservations had signed an agreement for each man, woman, and child to take an allotment of 160 acres and to sell the remaining lands to the United States to be opened to settlement. This agreement was to be valid only after it had been approved by Congress and for some reason that body never saw fit to approve it until June, 1900. The allotting of the lands began immediately and by March, 1901, had been completed. In addition to their allotments the Kiowa-Comanche tribes were to retain 480,000 acres of land in tribal ownership for their surplus livestock.[2]

On March 3, 1901, a federal law directed that these lands should be opened to settlement in such manner as the President might designate, but by this time it had become evident that it would be by some form of lottery. A couple of months later the ranchmen received notice that their leases would be cancelled in the near future, and that they should be prepared to remove their herds from these reservations within a few weeks. This meant that their pasture fences must be removed and the barbed wire rolled up and delivered

---

[2] The Big Pasture was a 480,000-acre reserve set aside for the use of the Kiowa and Comanche Indians. It was liquidated by auction sale to homeseekers in 1906.

at some central point from which it would be distributed to the Indians.

For many years my old Uncle Ike and his wife, Aunt Lou, had been living on his claim about nine miles north of Navajoe. They had a large comfortable home, a big peach orchard, excellent land, and were a most devoted couple, but the old man still retained his restless, roving nature. In consequence, he devoted far more time to freighting merchandise from the railroad to little inland towns, building fences, and plowing fireguards for cattlemen on the reservation than staying home and operating his farm. Knowing this I was not surprised when he came to Jay's and offered me a job.

"Ed," he exclaimed in his booming voice, "I've got me a contract with th' guv'ment to take down about two hundred miles of them pasture fences over in th' Injun Country an' so I have an' I want you to he'p me an' so I do. Kin you make it?"

"I'll be glad to, Uncle Ike," I replied.

"That's fine Ed. The blacksmith is makin' me some windlasses an' so he is. We'll start in right acrost th' river east of my place early Monday mornin' an' so we will. I've got me a purty good crew promised me, an' so I have, but I 'specially want you an' so I do. You kin cook or roll wire which ever you'd ruther do an' so you kin."

I started at daylight Monday morning on "Steve" and reached the place named to find Uncle Ike there with three wagons and seven men including his seventeen-year-old grandson, Casper Davis. This gave him a crew of eight besides himself. Casper was given the job of cook which pleased me a great deal and was quite satisfactory to him.

One wagon was required for the grub, bedding, cooking utensils, and tools while two men on foot followed the fence with hatchets to cut the wire loose from the posts and two more at each wagon set at right angles to the fence wound it up into rolls of approximately 100 pounds each. It was hard work and we were all ready to eat when we reached the chuck wagon which Casper had driven four or five miles down the fence and camped to prepare dinner or supper.

I worked about three weeks on this job and thoroughly

enjoyed it. Uncle Ike was a kind and jovial boss and the men were congenial company. Casper was a good cook and we fared well on his coffee, bacon, beans, sourdough biscuits, sorghum, and dried fruit. We played pitch on a blanket after supper or sometimes caught a mess of fish when we camped on a creek. In addition a couple of cowhands brought us a quarter of fat beef when they butchered a yearling. This added a great deal to our meals.

By about the first of July we had taken down around 150 or 200 miles of fence and Uncle Ike's first contract was completed. I was unable to help the old man on another contract because on July 4 the President issued a proclamation for opening these lands to settlement and I planned to register for a homestead.

Shorn of legal phraseology the proclamation provided that the area to be opened should be divided into two land districts by a line running east and west across the center of it. The northern one was known as the El Reno District and the southern one the Lawton District. Between July 10th and 26th a registration was held at El Reno, a small town near the northern border of the Wichita-Caddo reservation, and Fort Sill on the military reserve near the middle of the Kiowa-Comanche lands and about fifty miles east of Navajoe.

After deducting Indian allotments, school lands, indemnity school lands, the military reserve, forest reserve, and lands retained by the Indians for their surplus livestock, there remained only 6,500 homesteads of 160 acres in each district. Any person desiring one of them must appear in person at either of these registration points, except that honorably discharged soldiers or sailors might be registered by an agent.

Any applicant must certify under oath that he was qualified to receive a homestead and put on a card his address, age, height, weight, birthplace, and the district for which he was registering. To this the registration clerk added any distinguishing marks as a scar, mole, or crooked finger. The card would then be placed in a small envelope, sealed and stamped with the name of the district for which the person had registered. When the registration period ended the envelopes from Fort Sill were to be brought to El Reno and those for that District put in one huge box and those for the Lawton District in another. After being thoroughly mixed by rotating these boxes, they were to be drawn out one by one and numbered in the order drawn.

A land office was to be established for the El Reno District at that town and one at Lawton for that District. On August 6th the first 125 persons whose names had been drawn from the boxes of each district should appear at its land office and make formal entry of the 160-acre homesteads chosen. This was to be continued at the rate of 125 a day at each office until the first 6,500 registrants in each district had chosen a homestead or been given the opportunity to do so. The opening by lottery would then be over, and any land left because some of the first 6,500 failed to appear became part of the public domain.

The proclamation also stated that the region opened should be divided into three counties of Oklahoma Territory to be named Comanche, Kiowa, and Caddo, and that 320 acres were reserved as county seats designated as Lawton, Hobart, and Anadarko. These townsites had been surveyed and platted, and the lots were to be sold at auction to the highest bidder. The sale was to begin on August 6th, and after deducting the cost of surveys and sales all remaining funds were to be turned over to each county for its use in erecting public buildings and operating local governments.

To say that the President's proclamation created great excitement among the residents of our community would be a gross understatement of fact! Our chief interest was in the Lawton District which we knew so well and within twenty-four hours nearly everyone in our community eligible for a homestead was headed for Fort Sill to register. Just why we were in such a hurry is a mystery but there was a vague feeling that those who registered early might have a better chance of drawing an early number than would later registrants.

I started the next afternoon with four friends who supplied a wagon and camping outfit, but I saddled "Steve" and took him along so that I might return leisurely looking over land. We camped the first night about fifteen miles from home. We were up at dawn and after a hurried breakfast resumed our journey. When we reached the crest of a ridge, we could see scores of wagons, carriages, and men on horseback strung along the road both in front and behind us. In the early afternoon we passed an ancient rattle-trap wagon drawn by a dejected looking mule and a cow. An old lady wearing a calico dress and sunbonnet was driving this ill-assorted team while a gangling teen-age boy beside her wielded a long switch, and a couple of tousle-headed younger kids behind them peeped over the top of the wagon bed.

We reached Fort Sill just at sundown. I was riding "Steve" and stopped to watch soldiers at drill for a few minutes. Upon looking around for my companions in the wagon I found that they had vanished. I searched for them until dark without success for there were thousands of other wagons and men scattered about and I, at last, realized that my chances of finding them before morning were remote.

Fortunately I met an old friend who told me that he and three others had arrived early that morning and were camped not far away. When my own situation had been explained, he promptly asked me to spend the night with them, and his invitation was gladly accepted.

While I had never met my friend's companions, they gave me a cordial welcome, brought out grain and hay for "Steve," and announced that supper was ready. After we had eaten by lantern light and the dishes had been washed we sat on the grass to visit and they explained to me the method of registering. They said that when the office had opened for registration the proceding day the line of humanity formed in front of the building was half a mile long. Moreover, while one was being registered, at least half a dozen more persons arrived to further lengthen it. Clearly there would be a string of people two or three miles long, some of whom would have to stand in line for several days before they could be registered.

In desperation an army officer suggested a plan that all would-be-registrants form themselves into companies of one hundred persons and each company choose one of its number as as captain. He should give to each member a number from one to one hundred. All captains should then report to the registration officer every morning half an hour before it was to open. Here each would receive a number for his company and be told approximately when to have it in line before the registration building. Even after receiving a number for his company, however, every captain should report to the office each morning to be given such information as he might need. My hosts declared that the plan was working well and that some 2,000 had been registered the first two days.

The next morning we were all up at dawn, and after breakfast I mounted "Steve" and started in search of my lost companions. That great camp in the valley of Cache Creek just east of the Fort was a wonderful sight as the sun rose above the hills beyond it. As far as one could see to the north and south, were covered wagons and people stirring about cooking breakfast and feeding teams. The smoke of thousands of campfires hung over the valley like a thin fog, and the air was filled with the odor of burning wood. I sought diligently for my friends but did not find them until early in the afternoon.

New companies were being formed all the time and we were soon all "enlisted." I was in company 75 but others in our party were in companies of a slightly higher number. By nightfall over 120 companies had been formed and about 3,500 persons had been registered. Once we were in a company and a captain had been elected, he became largely responsible for getting us registered and we were free to wander about, see the sights, and visit with friends.

George had been away from home when I left for Fort Sill but he came in a couple of days later with three other men from Navajoe. The group with whom I had come returned home as soon as we had registered but I remained three days longer to go back with George and his party. After registering there was nothing for me to do but I was never bored. Church services were held under the trees almost every evening and I attended one evening of singing held in the camp of several farmers from Texas. At this meeting there were a number of women and girls.

The Fort Sill garrison consisted of troops C and D of the 8th Cavalry under the command of Major G. L. Scott. Soldiers patrolled the camp day and night and preserved perfect order. There was no drinking or gambling and one grafter who set up a "shell game" was promptly arrested by a trooper and lodged in the guardhouse. Even social card games were stopped by the troopers.

As soon as George's party had registered, we all returned to Navajoe, but George and I stayed only long enough to put a supply of food and bedding in our old wagon before we set out to explore the country to be opened. Every person who registered was given a registration certificate permitting him to go upon the lands and inspect them in order to be prepared to make the choice of a suitable tract in case his number was drawn. With the best maps obtainable and a pocket compass, we spent a week riding over the western part of the area locating corner stones, noting the quality of the land and the legal description as to township, range, section, and quarter-section. We then returned home to await the results of the lottery.

We had not long to wait. At El Reno on July 29 all envelopes containing registration cards were placed in two boxes ten feet long, two and one-half feet wide, and two and one-half feet deep. With an iron rod running through the middle of each to form an axis, one was labeled El Reno District, the other Lawton District. The boxes were rotated until their contents were thoroughly mixed. Small boys then drew out the envelopes one-by-one and they were opened, the names were recorded, and a card giving the number drawn was mailed to every person who had registered. This was to assure all registrants that their names were actually in the boxes although only the first 6,500 persons whose names were drawn from each box were entitled to choose homesteads under the terms of the lottery.

The number of persons who had registered for the two districts was approximately 164,000. As there were only 13,000 homesteads in both, this meant that a registrant had considerably less than one chance in ten of drawing a so-called "lucky number." George and I had agreed that if one of us drew a claim and the other did not, we would divide the land equally as soon as a patent to it was secured.

George was the lucky man. About six days after the drawing at El Reno had begun he received a card stating that his name was the 486th drawn from the Lawton District box and that he should appear at the Lawton land office on August 9th to make entry of his homestead. This gave us hardly a week in which to make a choice and we hastily prepared for another exploring expedition.

With a frying pan, coffee pot, and enough food for three or four days rolled up in blankets tied behind our saddles we set out at dawn on horseback. Some ten miles beyond the river we reached a small stream called Otter Creek on parts of which we had hunted and fished. We turned north up this stream, searching out corner stones, and making notes. We already had the legal descriptions of dozens of choice tracts of land, but in Western parlance we were looking for a place where "all the coons were up one tree," and eventually felt that we had found it.

On the morning of the third day we came to a lovely valley about a mile and half wide and extending approximately the same distance north to where Otter Creek emerged from a deep canyon in the mountains. The valley was open to the south but was hemmed in by low mountains on the east and west. We turned east and crossed the crystal clear stream flowing over a colorful mosaic of many colored pebbles.

As we looked to the north we were fairly dazzled by the prospect before us. Clearly this was it! A quarter of a mile farther east was a small tributary of Otter Creek. It came through a wide gap in the mountains to the northeast and between it and the main stream lay the loveliest valley we had ever seen. It was level as a floor and covered with grass reaching to our stirrups. We rode up the valley half a mile and returned following Otter Creek and noting the huge pecan, walnut, elm, and hackberry trees along its banks. Crossing to the west side of the stream, we began a diligent search for a corner stone.

We knew the township and range that we were in and gashes in the corner stone would enable us to determine the

78

number of the mile-square section. We soon found it a little over half a mile west of the creek. Two marks on the south side and four on the east indicating the number of miles to the township and range lines showed that we were at the southwest corner of section 21, township 3 north, range 17 west. The grass-covered valley between the streams was therefore on the eastern half of this section.

Our work was finished. If we secured either of these two 160-acre tracts, we felt that it would be like finding the end of the rainbow. There was little difference but we had a slight preference for the south-east one. We realized that 485 others would choose homesteads before George but were certain that most of these would select land as near Lawton as possible because it was almost certain to become the metropolis of southwestern Oklahoma. We must, however, make up a list of several more tracts in case both of these had been taken before George's number had been reached.

Once back at Navajoe we packed the old wagon and started for Lawton reaching it late in the afternoon of August 8th. When we crossed a ridge west of it we were astonished to see before us a city of tents. Any attempt to estimate its population would be only a guess but it must have been 15,000 or 20,000. All lived or carried on their business in tents of many shapes and sizes pitched in long rows with broad streets between them. We found later that the only buildings in Lawton were the land office, a long low wooden structure, and the First National Bank, which was a box-like shack about sixteen by twenty feet.

We camped just before sundown on a ridge half a mile west of the tent city but not liking to leave the horses unattended after dark did not go into town until early the next morning. In what might be called "the business sections" the tents were largely occupied by real estate men as "locators" who for a fee of $25 guaranteed to get any entryman a good homestead. Others housed saloons, cold drink stands, eating places, and shell game or wheel of fortune operators. The centers of attraction, however, were the land office and the platform from which auctioneers called for bids on town lots.

The land office was opened from nine until four except for the noon hour when it was closed for lunch. The holders of numbers, who were admitted in groups of ten, might each take with him an attorney or locator to assure his giving the correct legal description of the land for which he wanted to make entry. No one else except the land office staff was permitted inside the building. A crowd of men hung around the south window, however, and bumped heads as they observed a huge map on the east wall on which a clerk marked with a blue pencil across the tract chosen by each homesteader as his selection was made.

George was admitted to the land office soon after two p.m. and I paced back and forth outside as nervous as an expectant father in a hospital corridor. Half an hour later he emerged with a broad grin on his face and held out his homestead entry receipt.

"Well we got 'er Ed." he exclaimed with great satisfaction. I looked at the paper and read the numbers SE 1/4, S 21, T3N, R17W I.M. (Indian Meridian). I stifled a loud cheer. We had our first choice and all was "right with the world."

We "stayed not upon the order of our going" but hurried back to camp, hitched up our team, and headed for our new home. Upon reaching it the following afternoon we camped in a grove of big walnut trees near the bank of the creek. It was an ideal spot for a cold spring was only a hundred feet away. Here we remained for a couple of days spending our time walking about over the land. Closer inspection made us feel that it was even better than we had thought. We wanted to stay longer but grub was running low so we started for Navajoe to replenish our store.

With enough groceries for two or three weeks and our tent, under which we had been sleeping when at Jay's place, we then returned to our newly acquired land. Here we pitched the tent in the walnut grove by the spring. We wanted to build a house and had funds available for it as Bailey Brothers had paid only part of the purchase price of eighty acres of land we had sold them and the balance was payable on demand.

I discovered immediately, however, that my part in the

land lottery was not ended. The entry of lands at Lawton would not be over for six weeks and already a number of men in Greer County who had numbers coming up later had asked me to help them select homesteads. Others now came to our camp with the same request. As a result until about October first, I worked constantly as a "locator." If I had been willing to charge each of them twenty-five dollars as did the professionals, my return might have been very good, but I preferred to be paid by the day and put the price too low!

It would require a small volume to relate in detail all my experiences in locating men on 160-acre homesteads during the next six weeks. Some were residents of Greer County while others were from Texas or northern or eastern states. Many were from towns and cities and the helplessness of nearly all of these was pitiable. Not one in ten could use a map efficiently and less than one in twenty could read a corner stone but found the marks on one as mysterious as the characters on a Chinese laundry bill. Usually the party consisted of three to five men who were almost always in a covered wagon.

I accompanied them mounted on "Steve," found the corner stones of sections, made plats, took field notes, and prepared each man a list giving the legal descriptions of twenty or more tracts which they had seen and that I knew were vacant at that time. On one or two occasions I went to Lawton with them to see them through the land office. In most cases, however, each man was given a list and instructions to write on his entry application the first number on it that had not already been taken.

Most of these men I located on a broad prairie of rich soil fifteen or twenty miles southwest of our homestead. It had been avoided by many locators because the lands there had been surveyed many years earlier than the rest of the reservation and the corner stones were often difficult to find. By my providing each of my men with a lengthy list of numbers not one of them failed to secure a choice homestead. Many of them moved on to their land and began a home within the six months required by law but some relinquished to another a 160-acre tract that would now sell for $15,000 to $20,000 or more.

As the weeks went by it became evident that a considerable number of the 6,500 persons entitled to choose a homestead in the Lawton District would not do so. The reasons for their failure to appear at the land office and make entry varied. A few had died, others were ill, and a great many who had registered hoping to draw an early number, drew a late one and felt that all good land would be taken before their number had been reached. The reasons for these persons' failure to appear were not important, but the result would be that several hundred 160-acre tracts would be available for homestead entry when the sixty-day period for the lottery ended.

The land office closed at four p.m., October 4th, but it had been ruled by officials in charge that the sixty-day lottery period did not end until midnight. At that time all of these vacant tracts would become part of the public domain and could be claimed as a homestead by the first qualified person who set foot of them. This would mean a mad scramble for land on the night of October 4th.

I was eager to secure one myself but when an elderly Greer County man earnestly begged me to help him, and his son, daughter, and nephew to acquire homesteads, it seemed impossible to refuse. Between a row of sandhills and the North Fork of Red River I had discovered five or six beautiful quarter sections that had been overlooked. In addition I knew of a number of others northwest of our own place.

The Lawton newspaper published every morning the legal numbers of all homesteads entered the preceding day. This enabled us to check on our maps every day just what land was still available. This made it possible for me to make with George and Jay a plan of action. On the first of October I would ride to Lawton and keep my maps and lists of vacant land up to date. Jay, who was helping two or three friends from Navajoe, would camp with them where the Navajoe-to-Fort Sill road crossed Otter Creek three or four miles below our place. Finally, George would take my old man and his party to the Horse Creek crossing of the Fort Sill-to-Vernon road and wait there for me. He would then take my notes for the son and nephew to Jay and they would try to locate land in that area.

I rode into Lawton late in the afternoon of October the first, with some food rolled up in a blanket and a .45 Colt's in a shoulder scabbard inside my shirt. Clearly the fourth promised to be a busy day for all of us. George had expected me to leave Lawton on the fourth around two p.m. but I was determined to get the numbers of all entries made by staying until the land office closed at four. It was some thirty miles to his camp and about that many from there to the little valley beyond the sandhills but he had promised to bring me a fresh horse so I had no doubts about reaching it before midnight.

I was very hopeful of securing land for the girl, her father, and myself in the attractive valley on which my eyes had been fixed hopefully for several weeks.

My three nights in Lawton were spent with three of four Texans encamped about a mile north of town beside a big well from which they were selling water. They had a huge tank on wheels, equipped with hose, from which they would fill a barrel for a dollar, a washtub for fifty cents and a three-gallon pail for a quarter. Every morning I checked off the lands entered the previous day on three maps and marked out on three lists of vacant lands in the western part of the Lawton District all tracts entered as homesteads.

During the last few days lists of entries made in the morning had been posted on the outside walls of the land office at twelve when it was closed for lunch. This made it possible for me to get the information on my maps and lists complete up to noon, October 4th. At one p.m. when the land office reopened I was standing by the exit door with pencil and note book and "Steve," just fed and watered, was tied nearby. As each man came out I asked to see his entry receipt and no one refused. It took but a moment to jot down the land numbers and when the doors closed at four that phase of my work was done and my cherished little valley was still vacant.

Within three minutes I was mounted and riding west. When the Vernon road running southwest was reached, I followed it. Dozens of riders dashed by me, but knowing the many miles we must cover I held "Steve" to a moderate, steady pace. Soon a young chap on a bicycle sped by me turning his head to yell "goodbye." Three or four miles farther on I passed him sitting by the road mending a punctured tire and yelled my own goodbye but he only scowled. Within fifteen miles I began to pass the men who had left Lawton at top speed, some of them walking and leading their horses.

George mounted on "Claybank" met me about a mile from his camp, and we talked things over as we rode in together. Night had fallen but the stars were shining so it was not very dark. I gave George two lists and two marked maps, one of each for himself and for Jay. He studied them for a few minutes while the horses were being hitched to the wagon and I was shifting my saddle from "Steve" to "Babe" that George had brought me. All of this was done within ten minutes, and we were all on our way. George and the two young men riding for Jay's camp some fifteen miles distant and I, mounted on "Babe" and leading "Steve," headed southwest followed by the father and daughter in the covered wagon. It was around thirty miles to the little valley and after following the road for ten or twelve miles we had to leave it and travel the rest of the way across the prairie. Fortunately it was level and when we crossed the valley's rim, it still lacked half an hour until midnight.

I had been doubtful about finding the corner stone after night but a lighted lantern revealed that we had stopped the wagon within thirty feet of it. We drove the wagon, in which the daughter would sleep, a few yards northwest of the stone. Her father and I spread down our blankets on the grass northeast and southwest of it. Thus each of us slept on the land claimed as a homestead. We had neither seen nor heard anyone but I caught glimpses of lights north and west of us and feared that we would have company and competition when morning came.

One who rides sixty miles between four o'clock and

midnight needs no further sedative and I awoke at sunrise the next morning to find that my fears had not been groundless. Less than half a mile north of us was a group of four or five men and about the same number half a mile to the west. Moreover, "Steve" and "Babe" were nowhere in sight. Here was double trouble but having eaten nothing but an apple for eighteen hours my only consideration was breakfast!

A fire was quickly kindled and the big jug from the wagon supplied water for coffee. As we ate I "laid down the law" to my companions. We were on these lands at midnight and no one had a better right to them than ourselves. No doubt every man in sight would swear that he too was on them at midnight and might have been, but so were we. I must go and find my horses that had surely been too tired to go far but while I was gone the father must not go near these men or talk with them. If they came to our camp he should tell them that upon my return we would discuss the situation.

The old man glanced at the heavy Colt's .45 which had been transferred to my belt and vaguely remarked that he "didn't want any trouble" which I assured him we would not have.

I put my saddle on one of his horses and started in search of my own. "Steve" had never left me before but evidently "Babe" had wandered away and he had followed. Within two hours I had found them and was back at camp only to find that my instructions had been totally disregarded. Soon after I had left, the group of men west of us had joined those to the north and the old father could wait no longer but walked over to talk with them. When he offered to sell his and his daughter's rights for fifty dollars, it was plain that he was ready to quit and the men refused to negotiate further.

If he had not made such an offer I would have had some hope of acquiring at least one tract by tossing a coin with other claimants, or drawing lots but clearly the game was now over. Evidently the old man had visions of a gun battle and three or four dead men scattered about over the prairie for he earnestly urged that we leave immediately and try to find other land farther north. Reluctantly I agreed and was fortunate enough to secure the girl a fairly good quarter section of sandy land. George located the nephew on one, and Jay was able to put one of his friends on a fair homestead.

Within three days every 160-acre homestead worth taking had been occupied and George and I returned to our camp in the walnut grove on Otter Creek. Ahead of us lay the task of improving our beautiful tract of virgin land and making of it a productive farm. The Great Land Lottery was over but I always looked back to my share in it as one of the most interesting experiences of my life. For over four months I had not slept under a roof, unless the top of the canvas occassionally occupied could be so designated. During these months it had been my privilege to live almost exclusively with men of all types and from many parts of the country. Some were cultivated Christian gentlemen and some were rough and profane but what I remember most is their kindness. My close association with them in camp and the field added much to my education.

Teaching at Deep Red

The great land lottery of 1901 ended on October 4th, but the land offices at Lawton and El Reno were kept busy for several months. Many persons who drew "lucky numbers" and filed on homesteads were town or city dwellers who knew nothing of farming and had no desire to learn. Most of these sold their claims before the end of the six months' period at which time the law required them to make actual settlement on the homestead. Tracts of 160 acres were sold for $500 or $600 that were eventually worth $15,000 to $20,000.

If George and I had gone into the real estate business we might have done very well, but our only desire was to get settled on our own beautiful claim and start improving it. Obviously our first task was to build a house so we drew the rest of the money due us from the sale of our Greer County land. We then hauled the necessary materials from Hobart, twenty-five miles north of our claim, and hired a "jack leg carpenter" who lived near Navajoe. With our help he built us a box house sixteen feet long and fourteen feet wide. The site was some fifty yards from the middle of the west line of our land and about the same distance from the bank of the creek. We bought a small cookstove which we felt would also provide enough heat. Other furnishings included beds, chairs, a cupboard, cooking utensils, and dishes we brought from our former home near Navajoe for Jay and his wife had their own furniture and did not need that of our father's.

By the time we were settled in our new home it was mid-

November. George's leg was again troubling him so he returned to the hospital at Mangum. He was gone for three weeks and the day after he left a fierce blizzard struck bringing sleet and snow. As a result I lived alone in our new home for that entire time without seeing another human soul! We had neighbors less than a mile away but the weather was so bad that no one ventured out if it could be avoided.

Fortunately I had laid in an ample supply of food and by staying close to the little stove it was possible to keep warm. The first couple of days were lonely ones but I soon became adjusted to living alone. Three or four books, including a thick one-volume history of the United States and a copy of Longfellow's poems, were read and studied with great care. When tired of reading I sometimes found entertainment in writing verses of my own. Some of these were published a quarter of a century later in my little volume of verse, *The Prairie Schooner and Other Poems.* I would also occasionally venture out with my Remington rifle for a brief and slippery stroll along the timber-bordered stream hoping to bag a squirrel. Sometimes I was successful and found squirrel stew with drop dumplings a refreshing change from a diet largely of bacon, beans, sourdough biscuits, syrup, and dried fruit.

The long period of bitter cold ended at last, and the warm winter sun melted the snow and sleet. George came home in high spirits for his leg was much better, and I was delighted to see him after my three weeks of living by myself.

As we checked our resources, however, we found that building our new home and paying George's medical bills, added to living expenses, had left us again virtually penniless. Moreover, there seemed to be no way of earning money as cotton picking was over, and in the winter months neither farmers nor ranchmen needed help.

The long period of cold weather had reduced the fuel supply of many of the settlers in Greer County, and some of our former neighbors soon came to us asking that we sell them some wood. Living for years on the Greer County prairies had given both George and me a love for a growing tree equal to that of Joyce Kilmer. There were many dead or half dead trees along the creek, however, and some dry logs or branches on the ground. These we gladly sold and while we were not paid much for a wagon load of wood our income from this source was enough to keep us supplied with groceries for a few months.

In addition to reserving 320-acre tracts of land at the county seats of Lawton, Hobart, and Anadarko for townsites, the federal government had set aside three or four other townsites of 160 acres each. One of these was about three miles southeast of our place. Here the thriving village of Mountain Park had grown up. By November it had three or four general merchandise stores, a hotel, blacksmith shop, meat market, barber shop, and a population of nearly 1,000.

One day I rode over to Mountain Park to get the mail and have my hair cut. The barber had just finished with me, and I was putting on my coat when a long, lanky chap came in and said to him:

"Jim, if you're goin' up to Hobart this week I wish you'd ask that county superintendent of schools to send us a teacher. Our schoolhouse is just about finished, and we want to start school a week from Monday if we can find a teacher."

"Here's a teacher right here," said the barber, "and he's a good 'un. Mr. Dale, this is Dick Robinson."

As a matter of fact Barber Jim did not know whether I was a "good 'un" or not but only that I had taught a short term of school in Greer County. The rest of his statement was only guesswork.

Mr. Robinson explained to me that he lived about twelve miles southeast of Mountain Park and was one of the three trustees of the Deep Red School District. He added that the other trustees were in town for they had all come up to get a load of feed for their cattle. If I would consider teaching their school we could go and see them and settle the matter at once.

The idea appealed to me very much especially after meeting the other two trustees who seemed to be men of high type. Within fifteen minutes it was agreed that I should teach their school for three months at a salary of forty dollars a month to be paid in district school warrants. These would probably have to be discounted at the bank although they drew 6 percent interest until they were paid.

When I asked about a place to board, Dick Robinson said that he and his wife didn't have much room but if I didn't mind that, they would be glad to have me board with them. He added that they lived only a quarter of a mile from the school house. I assured him that I was not accustomed to "much room," and it was agreed that the Robinsons would board me for eight dollars a month which included payment for pasturage and feed for "Steve."

George received the news of my school teaching job with mixed feelings. Naturally he hated to be left to bach all alone but realized that we had to eat and, with the coming of spring, we would not be able to sell enough firewood to replenish our supply of groceries already alarmingly low. So the offer of forty dollars a month to teach school came like manna from Heaven.

On the Sunday afternoon before the Monday set for the opening of school I mounted "Steve" and with a sack holding my spare clothes and a few books tied behind my saddle, set out for my new job. It was easy to find the Robinson place but a bit shocking to realize that when Dick said he "didn't have much room" he had told the truth—and how! His house was a single room about eighteen feet long and fourteen feet wide. It was on the south side of a small hill and the rear half was largely underground although the floor was level with the front yard.

The furniture consisted of two double beds extending along the west wall. Between the footboards of these was only room for a couple of trunks. The cookstove was in the northeast corner of the room with a cupboard beside it. The dining table on the east side, half a dozen chairs, and a shelf east of the door with a water pail, tin dipper and washpan completed the furnishings except for cooking utensils.

Dick and his wife gave me a most cordial welcome and introduced me to their sister-in-law, who was visiting them. They brought forward their three children, Geneva, about eight years old, Elmer, who was six, and Clarence, four.

After a good supper we sat and visited for a couple of hours. The Robinsons were from Wise County, Texas, where Dick's father owned about 700 acres of land and a cotton gin. Dick had farmed some of this land as a renter but wanted a home of his own so had come out and registered for the lottery. Failing to draw a number below 6,500 he had bought this place for $500.

About nine o'clock Clarence was asleep on his mother's lap and Dick suggested that he and I go out to the well and get a cool drink before going to bed. He drew up a bucket of water and after drinking we sat down on the well curb and continued our conversation for about ten minutes. During this time we could hear the women moving about in the house and dropping shoes. Finally all was still inside and the light shining through the window grew dim so he remarked that he was sleepy, and we'd better get to bed.

When we got inside I saw that the two women and Geneva and Clarence were in the north bed and the south one, next to the door, had the covers turned back for Dick and me with young Elmer crosswise at our feet. Dick got in bed next to the wall and I blew out the lamp, hung my outer garments on a chair within easy reach, and slipped into bed on the front side. As was customary at the time, and for many years more, all men and boys slept in their underwear. No one in that region had ever heard of pajamas, and only an occasional very old man slept in a nightgown and cap.

The last thing I remember before falling asleep was wondering about how to get my pants on the next morning. It proved very easy. When I awoke it was broad daylight, and Dick was up and outside doing the feeding and milking. The women were both up and cooking breakfast, diligently keeping their backs toward me. I reached out and retrieved my trousers, slipped them under the covers, and hunched up my knees to make a small tent of the covers. Under this it was easy to pull on my pants and then sit up to put on my shirt, pivot around to get my feet on the floor, and slip on socks and shoes. I was then fully dressed and needed only to wash and comb my hair to be ready for breakfast.

It might be said now that for the next three months this was my method of dressing. By that time it had become a fixed habit, and even when there was no necessity for it I continued to dress in bed.

Immediately after breakfast Dick and I went to the schoolhouse. Except for a chair and small table for the teacher supplied by one of the school board members it had no furniture. The twenty by thirty foot room had been swept clean, and there was a water bucket and long-handled tin dipper in one corner, and a wood-burning stove in the middle of the room. There was also an axe and a pile of wood outside. Dick said that the children had been told to bring chairs or stools as seats, and the big boys would bring water from a nearby neighbor's well and chop wood. He added that the board would have some benches made as soon as the neighborhood carpenter could get around to it.

The lack of a blackboard troubled me a little but I had brought a thick pencil tablet with me and when Dick left me for his own work, I nailed this to the wall behind my table. Figures and exercises could be written large enough on this with a soft pencil and the sheet torn off when something else was needed. I also had a small bell, from my Clabber Flat teaching, for summoning the students.

About eight-thirty I saw through a south window two tall, lean teenage girls coming. Each was carrying books and an empty red powder can, evidently tossed aside by the construction crew building a railroad a couple of miles to the west. When they came through the door the girls both curtsied politely to me. They then placed their books on the floor, seated themselves on the powder cans, and were apparently ready for school.

Other children soon began to arrive each carrying a chair, stool, or short bench. In one of two instances parents brought the youngsters and chairs in a wagon but as a rule the children came alone bringing an assortment of textbooks and their lunches in tin pails. At nine o'clock I rang the bell and those playing outside trooped in. Two boys failed to bring anything to sit on but I found a couple of nail kegs and a short board outside which provided a precarious bench.

92

A count revealed that there were thirty-two pupils ranging in age from six to sixteen. From them I learned that the former home of most of them had been Texas. The Hash and "Widder Grubb" families that were closely related, however, were from the mountainous part of Virginia, the Mounts from Colorado, and the Thompsons from Indian Territory where Mr. Thompson owned and operated a large general store. He was regarded as well-to-do by his neighbors most of whom were quite poor.

It was not possible to do much the first day except get the names and ages of the children, find out how far they had gone in school, and organize classes. None of the very young had been in school before or knew the letters of the alphabet and some of the nine to eleven year-olds had attended school only three or four months and had not gone beyond the First Reader. Some of the older ones would now be classified as in the fourth or fifth grades and two or three might have reached the sixth. Without exception, however, every one of these thirty-two children appeared intelligent and eager to learn.

Within two or three days we had settled down to work in happy fashion. I liked these kids and they liked me. Their textbooks from various states were sent to town and the book dealer gave a generous price for them in exchange for the adopted texts used in Oklahoma Territory. In a couple of weeks the local carpenter delivered us ten long benches which solved the problem of seating. We still had no desks and no blackboard but we got along without them. Two of the benches were put in front of my table for the use of classes when called to recite and thick pencil tablets nailed to the wall served in lieu of a blackboard. The other long seats were placed well to the rear of the room in order that my reciting classes would not interfere too much with the studies of the other pupils.

About the first of May a tornado from the northwest struck the schoolhouse and moved it some thirty or forty feet to the southeast. Fortunately, it remained upright, but the seats were overturned and the kids and I all fell flat on the floor. The southside of the roof was split and a heavy rain which came behind the wind poured in. The youngsters, all crying and wailing as they got on their feet, earnestly asked me:

"Perfessor, will there be another 'un?"

I assured them that there would not be and looked them over to see if any were hurt. One boy had a small knot on his forehead, and a little six-year-old girl was sobbing that her back was hurt. I sat down, took her in my lap, unbuttoned the back of her little dress, and found a blue spot about the size of a dime between her shoulders. I rubbed it a bit, told her that she was not hurt, and she stopped crying. With the help of the boys we moved all the seats to the dry side of the room and when the children's anxious parents arrived, they found their offspring running and sliding on the wet floor near the south side of the room!

School was dismissed for a couple of days while the men restored the building to its foundation and mended the roof. However, for the rest to the term when a dark cloud appeared to blot out the sun, students became so fidgety and nervous that I had to call a recess and send them outside. Once out of the building where they could keep an eye on the clouds their nervousness vanished and they instantly began to play with enthusiasm a game of town-ball, shinny, or "blackman." Feeling that they were "playing me for a sucker," I would ring the bell and call them in, but immediately their nervousness returned and there seemed nothing to do but either give them another recess or dismiss school for the day and send them home.

Most persons today would view with horror the prospect of living for three months with a family of five in a house of only one fairly large room. They would feel that life under such conditions must be unpleasant. Nothing could be further from the truth. Mrs. Robinson kept the little home scrupulously clean and provided us with meals of plain, substantial food. The children were always quiet and well-behaved when in the house, but most of the time they played outside until dark and were put to bed soon after supper.

I have never known a more modest, kindly, and considerate family than the Robinsons. Once accustomed to dressing under the bed covers every morning and going to the well each evening for a drink of cool water while Mrs. Robinson retired, it became quite natural. Any preparations of lessons, reading, or grading papers could be done at the schoolhouse after four o'clock when the children had gone home. As to a bath, no one in the entire region took more than one a week, usually Saturday night, and very few that often. I usually went home on weekends where I could take a dip in the creek or in a wash tub in the kitchen if the water in the stream was too cold.

Teaching at Deep Red was a most happy experience. The children were as good as gold and even the beginners made a remarkable advance in this brief term of three months. The three or four to whom I had to teach the alphabet could read quite well by the end of the term and spell correctly every word in the *Primer* including "cylinder" which is more than can be said for some of my former college students!

The school term ended about the first of June. I bought about twenty pounds of mixed candy as a "treat" for the children and hid it in the barn. After the Robinson kids were sound asleep I brought this in and poured it on the table. Mrs. Robinson and Dick helped me to put it into the small paper bags which had been given to me. These were placed in a large wooden box and concealed under a bed, with Dick voicing some regret that Elmer could not have seen the "big pile of candy on our table."

School ended the next day with classes as usual until afternoon recess but this final period was devoted to a program of readings, songs, and the awarding of some prizes. These were attractive books with colored pictures that I had bought to award students for excellence in spelling and arithmetic and most progress in all studies. Then the bags of candy were distributed and goodbyes were said sometimes accompanied by tears of some of the older pupils and more or less sticky kisses from a few of the small fry. They were comforted a bit when I told that I had promised the school board to come back the next term which they hoped would be for at least four or five months.

Pleasant as my three months in the Deep Red community had been, I was very glad to get back to our Otter Creek home again and resume baching with George. He had been a bit lonely at times in spite of my frequent weekend visits and the fact that we now had neighbors all about us. The past six or eight months had brought great changes in this area and others soon followed.

The railroad extending south from northern Oklahoma had been completed to Vernon, Texas, and the village of Mountain Park grew rapidly. A little later a branch of the Frisco had been pushed southwest from Oklahoma City to Quanah, Texas, crossing this earlier railway line about three miles south of Mountain Park. At this intersection a new town called Snyder had been established which soon outstripped its neighbor to the north. Some ten or twelve miles west of Snyder, in Greer County, the Frisco also founded the town of Headrick. To this, Navajoe, only seven miles northwest, quickly removed "lock, stock, and barrel," leaving only the schoolhouse. This was torn down a few years later, and only the little wind-swept cemetery remained to remind the oldtimers of the flourishing little town that for over fifteen years had been an important trade center for a huge area.[1]

These rapid changes meant little to George and me. Our most pressing problem was how we were going to eat for the next few months! My so called "salary" of forty dollars a month had been paid in school district warrants, but there were no funds to pay them. In consequence they had to be sold and, although they drew 6 percent interest until paid, the banks refused to take them for less than a 25 percent discount.

This meant that my forty dollars a month was reduced to thirty dollars and after paying for my board and lodging I

---

[1] Navajoe is a case study in the effect of railroads on towns. Increasingly in these times towns followed the course of rail right-of-way; those situated a distance from the railroad faced extinction. Snyder is an example of a town which grew up at the Frisco Railway intersection. Headrick evolved as a railroad town; it was formed in large measure by business leaders at Navajoe moving their properties to the railroad.

had left only twenty-two dollars a month. It is true that little money was required. Bacon was only about ten cents a pound and twenty-five cents would buy enough steak to serve a family of four or five persons. Even so, all I had left of my teaching pay could hardly be stretched far enough to buy groceries from June to cotton-picking time in September. Until that time, getting a job was virtually impossible.

Luckily we happened to meet an old Yankee claimholder who sold us a second-hand mower to be paid for in six months. The bluestem grass on our valley land across the creek was almost waist-high so we made a wooden bullrake and began cutting and stacking hay. We put up several stacks, did a little cutting for others farther down the creek, sold two or three loads of wood, and pulled through until autumn. The fare was a bit slim sometimes but wild currants, plums, and fish we caught from deep holes in the creek added something to our diet so we were never hungry.

About the first of September Mr. Jenkins, whom we had known in Greer County, came to see us. He said that he had accepted a job as manager of a cotton gin in Washita County but had about thirty head of cattle on his claim some twelve miles south of us and asked George to live in his house and take care of them during the ginning season. This would be about three months and although the pay was low, George was glad to take the job for the work would be light, and Jenkins gave him the first month's payment in advance!

My term of school at Deep Red did not begin until the first of November so I was again left alone to keep bachelor's hall. It was not so lonely as it had been the year before as the weather was lovely and there were now neighbors who were frequent visitors. One had a large field of cotton and during October I joined Uncle Mike Smith's three boys in cotton picking. To save time I took a lunch to the field, and one of my clearest memories is of how good the food tasted at supper after picking cotton from soon after sunrise to sundown with only a cold lunch at noon. The sourdough biscuits, bacon, fried potatoes or canned corn, and sorghum had a flavor that only a long day of hard work in the crisp October air can give.

Of course I often rode down to see George on Sundays. He was looking after the cattle and cutting feed and putting it in shocks from time to time, but his most difficult task was keeping a few of the more perverse old cows from breaking through the pasture fences and raiding the nearby farmers' fields. He was quite comfortable most of the time, but Mrs. Jenkins had insisted on taking most of the furniture with them, including the cookstove. This made it necessary to build a campfire in the yard to prepare a meal and to bake biscuits in a Dutch oven. Cooking outside presented no problem except on occasional rainy days.

George was still at the Jenkins place when my school term at Deep Red began about the first of November. Mrs. Robinson's health was bad so I boarded with Mr. and Mrs. Worthy who lived about a mile northeast of the school house. Their home of five rooms seemed very commodious compared with the Robinson's one-room dugout and although they had three young daughters, ranging in age from six to eleven, they were able to give me a small room and still have ample space for their own family.

I was very glad to get back to the Deep Red school again. My former students and their parents all seemed delighted to see me and I quickly became acquainted with the half dozen or so new pupils. I rode over to see George once or twice but in less than a month Mr. Jenkins sent his family home and George returned to our Otter Creek cabin. After that until the term ended about the first of March many of my weekends were spent with him there.

As was the custom I dismissed school for a week as Christmas drew near, after giving the children a treat of candy and apples. The holiday was as welcome to me as to the youngsters for I had not been with George much for three or four months. We had Christmas dinner with our brother Henry and his family who had sold the hotel they had been operating in Cordell and moved to Mountain Park. Most of the holiday week, however, was spent on the claim, hunting a little along the creek but mainly visiting.

My school closed about the first of March with exercises as at the end of the first term, treats for the children, and awarding of prizes. Money had been available to pay my warrants, and the school board had promised to give me a six months' term the following year at forty-five dollars a month so I agreed to return.

It was good to be home again, and my first task was to plant a big garden on a plot of ground across the creek which we had plowed the preceding September. If we ever had any doubts as to the fertility of the soil they speedily vanished. Everything I planted grew amazingly well. We had far more onions, potatoes, beans, cantaloupes, watermelons, and other "garden truck" than we could use so we gladly gave the surplus to neighbors.

The months slipped by quickly. We cut and stacked a little more hay, sold a few loads of wood, and were able to buy enough groceries to eat fairly well. Yet we both had the feeling that, in our own language, we were only "spinning our wheels getting nowhere fast." We had lived here for nearly two years on one of the most beautiful and fertile 160-acre tracts of land we had ever seen. Clearly it could be made a most productive farm by the expenditure of a few hundred dollars, but we had no money and apparently no means of securing any. We could not give the land as collateral for a loan because a homesteader must live on a claim five years in order to receive a patent of clear title. Until then, the title was held in trust by the United States government.

One evening near the end of summer, George came up with a surprising suggestion. Under what was known as the "commuted provision" of the Homestead Act a homesteader might receive a patent or fee-simple title to his claim after fourteen months residence by paying a dollar and a half an acre to the federal government. George proposed that we do this instead of waiting some three more years to get the land free.

My first reaction to this proposal was little short of horror. We had borrowed money before with tragic results, and "a burned child dreads the fire." As we talked it over, however, my objections began to vanish. Unlike our short time cattle loan, this one would be for several years during which time the land was certain to increase in value, and the advance would be even greater because the money would be used for improvements.

Once we had agreed on this course, we became quite enthusiastic to put it through as soon as possible. It took some time to take care of all details but it was easy to get a loan of $800 to be paid in five years. George made the trip to Lawton, paid the $240 at the land office, and received his patent. This left us $560, a pitifully small sum by recent standards, but important money in Oklahoma Territory.

One of our first tasks was to move the house nearly a quarter of a mile south to a spot only a couple of hundred yards from the section line road along the south side of the land. This was done to avoid having to cross a short west branch of Otter Creek which caused us trouble after a rain. The move was not difficult as neighbors helped us and the task was finished in a few hours.

Before we were able to get much done toward improving the land it was time for my school to begin at Deep Red. I boarded with Mr. and Mrs. G. D. Thompson who lived a mile east of the schoolhouse. They had three sons and two daughters in school and a baby boy at home. They were a lovely family with an attractive two-story home. There were three beds upstairs where the boys and I slept.

School started off in excellent fashion for I now felt very much at home in the Deep Red community. It was about the middle of September and the weather was pleasant. When I rode home at the end of the first week, George and I talked about hiring a farm hand to break sod and build fences, corrals, and sheds.

Here I was able to help. The Hash family from the mountains of Virginia had, in addition to three children in my school, two grown sons at home. The older of these, Alex, impressed me as a nice quiet chap who would be just what George needed. When I got back to Deep Red I rode over to the Hash home to see him and explain our situation. He did not seem to mind eating bachelor's cooking and when I asked him what wages he would expect he said he "would try it a month for sixteen dollars."

No better choice could have been made. George and Alex liked each other from the first day and soon became fast friends. Alex was a tireless worker and by the time my school closed, the first of March, large fields had been plowed, pastures fenced, corrals and sheds built, a well drilled, and the yard fenced. For the next three years George had Alex with him a large part of the time and always declared that he had never seen a better farm hand.

While George and Alex were improving the farm, I was busily engaged in trying to improve the learning of the youngsters of the Deep Red school. The number of pupils had now risen to forty. We formed a lively literary and debating society, held a box-supper to raise money for the church, and attended other such suppers or debates at the Hilltop School six miles west of ours.

The Thompson home was a very pleasant one, but Mrs. Thompson was expecting a baby so a few weeks before it was due I moved in with Mr. and Mrs. Dysart for the last two months of the term. Living with them was very pleasant. The children in the household were two sons of Mr. Dysart's first wife, Wesley about fourteen, and John, twelve. A couple of years after their mother's death, Mr. Dysart had remarried and the second Mrs. Dysart had borne him a daughter, at this time hardly more than a baby.

My decision not to return to Deep Red was reached only after long deliberation and considerable soul searching. The community was very close to my heart and I felt a deep affection for my pupils which it seemed that they returned in full measure. With very few exceptions they had studied hard and made remarkable progress. Some ten- or eleven-year-old youngsters could barely read at the beginning of my first term of teaching the Deep Red School. Yet after only thirteen months of schooling they were equal to most sixth grade students in reading, spelling, writing, arithmetic, and geography.

It would have been a real pleasure to continue working with them, but it seemed that if I continued teaching it should be as principal of a school large enough to require two or three teachers. The members of the school board seemed deeply disappointed by my decision but did not blame me in the least.

The exercises of the last day included the usual treat for the children and the awarding of prizes. A number of the parents came and seemed to enjoy the program very much. When it was over, however, and the time had come to say goodby, a good many tears were shed not only by the smaller fry but by some of the older girls and boys. It must be confessed that my own heart was deeply touched and every summer for the next two or three years I paid several weekend visits to friends in the Deep Red community and always received a most cordial welcome.

Village
Schoolmaster and Student

With the close of school at Deep Red I hastened home to help George and Alex on the farm. I was a trifle soft and sappy after staying indoors so much for six months but hard work on the land soon toughened my muscles. The land plowed in October was in fair shape for growing crops and we now had farm implements with which to work.

Alex and I planted large fields of corn, feed, and cotton, did more fencing, and built a shed-room on the north side of the house. George did most of the cooking, milked the cow that he had bought, did other chores around the place, and helped with plowing the corn and chopping cotton. He also directed the work of building the shed-room as he knew a little about carpentry of which Alex and I were grossly ignorant.

While busy with farm work, I was also keeping in mind the problem of a school for the coming year. My brother John, who was teaching at Mangum, the county seat of Greer County, wrote me that the school board at Duke was in need of a principal for that two-teacher school. Duke was a tiny village about twelve miles west of Altus. It was some distance from any railroad so I rode out there to look over the situation.

It did not appear too promising. The area was in the process of changing from a ranching to a crop-growing community. The school building of two large rooms was on the prairie about a quarter of a mile from the little hamlet which consisted of one large general merchandise store, another much smaller one, a blacksmith shop, and three or four residences. The three members of the school board were all farmers. They greeted me cordially and after a brief visit, I agreed to accept their offer of sixty dollars a month for a term of six months. School was not to begin until very late in November after the cotton-picking season was about over for there was a good deal of cotton grown in the community.

In August I attended a summer normal which John conducted at Olustee, a little town some ten miles southwest of Altus. This seemed necessary because I would be teaching in Greer County and would need to secure a teacher's certificate from that county. The normal was much like that one I had attended some years before at Cloud Chief except living conditions were less primitive and the number in attendance larger. At its close the usual two days of examinations were held and I received a first grade certificate since my past teaching experience now exceeded twelve months.

After the close of the normal, I returned to the farm and helped George and Alex gather corn, pick cotton, and build more fences until late in November when it was time to open school at Duke.

I left "Steve" at home and went from Snyder by train to Eldorado, and from there to Duke by the daily stage which carried both mail and passengers.

Teaching at Duke proved very different from that at Deep Red. I boarded with Mr. and Mrs. Witcher who lived less than half a mile east of the school building. The family consisted of two daughters and one son. The older daughter, Beulah, was a very attractive girl about twenty years old. The younger one, Addie, about eight, was a nice kid but the son Grover, around twelve or thirteen, was a "holy terror!" Perhaps he was a "chip off the old block" for his father had a blazing temper and swore like a trooper although he was a very kind man. The other member of the household was a hired man of German extraction called Joe who shared a room with me. Joe was a Catholic and had a Bible on his table but apparently never opened it as long as he felt well. When stricken with a minor illness, such as a touch of indigestion, however, he read it diligently until the ailment had passed.

My assistant teacher was a young woman with the impossible name of Jerusha. She had all the younger children while I had all those above the third reader. Jerusha had taught only a few weeks when she was forced to resign because of the serious illness of her mother. Beulah Witcher took her place and the county superintendent of schools, at my request, issued her a temporary certificate to complete the term.

My memories of the six months at Duke are not particularly happy ones and the period could be dismissed with a very brief statement except for two episodes. Only one of these was related to my school work, while the other was a tragic event in the history of southwestern Oklahoma.

The younger children of the Duke School studied fairly well and presented no problem. Unfortunately there were half a dozen or more big youths from sixteen to twenty years old who apparently felt that proofs of manhood were the ability to ride wild broncs, swear fluently, play pitch, chew tobacco, and spit through their teeth! I knew the type only too well and expected trouble from some of them sooner of later.

It was delayed however for some four months. Then I was forced to suspend a nineteen-year-old youth for misbehavior and refusal to obey rules. My timing was bad for it was on a Friday afternoon that I told him to take his books home and not to come back until he was ready to promise that he would behave himself and give no further trouble. This gave him the weekend to secure a pledge of help from a couple of his cronies.

On Monday he appeared early and when the bell rang, came and took his usual seat near the door. When I asked if he had returned ready to promise better behavior he replied that he was making no promise but was staying in school and no one could make him go home.

Apparently there was nothing for me to do except take him by the collar, drag him from his seat, and throw him outside the open door.

As the girls fled to Beulah's room, the two husky reserves rose from their seats and moved in my direction. By the stove was an iron rod about three feet long and nearly an inch in diameter that served as a poker. I picked this up, pointed at the two would-be-reinforcements, and said: "Sit down!" They sat!

My attention was then given to my original opponent who had picked himself up and was coming through the door with a rock in one hand. As his comrades were now back in their seats I laid the poker down and caught the lad's wrists. Not able to get close enough to trip him without danger of being struck by the rock in his right hand, I loosened my grip on his left wrist and hit him on the jaw, knocking him down. It was then easy to twist the rock out of his hand and sit on him until he agreed to go home.

Instead of going home he sat down on the woodpile and Witcher, who came past on his way to Duke, arrested him and took him to the justice of the peace who lived there. The lad's father and big brother learned of this by way of the "grapevine telegraph" and rode into the village to sign a bond for his appearance in court.

After school was dismissed at four o'clock, the father, school board members, and three or four of the older students who had witnessed the "late unpleasantness," met with me at the schoolhouse. The father said that he had told his son to go back to school that morning and ask me to let him stay but to come home if I refused. He then admitted that the boy was "partly" to blame but insisted that I shared some of the blame, and that we should both plead guilty to assault and pay our fine! Upon my flat refusal he produced a warrant for my arrest. Witcher read it and the board members all signed a bond for my court appearance.

The aftermath of this affair was that the father went to Mangum to consult the county attorney. That official told him to hurry home, withdraw the charges against the teacher, and have his son plead guilty to assault. The father did this and paid the son's fine and court cost amounting to a total of about twenty-five dollars. The lad did not return to

106

school and his father seemed willing to regard the incident closed.

Rumors reached me, however, that the big brother was voicing threats that at the first opportunity he and two of his friends were going to beat me up in such fashion that my own brother wouldn't know me. As a result of such rumors for a few weeks I carried a .45 Colt's pistol in a shoulder scabbard under my shirt when I went to the village each Saturday. No further trouble came, however, and school ran along very smoothly to the end of the term.

I have always felt a bit ashamed of this incident in my work as a teacher but have never regretted the way in which I dealt with the situation. It was fortunate that the youth's two friends each had a yellow streak in his makeup wider than Michigan Boulevard for the iron rod I picked up was a lethal weapon. Faced with the task of defending myself against the attack of three big huskies, including one armed with a rock, I might have struck too hard and killed one of them.

The other event marking the six-months' period of my teaching at Duke that is memorable was the frightful tornado of May 10, 1905, which swept away a large part of the town of Snyder. News of this disaster reached Duke within a few hours together with a plea for help. Naturally, I was deeply concerned as to the safety to my friends in Snyder since it was only five miles from our home on Otter Creek. It was near the weekend so Mr. Witcher took me to the railway station early the next morning and by ten o'clock I reached Snyder.[1]

The situation there was horrible. In a town of some 1,200 people about 120 had been killed and that many more seriously injured. A vacant store building was taken over as a morgue and on the shelves and counters were laid the broken and mangled bodies of men, women, and children. Another large building was used as a hospital where doctors

---

[1] The Snyder tornado, 1905, which killed 120 and injured several hundred matched in destructive fury the storm which hit Woodward in 1947, killing 101 persons and seriously injuring over 1,000 survivors.

and volunteer nurses ministered to the injured as best they could.

Although many persons came from nearby towns to offer help, there also came a few underworld characters hoping to profit by this disaster. I therefore joined with a dozen men serving as special police officers acting as guards to prevent looting of wrecked buildings, especially at night. On the following day my work was in the little cemetery where we buried eighty bodies in the afternoon. It was a gruesome task and I can never forget the pitiful sight of one small boy who sat sobbing beside the long grave as we buried his father, mother, grandfather, grandmother, brother, and sister. From a household of seven he alone had escaped death protected in the dugout back of the house.

After the mass burial and the appearance of a national guard troop to preserve law and order I went out to the farm before returning to Duke. Here I found George and Alex diligently engaged in constructing a storm cellar! Virtually every family in Snyder and the surrounding country lacking a storm cave dug one within a few weeks. These refuges were commonly called "fraidy holes" and were often furnished with a bed, two or three chairs, and a lamp or lantern.

Some three weeks after the Snyder disaster my school closed, and I returned home to help George and Alex on the farm. There was also the problem of finding a school for the coming year. The Duke school board had urged me to return at an increased salary and a number of my students seemed deeply disappointed when I told them that I would not be with them the next year. I was fond of many of these youngsters and their parents but I missed the warmth and hospitality of the Deep Red community and also I wanted to be in a larger school.

The problem of another school was soon solved. While riding over to Greer County to visit my brother Tom, I met a member of the Headrick school board who stopped me to ask if I would take a place in the Headrick school. He said that they had employed the principal but wanted another man as the other three teachers were women.

Headrick was a thriving little town with a bank, one large

general merchandise store, two or three smaller ones, a restaurant, hotel, drugstore, barber shop, meat market, and a small newspaper. The school employed five teachers for a seven-month term. The prospect of teaching there pleased me very much. Several of the leading citizens of Headrick had been businessmen at Navajoe before the sudden death of that little town and were my good friends. I accordingly called on the other two members of the school board and was quickly employed as the "second man" in the school at a salary of sixty-five dollars a month.

Most pupils of the Headrick school came from farm homes as it was one of the first two consolidated school districts in Oklahoma Territory. Transporting children by bus lay far in the future but many pupils came in buggies or light spring wagons. A long shed on the school grounds provided shelter for the animals and the youngsters brought grain and hay for them and lunches for themselves.[2]

The chief crop in the area about Headrick was cotton which until fairly recent years has so interfered with education in the South. This meant that our seven months term did not begin until late in November, after most of the cotton had been picked. The late opening of school pleased me for I could stay at home and help harvest our cotton, corn, and feed crops.

Before my work began at Headrick, I had been either the only teacher in the school or at Duke the "head man" with an assistant. In consequence, it was natural for me to worry a bit at the thought of being in a secondary position. I soon found that there was no reason for such worry. Our superintendent, Mr. Dennis, was a very kind and sensible person who showed me every possible consideration. In fact, it was something of a relief to have little responsibility for any students except those of my own classroom.

It was not long, however, until my situation changed. Within two or three months Mr. Dennis resigned to become

---

[2] This represents a pioneer effort at consolidating schools to improve quality of instruction; this step in educational reform did not become a statewide policy until the late 1930s and 1940s.

bookkeeper for the town's biggest store, and I was appointed superintendent by the school board. This boosted my pay to seventy-five dollars a month and made me the teacher of the most advanced students. These had never been placed in definite grades but would now be in junior high school although far older than most junior high students of today.

The responsibility of teaching these young people made me feel keenly my own limitations. Up to this time my formal education beyond the eighth grade had consisted of only two four-weeks' terms at summer normal institutes conducted by my brother John. True, I had read widely and probably had as much knowledge of history and literature as most college graduates. Clearly, however, if I continued teaching it was necessary for me to begin at once a program of high school and college training.

My brother, John, had graduated from the Central Normal School at Edmond. This was a two-year college primarily for teachers and each of its graduates received a diploma which constituted a life-time authorization to teach in any Oklahoma public school without further examination. As John had told me a great deal about this school, I quickly decided to continue my education there.

Immediately after the close of school at Headrick, about June, 1906, I took the train for Edmond. Except for the two normal institutes, I had never attended any school of more than two rooms so the two large brick buildings of Central Normal filled me with awe and admiration. I enrolled in beginning Latin, algebra, plane geometry, American history, and English. Chapel was held every day and it was a great thrill to find myself a member of the student body of what seemed to me a great educational institution!

I was fortunate to find room and board at the home of Mrs. Barlow who lived with her son and two daughters near the campus. My roommate was the college librarian, Luther L. Dickerson. He was a very pleasant young chap about three or four years younger than myself.

Latin and mathematics were difficult for me but history and English were easy. By hard work I was able to make fair grades in the more difficult subjects and excellent ones in

English and history. By the close of the summer session the first of August, I had become fairly well adjusted to campus life and had made a number of friends among the students, most of whom were either teachers or prospective teachers.

With the close of the summer session the first of August, I returned to Headrick for the short pre-cotton-picking term but was back in Edmond around the middle of September for the fall term. This made it possible for me to witness the ceremony of ushering Oklahoma into the Union as a state which came on November 16, 1907. On that day a huge celebration was held at the capital city of Guthrie. A mock wedding united "Mr. Oklahoma Territory" and "Miss Indian Territory" in marriage. Charles N. Haskell was inaugurated as the first governor of the new state, and all other state officials took the oath of office. Prohibition was to go into effect at midnight and just before that hour the Edmond band lined up before the town's largest saloon and played, "Shall we Gather at the River."[3]

My stay at Headrick intermittently from September, 1905, to the first of June, 1908, was one of the happiest periods of my life. The pupils were, as a rule, studious, eager to learn, and respectful to their teachers. They presented few problems in the matter of discipline as their parents were, with few exceptions, honest, hardworking, God-fearing men and women who had given their children excellent home training. It was a joy to work in such a community. After the first year, I lived in the home of Mr. and Mrs. D. H. Hamilton on a tract adjoining town and it pleased me greatly when the Thompsons of Deep Red sent their son, Fred, over to room with me and attend school.

It was a privilege to take three or four of my best students with me to Edmond every summer session and for the fall term. Their parents might have hesitated to send them so far from home alone but were glad to let them go with me

---

[3] Oklahoma statehood represented a national political anomaly in that for partisan reasons, as well as others more compelling in the long run perhaps, the twin territories were fused, gerrymandered, into the single state of Oklahoma. Congress, on the other hand and also for partisan reasons, gerrymandered Dakota Territory in 1889 into two states, North Dakota and South Dakota.

Physical Science laboratory, Central State Normal School, Edmond, Oklahoma, 1908. Edward Everett Dale is standing at right. (Courtesy Western History Collections, University of Oklahoma Library)

assured that I would find them a good place to live, help them in enrolling, and with their school work if necessary.

It was a pleasure to look after these young people. Usually they lived in the home of Mrs. Barlow but if she did not have room for them another friend of mine nearby was glad to have them. When I left Headrick in June, 1908, about one-third of the thirty high school students had spent one or more terms at the Edmond school. One or two of these returned later and remained until they had finished and received their diplomas.

When school closed at Headrick about the first of June, 1908, I tendered my resignation and returned to Edmond determined to stay until I graduated. A check of credits indicated that by hard work this goal might be reached by August, 1909.

By this time I had become accustomed to college life as it was then in an Oklahoma normal school. Obviously, it was very unlike campus life today. There were no fraternities or sororities, we had no stadium; football spectators lined up along the sidelines moving along with the ball and shouting encouragement to the home team. There were no dances and no smoking of cigarettes by men, let alone by women. It was a glorious year, and when I received my diploma at the August commencement it was with a feeling that the world was mine.

The first legislature of Oklahoma had established three new normal schools all located in the Indian Territory part of the state. As buildings had to be erected and furnished, these did not open until September, 1909. Naturally there was a scramble for jobs in these institutions which were under the control of the State Board of Education. I was thirty years old and had been an assistant in the department of chemistry and physics at Edmond during my senior year. At the suggestion of my professors I promptly applied for a position as teacher of these subjects in the new normal schools.[4]

---

[4] The three normal schools established in the Indian Territory portion of the state were Northeastern at Tahlequah, East Central at Ada, and Southeastern at Durant.

This was the valor of ignorance. I should have known that I was incompetent to teach chemistry and physics in college or any other subjects with the possible exception of history and English. Yet in choosing teachers for these new schools, competence seemed to be less important than political pull and perhaps my qualifications were as good as those who received appointments.

There was too much competition, however, and when it became certain that there was no place for me in one of these normals, I secured the job as head of the school at Roosevelt, a small town about twelve miles north of the Otter Creek farm. My salary was $100 a month and the school board had already employed the four women teachers, one of whom had taught in the school for several years.

I was pleased to have this position as it would be easy to go home any weekend. Also the attractive new school building, which had been finished just before the opening of school, had a nice office for me on the second floor. Finally, there was little cotton grown in the district so the term began early in September and continued for nine months with no break except for the holidays.

In spite of the new building, an attractive office, a slightly higher salary, and a longer term than I had ever had before, my memories of the year at Roosevelt are not especially happy ones. Yet on the whole it was a good year. I boarded at the home of Charles Sims, manager of the lumber yard. He and his wife were kind to me as were the members of the school board and everyone else, but the people of Roosevelt were quite unlike those of Headrick. Many of them were from the North. Interest in church and sunday school seemed comparatively slight, and I missed this as well as the warm hospitality of residents of the Headrick community.

Most of the students were bright but they were far more sophisticated than the youngsters I had taught, and many of them did not show proper respect for their teachers or parents. Only one or two were actually tough, and we had few disciplinary problems, but not many seemed to have the desire to learn as had most of my students at Deep Red and

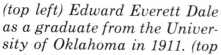

(top left) Edward Everett Dale
as a graduate from the University of Oklahoma in 1911. (top
right) Arthur Grant Evans, president of the University of Oklahoma,
1907-1911. (below) The University of Oklahoma Campus in 1909.
(Courtesy Western History Collections, University of Oklahoma
Library)

Headrick. Moreover, the work was hard as I had to teach Latin, algebra, and geometry.

While church work did not seem to appeal much to the men of Roosevelt, they had a very active chapter of Knights of Pythias Lodge which I joined soon after school opened and never missed a meeting. This was my first fraternal order, and I thoroughly enjoyed working in it and was soon elected an officer. The membership was large for a town the size of Roosevelt, and the Lodge rendered assistance to the needy in the community. I felt very close to its members at the end of the school year, as well as to many of my students. I had fully decided, however, to enter the University of Oklahoma as soon as school closed and it was with some regret that I declined the school board's request to return the next year.

A few days after school closed at Roosevelt I enrolled in the eight weeks' summer session of the University of Oklahoma. This was my first time to be on the campus of that school but I was now accustomed to college work so did not have the feeling of awe which had characterized my first few days at the Edmond Normal. The registrar gave me sixty-four semester hours of advanced standing for my work at Edmond which left me sixty more to complete the requirements for a Bachelor of Arts degree.

After some hesitation I decided to major in history and to minor in government. My ambition was to graduate in one full year and two summer terms. This meant that it would be necessary to enroll in as many hours every term as university regulations allowed and take an extension course in August, 1910. In the first summer term I took German I, five hours, a two-hour course in English history and two-hour course in classical archaeology. German was very hard for me but I scraped by with a grade of C. The other two courses presented no difficulty nor did four hours extension taken *in absentia*.

The next year was a pleasant but very busy one. Nineteen hours each semester left little time for athletics or social life, but I enjoyed the work and made excellent grades in all but one or two courses. Naturally I would have been glad to graduate at the June commencement but knew that this was impossible so did not worry about it.

Two months later, at the end of the summer session, I received my bachelor's degree. There were some eighty graduates in June but at this August commencement there were only two. The other was Dorothy Bell, a spinster perhaps only a few years younger than I.

The President of the University was Dr. A. Grant Evans, a Presbyterian minister. When he called for the candidates for the degree of Bachelor of Arts to come forward, Dorothy and I rose, marched down the aisle, and stopped facing the preacher. The same idea evidently came to each of us for I saw her look wildly at the nearest open window. Dr. Evans smiled quizzically before speaking, but his first words were correct. He said: "By virtue of the authority vested in me, I hereby confer upon you...." If he had said: "Dearly beloved we are assembled here in the presence of God and this company..." no doubt Dorothy would have jumped through one window and I through another!

The fact that my attendance at the University of Oklahoma was limited to one year and two summers prevented my forming as many close friendships with my fellow students there as I did at Edmond where my work was spread over a period of three years. This I have always regretted for while normally a member of the Class of 1911 only one or two of these classmates became my intimate friends.

Graduation from the University of Oklahoma gave me a great thrill. College graduates in western Oklahoma were extremely scarce at this time. The fact that I was flat broke did not worry me. The school board at Blair, a thriving little town ten miles north of Altus, had accepted my application for the position of superintendent.

The prospect of becoming head of the Blair school pleased me very much. The school building was a two-story brick structure, the term was for nine months, and the staff consisted of nine teachers including the music teacher, Mr. Burt, who was given a studio in the building. He was not paid by the school board but by the parents of those who took music lessons. He also organized and conducted an orchestra composed partly of older students, and was considered a member of the faculty.

What pleased me most about Blair school, however, was that Ural A. Rowe, my closest friend and roommate at the university, was to be my "second in command" as high school principal. Rowe's parents lived on a farm half a mile or so north of Blair. They were kind and hospitable Christian people, very proud of Ural and his brother, Otis, a lad about twelve years old.

The two school years of 1911-12 and 1912-13 spent at Blair were my final years of public school work. They were also among the happiest and most fruitful years of my life. The little town was the center of a remarkable community. With very few exceptions it was composed of kindly, industrious, and deeply religious people who tried earnestly to bring up their children "in the way they should go." Almost completely free of the petty feuds and factions which characterize so many small town communities, they were unanimous in giving whole-hearted support to the school.

It was quite worthy of support. Every teacher was well-trained and had ample experience; all but one of the women teachers had taught in this school the previous year and at least two of them for several years. The older students were eager to learn, worked hard, and the smaller children were well-behaved so there were few problems with respect to discipline. Most of the senior high students were in my room and I sought to train them in good study habits by going out and closing the door for a few minutes. By gradually increasing the length of my periods of absence it became possible for me to leave these young students without any supervision for twenty or thirty minutes while I did an errand in town.

Naturally I was much pleased when two of my best male students in the Headrick school came to Blair to continue their education under my direction. It must be confessed, however, that my happy memories of Blair are largely due to Ural A. Rowe, who for two years was my right arm, taught me much, and became the closest friend of my entire

Ural A. Rowe, Edward Everett Dale's closest friend during his days as an educator in southwest Oklahoma and as a student at the University of Oklahoma. (Courtesy Western History Collections, University of Oklahoma Library)

life. In appearance we presented a marked contrast. I was six feet tall and thin as a rail while he was equally tall, weighed over two hundred and as some girl said: "Looked like the baby on the chill tonic box." His mind was razor sharp, his sense of humor equally keen, and his judgement sound as a dollar. Since he had been reared in the community all of the older students called him "Ural" but had for him the highest respect and a considerable measure of affection.

Once school was well under way, Rowe and I looked about to see what could be done to promote extra-curricular activities. Basketball seemed to be the only game that had been played much in the past so we formed both a boy's team and a girl's team and played nearby schools. We also helped organize debate teams and matched debates with schools in several towns in the county.

We soon discovered that the young people of the three leading churches had a Chistian Endeavor, a B.Y.P.U. (Baptist Youth Peoples Union), and an Epworth League. All of these were literally dying on their feet. We accordingly asked the president of each of these groups to call a special meeting of the members the following Sunday afternoon at the Methodist Church.

At this meeting we proposed that the three organizations be combined to form a young people's Christian Society. We assured them that it should be strictly their own affair, but we would gladly give advice and help when asked to do so. Somewhat to my surprise they approved the idea with enthusiasm. Officers of the new society were elected, a committee appointed to draft a constitution, and another to arrange programs.

Just how long this organization flourished it is not possible for me to say, but for the two years that Rowe and I remained at Blair, it was a great influence for good in the community. Devotional meetings were held in one of the churches every Sunday afternoon. At these a leader appointed by the program committee presented a program consisting of a Scripture reading, a prayer, a couple of songs, a five-minute talk, a final hymn, and benediction.

Social meetings were held every two weeks on Friday

evening at the home of some member. They were opened with a Bible reading and brief prayer. "Parlor games" were then played with much fun and laughter until about ten p.m. when refreshments were served. Two or three guests were always invited to every social meeting. Usually these were young fellows who were not in school but were either farm hands or the sons of farmers. They were not tough, but did not go to church or Sunday School so were lonely and were delighted to accept an invitation to one of these social meetings. After attending two or three of them they began to come to the devotional meetings too. Within six months most of them were going to church and Sunday School every Sunday. It seems possible too that merging the three young peoples' societies into one made these youngsters and parents more tolerant of the others' beliefs.

Before the close of my first year at Blair in June, 1912, President Charles Evans of Central State Normal offered me a job teaching history in his eight weeks' summer school. The salary was low but I gladly accepted the offer to work in the institution from which I had graduated in 1909. Rowe went with me to enter Central as a student. His ambition was to study law. The University of Oklahoma Law School required two years of college work for admission and he still lacked half a year.

We roomed together at Edmond and ate at the same boarding house. During the entire term we were inseparable. He took my course in Oklahoma history so for eight weeks he was my student. When the term ended about the first of August, Rowe returned home, and I had a short vacation visiting my sister Mattie and her family in Wichita, Kansas. Her husband had a fairly good job there and her two daughters were working in offices.

School opened at Blair again early in September, 1912. The second year was, if possible, more enjoyable than the first. Those who had been strangers a year before were now near and dear friends. School ran smoothly, and my pay had been boosted from $125 to $140 a month. I knew Rowe would be at the University of Oklahoma the following year and without him the school would never be quite the same.

Perhaps this was one factor in my decision not to return to Blair the following year. I loved teaching but could see little future, for me at least, in public school work except in administration which I did not especially like. To teach history in a college or university would require my doing graduate work in some university perhaps for two or three years, but why not? A bachelor nearly thirty-four years old with no dependents and $1,000 in savings should be able to spend one year at any American university.

There was never any doubt in my mind as to the choice of a university. It was Harvard. Among the scholarships listed in its catalogue was the Austin Teachers' Scholarship of $250. I sent in my application accompanied by letters from my teachers at the University of Oklahoma, three or four of whom had Master of Arts degrees from Harvard.

A couple of months before the end of school I received notice that the scholarship had been awarded to me. The school board offered to give me a year's leave of absence but I declined this. My books, papers, etc., I carted down to the farm. George had married a year or more before this time so he no longer needed me to keep him company. I was to teach at Central Normal again that summer and Rowe went with me to finish enough hours of academic work to be admitted to the O.U. Law School in September. Once more we roomed together and ate at the same boarding house and the weeks slipped all too quickly. About August first came commencement which meant much to every graduate but perhaps even more to me because it was a turning point in my entire life.

Chapter IX

Fair Harvard

Looking back over a period of more than half a century I am appalled by my colossal nerve in going to Harvard to work in the graduate school for an advanced degree in history. True, the University of Oklahoma had awarded me a Bachelor of Arts degree in 1911 but that institution had only about 800 students. The Department of History had three teachers, two of whom had M.A. degrees and one a Bachelor of Science. The library facilities were about what one would expect in an institution which had been opened only about twenty years earlier with a faculty of four and a student body of about fifty-five, all but a few in the Preparatory Department.

As a matter-of-fact it was ignorance rather than nerve which prompted my decision. At thirty-four years of age I had never been outside the states of Texas and Oklahoma except for a brief visit to Mattie in Kansas and another to relatives in Nebraska. I had never been in any city larger than Fort Worth, Wichita, or Oklahoma City. Nor had I seen a larger body of water than Oklahoma City's Belle Isle Lake. Finally, until seven years ago my formal education had not extended beyond the eighth grade. Truly I was an innocent "babe in the woods" when I started for Harvard but "fools rush in."

The depths of my ignorance were revealed by my preparations for the journey and for my year in New England. Soon after receiving notice of the scholarship award, I purchased a strong steamer trunk and two of the heaviest suits of woolen "long johns" underwear that could be found in Oklahoma. I also bought a large suitcase to carry with me. Into this I packed all my summer clothing and my blue .45 Colt's revolver, while my winter suits, overcoat, new underwear, and heavy woolen socks were placed in the trunk.

At the end of my last class my students gave me a beautiful leather bag to which I transferred my gun, razor, toilet articles, extra shirts, socks, and underwear. This was a great convenience but my crowning act of folly was to take my old typewriter. It was of the old fashioned "invisible" variety which someone suggested should be called "baby typewriters" because you had to keep turning them up every few minutes to see if anything had happened! The name was a fitting one but mine was a husky infant to carry on a long journey. It could be done, however, by buckling a leather strap around it.

As I had made a recent trip to the farm to leave a little surplus stuff, pick up a few things, and say goodbye to George and Anna there seemed no reason why I should not start for the East as soon as school closed. There was no reason for me to reach Cambridge until after the middle of September for enrollment at Harvard did not begin until about September the 20th, but my plan was to stop in Washington for a month to do some research, and also to stop off for two or three days in both Philadelphia and New York on the journey from Washington to Boston. My first stop, however, was to be Chicago to visit a couple of days with my nephew Phillip Dale who had graduated from Rush Medical School and was an intern at the Cook County Hospital.

One day after commencement I said goodbye to Rowe and the other Edmond friends, checked my trunk and big suitcase and, with my smaller bag in one hand and the "Baby" in the other, boarded the train for Chicago. It was a day run, reaching Chicago about nine p.m. but neither by night nor day did I have any thought of traveling by Pullman. I had slept on the prairie every night for months free, so paying four or five dollars for a berth seemed incredibly extravagant. Also paying a dollar and a half or two dollars for a meal in the diner seemed equally foolish to one accustomed to getting a good dinner for a quarter and never more than fifty cents even at the "drummer's" table.

Obviously my stay in Chicago must be at a hotel, so on the train I made some inquiries as to hotels in that city. One fellow traveler told me that he usually stayed at the "Sherman" which he said was a very nice small hotel and not as expensive as the larger ones. When we reached Chicago I followed his suggestion and after depositing the "Baby" at the checkstand took a taxi for the Sherman. It looked anything but "little" to me and the cheapest room available was four dollars which made me wonder what the price of a room at one of the "larger" hotels would be!

The room was very nice, however, and after a good night's sleep and breakfast I called Doctor Phillip. He was the oldest son of my brother Frank who had died about 1910. I had visited Frank's family in Nebraska in August, 1912, but Phillip was in Chicago at that time so I had never seen him. He was free to leave the hospital when he got my telephone call so he came over to the hotel at once. He was only three or four years younger than myself and we became fast friends within a few hours. Phil suggested that I check out of the hotel and stay with him at the hospital. He explained that he roomed there with two other young interns, but one of them was away on vacation and I could have his bed. The suggestion seemed a good one so I spent two nights there. I usually took Phil to lunch and dinner and he arranged for me to put on a gown and go into the operating rooms to watch surgery. This was all very interesting to me and the friendship formed with Dr. Phil in this brief time continued until his death in 1968.

After a couple of days I resumed the journey to Washington by day coach. I could sleep pretty well leaning back in the seat but it was near the time of a full moon and there was so much to see, even at night, that it seemed too bad to miss anything by sleeping. The wheat fields of Ohio were like a sea of gold. We reached Pittsburgh at night and a note in my diary states that: "It looked like Hell with the lid off." In marked contrast, the Potomac at Harpers Ferry by bright moonlight seemed to me as glorious a night as Heaven itself could ever show.

We reached Washington early in the afternoon and after leaving my wretched old typewriter at the checkstand, I took a streetcar headed in the general direction of the Capitol. My first objective was to find a not-too-expensive hotel where I could stay for a day or two while looking for a room in some home. My quest ended at the old National Hotel, and after depositing my bag I took a long walk to see the sights around the Capitol and Library of Congress.

Washington in 1913 was a sleepy southern town of about 375,000 people. Woodrow Wilson had been inaugurated President the preceding March, and hopeful Democrats seeking appointment to office still lingered about the hotel lobbies. There were plenty of rooms available, however, and the following day I rented a large, luxuriously furnished one on C Street N.W. not far from the Capitol for four dollars a week! A very nice smaller one could have been had for three dollars but the big one was light and airy, very near a bathroom, and had a desk, floor lamps, and three or four easy chairs. Having chosen a room I had my baggage sent up from the station and settled down for a month in Washington.

It proved a most interesting period. My ambition was to write a history of Oklahoma and I hoped to collect material on the Five Civilized Tribes and their removal to Oklahoma. This meant working in the files of the Office of Indian Affairs and perhaps in the State Department for the creation of the National Archives lay far in the future.

I accordingly called upon Claude Weaver who had given our commencement address at Blair when my first year there closed and had been elected to Congress in November, 1912. He seemed delighted to see me, especially when he learned that I was not seeking an office but only a letter of introduction to the Commissioner of Indian Affairs. He urged me to make his office my headquarters while in Washington and to give him a list of any books I needed from the Library of Congress. He said he would have them sent to his office where I could get them.[1]

While in the House Office Building it seemed well to call on Bill Murray who had also been elected congressman-at-large from Oklahoma the past November. I did not know him at all and found him considerably less cordial than Claude but he gave me a letter to the Indian Office and the State Department. Equipped with letters from two members of Congress I felt that there would be no difficulty in getting access to the files in which I wanted to work and this proved true. Officials of both the Indian Office and the State Department showed me every possible courtesy and consideration, and for four weeks I spent much time nearly every day reading documents and taking notes.[2]

Most of this work was done in the Office of Indian Affairs but I found the early treaties for removal of the Five Civilized Tribes in the State Department and was assured that photostatic copies of any of these would be made for me at cost. I also spent a good deal of time reading in the Library of Congress. The work done during these weeks in Washington later proved of great value in my study at Harvard.

For the first few days I ate at various small restaurants. This proved most unsatisfactory so I found a good boarding-house not far from my room which served breakfast and dinner for $4.50 a week. There were about twenty persons, all of them government employees, who ate there. Some of them got their lunch at a small eating place near the building in which they worked. For others the boarding-house lady prepared a lunch to take with them. The cost was only twenty-five cents so I often asked her to prepare one for me.

Although I did a great deal of good work during these four weeks in Washington there was so much to see and so many interesting places to visit that my reading of old documents

---

[1] Claude Weaver, Fifth District Congressman.
[2] William H. Murray, Fourth District Congressman; governor of Oklahoma, 1931-1935.

127

and taking notes was sometimes neglected in favor of more congenial pursuits. These included a boat trip to Mount Vernon, a visit to Arlington and to Alexandria, and spending much time sitting in the galleries of the House and Senate watching the work of our lawmakers.

The beauty of the interior of the Library of Congress and the White House impressed me very much as did the view from the top of the Washington Monument. I visited various parks and public buildings, met a few distinguished men, including Senator Robert L. Owen of Oklahoma, and was standing on the east steps of the Capitol when President Woodrow Wilson came to address a joint session of the House and Senate on the Mexican situation. All of these things seemed to me a part of my education.[3]

Early in September I left Washington for Philadelphia but spent only a couple of days in that city, sightseeing and taking notes on the historic places visited. My chief interest was Independence Square where I saw the Liberty Bell, and made a careful sketch of the interior of Independence Hall. In addition, I took the elevator to the top of city hall in order to see the city spread like a map below me and try to locate sites of battles fought during the American Revolution. A visit was also made to Fairmount Park and to one of the art museums.

My short stay in Chicago, four weeks in Washington, and two days in Philadelphia had greatly increased my confidence in my ability to find my way around a large city. At least I had learned that the first thing to do upon reaching a city is to buy and study a map of it. My work during the opening of the Kiowa-Comanche Indian reservation, which required the constant study of maps, was very helpful to me in becoming acquainted with the overall picture of Washington, Philadelphia, and New York, which was my last stop.

My four days in New York were very busy ones. I stayed at a hotel on 72nd Street which someone in Washington had

---

[3] Robert L. Owen, elected to the United States Senate from Oklahoma in 1907, served until 1924.

recommended. It was a very pleasant place but my time was spent in seeing New York. My first venture was to take the cruise around Manhattan Island during which a spieler with a megaphone called the attention of all bug-eyed passengers to points of interest.

The rest of my stay was devoted to a close-up view of those things which the average tourist wants to see on his first visit to New York. These included Central Park, Battery Park, the view from the top of the Woolworth Tower, Wall Street, where I dropped a half a dollar on the sidewalk and promptly retrieved it in order to be able to say truthfully that I had "picked up a little money on Wall Street!" Finally came a trip to Coney Island, one evening at the theater, and I was ready to start on the last lap of my journey.

The mighty Hudson River and the ships at the piers had greatly impressed me. Possibly my love of ships and the water was inherited from seafaring ancestors. At any rate I decided to take the boat which made the day run to Albany, spend the night there, and go from Albany to Boston by train. It proved to be an excellent idea. The weather was perfect so I spent virtually the entire day on deck enjoying to the fullest every minute as we passed the Palisades, the region made famous by Washington Irving, West Point, and numerous magnificent homes.

About six p.m. we reached Albany and I found a modest hotel near the railway station. I would have liked to see a little of New York's capital city the next day but there was not enough time as my train for Boston left fairly early in the morning. There was much of interest to see from the car window as we rolled eastward across Massachusetts. The Berkshire Hills were picturesque and the entire countryside was beautiful. I was glad, however, when we rolled into Boston and my long journey was at last ended.

My first night in Boston was spent at the Quincy Hotel. I bought a map of Greater Boston, studied it carefully, and the next morning took the subway at Park Street Under for the eight-minute ride to Harvard Square. Needless to say my first sight of Harvard gave me the greatest thrill of my life. I entered the yard and gazed with awe and admiration at the buildings. Not one of them was as pretentious as the administration building of the University of Oklahoma for the Widener Memorial Library was in the first stages of construction. Yet I sensed that these buildings had about them the intangible dignity of age. The shady elms, gravel walks, and inscriptions over the main gate and near the eaves of some buildings impressed me. No doubt every prospective student seeing Harvard for the first time is inspired by the inscription above the entrance of the gate: "Enter to Grow in Wisdom." It was crystal clear to me that I had ample *room* to grow in wisdom!

It was only a few days until registration so after spending an hour walking about the yard and outside it to see the statue of John Harvard, Memorial Hall, the Union, Law School, Divinity Hall, the Peabody, the Germanic Museum, and various other buildings, I began the search for a place to live.

Phillips Brooks House was open and its secretary, Arthur Bean, was very helpful. I had already decided to room in a home rather than in one of the residential halls and after some search located one at 76 Hammond not far beyond the Peabody Museum and Divinity Hall. It was a very pleasant little room on the second floor of the east side of a three-story two-family house owned by a widow lady, Mrs. Elder, and her old-maid daughter. They occupied the first floor and rented rooms on the second and third floors to graduate students.

While my room rental was only three dollars a week it was furnished with a comfortable single bed, desk, a couple of chairs, and small book case. There was a gas lamp on the desk, a hot water radiator to furnish heat, and the bathroom was very near as there were two other rooms on that floor. The location was excellent for it was only a few minutes' walk to Memorial Hall where I planned to eat.

By the time I was well settled and had answered most of my letters from Oklahoma it was time to register. To my surprise this was very easy. G. W. Robinson, Secretary of the Graduate School, and Dean Charles Homer Haskins (commonly refered to by students as the Duke of Normandy) were both most helpful.

130

Frederick Jackson Turner, Professor of History at Harvard University, advocate of the Frontier Thesis of American History, and Edward Everett Dale's mentor. (Courtesy Western History Collections, University of Oklahoma Library)

Dean Haskins said that it would probably take me a year and a half to complete the requirements for a master's degree. To this I replied that one of my classmates at the University of Oklahoma, Mr. Williamson, whose academic record was not better than mine, had received the degree in only one year. The Dean asked Mr. Robinson to bring him Williamson's card and, after looking it over, he agreed that it might be possible for me to receive the degree at the end of the year.

Tuition at Harvard was $150 a year. Of this ninety dollars was payable at registration and the remaining sixty dollars at mid-year. Every student who lived in university housing presented a bond of $400 signed by two sureties but for those who did not occupy a room in one of the university halls the required bond was only $200. The bursar checked off tuition charges on my scholarship award notice and I paid a bonding company five dollars to guarantee my bond.

With these preliminaries out of the way I hastened over to a large hall where faculty members sat to advise students and approve courses. It was here that I first met the man who, in a great measure, directed my work during my entire stay at Harvard and who, as long as he lived, remained "my guide, philosopher and friend" in all my scholarly work, Professor Frederick Jackson Turner.[4]

I registered for two courses throughout the year with Professor Turner. One was History 17, *History of the West*, which met three times a week, and History 20K, an individual research course in American history, which normally met only once a week. My other courses were History 14, *The French Revolution and Napoleon*, a half-course in *Latin American History* the first half-year, and a half-course in *American Economic History*, the second half year. My program was sent to the graduate office and within a week or so I was notified that it was approved and if

---

[4] Frederick Jackson Turner, historian and interpreter of the pioneer experience, introduced the seminal theme of American Frontier as principal determinant of national character in his famous oration and essay presented in 1893.

completed with distinction I would be awarded the master's degree.

Turner's class in *History of the West* was a large one with fifty students. I sat next to Avery Craven, later a distinguished professor at the University of Chicago. Here a friendship began which has continued to the present time. Other men in this class who later became well-known in America were Nicholas Roosevelt and Junius Spence Morgan. Probably there were more.

It is not too much to say that this course opened to me a new heaven and a new earth in the field of American history. When Turner spoke of the lack of respect for the law *per se* on the American frontier I recalled that even ministers of the Gospel living near Navajoe cut and hauled wood from the Indian reservation across the North Fork of Red River, keeping an eagle eye out for United States marshals or Indian police.

His discussion of extra-legal associations brought to my mind memories of the livestock associations that existed in Southwest Oklahoma which employed livestock inspectors to check on brands, stop theft of cattle and horses, arranged roundups, and made rules with respect to them. His mention of settling disputes by arbitration reminded me that two of our neighbors in the Texas Cross Timbers came to my father and asked him to join them in settling a dispute between two men of the community. Turner's mention of the fact that a man on the American Frontier frequently worked at various vocations called to mind that I, myself, had engaged in half a dozen types of work. It was a shock to realize that all of these things were a part of history.

My other courses were all very interesting. Professor Johnson was distinctly a military historian. He was a classmate of Rose at Cambridge and the course, which began with the meeting of Estates General in 1789, ended with the banishment of Napoleon to St. Helena in 1815. This was intensive study of history for every student was required to write a short paper on some phase of the French Revolution or Napoleon's career every three weeks.[5]

---

[5] John Holland Rose, eminent British scholar.

Professor Merriman was a remarkable lecturer for he was extremely dramatic and had a rare gift for speaking. Dean Gay of the Graduate School of Business Administration was also a good lecturer and his course was interesting. In my research course with Turner, I presented two long papers. The first was on "The Indian Territory in 1888" and the second dealt with "The Opening of Oklahoma to White Settlement." I met with him for an hour once a week throughout the school year and learned much about historical research, of which at first I was woefully ignorant. Turner was always very patient and kind and, probably because I was much older than most of his students, met me on a more or less "man-to-man basis."

My room was very comfortable and I soon became well acquainted with my fellow roomers. Masterson, a tall rangy Texan, occupied the room next to mine on the south. He was studying education and took his master's degree later in the year. Jacoby, who was working for a doctor's degree in English, had the third room on that floor which was just north of mine. On the third floor there were only two rooms. One of these was occupied by Stellwagen, who was a graduate student in social work, and Kintner, whose field of work I have forgotten occupied the other.

Masterson and I ate at the same table in Memorial Hall. This was the larger of the two dining halls. It provided excellent meals three times a day for 1,000 men at a cost of $5.25 a week. At Foxcroft Hall with somewhat fewer men the service was *a la carte* and the student who ate a bit sparingly and chose the cheaper foods could get by for about $4.00 a week. Service at Foxcroft was provided by student waiters while those at Memorial Hall were Negroes, usually from Barbados or Jamaica. The head waiter was a handsome, very light-complexioned Negro, and there were three "captains," each having general supervision of the waiters in one third of the hall.

As every student had filed a bond with the Bursar, bills for meals at the dining halls were not sent out until the end of the first half-year. Also, those who ate at Memorial Hall could charge candy, tobacco, and cigarettes at the little stand just inside the front door, and the purchases were added to bills for meals.

The food was excellent and included both fruit and cereal for breakfast, followed by eggs, fish, or meat. Either meat or fish was served at lunch and dinner. We were told that a wealthy woman, whose son did not get enough milk at Memorial Hall, had left by her will a large sum of money to the dining service on condition that there should always be milk and cream on every table. As a result when a milk or cream pitcher had been emptied all one had to do was to hold it up and a waiter came on the double quick to refill it.

I was very much "afraid of my job" and with very good reason, so I buckled down to work determined to make good grades if it were at all possible. No time was spent on recreation for I recall attending only one show during the entire school year. That was late in the year when one of the men at our table insisted on my going with him to see Elsie Janis in *The Lady of the Slipper*. For exercise I walked quite a bit, went to the gymnasium about three times a week for a workout with a class, and also did a little boxing.

Social life for me simply did not exist. During the entire year I did not have a "date" with a girl. In fact I cannot recall meeting but one young woman, except at the teas at Phillips Brooks House where I was introduced to three or four faculty daughters, and talked with them for a few minutes.

These teas were held every Friday afternoon from about four to six from November to April. Some faculty wife was responsible for each, although she probably had two or three assistants. Half a dozen or more students, usually seniors, were chosen to act as receptionists and tried to see that every student met all faculty people and any distinguished visitors.

It seemed to me that attendance at these teas would contribute a great deal to my education so I seldom missed one. No doubt it did for President Lowell usually came and Mrs. Lowell was always there except upon the rare occasions when she was not in Cambridge. Among other interesting persons I met at Phillips Brooks House teas were Mrs.

Turner and her daughter, Dorothy, Professors Josiah Royce, Hugo Munsterburg, and his daughter Alice Longfellow, who lived in the old home, Craigie House, Dean LeBaron Briggs, who was not only Dean of Harvard College but President of Radcliffe, and many others.[6]

What impressed me most with respect to these people was their simplicity, kindness and courtesy. When someone introduced me to Dean Briggs as "a student from Oklahoma," the Dean said: "Let's sit down over in this corner, Mr. Dale, and you tell me something about Oklahoma while we drink our tea. I've never been there and would like to know more about your state."

For some fifteen minutes he asked me questions about Oklahoma, its Indians, ranches, oil wells, and many other features. He urged me to come to see him. "Every Wednesday from four to six is set aside for student visitors," he added. "You might find a freshman or sophomore there or maybe an upper classman or you might not find any other visitors but I'll be glad to see you. I live in a big rambling old house. It's quite a pleasant place to live but hard to keep warm enough in winter."

It was my firm determination to accept the Dean's invitation and pay him a visit some Wednesday afternoon but there were so many things to do that I never found the time for it. I found, however, that many professors set aside two or three hours of one afternoon every week to entertain any of their students that cared to come. President and Mrs. Lowell also held open house for students two hours every Sunday afternoon that they were in Cambridge. If they had to be away from home a notice to that effect was published in *The Crimson* the latter part of the week. This custom of the president, deans, and leading professors at Harvard of inviting students to their homes for a couple of hours at a specific time and day of the week has always seemed to me one worthy of consideration by other American colleges and universities.

---

[6] Abbott Lawrence Lowell, President, Harvard University (1909-1933).

On Christmas Eve President and Mrs. Lowell entertained "left over" students in their home. This was to me a most enjoyable evening. We sat on the floor and admired the beautiful Christmas tree while President Lowell read from St. Luke, the story of the first Christmas. It was most impressive for he had an excellent voice. We then sang all the familiar Christmas Carols,, and each of us received a charming little calendar for 1914 bearing the seal of Harvard, and inscribed, "With the compliments of President and Mrs. Lowell." The dining room doors were then opened to reveal a long, beautifully decorated table loaded with sandwiches, cakes, cookies, and candies, and we were all urged to help ourselves to the wealth of Christmas goodies.

The following day I was invited to Christmas dinner at the apartment of Mr. and Mrs. Arthur Bean. It was a lovely dinner with only one other guest. Mrs. Bean was just out of the hospital where she had gone for the birth of her first baby. She came to the table for a little while but the nurse took her away before dessert was served. My fellow guest and I left soon after dinner for we both felt that we should not linger.

That evening a party for "left over" students was held at Phillips Brooks House. The committee in charge had arranged a program of songs and readings, and Professor Palmer, who had retired a year or so earlier, had reluctantly agreed to come and give a brief talk. Here we again sat on the floor during the program and at its conclusion were ushered into the big dining room. Here we found a long table spread with platters of turkey and dressing, bowls of cranberry sauce, plates of cake, pies, nuts, salad, candies, plum pudding, etc. All this had been sent by the wives of Harvard faculty members and must have been a large part of the food remaining at the conclusion of their Christmas dinners. This struck me as another custom well worth adopting by colleges in my own state!

Although football tickets might seem an extravagance I felt that attending the games was part of life at Harvard so I did not miss any of those played in Cambridge. While not a great fan I found them all thrilling, especially the one with

Yale in which the five field goals drop-kicked by Brinckley, including one from the fifty yard line, were the only scores made. I went to only one or two of the baseball games, for in the 1913-14 school year at least Harvard's baseball was as disappointing as its football was brilliant.

Membership in the Harvard Union at that time cost ten dollars but several lectures were to be given there so I joined, but made little use of its library or other facilities it offered. I attended several lectures given by distinguished visitors, however, so I felt that my money was well spent. The speakers that appealed to me most were Major General Leonard Wood and Booker T. Washington.[7]

It was not long after Christmas until we reached the end of the first half-year. Although three of my courses were for the entire year, examinations were given at mid-year in these, except in my research course with Turner. My grades in all courses were B or better, although this only indicated the quality of work up to that time. These grades gave me confidence so I felt more comfortable during the second half year.

Except for one terrific blizzard of short duration, the winter had been much milder than I had expected and as the first warm days of spring came I began to give more thought to visiting places of historical interest. In the autumn and winter a good many had been visited, but while living in the midst of so many historic spots and shrines of American literature it seemed too bad not to take advantage of my opportunities.

Before the coming of winter I had climbed to the top of the Bunker Hill Monument, seen the Old North Church, visited Craigie House, Mount Auburn Cemetery, Faneuil Hall, Salem, to see the House of Seven Gables, and Plymouth, where I stood on Plymouth Rock and spent some time in the cemetery on the flat-topped hill reading the inscriptions on the gravestones. I also visited the Standish Shore and

---

[7] Major General Leonard Wood, commander of 1st Volunteer Cavalry in Cuban campaign of Spanish-American War; later chief of staff, U.S. Army. Booker T. Washington, black educator and social reformer; founder of Tuskegee Institute in Alabama.

climbed the monument to the foot of the statue of Miles Standish who was one of my boyhood heroes.

The United States Navy yard at Charlestown was of very great interest to me. I visited it two or three times and went aboard two or three of the big battleships as well as "Old Ironsides," as the frigate *Constitution* was called. It was of special interest to me, as before the age of ten I had memorized the poem of Oliver Wendell Holmes beginning with the words: "Aye, tear her tattered ensign down. . . ."

My first trip after moving into my room at 76 Hammond Street was to Lexington and Concord and during the year I made two more trips, the last on the 19th of April which is a holiday in Massachusetts. Re-enacting the ride of Paul Revere was a part of the celebration, so I left the trolley at Lexington and waited until Paul, dressed in colonial costume, rode in accompanied by three or four state troopers. Although the original Paul Revere rode on to the outskirts of Concord before being captured by an advance guard of British troops, this one stopped and called it a day at Lexington.

After seeing him ride in, I walked on to Concord which has always seemed to me the most interesting little town in America. Here, on this and later visits, I saw what was said to be part of the first Concord grape vine originated by Ephraim Wales Bull in 1849. Here I gazed with awe and admiration at Emerson's home, Orchard House, where Louisa M. Alcott lived from 1857 to 1878, and among the trees just back of it, and the Concord School of Philosophy organized by Bronson Alcott and his friends.

Next to the Alcott home was Wayside where Hawthorne lived for some twelve years the latter part of his life. Beyond the river was the "Old Manse" where Hawthorne brought his young bride in 1842. Here he lived for nearly four years during which he wrote "Mosses From An Old Manse." The Old North Bridge, where the first British soldiers were killed on that 19th of April, 1775, the battle monument at its east end erected in 1836, and the statue of the Minute Man by Daniel C. French at the west end, all impressed me deeply. Both there and in Sleepy Hollow Cemetery where Emerson,

Hawthorne, Thoreau, the Alcotts, and other famous persons are buried, I felt that I was standing upon holy ground.

It was not long after April 19th until most Harvard students began preparing for final examinations and had little time for anything else. Two seniors in Turner's History of the West asked me to help them review the work in that course in which my grade at the mid-year had been B. They said that they believed I could help them more than could the professional tutor across the avenue commonly called "the widow." It never occurred to me to expect payment for my help but after reviewing the course for four hours they sent me a check for ten dollars which was an unexpected windfall. Exams were long but I passed them all with B or A- which entitled me to the master's degree.

The commencement ceremonies were to me most impressive. They included the class reunions held in the yard, the Ivy Oration in Latin at the stadium, the procession of the faculty and students to the auditorium, and the conferring of degrees. The colorful gowns and hoods of the professors who came from various American and European universities were truly a thrilling sight to an Oklahoman from a university that had fewer students than Harvard had faculty members.

I was indeed proud of my degree and, in common with virtually all of my fellow students, was eager to start for home. Two or three months earlier my major professor at the University of Oklahoma, Dean James S. Buchanan, had written to tell me that he had recommended me for a job as instructor in the Department of History. Professor Roy Gittinger was taking a year's leave of absence to complete work for the Ph.D. degree and I could take over his classes. The appointment would be nominally for only one year but the Dean said that he was certain it would be permanent for enrollment was increasing so fast that the History Department would need another man within a year.

The prospect of returning to my *alma mater* as a member of the faculty was most pleasing. The only "fly in the ointment" was that the salary of an instructor was only $900 for the school year and my salary for my second nine months term at Blair had been $1,200. I pointed this out in my reply and President Stratton D. Brooks reluctantly yielded to the urgings of Dean Buchanan and agreed to pay me the $1,000 a year which I had asked.

With a job waiting for me in September there seemed no reason to hurry home so my love of the sea made me decide to go from New York to New Orleans by ship and from that city to Oklahoma by train. A firm on Washington Street quickly arranged my passage from New York to New Orleans on the Morgan Liner *Antilles*, and day coach travel on the Illinois Central to Memphis and thence to Oklahoma on the Rock Island. The man preparing my tickets suggested second class on the *Antilles*, asserting that first class passengers would be expected to wear formal dress at dinner. His suggestion, however, was firmly rejected. This would be my first ocean voyage and, by golly, I was going to make it in style!

As this was before the construction of the Cape Cod Canal, I had to take a train to a port on the south shore where I got a ship for the night run to New York. Here I boarded the *Antilles* which in marked contrast to the weather-beaten old hulk that I had just left was a beautiful ship. As it was near the first of July and not many people were going to New Orleans, there were only about forty first-cabin passengers, and eight second-cabin, at the rear, while forward in the steerage there were only an Italian with his wife and little girl, two Russian brothers about seventeen and fifteen years of age, and one lonely Spaniard from Galicia.

The first morning after leaving New York we picked up a big Italian tramp steamer with a broken propeller shaft. Her captain had asked to be towed into Norfolk so a line was made fast to her bow and we headed for that port. The Italian was very heavy and again and again the line parted and some of our sailors had to launch a boat in order to pick up the ends and splice them. How many times it had to be done I have forgotten but it was ten o'clock at night when we reached Norfolk Harbor, where the Italian anchored and we got under way again for New Orleans.

This salvage operation extended what was usually a five-day voyage to six. Personally, I was delighted to have an additional day. My cabin was a large, luxurious one, the food was delicious, and the weather fine. My fellow passengers were kindly, pleasant, quite informal people. Apparently the idea of "dressing for dinner" never entered anyone's head. We played deck quoits, watched flying fish and dolphins leaping out of the water and turning somersaults, and were thrilled by the sight of a whale spouting water high in the air. Also, I went down to the forward deck to improve my Spanish by talking with the lonely Spaniard.

As we rounded the tip of Florida we had a glimpse of Key West in the distance, the only land we saw until we reached the mouth of the Mississippi where we took on a pilot to conduct us up the river to New Orleans. Darkness was falling before we had gone very far from the mouth of the river. I had been sitting in my deck chair to view the apparently endless marsh lands but with the coming of night there came a great chorus from the insect life mingled with the voices of frogs and night birds.

I spent only one day in New Orleans but it was a busy one for there was much to see. The river front with Negroes loading and unloading ships was very interesting. Canal Street impressed me a great deal, and so did Jackson Square where an elderly Negro paused in his work of clipping grass around the base of the equestrian statue to greet me cordially.

"Cap'n doo's you have a stamp?"

"I'm very sorry," was my reply, "but I don't have one."

"Well, I declare Cap'n, I us hopin' you did for I wants to write to my mothah. Ain't writ to huh in a long time an' I spects she's gittin' worried 'bout huh boy. Ain't got a nickel eigheh is you?"

Such an approach seemed to deserve some reward so I handed him two nickels!

The next morning I boarded a day coach of the Illinois Central train for Memphis. The journey was quite uneventful but the Mississippi countryside, with its broad cotton fields, Negro cabins, and an occasional old Southern mansion, was interesting. After only a brief wait in Memphis, I was able to get to a Rock Island train for Oklahoma City only half an hour's ride on a Santa Fe train from Norman. It was good to be home but looking backward it had been a year in which I had been introduced to a "brave, new world." I was not a part of it yet but was on the way and traveling fast.

(top) Stratton D. Brooks, president of the University of Oklahoma, 1913-1923. (below) James Shannon Buchanan, acting president of the University of Oklahoma, 1923-1925. (Courtesy Western History Collections, University of Oklahoma Library)

Fledgling Instructor

The summer schools of both the Edmond Normal and the University were still in session when I reached Oklahoma City in July, 1914. Naturally, I went to Norman first to report to Dean Buchanan, to see faculty friends, and to call on President Stratton D. Brooks whom I had never met. Dr. A. Grant Evans had been replaced in September, 1911, by Dean Julien C. Monnet of the law school as acting president. He had served only one year when the University Board of Regents appointed Dr. Stratton D. Brooks, Superintendent of the Boston City Schools, president.

Dean Buchanan seemed delighted to see me as did Professor Gittinger, whose courses I was to teach during his absence. Others who had been my teachers welcomed me to the faculty as did President Brooks, who impressed me not only as a very able executive but also as a man of much personal charm. My friend Ural Rowe had written me that he was in the law school, but was spending the summer at his parents' home near Blair.

After a few days in Norman and a visit with friends in Edmond, I went by train to southwestern Oklahoma to spend two weeks with George and Anna. My brother Henry had sold his hotel in Cordell and brought his family to Mountain Park where he built a home on a tract of land at the edge of town and established a small dairy.

After visiting Rowe and other friends at Blair and Headrick, it was time to return to Norman to get settled and prepare for the opening of the University early in September.

As a student I had taken my meals with Mrs. McGuire who lived not far from the University campus. She had moved to another house near the school but it was small so she had only two double rooms to rent, although she furnished meals to several other men who roomed nearby.

She gladly rented one of these two rooms on the second floor to Rowe and me and the other to Mack Heath, a friend of Rowe's, who had taught school near Blair, and to Jesse Thompson, one of my former students at both Headrick and Blair. The rooms were large and each was furnished with a double bed, study tables, and chairs. We put both beds in one room and used the other as a study.

For these rooms and three meals a day we each paid twenty dollars a month. This seems ridiculously little today but only a small coal-burning stove provided us with heat. For it we bought the coal and kindling and took turns getting up in the morning and building a fire. Also the bath was in the hall and was not exclusively ours, but was used sometimes by members of the family. The meals often reminded me of those at Harvard's Memorial Hall—they were so different! Yet, they were well cooked and surprisingly good for the amount we paid for them.

My so-called "teaching load" was sixteen hours a week which many university teachers today would consider far too heavy. To one who had been accustomed to spending over forty hours a week in a classroom and office of a village school it seemed very light.

Professor Gittinger's courses which I took over the first year were *Greek and Roman History, English History, The American Colonies*, and the *Early Middle Ages*. In addition were *Oklahoma History*, a course in *History of the West*, and one section of a freshman course in *American Government*, required of all students in the College of Arts and Sciences. In 1914-15 we had three sections each semester and I usually had the ten o'clock section. This seemed to be a very convenient hour for most students as more than eighty enrolled in my section the first semester.

None of these courses worried me too much for I had taught Ancient History in high school, had done some work

146

The Carnegie Building, the old library at the University of Oklahoma. (Courtesy Western History Collections, University of Oklahoma Library)

in most of the other subjects either at Edmond or O.U., and had all of my lecture and reading notes on Turner's course on the West at Harvard. My knowledge of the early Middle Ages and some of the other courses was far from great but I had read a great deal in the history of both Western Europe and America.

Teaching junior college-rank students for two summers at Central State Normal helped me make the transition from high school to university teaching. In fact I never felt the slightest embarrassment or nervousness in dealing with my students.

My age and experience in public school work were also important factors in enabling me to establish cordial relations with members of the faculty and to fit easily into the academic and social life of the campus. At thirty-five I was as old as some who were professors or associate professors and my master's degree from Harvard indicated that my training was equal to that of most of my colleagues because doctoral degrees were few at the University of Oklahoma in 1914.

I found considerable changes at O.U. since my graduation. The administration building had been completed and the law building erected. Many classes were still held in the wooden structure called Park Row and the only gymnasium was the large frame building in use during my student days. President Brooks was a great builder, however, and during the twelve years of his administration a large number of new buildings were constructed.

Nothing startling happened my first year as a member of the O.U. faculty. I worked hard and saved my money for I wanted to return to Harvard as soon as possible to start the Ph.D. degree. This had been discussed with both Professor Turner and Dean Haskins. They agreed that my chief handicap was my age but that in my case this was not too serious. They urged me, however, not to delay any longer than was absolutely necessary.

Although I worked very hard to prove myself a good teacher there was time for some recreation and social life. On the average campus an unattached bachelor is likely to

148

receive a good many invitations from hostesses who need an extra man at a tea or dinner party. I soon discovered that there was sometimes more formality at a small newly established Western university than at a large and very old Eastern one. Apparently some educational institutions, like individuals, go through a period of adolescence in their growth.

At any rate in order to "keep up with the Joneses" I soon bought myself a gorgeous dress suit with white vest, tie, patent leather shoes, and all the other "fixin's." A majority of the members of the faculty had similar attire which we wore more often in the next two years than most of us have worn even a tuxedo and black tie in the last quarter of a century.

As spring approached I also bought a second-hand Ford roadster for $300. Here I was far in advance of my colleagues for there were not more than three or four other faculty members who owned a car. This was not saving money for my return to Harvard but I bought the little car at a bargain price and felt sure that it could be sold without much loss at any time. I had never driven a car but a friend who had sold his Ford gave me a few lessons and in a week I was a fairly competent driver.

The second semester slipped by all too soon and for several days students and teachers wrestled with the pains and perils of final examinations. I was to teach in the eight-weeks' summer session. The law school had no summer term, however, so Rowe would spend the summer months with his parents in their home near Blair. It had been a joy to have him as a roommate again but the regret felt in parting was tempered by knowing that we would be rooming together again the following year.

Dr. Harry Gossard who taught mathematics was to teach in the summer school but his wife had planned to spend the summer with her parents in Pennsylvania. The Gossards lived in a neat little cottage near the University. Not wanting to live alone, he asked me to live with him during the summer session and I was glad to accept his invitation. He was about thirty years old and a delightful companion for he had a great deal of personal charm and a keen sense of humor. We had a happy eight weeks together and I felt a little sorry when the summer term ended about the first of August.

As the end of the summer term approached, I began to consider how to earn some money between its close and the opening of the first semester in September. Dr. Joseph W. Scroggs, the head of University Extension, was at this time deeply interested in visual education. He had employed a young Mr. Phelps at a salary of $100 a month to sell illustrated lectures to village and rural schools. As one man could not possibly cover the entire state, and I was the proud owner of a Ford roadster, I called on Scroggs to ask for a similar job. He seemed much interested but said that he lacked funds to pay me a salary. He would pay my expenses, however, and a commission of six dollars for every sale I made. This seemed generous and I accepted the job on these terms.

The plan was to provide rural and village schools with mimeographed lectures and colored lantern slides. The school was to supply a small cheap projector and a screen, but no doubt local businesses would buy these for a number of blanks slides were provided on which advertisements could be written. My recollection is that the cost was only twelve dollars to the school for the entire series of lectures. On each one sold by me, Scroggs would have barely enough left to pay the postage on the slides sent out each week, but he brought wholesome entertainment and increased the knowledge of thousands of persons.

As soon as my final examination papers were graded, I packed a simple little projector and silver screen into my "tin lizzie" and started for southwestern Oklahoma. The lecture I had chosen was *Historic and Literary Boston* from the series, *See America First*. For this there was no need for a mimeographed lecture. Boston had made such an impression on me that it was a joy to show pictures of Boston Common, Lexington, Concord, Plymouth, Craigie House, Harvard University, the Old North Church, Orchard House, etc.

No schools were in session but there was a County Normal at Hobart which I visited. At a picnic in a grove near one little town, many stayed to dance or ride the merry-go-round until ten or eleven at night. Here I hung the screen up against a tree and held forth on *Historic and Literary Boston* to a large audience. I had a carbide gas tank on the running board of the Ford and at country schoolhouses and other places without electricity used it for projector.[1]

The venture soon proved quite profitable. The first week I sold six courses and collected thirty-six dollars. The number sold increased every week, and in the fourth and last week I sold fourteen, for which I received eighty-four dollars. The total amount collected for the four weeks was $228, which was far more than my summer school salary. Moreover, it was all profit since Dr. Scroggs paid my expenses. I was almost ashamed to let him do this for the four weeks had been like a vacation. Best of all, when class work began at the University in September, 1915, Harvard in 1916-17 seemed assured.

My second year as instructor at O.U. was not too different from the first. Professor Gittinger was back with his Ph.D. from the University of California and relieved me of his courses. I continued to teach the other courses and added the *French Revolution and Napoleon* and *History of Spain*. Rowe and I again roomed together at the McGuires with the same arrangement as in the previous year, except Thompson did not return to school, and Jack Boatman, a law student, replaced him. This was Rowe's senior year in the Law School.

During this second year, however, I found myself engaged in far more "outside activities," to use a term coined by the students, than in my first year as instructor. Upon my arrival at O.U. I found two clubs composed of members of the faculty. One was the Popular Science Club. Its member-

---

[1] This generator tank contained carbide, gravel-sized pieces of carbon compound, and mixed with water produces gas which, when ignited, yields a bright light. This light reflecting from mirrors in the "magic lantern" (ancestor of the slide projector) projected images from slides onto the screen.

ship consisted of the twenty men oldest in service. Naturally, it was dying on the vine for the members read and discussed papers in their fields! Obviously, a chemistry professor's papers would be a powerful sedative to any English, government, or history professor and *vice versa*. As a result this club faded away.

The second faculty organization was the Newcomers Club of which every fulltime faculty member of the rank of instructor or above was a member. It derived its name from its primary objective, which was to welcome all newcomers to the faculty and to give them and their wives an opportunity to become acquainted with their colleagues as soon as possible. In a fast-growing institution such as O.U., there was usually a number of new appointees every year, so the Newcomers' Club in time became so large that finding a meeting place became a serious problem.

The Popular Science Club members seldom attended meetings of the Newcomers, so the leaders of the latter group rarely arranged serious programs. Instead they planned hilarious programs such as an indoor field meet, an informal opera—a take-off on *Carmen*, or poetry contest.

A third club called Wabunaki was formed very early in that year by faculty who believed that there was need for an organization which would give teachers in the various departments some idea of the work of their friends in other departments. The papers or talks were informal and might deal with some experience of the individual. For example, a former Rhodes Scholar who taught mathematics might give a paper or talk on Oxford. The name "Wabunaki" is an Indian term meaning "morning light" or "the dawn."

It was my misfortune to be elected president of the Newcomers' Club and secretary of Wabunaki. I accepted both offices before discovering that the president of the Newcomers was to find places for the meetings, appoint the program committee, meet with it to plan the meetings, find persons who would participate, arrange for the refreshments, etc., while the secretary only read the minutes of the last meeting. The secretary of Wabunaki, however, did all these things, while the president had virtually nothing to do but preside and introduce the speaker.

152

Onerous as were my duties in these two clubs, they gave me an opportunity to meet colleagues and their wives. As a result, at the end of my second year as instructor at O.U., I knew every member of the faculty and his wife, if he had one. The faculty was small in 1916; but as the student body increased in numbers, more teachers were employed. In consequence when I returned to O.U. after my second year at Harvard, there were so many "Newcomers" to the faculty when school opened in September, 1917, that I have never known all of them and their wives or husbands since.

At some meeting of a faculty group, possibly the Newcomers' Club, I had made a speech on the "Folk Lore of the Cowboy." It included some experiences of my own life and to my surprise seemed to make a great hit. Dr. Brooks heard of this and later heard me give a talk on "Folk Lore of the Prairie Homesteaders."

In addition to sixteen hours of teaching and my club activities, I did a bit of public speaking. Chapel was held regularly at which a member of the faculty gave a talk. I spoke two or three times at these chapel services. I also made a three-day trip to Eastern Oklahoma to speak to the students in the schools of three or four small towns, and later gave the commencement address to the graduating classes in two or three schools near Norman.

Upon receiving notice that my application for another Austin Teacher's Scholarship of $250 had been granted, I began to make definite plans for my next year of work at Harvard. Even before receiving notice of the scholarship award, I had made some attempt to satisfy the language requirement. Harvard demanded of all doctoral candidates a reading knowledge of German and French. I had as an undergraduate two years of German and about three of Spanish but no French. Dr. Lucille Dora was offering in the second semester a course in French. It was for her major students, usually juniors or seniors, who taught a class in French I, presumably under observation.

It was my good fortune to enter this class which was taught by Dr. Dora's assistant, Rosalie Gilkey, a pretty young woman about twenty years old. After the first two or three days, Dr. Dora seldom dropped in, even for a few minutes, and her young assistant was left in complete charge. I worked hard in this class but it ended all too soon for me to feel that my knowledge of French was sufficient to pass the Harvard examination.

I was sorry to see the second semester end. Rowe received his law degree and most of the prizes awarded for superior scholarship. Except for my year in Cambridge, we had worked together or had been roommates for five years. It was hard to say goodbye knowing that our close association for so long a period was ended.

I was to teach in the summer session but was eager to continue my study of French, so I asked the young woman who had taught our class if she would give me private lessons in reading French for a couple of months. She readily agreed and during the eight weeks of summer school she met me three evenings a week in a seminar room at the library for two hours to read French. Her fee was fifty cents an hour which the canniest Scot in all Christendom would not have called exorbitant!

She was a lovely girl as well as an excellent teacher, so it was not surprising that I began to look forward to these sessions with more interest in the teacher than in the subject taught. Reason whispered that no beautiful and sensible girl of twenty could ever develop a romantic feeling for an old bachelor of thirty-seven.

Hope springs eternal, however, and when our lesson closed one extremely warm evening I summoned up enough courage to suggest that we take a little drive to "get a breath of fresh air." She seemed to hesitate for a moment before accepting but we had a pleasant half-hour's drive. This seemed to break the ice a little and led to other drives and a dinner at her home. By the end of summer school and my leaving for Cambridge, we were good friends but nothing more!

Immediately after the close of summer school, I drove down to southwestern Oklahoma for a brief visit with my relatives and friends. Here I sold my little car for $210 plus the price of train fare back to Norman. Once there I packed up and a little before the end of August started for Cambridge. This was earlier than necessary, but I planned to take a little vacation at some place by the sea.

Having seen the Northeast, I wanted to see something of the South so I took a train for Memphis and from that city traveled by the Southern Railroad to Norfolk, Virginia. My former trip had taught me a great deal. The "Baby" had been given to some student before starting home from Harvard in the summer of 1914 and I took much less other stuff than on the previous trip. Paying several dollars for a Pullman berth still seemed gross extravagance but riding in a day coach of the Southern Railway in the summer of 1916 did much to modify that opinion.

Norfolk proved to be a most interesting town. After a long night's sleep, I visited the great navy yard, Fortress Monroe, and other historic places. This took only a couple of days. Then someone told me of Virginia Beach so I decided to go there for a week or so before going to Cambridge.

In 1916 Virginia Beach was only a string of cottages facing a beautiful beach, a life-saving station, and a dancing pavilion covered by a shingle roof. The season was over so there was not a vacationer in sight. It seemed an ideal spot to rest for a few days, and I found room and board at the Paine Cottage almost next door to the life-saving station.

The elderly Mr. and Mrs. Paine gave me a cordial welcome and for over a week I did almost nothing but rest, read, and swim. The food prepared by the Negro woman in the kitchen seemed out of this world when compared with the sandwiches, cookies, fruit, etc., on which I had subsisted while traveling in a day coach of a Southern Railway train that seemed to have only two speeds—very slow and full stop! Now we were having *Virginia Spots*, one of the most delicious fish that swims, crab meat, chicken, hot biscuits, Smithfield ham, and numerous other good things.

The water was fine for swimming—pleasantly cool but not cold, and not soupy warm like that of some lakes and ponds of Oklahoma in August. Here I saw at night the most glorious phosphorescent sea that ever met my eyes before or since. The Paines' fifteen-year-old grandaughter and her chum one evening invited three or four other girls and the men from the life-saving station for a square dance. It was fun for all of us, but time was running out for me and a day or so later I returned to Norfolk. A ship was sailing for New York that evening; so, true to my inborn love for the sea, I boarded it and within an hour after reaching New York was on a train bound for Boston.

Upon reaching Cambridge, I hurried over to 76 Hammond Street hoping to get a room at the home of Mrs. Elder. Luck was with me for my old room on the second floor was vacant, and Mrs. Elder and her daughter seemed much pleased to have me occupy it again. Harvard seemed little changed except that the Widener Memorial Library, under construction two years before, was completed and the books were all housed there. In 1913-14 they had been widely distributed—some in Massachusetts Hall but many in two or three other buildings.

It was a great thrill to be back at Harvard again. By the time I was well settled the other roomers on that floor had arrived. They were all senior law students. John Edwin Peakes and Nate Tufts were good friends from Maine where John had taught school for a year or so. Abe Feinberg was from some town in Massachusetts. These three soon became my warm friends. The fourth man's name was Marrs, but none of us knew him well as his best friends were apparently unknown to the other three law students.

Turner had written me that he was to be on sabbatical leave that year. This was a great disappointment to me; but he had approved the subject of my dissertation, "The Range Cattle Industry in Oklahoma." This made it possible to work on it in government documents if my course work left me any time for it.

It must be confessed that it left very little. I registered for Professor Channing's Seminar, a full course for the entire year; for his half course in printed materials for American History; and audited his half course in the American Colonies. My other courses were Professor Hart's Government 12, which was for the year; Julius Klein's Spain in North America the first half year, and History of South America the second half; and Dean Haskins's Historical Bibliography and Criticism, a half course throughout the year. I also audited Professor McIlwain's Constitutional History of England to the reign of Henry VII.

This meant four full courses and auditing two more, but I was now accustomed to work at Harvard and was not "afraid of my job" as I had been two years before. Clearly my program would require a great deal of hard work; but it could be done for my grades in 1913-14, while not startling, had been good.

My financial situation was not as good as it had been in 1913-14 in spite of my success as a salesman for Dr. Scroggs and a $100 increase in salary my second year at O.U. In consequence, I decided to eat at Foxcroft Hall instead of Memorial. I found the food very good at Foxcroft and surprisingly cheap, but the service was slower with student waiters than it had been at Memorial where the Jamaican Negro waiters moved with astonishing speed. Yet, by using care in ordering, a moderate eater could probably save a dollar a week and still have fairly good and well balanced meals by eating at Foxcroft.

O.U. and Beacon Hill

It seemed to me that Harvard had not changed much in the past two years except that the completion of Widener Memorial Library with stalls in the stacks for graduate students greatly facilitated all work in research. The teas at Phillips Brooks House were held every week just as they had been formerly. President and Mrs. Lowell were "at home" to students once a week for a couple of hours and entertained the "leftovers" Christmas Eve. Morning prayers were still held every morning for some fifteen minutes. Phillips Brooks House also entertained the leftover students the evening of Christmas Day and many professors set aside two or three hours of one afternoon a week for students to visit them in their homes.

Eating at Foxcroft gave me the opportunity to meet far more students than at Memorial Hall where I saw only the same men every day except when one of them might have a guest. The law students rooming at 76 Hammond were very interesting men, especially John Peakes, Nate Tufts, and Abe Feinberg. I also soon came to know men in my classes, especially Fred Merk of Wisconsin, Charles Harris of Maine, and Richard Morton of Virginia.

Soon after settling down to work it was my good fortune to make new friends in Greater Boston, due to the kindness and courtesy of President and Mrs. Brooks. During my second year at O.U. I had come to know Dr. Brooks quite well. Upon one occasion I had made a speech to a group on the campus on "The Folklore of the Cowboy." Evidently Dr.

Brooks liked this talk, for one day I received a letter with a Boston postmark. Curious to know who might be writing me from Boston, I opened it and read:

Dear Mr. Dale:

I have received a letter from our mutual friend, Dr. Stratton D. Brooks. If you know half as much as he says you do, you know a damned sight more than I do; and if you are half as good a fellow as he says you are, you are a damned sight better fellow than I am.

Anyhow, I want you to be my guest at the dinner of the Puddingstone Club next Wednesday evening at 6:30 and tell us a little about cowboys. Please come to my office about six. Sincerely,

Nathaniel C. Fowler, Jr.

That and his office address was all. There was nothing to indicate who the writer was or what his business might be. Moreover, I could think of no one who could give me any information and the idea of turning to *Who's Who* never entered my head. So it was with complete ignorance of my would-be host and of the Puddingstone Club that I wrote Mr. Fowler a brief note accepting his invitation.

Later I was to learn that he was sometimes called the "Dean of America Advertising." Born in 1858, he was publishing a small newspaper when only a boy. Later he had been a newspaper columnist, business adviser to many large firms, had directed selling campaigns, had written nearly a dozen books, and was conducting a "business laboratory." His best known ad is that which he did for the Prudential Life Insurance Company, "The Strength of Gibraltar." He once told me that for this he had received $1,000 and should have had more.

My knowledge of all this came much later. When the time came for me to keep my engagement, it is not surprising that I should have felt a bit jittery as to what lay ahead, for the unknown is usually frightening. Nothing had been said as to dress but it seemed that my evening suit might be in order, so clothed in my best "bib and tucker" I reached Fowler's office at 6 p.m.

He greeted me cordially and in five minutes my nervousness was gone. Clearly Nat Fowler was a remarkable character with a razor-keen mind, a charming extrovert, who had a great sense of humor, and in five minutes could make even a complete stranger feel that he had met a long lost friend. He said that we would walk to the meeting place of the Club, but it was only a few blocks, so we need not start for ten or fifteen minutes.

"I don't mean to insult you," he said earnestly, "but you're to give us a little talk on cowboy life this evening so maybe you should know that we don't tell dirty stories in the Puddingstone Club. Oh, we say hell and damn of course, they're all right, but what I mean is sex stories or jokes. Don't let me insult you now, but it seemed I should tell you this."

I thanked him for the tip and assured him that in the many speehes made to men's clubs I had never told a story or joke of the type he had indicated and never would. Hell and damn were in my vocabulary, too, but rotten or obscene stories had no place in any meeting of men and any man who had to depend on such stories to interest an audience was, in my opinion, incapable of making a speech worth hearing.

As we walked over to the meeting, he told me a little about the Puddingstone Club. It had a membership of some forty men, many of them listed in *Who's Who*. Apparently it had no officers except Fowler who was secretary. He appointed some member to be responsible for each program. He also sent out the notices giving the program and requesting that any member who could not come notify him. It seems, too, that he or his secretary planned the menu for every dinner.

When we reached the meeting place, several of the members were already there. Fowler introduced me to them and to the others as they came in. All wore business suits and Nat apologized for my evening clothes, saying that he had failed to tell me to wear ordinary garb. He added that since the fault was his, they should not write their names on my shirt front as they did when one of their members came in wearing a dress suit because he expected to go to a formal reception later in the evening.

160

To say that Nat Fowler's introductions were unconventional is truly a gross understatement of fact! When Reverend Edward Cummings came in, Nat said, "Mr. Dale, this is Ed Cummings. He's the pastor of Edward Everett Hale's Church, but he's damned good fellow, aren't you Ed?" Most of the other introductions were in the same general vein, for always something was said as to the member's vocation and usually I was referred to as, "from Oklahoma where our former member, Stratton Brooks, holds forth."

While I cannot recall what we had for dinner, except that it started with half a grapefruit, I know that it was an excellent one as were all the Puddingstone dinners. My speech on cowboy life was well received for it included several humorous stories. I also gave an account of my being snow-bound for three weeks with two other cowhands and of our efforts to entertain ourselves by a verse writing contest. The men seemed to like my talk a great deal. At least they all said so at the close of the meeting as they shook hands with me and urged me to come again.

The next day I received a very flattering note from Mr. Fowler praising my talk and asking me to be his guest again at the next meeting. I learned eventually that this was his fixed practice. During the entire year he asked me to speak to students in his business laboratory or to some other group, three or four times. On the following day, I always got a flattering note of thanks, so soon as to make me wonder sometimes if it had not been written before the speech was made!!

Of course I was delighted to accept Fowler's invitation to come to the next meeting of the Puddingstone Club, provided he would let me pay for my dinner which he reluctantly agreed to do. Apparently members seldom missed a meeting for the dinner was always perfect and the program fun.

Just which member of the Club was responsible for the next program I cannot recall, but it was a most enjoyable one for me because, unlike the previous meeting, I felt free to sit back and relax, secure in the knowledge that *MY* speech had been made at the former meeting. After a male quartert had given a few numbers and a club member a piano solo, the master of ceremonies for the evening began: "We will now hear from a young man who comes to us from the far off western plains, although he bears a name honored by all true Bostonians-and—." He had gotten that far in his announcement before I froze with horror at the realization that he was talking about *me!*

As he completed his sentence, I staggered to my feet and there came to mind some of the old rhymes written years before. Maybe these verses might pull me out of this crisis.

"Gentlemen," I said, trying to keep my voice steady, "I have no speech for you this evening but in my old cowhand days, living all alone in a dugout camp, I used to write verses for my own amusement. So maybe a few of these crude rhymes might interest you. Upon one occasion, after a hard day's ride, it seemed everything had gone wrong that day. Then it appeared that everything went wrong *every* day. So while in that mood, I wrote these verses and called the finished product *Butter-Side Down.*"

When I was just a little kid and always in the way
My Ma would spread a slice of bread and send me out to
play,
I'd play about beneath the trees with marbles, bat and ball,
Or climb upon the orchard fence, or on the garden wall,
But if that bread should drop from out my little hand so
brown,
It always struck the dusty earth
Butter-Side Down.

I grew a little older and to college went a way,
I studied hard each lesson never taking time for play,
I burned the oil of midnight o'er my Latin and my Greek,
I toiled both late and early through each long and weary
week,
But when examination day at last came rolling round,
I always dropped, yes sadly dropped,
Butter-Side Down.

162

I courted a fair maiden, her heart I hoped to win,
For candy, books, and flowers spent all my surplus tin,
She had another fellow, a tall and ugly guy,
With hair as red as blazes, and a wicked looking eye,
But just about the time I thought I had him done up brown,
She married him and let me drop,
Butter-Side Down.

And so it's been throughout my life, I've met Dame Fortune's frown,
For all of my investments went Butter-Side Down,
I quite believe that when I leave this world of doubt and sin,
And reach that Golden City that the righteous enter in,
When that good old man, St. Peter, presents my shining crown,
I'll drop the everlasting thing,
Butter-Side Down.

The vigorous and sustained applause which followed this foolish rhyme was astonishing. Clearly my audience wanted more so for fifteen or twenty minutes, I continued to recite so-called "poems," mostly in child dialect, which I had written some years earlier. When I at last sat down, the almost thunderous applause convinced me that Lady Luck or Dame Fortune had helped me to turn what had appeared to be complete disaster into triumph.

It was evident that the men had been amused by these crude verses. At the close of the meeting, they all came up to shake hands and tell me so. They also told me to consider myself a member of the club as long as I was in Boston. Nat assured me that he would send me notices of all meetings and urged me never to miss one. He also sent the "Butter-Side Down" rhyme to the *Boston Transcript*, which published it, and Nat had it printed on slips of paper and sent a copy to all club members.

For the remainder of the year I attended every meeting of the Club including the "Outing" which was held at the country estate of Henry Harriman late in May.

The membership of Puddingstone Club was a group of the most remarkable men I have ever known. Among them in addition to Nathaniel Fowler and Rev. Ed Cummings were Denis McCarthy, who came to America a shy Irish lad and wrote four volumes of lyric poems about his native land. Others were Bill Crawford, head of a boys manual arts school; John Orth, pianist and composer whose compositions "To a Portrait" and "By the Ocean" were well-known half a century ago; Nixon Waterman, poet and newspaper columnist; Farley Brothers, wholesale dry goods merchants with literary leanings; Nathan Haskell Dole, and Dr. Paul, both writers; Henry Harriman, at one time head of the U.S. Chamber of Commerce, and many others.

Just how long the Puddingstone Club continued, I do not know. Nathaniel C. Fowler died in November, 1918, but his place as secretary was taken over by another member, probably Bill Crawford. At any rate, the club was still going strong in 1922 and probably for some years more.

Except for Fowler, my closest friend of the Puddingstones was John Kennedy Lacock, an old bachelor who lived on Buckingham Street in Cambridge. He had a master's degree in history from Harvard and wrote some excellent guide books for Boston and nearby towns. He also led a party of historians, headed by Professor Albert Bushenell Hart, on a trip to explore and map the route of General Braddock's army in its ill-fated campaign having as its objective the capture of Fort Duquesne. The party found and marked every night's camping place and Lacock published a small book and a set of cards describing the line of march.

My association with the Puddingstone Club and the friendship of Nathaniel Fowler soon brought me contacts with other Boston organizations. One of these was the Twentieth Century Association. It was a very large group, which someone said, "Had in its membership about all of the old Boston that 'was left'." It had a large clubhouse at Joy Street, a fulltime secretary, and held a luncheon meeting every Saturday from October to May. After lunch came a speech, usually upon some timely topic.

The club had so much prestige that it seldom had any difficulty in obtaining an able and often distinguished speaker. Visitors from Europe, especially Great Britain, accepted invitations to speak to the club, as did United States senators, cabinet members, and well-known authors or university presidents from outside the city who might be visiting Boston. If none of these were available, there was much local talent in Greater Boston itself.

Soon after "rhyming my way" into the Puddingstone Club, I received an invitation to attend a meeting of the Twentieth Century group. Knowing that many members of the club belonged to the oldest and most aristocratic families of Boston, I had expected an elaborate luncheon. To my surprise, the dishes were blue willowware, and the lunch consisted of corned beef hash topped by a poached egg, scalloped potatoes, apple pie with a sliver of cheese, and tea. That was all except bread and butter. It was excellent food, well cooked and satisfying, but not what the average well-to-do Oklahoma hostess would serve.

After lunch the dishes and tablecloths were removed, and the tables were revealed as wide flat boards resting on "saw horses." When all these were stacked around the rear wall, the speaker, a distinguished member of the British Parliament, was introduced by President John Graham Brooks. At the close of his speech, some thirty minutes were given to questions directed to the speaker by those in the audience who wished to have some point in the address clarified or discussed further. I found later that after a meeting had adjourned, the speaker was often invited to accompany those club members especially interested in his subject to a smaller room upstairs. Here he was assured that he could speak freely as no reporters were present, and what he said would be held in strict confidence.

It was my good fortune to attend many meetings of the Twentieth Century Club as the guest of Nat Fowler or some other friend. The meetings were not as much fun as those of the Puddingstoners, but they were most educational and afforded me the opportunity to meet many remarkable men of great talent. Among the members who became my good friends were Dr. Samuel S. Curry, head of the Curry School of Expression, and Dr. George L. Perin, a distinguished clergyman of the Universalist Church, who had founded the

Franklin Square House, a home for working girls, and was trustee of various charity or cultural institutions.

Eventually I was invited to become a member of the Twentieth Century Club. The invitation was gladly accepted for I considered it a great honor and the dues for a nonresident were only half the sum for a member residing in Greater Boston, so were virtually negligible even to a needy graduate student. This membership I still retain and have paid my small dues regularly for over forty years without attending a meeting, yet the programs and announcements are well worth the small cost.

A third organization which I attended several times that year as a guest was the Boston Authors Club. Many of its members such as Denis McCarthy, Nixon Waterman, and Nathan Haskell Dole were also members of the Pudding-stone, Twentieth Century Club, or both. The Boston Authors Club is an old organization founded in 1900, which has always had among its members some of the best-known writers of America. I thoroughly enjoyed the meetings, met many charming people, and was flattered when asked to read some of my western verses. Upon returning to Cambridge in 1919 Basil King was president. Of the honorary vice-presidents, William Dean Howells had died on May 10, 1919, but Garriet Prescott Spofford was still living and writing, as was Robert Grant. Others who were well-known at that time were Alice Brown, Eleanor H. Porter, Dallas Lore Sharp, Arthur Stanwood Pier, Caroline Ticknor, William Dana Orcutt, and Amy Bridgman.

I worked very hard and my grades were higher this year than they were my first year at Harvard, largely because I knew what to expect and worked more efficiently than in 1913-14 when I was desperately "afraid of my job." The completion of the new library also helped a great deal, as it housed all the books which in my first year were scattered about in three or four buildings. Finally, two years of teaching American history and government to under-graduates and graduates at O.U. had made me thoroughly familiar with the *facts* of these subjects and had given me confidence.

166

My courses with Professor Channing were fascinating. His seminar had ten students, all from different universities. Richard Kendig was from Amherst; Frederick Merk, from Wisconsin; and Richard Lee Morton, from William and Mary. These became my special friends, especially Merk and Morton. Others were from various colleges, including one from Harvard College.[1]

Each of us was to give three lectures on the topic chosen for the half-year from an outline of only one page. A copy of this outline and of the bibliography was to be given to each student and to Professor Channing. He assured us that he and the rest of the class would judge the college from which each man came by the quality of his work in the course. This was a pep talk worthy of any football coach! At the end of the year, Channing told me ruefully that the chap from Harvard College made the lowest grade in the class!

Each student in this seminar was given a fifteen minute conference period with Channing in his office once a week. Mine was from twelve noon till twelve-fifteen every Wednesday. We discussed any problems with respect to my topic but if there were none, talked of anything pertaining to American history. Fifteen minutes may seem to be a very short time, but it amounts to nine hours in thirty-six weeks and in these conferences I learned much.

He was a remarkably good lecturer and auditing his course in The English Colonies in America enabled me to reorganize my own course in colonial history and make it one of the most popular history courses offered at O.U. At least the class grew from twelve or fifteen students to fifty or more.

Channing was said to have a bad temper and showed it once or twice by laying out, in no uncertain terms, some member of the big class in the American colonies, which consisted largely of sophomores. In each case, however, the lad was whispering to his neighbor or trying to read a newspaper during the lecture and fully deserved a repri-

---

[1] Professor Edward Channing.

mand. To me Channing was always most kind and even had me spend an evening in his home.

The half-course in Historical Bibliography and Criticism given by Dean Haskins met once a week for two hours throughout the year. It was for me one of the most valuable courses I ever had. Haskins was the best lecturer that it was my privilege to have at Harvard, with the possible exception of Merriman, and the breadth and depth of his knowledge of history was amazing. At the end of the year when the grades were in, George Washington Robinson said to me in his precise New England accent: "If I weah you, I should be very proud of the A you made with Professah Haskins. For a man in the field of Amehican Histoah, that is most unusual." Believe me, I *was* very proud![2]

My course in American Government with Professor Hart was very easy, probably because I had taught American government repeatedly five or six times to freshmen classes at O.U. This course was graduate level, but my factual knowledge gained by teaching it so many times helped a great deal. Hart's lectures were unpredictable, sometimes rambling, at other times brilliant, but he was most kind and helpful to his students and former students. He had me to dinner at the Harvard Club once and invited me again, but another engagement prevented my acceptance. Many years later he was a dinner guest in our home at Norman.[3]

I enjoyed all my courses a great deal and finished the year with four grades of A and two of B. Both Merk and I made A in Channing's Seminar. This was a considerably better record than for my first year at Harvard, in spite of my outside activities. Possibly such activities actually helped me to do better class work for the steady grind the former year resulted in my becoming nervous and having some eye trouble for several weeks. Also, it is certain that my association with clever and distinguished members of these Boston clubs gave me inspiration and encouragement.

---

[2] Professor Homer Haskins.
[3] Professor Albert Bushell Hart.

Some other activities of that year were giving a lecture on the Cow Country to a woman's club of which Mrs. Stratton D. Brooks had formerly been a member. This was "Husbands' Evening" and the club paid me a very acceptable fee of twenty-five dollars.

Not long after the closely contested presidential election of November, 1916, a lady belonging to an old Boston family asked me to meet a group of young women for an hour one evening a week. She said that they were much interested in current events, but needed someone to talk to them and explain what they had read in the newspapers. The meetings would be held in a room at North End House in North Boston near where the Italian and Yiddish quarters met.

The lady said that these young women were unable to pay for this service but would insist on giving me a small sum for transportation. Since a scholarship holder is usually pledged not to work for money without the consent of the Dean of his school, I told Dean Haskins of this request. He said that it was quite all right for me to do this, so for the next couple months or more I met with this group every Thursday evening from 7:30 to 8:30.

It was a very interesting experience. North End House, situated in the middle of the so-called slums of this section of the city, was a busy place every evening for although social service was then largely in its infancy, there were night classes in various subjects, panel discussions, lectures on numerous themes, and recreational games and chaperoned dances every evening. Most of these activities were carried out by volunteer "Do-gooders" but were sponsored and directed by professional workers.

My class in current events was made up of some two dozen young women ranging in age from about eighteen to the mid-twenties. Probably all of them had been born in this country of immigrant parents. They all spoke English with comparatively little accent although this was doubtless not true of their parents. They were all clean, neatly dressed, well-groomed girls who worked in factories or shops in this part of the city. Some were Italian, others Jewish, and perhaps still others Czech, or of Polish descent, but all were intelligent and eager to learn. It was a pleasure to teach them more about national and world affairs and to do my best to answer their questions. They seemed most grateful and when I was forced to end the meetings because the first half-year exams were drawing near, they insisted on giving me an envelope containing several dollars in currency as a "thank-you offering."

I accepted this with some reluctance for they were poor, and besides meeting with them once a week had taught me more than I had taught them. It had given me some understanding of the lives of these immigrant families in the slums of our large cities. It was my custom after most meetings to stop for a cup of coffee at a cheap little restaurant before returning to Cambridge. Here the number of human derelicts that came in to ask for a little something to eat made me realize why most New Englanders believed it a sin to waste food.

Mention had been made of John Kennedy Lacock. His Cambridge home was a huge old three-story house with a basement and sub-basement. It was on a steep hill facing Buckingham Street where it joins Concord Avenue near the Harvard Observatory. This was only a short walk from my rooming place at 76 Hammond Street. Soon after our first meeting at the Puddingstone Club, he asked me to come to his home to meet a few friends that he was having for a little party. I gladly accepted and we soon became fast friends.

We had much in common. We were both bachelors, although he must have been a few years older than I. The chief interest of both was American history, and we both had master's degrees in that subject from Harvard. Most important of all was the fact that "the vibrations were right." We thoroughly enjoyed each other's companionship, had the same interests, liked the same things, and the same people. The friendship formed that year was to continue until John Kennedy Lacock's death some twenty years later.

John's guidebook to Boston and the nearby towns must have brought him some income. He had given some illustrated public lectures on the life of Lincoln, General

Braddock's Expedition, and perhaps some other subjects. He rented three or four rooms in his big house to persons that he had known for many years. Among them were Miss Harriet Gardiner, who must have been around eighty years old, and Mildred Prescott, a nurse probably in her thirties, and at various times one or two others.

He must have had other income from stocks or bonds for he never seemed to lack funds, drove a small coupe of popular make, and belonged not only to the Puddingstone, but to one or two other clubs in Boston. He also entertained quite a bit, but his parties were of a type that cost very little or nothing. At this time movies were in their infancy. John used his excellent record player to entertain his guests.

He not only gave illustrated lectures but illustrated old popular songs by operating the projector to throw on the screen suitable pictures for the song coming from the record player. He also brought some of his artist friends to furnish entertainment. On my birthday, for example, he invited the parents of a six-year-old girl, who was a marvelous dancer, to bring her to the party to dance for me and the other guests. I recall that on another occasion a male quartet which sang at one of the largest and richest churches in Boston came to one of John's parties and sang several numbers. These men were well-paid by the church for singing every Sunday, but John was a good friend so they came to his home to help make the party a success.

It was not long until John discovered my skill in cooking, especially "flapjacks." He seemed intrigued by my ability to flip them over without the benefit of a pancake turner or broad-bladed knife. As a result, he laid in a supply of maple syrup and upon a number of occasions invited three or four men in for a "flapjack" supper. These were usually some of our mutual friends as Dr. Curry, and others of the Puddingstone or Twentieth Century Clubs.

The procedure was to put a two-burner gas plate on a small table in the dining room near the large dining table at which the guests were seated. To this I would bring two light griddles and a huge bowl of my own carefully blended pancake batter. After rubbing the hot griddles with the

171

freshly cut end of a potato instead of greasing them, I would put enough batter on each griddle to make a flapjack six to eight inches in diameter. It browned on one side in a minute or less and could then be tossed with a twist of the wrist which landed it in the center of the griddle with the browned side up.

These little "stag" parties were great fun. As only two flapjacks were cooked at a time, and the average husky male was likely to consume six to eight, supper was a leisurely affair with ample time for talk, jokes, and laughter. Yet it is surprising how quickly three or four dozen pancakes can be baked and served. Accompanied by crisp bacon or sausage, and plenty of maple syrup, butter, and strong coffee, five or six flapjacks make a satisfying and wholesome meal. Moreover, the guests, apparently fascinated, watched me flip them over and expected me to land one on the floor but my luck held and I always had a perfect score!

John Peakes and Nate Tufts, who occupied the room adjoining mine, were good scouts and I became very fond of them. They were both from "down in Maine" though the map would suggest that "up in Maine" would be more nearly correct. John's "Aunt Prudence," who was a widow, lived with her two or three daughters on a small Maine farm. John occasionally spent a weekend with her and the girls, always calling her first to be sure she would be at home and that she was not expecting other guests for the weekend.

The "Prudence" struck me as a trifle peculiar, but I eventually discovered that parents in old New England families sometimes named their daughters for one of the cardinal virtues. This custom had descended from the early Puritan settlers of Colonial New England who often named their girl babies Patience, Honor, Faith, Hope, Charity, Prudence, and even Obedience. Perhaps they expected the child to grow up with the quality suggested by her name. Some clever chap has asserted that if far-sighted parents today named their girls on any such basis they would christen them Jazzina, Gadabouta, Extravaganza, and Hysteria.

As indicated, I met few girls during my first year at Harvard. At the Phillips Brooks House teas I was introduced to a few Harvard professors' daughters including Dorothy Turner and Miss Munsterberg, but that was about all. In addition to these, I can recall only one other young woman. She was a teacher named Helen Warren who lived with her parents in Arlington Heights and taught in a grade school near her home. While our acquaintance was slight that year, it was renewed my second year and we soon became good friends.

Helen was in her middle twenties, perhaps, and while not beautiful was a nice looking girl, neat, well groomed, and always "sensibly" dressed. She was modest and shy as a nun and as typically old-time New England as a character in one of Nathaniel Hawthorne or Louisa M. Alcott's books. In short, she was as naive and innocent as any little girl four or five years of age.

Once she and I took a walk from her parent's home to the James Russell Lowell House which I had expressed a wish to see. The house was closed but we admired the exterior and garden. Nearby was little Lowell Park with half a dozen or so benches. Helen hesitated a moment before she asked, "Do you ever sit down on a park bench?"

"Surely, I sit down on a park bench," I replied. "I sit down on a park bench, rock, log, the ground, or anything else when tired, why?"

"Well, some people never do. I thought if you ever sat on a park bench, we might sit down and rest a few minutes before we start home."

Helen and the persons with whom she was most closely associated had many inhibitions but apparently sitting quietly on a park bench was not one of them!

During my first year in Cambridge I had made a trip or so to Revere Beach, a small imitation of Coney Island. It was reached from Boston in 1916 by a thirty-minute ride on the train running on a narrow gauge railroad. The broad sandy beach was an attractive one and the temperature of the clear blue water was just right for swimming on a warm day. Behind the beach was an amusement park, including hotdog and hamburger stands, shooting galleries, doll racks, a ferris wheel, merry-go-round, and roller coaster.

One warm day about the first of June it occurred to me to ask Helen to go out there with me on a Friday or Saturday evening. She seemed a little surprised but said she was not sure she could go. The following evening she telephoned me that she would be glad to go as she had never been to Revere Beach.

It was a warm, pleasant evening and Helen was as excited as a little girl on her first visit to a circus. We did not swim but rode on the roller coaster and merry-go-round. I tried my skill in shooting. There was a full moon and we sat on the beach to observe the swimmers, watch the tide come in, and listen to the music of the orchestra at the dancing pavilion far down the beach.

Helen told me later that it had been an enjoyable evening for she had never before visited a place like that. She added that her mother, when told of my invitation, had replied: "Oh yes, go with him if you'd like to. It might be good for you to learn more about how other people live and what kind of entertainment they enjoy most."

It was my privilege to have Thanksgiving dinner with Helen's parents. They were kindly and hospitable people who made up for the simple fare of every-day life with a truly sumptuous feast at New England's original holiday— Thanksgiving. I do not recall what the father's job was but apparently it was clerical work of some kind with a Boston firm. The mother was a lovely old lady apparently a trifle less conventional than Helen, but a true New Englander. The only other guests were the young daughter, Reba, her lawyer husband, and their baby daughter. The table, with its magnificent centerpiece, the dinner, and the charming hosts made the day one that could never be forgotten.

It must be confessed that I did not take Helen out very much because, in addition to work in my history courses, much time was spent in the study of French and German. I took her to the Castle Square Theater a couple of times. It was leased by John Craig and his wife, Mary Young, who had their own stock company and tickets were cheap. Once we saw a sweet little romantic play dealing with a poor writer and a young princess. On another occasion we saw

Midsummer Night's Dream. It seemed to me very well done although Mary Young may have been not quite young and slender enough for a perfect Puck.

After the show we started for the subway and came to Child's Restaurant with a man inside the window diligently flipping hot cakes. This made me hungry so I proposed that we go in and have some coffee and flapjacks to sustain us on the long ride home. Helen agreed and seemed to enjoy the little snack as much as I did. Much later, however, she told me that it was a new experience for she had never before been inside a Child's Restaurant.

I remained in Cambridge until the early part of July. The city was to have a great display of fireworks on Boston Common July 4, and I asked Helen to go with me. We reached the Common early and found a well-located park bench. By the time it was dark enough for fireworks, a huge crowd had assembled. When a boy passed by selling popcorn and peanuts, I bought a couple of sacks of each and we contentedly munched as we watched the brilliant display. Helen seemed to enjoy everything, but on the way home confessed that this was the first time in her life she had ever sat on a park bench and eaten popcorn and peanuts! My only response was that she didn't know what she had been missing, which she agreed was true.

Helen was to me the most interesting girl that I have ever known. She once told me that she had learned more from me than from any other person. Perhaps she had, for our backgrounds were about as different as those of any two individuals of the same race and nation could be.

Teaching, however, is a two-way street. If I had taught Helen something, she also taught me a great deal. She had given me a far better understanding of the "New England Way" than I had ever had before. Probably if I had been born and reared in Greater Boston with its slums filled with people of so many different types and languages, who flocked to Revere Beach, the public parks, and Child's Restaurants, these places might have been considered as "off limits for me and my friends," too.

When World War I broke out in Europe in the summer of

1914, it attracted more attention in Eastern Seaboard states and those bordering Canada than in the inland states of the West. Industrial and commercial New England, New York, and Pennsylvania felt the impact of the conflict raging in Europe far more than did Oklahoma; and by September, 1916, when I reached Cambridge, it was plain that many persons feared that the United States would inevitably be drawn into the struggle.

When Congress declared war on April 6, 1917, the effect upon Harvard was startling. In my course with Professor Hart in American Government, for both undergraduates and graduates, the class of over sixty students dropped to about twenty within a week. No one left my classes in the courses for graduates only, as Channing's Seminar, his *Materials for American History*, and the course in *Historical Bibliography and Criticism* with Haskins. John and Nate waited for a few weeks and then left to enlist in the ambulance corps. John was back in a week or so because the medicos found a slight heart murmur and rejected him. Nate, however, I never saw again.

Within a month the excitement due to our being in a war had passed and the remaining students at Harvard had settled down to finish the year's work. I was eager to take my general examination but first had to demonstrate my ability to read French and German. Professor Ferguson, who taught Ancient History, gave the examination for that department. I had reviewed very carefully and made an appointment to take the examination in his home.[4]

On the day set, I walked over to the Ferguson home and the Professor received me cordially in his study. He offered me a cigarette which I declined as I did not begin smoking until two or three years later. He tried to put me at ease, for I was plainly nervous, by saying that he did not smoke much at home but smoked a good deal in Greece because a Greek who offered you a cigarette was likely to be offended if you refused it.

---

[4] Professor William Scott Ferguson.

After a few minutes of conversation he took a French book from his shelves and after looking through it a little indicated a page and said, "Look over this page a minute or two and then read it to me in English."

I had little difficulty with it so he handed me another French book, indicating the page to be translated. This, too, gave me but little difficulty. After I read aloud my translation with comparative ease, he said, "it seems that your French is all right, Mr. Dale. Now let's see what you can do with German."

I breathed a brief prayer asking Heaven to bless my little brown-eyed French teacher at O.U., as the professor handed me a German book and suggested that I look over the page that he indicated before reading an English translation aloud for him. Here I met my Waterloo. My German reading for the past few weeks had been Beiloch's *Ancient History*, while the book handed me was a volume on the German U-Boats and their role in submarine warfare.

This was bad enough but to make it worse, looking over the page for two or three minutes hurt more than it helped. It revealed a number of unfamiliar words which made me even more nervous. I stumbled through it in halting fashion but it was clear even to me that my German was very weak. Perhaps I did a little better on the pages from the next books, but not enough to prove even to myself that I had an adequate reading knowledge of German.

Professor Ferguson was very kind. "You read French very well, Mr. Dale," he said courteously, "but I think you should give another five or six months to the study of German. If you will do that I am sure you will be able to read it well enough to pass a satisfactory examination. I will say this in my report to the Dean."

It was with some embarrassment that I entered the office of Dean Haskins a day or so later. "What do you intend to do?" he asked.

"Buckle down to work on German, regardless of where I am or what my work may be."

"That is good," said Dean. "We have decided to let you take your general examination even though you do not have a reading knowledge of German. You should prepare to pass a satisfactory examination in German, however, as soon as possible even if it delays finishing your dissertation."

Soon after this a date was set for my general examination. At that time the Harvard General Examination of candidates for the Doctor's degree in history was entirely oral. It included all of six fields chosen by the student except the one in which the thesis was to be written. Only five of the fields could be in history. The remaining one must be in a closely related subject, usually government, economics, sociology, or anthropology.

My fields were: American History, first half, American History, second half, History of Spain, History of Latin America, English History, first half, and American Government and Constitutional Law.

Haskins was chairman of my board as Turner was on leave. The other members were Professors Channing, Hart, Merriman, and McIlwain, truly an imposing group of historians for an ex-cowhand from Oklahoma to face for a period of two hours, which seemed much longer to me.[5]

Every member of the examining group was very courteous but I have never felt proud of my showing. Possibly it was better than I thought but when it was over and Professor Haskins asked me to wait in the corridor for a few minutes, I was far from happy. At last the door was opened and the Dean asked me to come in.

"Well, Mr. Dale," he said kindly, "we have agreed to accept your examination. Let me congratulate you!" They all shook hands with me and offered their congratulations and I breathed a great sigh of relief. The greatest ordeal of my life was over but I was still unhappy because I had not done better. Then and there, I "highly resolved" to justify the confidence that these distinguished scholars had shown in me by making excellent grades in my classes and a far better showing on the final examination in my special field.

With the dreaded general examination behind me, there

---

[5] Professor Charles Howard McIlwain; Professor Charles E. Merriman.

was more time to review carefully for the finals in my courses. I worked very hard at this and, as stated earlier, made far higher grades than in 1913-14. Two grades of A with Channing, an A in my course with Hart, and an A with Haskins did much to strengthen my morale which had been badly shaken by the General Examination.

Ever since the United States had entered the war I had been eagerly looking forward to the close of school when it might be possible for me to enter the armed service. I talked with Dean Haskins and G. W. Robinson about this and they agreed that it might be all right if I could get a commission as a line officer. To my suggestion of enlisting as a private, the Dean almost held up his hands in horror. He earnestly urged me not to consider it, adding that men well trained in history would be sorely needed to teach soldiers war issues, geography, and many other subjects.

Soon after commencement the first examinations were held for admission to officers training camps. Along with scores of others, I took this examination. Apparently, heart, lungs, etc. were O.K. but after measuring my height as six feet the doctor shook his head. "Six feet high and weight only 138 pounds," he exclaimed. "There's no use to send it in. You've too much altitude for your latitude." Upon my protesting that my health was perfect, he grudgingly agreed to send my application in but was sure it would be rejected which proved true.

One of the outstanding members of the Puddingstone Club was Herbert F. Jenkins, Editorial Director of Little, Brown and Company. Soon after I had read some of my rhymes at the club, he asked me to get all of these so-called poems together, write a suitable introduction, and send them to him. Little, Brown had published the poems of Denis McCarthy in four volumes. Obviously, I was thrilled by the thought of having a book of verses issued by such a distinguished publishing house.

Of course I could not get these rhymes together and in form for publication until vacation time. After commencement, however, I decided to stay over for two or three weeks and get the little manuscript of verse in form to send to

Little, Brown and Company. John Peakes and Abe Feinberg had graduated from the Law School and were staying on to study for the Massachusetts bar examination which they must pass before they could practice law in that state. I would, therefore, have company of these two friends for Mrs. Elder gladly allowed the three of us to retain our rooms for as long as we wished at the rate per week we had been paying.

It was a pleasure to live a few weeks more in my room so near to those occupied by two such close friends. We never interrupted each other's work but always ate breakfast and dinner together, usually at a little restaurant at Harvard Square. On one or two occasions we took the subway into Boston and had dinner at Durgin and Parks, a world famous restaurant on North Market Street near the Fanueil Hall Market. For lunch one of us bought cheese, crackers, potato chips, bananas, or other fruit, etc., which we ate on my desk. Once I brought back ham sandwiches and kept urging Abe to have one since he was eating only cheese, crackers, and potato chips. Not until I saw John struggling to keep from laughing, did I suddenly realize that Abe was a Jew!

We had plenty of time to visit going to and from breakfast and dinner and during the lunch hour. Abe and I had a lot of fun kidding John who had accepted a job, beginning September first, with the distinguished law firm of Dunbar, Nutter, and McClennen at a salary of $50 a month. This was the old Brandeis firm, and John was fortunate to be employed by it. He was advanced rapidly and in a few years became a member of the firm. This could not be foreseen in 1917 so Abe and I earnestly urged John to eat more and store up fat to sustain him during the coming year when he must live on $50 a month!

Before the middle of July the manuscript of the book of verses was finished, delivered to Herbert Jenkins, and my scanty baggage packed for the long journey home. I called to say goodbye to Helen and her parents, gave a lingering handshake to Abe and John, wished them luck in the bar examination, and took the subway for South Station. My

180

little trunk had been sent down and checked the day before when I bought my ticket so all I had to do was board the train.

At long last I had learned to take a Pullman for a long trip, so did not waste my time in endless conversation with the more garrulous of my fellow travelers in the day coach, as I had done the previous summer on the journey from Oklahoma City to Norfolk, Virginia. Instead, my time was given to reviewing the events of the past year and planning for the future.

Sitting "alone with my thoughts," as the train rolled westward and seeking to recall the things that past year "had brought" was entertainment enough. It seemed to me then, as it seems to me now, more than half a century later, that the period from July 15, 1916, to July 15, 1917, might be regarded as the most fruitful year of my life. It is true that my first year at Harvard had introduced me to a new world, but this second year had made me a part of it, or at least completely at home there.

It had brought me many new friends as near and dear as those whom I had known for many years. Most of them were well-known in Greater Boston and a few throughout the nation and in Europe. They included some not previously mentioned such as the sculptor Cyrus Edwin Dallin, whose *Appeal to the Great Spirit* stands in front of the Boston Art Museum. And Ralph Davol, a writer of pageants, had a small group of us, including Dr. Curry and John K. Lacock, to a stag dinner one Sunday at his home near Dighton Rock.

Most important of all had been my academic advancement at Harvard, and passing my general examination, and the examination in French. My confidence had been greatly strengthened by discovering that I could make a grade of A in graduate courses taught by such distinguished scholars as Edward Channing, Charles Homer Haskins, and Albert Bushnell Hart.

It had been my privilege to dine with Professor Hart at the Harvard Club and to spend one delightful evening in the home of Dr. and Mrs. Samuel McCord Crothers, where I met Dudley A. Sargent, head of the Sargent School of Physical

Education for Women. Also, I accompanied Helen Warren to the annual exhibition of that school. To me the girls' feats in athletic stunts, including wall scaling, were amazing. In addition, on one occasion I sat for an hour or more entranced by the magic voice of Professor Copeland as he read the immortal story of "Bimi." "Copey," as he was called by students, could thrill an audience by reading a few pages from the *Congressional Record*![6]

As my mind turned back to review the colorful events and experiences of the past year, I also looked to the immediate future. Seeing so many of my friends rushing to enlist in the armed forces only increased my first impulse to have an active part in serving my country. Being rejected for the first officers' training camp was a bitter disappointment but already there were rumors that another examination was to be held soon, and other camps were to be established.

Surely, sooner or later it would be possible for me to secure a commission in the field artillery or any other branch of the service that would get me overseas to do my bit. Once the war was over, assuming that I came through it safely, I would get back to Harvard as quickly as possible to complete the work for the Ph.D. In the meantime, whether in the army or teaching, every leisure hour must be given to work on my dissertation and the study of German.

These reflections on the past year's experiences and thinking over plans for the following year so occupied my mind that it is impossible for me to recall anything about my homeward journey. Probably, there was nothing to recall. I reached Norman about the 20th of July, while summer school was still in session. My first impression was of the intense heat, while the second was that the student body was made up mostly of girls and older women who clearly were school teachers.

---

[6] Professor Charles Townsend Copeland.

Two Busy Years

When I reached Norman about the middle of July, 1917, most of the able-bodied men of the university faculty were in the armed forces, and it had been necessary to bring in a few instructors from other universities to teach in the summer session. Among these was Dean George Mitchell of the University of New Mexico.

I located a room to stay for a week or so until I could find permanent quarters and discovered a boarding house nearby which served excellent meals. Mrs. McGuire and her family had removed to Edmond and my friend Rowe was practicing law in Okemah, a small county seat town in eastern Oklahoma. He had married Juanita Snow, a former teacher in the Blair School. President Brooks had been appointed Food Administrator of Oklahoma which, added to his work as President of the University, kept him extremely busy.

Soon after reaching Norman, Visiting Professor Mitchell came to see me. I thought it only a friendly call possibly due to the fact that I was a good friend of Dr. David R. Boyd, at that time President of the University of New Mexico. It was, therefore, a great surprise when a week or so later I received a letter from Dr. Boyd offering me a position as head of the Department of the History at $1,600 a year.

To me this was an attractive offer. Dr. Boyd was the first president of the University of Oklahoma. He had served in that capacity from 1892 to 1908, when he and a number of his faculty members had been dismissed by the first governor of the new state. During most of the years as President of O.U. Boyd had also been President of the Territorial Board of Education which prepared all the examination questions for county teachers' certificates and also for graduation from the eighth grade.

Needless to say, I was much flattered by this offer. My salary as instructor was $1300. To exchange the rank of instructor to that of professor with a $300 raise in salary was most tempting. In addition was the family trait of restless feet itching to scratch strange gravel. Much as I liked teaching at my *alma mater*, it seemed that the offer was too good to refuse.

Naturally Dean Buchanan and President Brooks had to be consulted before resigning my position at O.U. and accepting Dr. Boyd's offer. When I presented the matter to them, both earnestly urged me not to go. They pointed out that while New Mexico was a large state, it had much fewer people than Oklahoma and would never have a large population because of the lack of rainfall and the fact that it had so many forest reserves, national parks, and Indian reservations.

Finally President Brooks said that if I would take over the administration of a small Indian museum in the basement of the Law Building he would recommend my being advanced in rank to assistant professor at a salary of $1600 a year. Since this was the same amount offered by President Boyd there seemed little reason to go to New Mexico so I wrote Dr. Boyd thanking him but declining his offer.[1]

With the close of the summer session I spent a week or so visiting relatives in Southwest Oklahoma. News of another examination for admission to officers' training camp brought me back to Norman. The notice of the examination stated that there was need for some older men which was encouraging. My weight was only 139 pounds, however, and again the army doctor said, "No use to send it in." I insisted

---

[1] The small Indian museum mentioned here is the beginning of the ethnology collection for Stovall Museum of Science and History on the University of Oklahoma Campus.

that he should send the application and data to the final authority, but again it was disapproved.

Then a notice was sent out of an examination at Camp Bowie, near Fort Worth, for commissions directly from civilian life in the quartermaster branch of the army. I had no desire to serve as quartermaster but hoped once in the service it might be possible to be transferred with the same rank to some other branch.

It was well worth trying so at the proper time I took a train for Fort Worth and a bus from that city to Camp Bowie. Apparently I passed the physical examination. Then came a written examination which did not seem too difficult although some of the arithmetic problems were a bit tricky. Finally there was an oral examination.

For this I was ushered into room and seated at a table where a captain and a major gave me the examination. The captain with my application before him began.

"Mr Dale I see that you are a history teacher. Who was Hamilcar Barca?" As history of Spain was one of my fields for the doctor's degree, that one was easy. "What was the Mason and Dixon Line?" Again I snapped back the answer. "What did Oliver Cromwell die of?" Not being in the army yet I could speak freely. "Captain, do you really think that it is essential for a quartermaster officer to know what disease caused Oliver Cromwell's death? He's been dead a long time you know."

"By the way, Captain," said the Major, "what did Oliver Cromwell die of?"

"Spanish flu. I just learned it myself yesterday. Mr. Dale, you know too much history for me. Unless you would like to ask some questions, Major, that is all." The Major replied that he had no questions, and the examination was over.

I took the first train for Norman and in a couple of weeks reveived a letter stating that my education and previous training and experience seemed not to have been of the type to make me fitted for quartermaster. It must be confessed that this did not disappoint me too much. What I wanted was a commission as a line officer in the field artillery, cavalry, infantry, or any other branch of the service that would get me overseas with combat troops.

With the opening of school I was too busy to worry about anything but my work. Dr. Gittinger had returned the previous year and resumed teaching his course in *Ancient History*, *English History*, and *English Institutions*. I had been teaching *History of the West*, *Oklahoma History*, *French Revolution and Napoleon*, and now added the *American Colonies*, *History of Spain*, and *Spanish American History north of Panama including the Spanish Islands of the West Indies*.

The little Indian museum, which was my responsibility, also required a great deal of work for it had been neglected for two or three years. New display cases had to be bought or made in the university shops. In addition, new specimens which came in had to be labeled and efforts made to add to the collection.

Although many of the men students of the past year were in the armed forces, so were a number of the younger men of the faculty. As a result, classes were largely made up of young women. Everyone was eager to help promote the war effort. The women were busy knitting sweaters and socks for soldiers. Also several members of the faculty visited Camp Doniphan near Fort Sill to give lectures to enlisted men.

It was my privilege to spend several days at this huge camp giving illustrated lectures on France. My work with Professor Johnston at Harvard helped me in preparing these which were given at the request of the camp's YMCA.[2]

It was flattering to me that the soldiers listened attentively to these lectures and seemed to enjoy them. This was not true in the case of some speakers who complained that many men of their audiences seemed to have extremely bad colds and coughed incessantly during a lecture!

Although teaching, grading papers, and preparing lessons took most of my time, I still attended Wabunaki and the Newcomers Club once every two or three weeks but tried to give some time every day to the study of German. I had

---

[2] Professor Robert Matteson Johnston.

186

found a pleasant room not far from the University and a boarding house which served good food. This was important for my fondest hope was to gain weight in case another examination for officers' training camp should be given.

It must be admitted my study of German did not take *all* of my spare time. Some of it was given to wooing the young woman who had been my French teacher. She had graduated from the University in June, 1917, and secured a job teaching in the high school of a small town about thirty miles south of Norman.[3]

During the past year at Harvard I had written her a good many letters but her replies were long delayed and to me seemed short and far from satisfactory! Now that she was teaching at a town thirty miles away she came home every four or five weeks for a weekend with her parents. Also, I could go down there once in a great while, but though she always seemed glad to see me, any sign of a romantic interest was completely lacking.

As the school year drew to a close I decided not to teach in summer school but to return to Harvard and spend most of the summer working on my dissertation. Professor Turner had approved the subject, "The Range Cattle Industry in Oklahoma," and I had done some work on it at Harvard.

Clearly a great deal of information could be found in public documents because until April, 1889, all of Oklahoma, except the Panhandle and Greer County, was Indian Country. As the Constitution of the United States had given Congress the control of Indian affairs, a study of federal documents would doubtless reveal information about grazing cattle on Oklahoma's Indian reservations.

The O.U. Library had few government documents while Harvard's Widener Memorial Library had an enormous number. Accordingly, after the close of school early in June I made a trip to southwestern Oklahoma to visit relatives,

---

[3] Rosalie Gilkey Dale was born on a farm northeast of Norman in Cleveland County homesteaded by her father in the Run of 1889. A modern languages major at the University of Oklahoma, she taught at Wayne High School in Grady County and at Chickasha High School in Grady County.

then about the first of July took the train for Boston. At Cambridge I was lucky enough to get my old room at 76 Hammond Street. The Harvard dining halls were closed during the summer but a woman living not far from my lodging place was serving good meals to six or seven students in the summer school, and she added me to the list.

G. W. Robinson, secretary to the Dean of the Graduate School, signed my request for admission to the library. He said he was leaving in a few days to spend most of the summer on his farm home in New Hampshire about 100 miles north of Boston. He added that he owned another small farm nearby and would be glad to sell it to me at a low price. At any rate, he urged me to come up and see it some weekend.

Once located in the library with a stall in the stacks near the documents, I plunged into work on my dissertation. Most of the people I knew were away on vacation. Professor Turner and his wife were at their summer cottage at Hancock Point, Maine. Professor Ferguson and wife were vacationing in New Hampshire, and the Channings were at their summer cottage at Catuit on Cape Cod. Professor Merriman was in the army, and Nathaniel Fowler was living in a summer hotel on a lake in New Hampshire, while Helen Warren was visiting an aunt who had a cottage at Ocean Grove, Maine.

John Kennedy Lacock was also away on vacation but returned before I had to leave for Oklahoma, and I spent several pleasant evenings in his home. In addition my friend Fred Merk who had been in Channing's seminar with me was living in Conant Hall. He was my closest friend among the Harvard graduate students, and I was delighted to see him again.

Fred was a brilliant scholar. He was a graduate of the University of Wisconsin and his parents lived in that state. He had finally persuaded them to make their home in Cambridge and was diligently looking for a suitable house which he could rent for them. He asked me to help in his search which I was glad to do. At last we found one only about ten minutes' walk from Harvard Yard. His father and mother came to occupy it but did not arrive until after my return to Oklahoma.

One of Fred's good friends was James McDonald on the faculty of Indiana University. He had spent the previous year in Spain, was teaching in the summer school of Boston University, and also was working on a doctoral dissertation directed by Professor Merriman. He roomed in Cambridge near the Library as it was less than ten minutes by subway train to Boston. He was a pleasant companion who visited Fred at Conant Hall quite often.

I also visited Fred every day or so. Sometimes we would boil Maine sweet corn on a gas plate in his room and eat it with butter and salt. This was contrary to all the rules of Harvard which prohibited cooking in dormitories. McDonald was never in on any of these illicit feasts, but went with me once or twice to dinner at Durgin and Parks.

There is little of interest to tell about the next few weeks. Immediately after breakfast I went to the library and plunged into work on my dissertation, reading documents, making notes, and composing an outline giving the chapters of the study and a synopsis of the contents of each.

It was hard, monotonous work in spite of my taking an hour off for lunch and going for a walk every evening after dinner. After three straight weeks of this steady grind, I proposed to McDonald that we take a weekend off for a hiking trip. He readily agreed so we each made up a little pack containing pajamas, extra socks, and shaving equipment. In addition, I had a canteen and army mess kit which had a small frying pan with a folding handle, a tin pan, cup, spoon, fork, etc.

So equipped with an additional item or two, including a small billy can to make coffee, we put on hiking clothes and bought tickets to Portsmouth, New Hampshire. We left North Station early Saturday morning. It was a beautiful summer day. The sky was a turquoise blue, and a few fleecy white clouds were reflected in the water of every stream we crossed. We reached Portsmouth in an hour or so and headed south on a country road near the sea.

We walked leisurely admiring the ocean on our left and the countryside on the right. When we came to a little village about eleven o'clock, we bought a few slices of bacon, some eggs, a slice of cheese, a few buns, and some fruit. About noon we stopped and built a fire of driftwood. I had salt, sugar, and coffee in my pack so we had an excellent lunch. The long walk and cool sea breeze had sharpened our appetites and the crisp bacon, scrambled eggs, toasted buns, cheese, fruit, and hot coffee tasted better than any meal in a dining room.

After an hour's rest we continued our journey. We passed several little villages and about six stopped for supper which did not differ too much from lunch. We walked on for about an hour after dinner and spent the night at a small village hotel. We had breakfast there after a long night's sound sleep for, not accustomed to much exercise, we were exhausted from the long walk.

After a good breakfast we resumed our journey. We left the sea at Newburyport and turned southwest through a region of beautiful farm homes. It was Sunday and all the stores were closed, but we had enough food left from the evening meal the day before to provide a good lunch. With only enough water in the canteen for coffee, McDonald wondered how we were going to clean the frying pan, tin cups, and plates. We had stopped among some sandhills and I showed McDonald a trick which I had often used in Oklahoma of dry-cleaning cooking utensils with sand. We wanted to get back to Cambridge fairly early so when we came to a town about two-thirty, we boarded a train for Boston.

We felt so much refreshed by this little jaunt that we repeated it about three weeks later. This time we went to Cape Cod and followed the seashore back toward Boston. There was little to see except sand and sea but it was cool and pleasant walking along the beach near the edge of the water. It was easy to find driftwood to cook our lunch and the salt sea air was always refreshing.

At the end of the first day we reached Plymouth just at dark. On our trip in New Hampshire we had slept at a small hotel in a little village, but Plymouth hotels seemed to be big as we looked them up in a telephone directory. McDonald called one and asked about a room. The reply was that there was only one left and the price was four dollars for two persons. We agreed that we could stand that and told the room clerk that we would be there in a few minutes.

Once inside the lobby we both realized that we were in quite a swank place. When we reached our room, we understood why it was only four dollars. It was an attic bedroom, directly under the roof. It was neat and clean with a good bed, and we agreed that we would make amends for our extravagance in paying so much for a room by having only toast and coffee or hot cakes for breakfast.

We were up early the next morning, shaved and dressed quickly, and went downstairs. The dining room was large but it was Sunday morning and evidently most of the guests were still sleeping for only two or three were being served. We sat down at a table for two prepared to order only coffee and a roll or its equivalent in price. An attractive little waitress brought us each a glass of water and a menu. We looked it over and hoped we did not show our shock when we saw that there was no *a la carte* service but only *breakfast*, and the price was a dollar and seventy-five cents!

If the expression on our face changed, the girl did not seem to notice it as she asked would we have fruit or cereal? We replied that we would have fruit *and* cereal, some red raspberries and corn flakes. When she said that she would have to give us maple syrup on one of these, because of the war, we assured her that we doted on maple syrup. She then asked would we have meat or eggs. We answered that we would have meat *and* eggs, one of those breakfast steaks and eggs scrambled. When we had finished all of this, we had a stack of buckwheat cakes and a second cup of coffee and felt that we had really got our money's worth.

It was still quite early when we left the hotel feeling that we had eaten enough to last us all day. We passed the plant of the Plymouth Cordage Company and followed the sea around the bay to the Standish Shore where we climbed to the top of the Miles Standish monument. We admired the statue of the stalwart Captain of Plymouth standing on the top of the monument gazing across the bay.

From the monument we continued our journey still keeping fairly close to the sea. By noon we began to feel hungry again in spite of the big breakfast. We had a small can of potted ham, a little glass jar of jam, and a block of cheese but no bread, rolls, or crackers. We passed several stores in small villages but all were closed. At last we came to a store with a boy about twelve near the door. "Son," asked McDonald, "do you know any place where we could but a loaf of bread or a box of crackers?"

"The store's closed," replied the youngster, "but I've got a key and will open it to get you some bread."

He produced a key and stepped up to the door but at that moment a woman came running around the corner of the building and snatched the key out of the lad's hand.

"That key got out of my hands by accident," she asserted wrathfully. "This is the Sabbath and the store remains closed. The Lord had said: 'Remember the Sabbath day to keep it holy,' and I always do."

McDonald remarked that He also said something about feeding the hungry, too, but the woman had already turned her back on us and started back to the house some fifty yards behind the store. As for the boy, he had disappeared as soon as the woman had snatched the key out of his hand. Although disappointed by her zeal, we had the good fortune to find, less than a mile farther on, an ice cream stand in a cool shady nook under some trees. Here the genial proprietor not only sold us a dish of ice cream but also a box of crackers. In addition, he insisted that we sit at a small table in the shade and eat our lunch with the ice cream as dessert. Refreshed by our lunch, we walked on until about three in the afternoon when we took a train for Boston. This was my last walking trip with McDonald for he left Cambridge a week or so later and I never saw him again.

It was now late in August and it seemed high time for me to make a little trip to New Hampshire to see G. W. Robinson and the little farm he wanted to sell me. He had written me a second letter urging me to come any time, so I replied saying that he could expect me the following weekend probably early Saturday afternoon. This was some three weeks after the trip to Cape Cod and the steady grind of work on the dissertation made me feel that a short break would be welcome.

I took the train at North Station Friday aftenoon with a ticket for The Weirs on Lake Winnepesaukee. The map showed that this little town was only a few miles south of Meredith which was the postmark on Mr. Robinson's letters. He had given me no directions, but it seemed that someone in Meredith would surely be able to tell me just how to reach his place.

The run of about 100 miles along the Merrimac River was a very interesting one. The grass, trees, and shrubs were a vivid green, and the fluffy white clouds in the blue sky were reflected in the crystal-clear water. The train was slow which pleased me for it gave me more time to view the beautiful scenery. At last we came in sight of the lake, and a few minutes later reached The Weirs.

It was an attractive little town on the southwest shore of Lake Winnipesaukee. There was a large and imposing looking hotel 100 yards or more west of the lake on the side of the hill back of town. Memories of the swank hotel at Plymouth made me decide to seek lodging elsewhere, especially since I was wearing a light flannel shirt, riding breeches, and tweed jacket.

Walking down the street a short distance, I came to a long low building with a wide porch in front and a sign above the door reading: "Winnipesaukee Cottage, Rooms." A rugged looking individual was sitting in a rocking chair on the porch smoking a pipe and reading a book. To my inquiry as to the proprietor, he said that she had "stepped out" a little while ago but would be back in a few minutes. He asked me to sit down as he was sure she would be back very soon.

I gladly sat down to wait and asked him if he had been here for some days. He said that he had come about two weeks before and expected to stay another week. He added that the rooms were nothing to boast about, but they were neat and clean. In a few minutes the landlady appeared. She was a neat, pleasant looking woman apparently about forty years old. To my inquiry about a room, she said that she had some vacant, but they were not made up. If I would wait ten minutes, she would make one ready and show it to me. Ten minutes later she returned and escorted me up one flight of stairs. The room was the "bowl and pitcher" type, but the bed and towels seemed clean so I paid the lady a dollar which was the price per night.

Clearly it was about time to eat so after washing and combing my hair, I put on a clean shirt from my small bag and sallied forth in search of food. The Lakeside Hotel looked promising so I ventured in and sat down at a small table in the dining room. One look at the menu proved that appearances are deceitful! The fish in cream and corned beef hash were impossible, or at least highly improbable. I was able to eat the cold sirloin of beef, fried potatoes, and the sample of sliced peaches.

I was still hungry, so after leaving the waitress a dime and paying the cashier a dollar, I crossed the street to a little stand and had a dish of ice cream and bought a cigar. It was too early for bed so I returned to the lobby of the Lakeside Hotel to smoke the cigar and write three or four letters before returning to my room at the Winnipesaukee Cottage and getting in bed. It was not quite ten, but tomorrow promised to be a busy day with "miles to go before I'd sleep" again. It was my good fortune not to know how many!

It was about seven when I awoke the next morning and after a shave and sponge bath, my first thought was to find some place other than the Lakeside Hotel for breakfast. My landlady, who was sweeping the front porch, spoke cheerfully and to my question as to a good place for breakfast, suggested the Chateau du Lys only a couple of minutes walk north. She added that most of her lodgers ate there.

This sounded good so I thanked her and headed north. She was quite right as to the distance, for a couple of minutes brought me to an attractive building with a sign "Chateau de Lys." The tables were laid so I went in and sat down opposite an old soldier. The waitress brought me half an orange, a bowl of oatmeal, a breakfast steak, baked potato, and coffee, all for thirty-five cents. This shocked me into leaving the girl a dime although she obviously did not expect a tip.

Returning to the cottage, I gave my landlady a dollar for another night's lodging, put on my flannel shirt and puttees, and started north for Meredith. I had received specific directions so after a steep climb to the top of the ridge behind the town, I reached the state road running northwest. A man told me that it was four miles to Meredith so it seemed wise to hasten along. Once in Meredith someone, no doubt, could tell me how to get to Robinson's place.

There was very little traffic, but two young fellows in a Ford asked me to ride, but I refused. After walking about two miles, I came to a white farmhouse with a tall elm tree beside it to which was affixed a sign stating, "This Place for Sale." This caused me to stop and interview the owner. He greeted me cordially when I introduced myself and was eager to show me the farm.

After looking over the big barn and the spring, which supplied the house, he took me to the fields planted with beans, corn, clover, and vegetables. From here we could see the lake less than half a mile to the east. He said that he had a right-of-way to it and added that the farm consisted of fifty-eight acres, part of it on the other side of the road. That portion included a good small farmhouse, a fenced pasture, big garage, tool and carriage house, and some large apple trees loaded with fruit. He said that his chief money crop was beans. He had made thirty bushels the past year and sold them for twelve dollars a bushel. He added that he also milked six cows, and sold thirty pounds of butter a week for fifty cents a pound. He asked $7,000 for the farm but might take less.

With all this information as to New Hampshire farming and after taking the man's name and address, I resumed my journey to Meredith which he told me was only a mile and a half away. It proved to be a pretty little town on the lake. The postmaster did not know Mr. Robinson or where he lived, but the proprietor of a grocery store was more helpful. Yes, he knew G. W. Robinson well. He lived about four miles beyond Meredith Center. This was North Meredith. Meredith Center was about four miles southwest. It must be eight or nine miles to Robinson's house.

Then and there I learned that a New England town is still a land unit for local government which may have three or four villages within its borders, as North Newton, South Newton, East Newton, Newton Center, etc. Also, I recalled that a couple of miles back I had seen a small cluster of houses which must be Meredith Center.

It was then a little past eleven, and hunger pangs were beginning to assail me. I started down the street toward the west and passed an old man. "Is this the way to Meredith Center, Sir?" I inquired.

"Straight ahead about four miles," was the reply.

"Can a man get something to eat there?"

"Yeah, there's a man at the store that'll feed you."

This made me decide to pass up the tempting wares of the bake shop across the street for a meal at Meredith Center. At the edge of the village my road left the main highway and became a country road running southwest. I had walked briskly for a couple of miles when a man in a truck came along and gave me a ride for a mile and a half, or until the road to Meredith Center turned south.

This helped for I was both tired and hungry. I left him with many thanks for it was not much over half a mile to the Meredith Center store. I hurried along past a white house with a sign, "Center House" beside the front door. A couple of hundred yards more brought me to the store.

A plump black-haired woman behind the counter told me exactly how to get to Robinson's home which was about four miles west. To my inquiry as to some place to eat, she said the Center House kept summer boarders and might feed transients. I thanked her and started in a lope up the road to the Center House. Two maiden ladies of uncertain age, but with "School marm" plainly written on their faces, were sitting in the shade of a tree beside the house. I bowed and asked if the landlady ever served dinner to travelers. I had walked far and was quite hungry.

The women seemed interested and hurried into the house, leaving me to wait patiently. In a few minutes they returned with the bad news that the proprietor had prepared lunch only for her regular guests. They added that she was not feeling well and had her regular boarders and could not take another. I was not feeling well either at this news. The young women were sympathetic. The landlady was out of sorts today about something they said and added that she was a bit cranky most of the time.

Dolefully I suggested that perhaps I could get some cheese and crackers and a can of salmon at the store. "No," replied the girls, "the store closes at noon and does not open again until about three." Then one of them said that the landlady's maid had told her that Mrs. Kimball, who lived a short distance east of the store, had sometimes fed travelers. I thanked them and said good-bye. It seemed well to go to the store first to see if it was open.

A dejected looking individual was sitting on a wooden box in front of the store building looking disgustedly at the closed door. I greeted him cordially and asked if there was a restaurant or other place where one could get a meal.

"Hell no," was his response. "There ain't nothin' here but this store; it'll be closed until three o'clock."

"Can you tell me where Mrs. Kimball lives?"

"Sure can. She lives in the first house beyond where you see them kids a playin'."

As he spoke he pointed east to three or four small fry playing in the sand beside the road.

I thanked him and headed down the road. The children looked at me with some curiosity but responded politely to my cheerful greeting. Another hundred yards or so brought me to a fairly large white house on the north side of the road. It had a wide porch where a gangling boy about fourteen was industriously working on his fishing gear.

When I spoke to him he answered in stuttering fashion, and Mrs. Kimball, a stout, elderly woman appeared at the door. My hat came off, and I bowed low and introduced myself and said, "Mrs. Kimball, would it be possible to get some dinner? I've walked all morning and am very hungry."

Mrs. Kimball's voice was of a deep masculine variety, but it sounded like the sweetest music as she replied, "Oh, I guess so, if you can eat what we do. Set down. My pertaters are on a-bilin' and must be about done."

I assured her that I could eat what they did and more. The boy tried to talk to me, but his stuttering speech made it hard to understand him. In a few minutes an elderly man, evidently Mrs. Kimball's husband, came around the corner of the house. He spoke in friendly fashion and went inside but was back in a few minutes and sat down on the edge of the porch. He seemed surprised to learn that my home was in Oklahoma, but before we had time to talk, Mrs. Kimball came to the door to say dinner was ready.

"Come right in and set down there," said Mrs. Kimball, and I speedily obeyed. The table was covered with oil cloth and the dishes were blue willow ware. This was interesting, but of far greater interest to me at the moment was the abundance of food on the table.

No grace was said, but the old man asked, "Will you have some of this here johnny cake?"

"This here johnny cake" was a thick cake made of yellow corn meal cut in triangular slabs. Garnished with plenty of fresh country butter it seemed to me the last word in food. Then there were the "pertaters," big mealy ones bursting out of their jackets, fried salt pork "scrap," round cakes of bread which the boy called "wolls," string beans, dough-nuts, pear preserves, tea with real cream and sugar, and last, but not least, a big saucer of Indian pudding with raisins in it.

At last having put away two slabs of "this here johnny cake," a couple of "pertaters" and everything else in proportion, I was in the same status of the small boy who said he "could still chew but couldn't swallow." I pushed back my plate, rose to my feet, and asked Mrs. Kimball how much I owed her.

"Oh, I guess about a quarter."

"A quarter! No, no, Mrs. Kimball, you can't feed me for a quarter. Back at Weirs last evening I paid a dollar for a meal not half as good as this one."

"A dollar," she exclaimed, "ain't that redicolus!"

"Not as ridiculous as paying you only a quarter for all that I ate today. Please let me pay you a dollar, at least."

She steadfastly refused to take the crisp dollar bill which I tried to put in her hand insisting that a quarter was enough but finally accepted thirty-five cents which was all the silver I had.

Although eager to start on the last lap of my journey, I had to stay long enough to answer a few questions of the old gentleman about Oklahoma. He said that I was certainly a long way from home. He added that travel was so expensive that he and his wife had done very little of it. They had a daughter living in Connecticut whom they had not seen for three or four years. They planned to visit her next summer, but it would probably cost them twelve or fifteen dollars and maybe more.

It would have been pleasant to stay longer and visit with this old couple, but it was four miles to the Robinson place which meant a full hour of brisk walking. So I shook hands with them and the stuttering boy, thanked them again, and started west feeling like Jesse James *should* have felt but probably didn't. Surely it was at least *petty* larceny to stow away so much good food and pay only thirty-five cents for it.

The store was still closed when I passed it, and the two school marms were sitting under the big tree evidently having just finished dinner. I waved and called that, thanks to them, I had just eaten a good dinner at Mrs. Kimball's house. They expressed their pleasure and I bade them goodbye and hurried on.

The road wound upward through the hills, at times through thick woods, and at others open pine forests. There were few houses. At last I came to piles of lumber and a saw mill. The road grew steeper and I passed a little schoolhouse and a little farther on a little cottage. An old man sitting on the front porch replied to my inquiry about the Robinson home, "Half a mile straight ahead."

I thanked him and pushed on through the woods. The road was steep and sandy but at last I came to a clearing at the top of the ridge. To my right was a low rambling house with a huge elm tree in the yard and a well and pump beside the house. Across the road was a pasture with a fence made of stone and rails.

At my knock the door was opened by a pretty little blue-eyed girl about fourteen years old. She shook hands and smilingly asked me to come in. She said that they had received my letter the day before so were expecting me. She added that her name was Hilda and that her father was helping "the boys" down in the pasture but for me to sit down and she would call him. She opened the door, took a megaphone hanging from a nail beside it, and stepped out on the porch. Her clear voice rang out: "M-i-s-t-e-r D-a-l-e is h-e-r-e."

She seemed certain that her daddy heard her for she came back and sat down to visit with me. The living room had heavy beams below the ceiling, there was a wide fireplace on the north side in which a bright fire was burning, and I spoke of how attractive it was. She said that they had a fire almost every evening all summer. She then asked if I liked pictures. Upon my assuring her that I did, she said that she was studying painting with the artist who lived in the little cottage half a mile down the road and would show me some of her work. To me her pictures, mostly landscapes, seemed very good.

A step on the porch indicated that her father had arrived. He came in smiling, apparently much pleased to see me. he was wearing rough working clothes. I told him that I must return to The Weirs that night so after a few minutes we went out to harness the horse and hitch him to the carriage which would transport us over to the little farm. He told me that Professor Ferguson was living that summer only about a mile away and we should go by his place and ask him to go with us.

Hilda helped roll out the carriage and hitch the tall bay horse to it. Her father returned to the house to change his clothes while Hilda and I finished dusting the venerable "jump seat" vehicle which apparently had not been used for a year or more. When we finished dusting, Hilda showed me her rabbits. There were three or four big ones and about a dozen babies that were most cunning.

Mr. Robinson was back in a few minutes clad in more gladsome raiment. My goodbyes were said to Hilda, and we drove about a mile southwest to the summer home of Professor and Mrs. Ferguson. It was another low, rambling house back some distance from the road in a pasture.

Professor and Mrs. Ferguson seemed delighted to see us and insisted that we have tea and then they would go with us to see the little farm where Professor Ferguson had planted several rows of beans in one of the fields. We entered the big living room with a wide fireplace in which a log fire was burning. Mrs. Ferguson poured the tea and a maid brought in a plate of "war cake." The small daughter about eight years old passed the cream and sugar.[4]

After tea they insisted on taking us outside and to the west side of the house to show us "the native home of the blueberry." Walking a few steps west of the house where we could get a good view of the pasture, we saw what seemed to me hundreds of acres covered with blueberries. There were some low bushes only a foot or so high and others three or four feet tall black with fruit. There must have been thousands of gallons in sight, and they were selling for thirty cents a quart in Boston.

Returning to the house we left the small daughter in care of the maid, and Professor and Mrs. Ferguson went with us to see the little farm which Mr. Robinson wanted to sell me. It was less than a mile drive through the woods. In the clearing we saw a house, barn, and "sugar house." There were some lovely apple trees loaded with fruit and three small fields, two of them in grass and the third planted in Professor Ferguson's bean crop of thirty rows.

The house had five rooms and a big woodshed attached. With a little work the house could be made into a very cozy summer home. The large barn was in need of repair. I ate one of the apples and found it delicious.

---

[4] "War cake" was a dessert popular during World War I, mixed with little or no sugar to support the military effort and assure essential provisions for the troops overseas.

We left the house and walked through the woods about two hundred yards to the lake. This was Lake Winnisquam, small compared with Lake Winnipesaukee, but a considerable body of water. The trees came to the water's edge, but it would be easy to construct a landing. About four miles south, at the lower end of the lake, was Laconia, one of the larger towns of New Hampshire, which could be easily reached by motor boat.

The sun was low when we reached the house where we had left the horse and carriage. Determined to return to The Weirs that night I refused invitations of Mr. Ferguson and Mr. Robinson to spend the night. I told Mr. Robinson that, in my opinion, the little farm was well worth the $7,000 he asked he asked for it, but it was a long way from Oklahoma. In addition, my own situation was doubtful because of the war. He could rest assured, however, that I would write him my decision soon.

They drove me through the woods to the main road where I expressed my thanks and said good-bye. It had been a long day and there were still eight miles to go before reaching The Weirs. Fortunately, a man and woman in a car came along before I had walked more than a mile and gave me a ride as far as Meredith Center, only four miles from The Weirs.

By this time it was growing dark, but there were no clouds and the stars were unusually bright. A road always seems longer at night. Two miles of brisk walking brought me to a paved highway and a mile and a half more to the top of the ridge from which the lights of The Weirs could be seen. I passed a small summer hotel and a hundred yards beyond it overtook four girls. As I passed them they gave a startled little scream. But it was only mock fear. They said that they had not seen a man for so long that even the sight of one startled them.

The invitation seemed obvious so I dropped into step with them and we walked along chatting and laughing like old friends. They said that they were going to a dance at the pavilion at the shore of the lake. When we reached The Weirs and passed under a street light, they looked at me with some curiosity, and I looked at them. Two were quite pretty girls, but my impression was that the other two were likely to be wallflowers. When we reached Main Street, I said good night and turned left while they turned right to the dancing pavilion.

It was about nine o'clock and a late supper seemed in order. A little restaurant was still open and after ham and eggs and a dish of ice cream, I walked over to the cottage and sat on the front porch long enough to smoke a couple of pipes of tobacco before going to bed. I was asleep in a minute or two and did not awaken until seven o'clock.

It surprised me not to be stiff and sore after the long walk of the day before. After a good breakfast, I walked down to the pier to view the lake which was clear as glass as there was no wind. I sat down on the pier and hung my feet over the water. There were several motor launches tied up at the pier, but none on the lake for this was Sunday and officials in Washington had issued an edict to conserve gasoline. Many tourists had put their cars in parking lots and were staying over until Monday.

Two girls in fresh summery dresses appeared out of nowhere and sat down on the edge of the pier a few feet away. They stretched out their feet revealing a generous length of silk hose. They chattered like magpies. A large steamer came around a wooded point of land headed in our direction. As it came nearer they turned to me, "Oh, is it coming here? Are we going to have to get up?"

I professed my ignorance but hoped not. It was very comfortable here.

"Oh! Aren't you from the South?"

I acknowledged it and asked how they knew.

"Oh! I knew just as soon as I heard you speak. I'm from Tennessee. She's from Nawth Calinah. I call her Caholine and she calls me Tennessee. We came in on the twelve o'clock train last night and we've got to stay all day for there's not another train until six this evening. How we'll live through the day I don't know."

I didn't either and would not worry too much if they *didn't*.

We talked for a little while but not long. Caholine was a fairly pretty girl and reasonably quiet. Tennessee was impossible. Her clothes were too "fussy," she wore too much makeup and talked too much.

After leaving the girls, I walked over to the post office. It was closed, of course, but I had cards to mail. There was still time to row an hour on the lake so I returned to the pier, rented a boat, and rowed for nearly an hour. The wind was rising and the water was getting rough so it seemed advisable to pull for the shore as my skill in handling a boat, even in still water, was poor.

It would be possible to get a train for Boston at six p.m., but the big excursion steamer was to leave at one for a five-hour tour of the lake. My love of ships and the sea made me eager to go on this trip so I decided to spend another night at the cottage and take the early morning train.

Once back at the pier I paid for the use of the boat and hurried over to the Chateau for lunch. I ate quickly in order to get back to the pier and board the steamer which left promptly at one. It was a large and beautiful craft and a fairly big crowd was waiting to go aboard. The trip was about fifty miles which required nearly five hours as there were several stops at towns on the shore.

I found a good location on the deck near the bow on the side away from the wind and sat down as we pulled away from the pier. The view was magnificent. There were summer camps along the wooded shore and almost every island, no matter how small, had at least one house on it. We stopped at a small town and took on some more passengers. It was a beautiful village with quaint, old houses, and a background of lovely green ridges with farmhouses, orchards, and sleek cattle.

In only a few minutes we were again under way and continued to pass cottages and summer camps. It struck me how pleasant it would be to spend an entire summer in one of these little cottages. I recall thinking that if "the right girl" should sometime agree to share my life, I would bring her here. What a delightful summer it would be with exactly the right person fishing, swimming, and wandering over these green hills picking blueberries.

We stopped at another town and then reached a place where the lake became very rough. The waves ran high and threw spray upon the lower deck, drenching some persons standing by the rail. Four old maid school teachers came up and sat down near me. They talked a streak all the time. I figured that in a few weeks they would be back in their village schools. Worst of all they appeared to be doomed to such employment forever. Certainly one of them was. She had a red nose and an unusually homely face. Even so, her face was more attractive than her dress which looked like she might have cut it out blindfolded on a bet and lost the bet!

I moved to the other side of the deck feeling the scenery would be better there. We stopped at North Meredith and I had a good look at the little town from the lake. It was growing cold and I was glad when we came in sight of The Weirs. It looked very pretty as we approached it from the lake. The train had pulled in and was waiting for pasengers from the ship. No doubt Tennessee and Caholine were on it if they had "lived through the day" for they were not on the ship.

The voyage had made me hungry so once ashore I headed directly for the Chateau du Lys for an excellent supper. Afterwards I lighted a cigar and strolled about the town for awhile and then dropped into the ice cream place and had a banana split. The four girls that I had passed the preceding evening came in and sat down at the table. They spoke in friendly fashion. We talked for a few minutes and I said goodnight and returned to the cottage and went to bed early for my train left at eight next morning.

I was asleep in a minute or so and did not wake until seven. It took only a few minutes to shave, dress, pack my bag, and get downstairs for breakfast. Even so it was nearly train time when I reached the station. My car was not crowded which pleased me for I had a seat to myself and could again admire the green hills and sparkling streams without interruption. At last Bunker Hill Monument came in sight and the train slowly pulled into North Station. It was only a short walk to the subway so in half an hour I was in my room in Cambridge at 76 Hammond Street.

It had been a weekend never to be forgotten, but it was good to find myself at "home" again. After bathing, changing clothes, and reading my mail, I walked to my boarding house for lunch. Probably the landlady and fellow boarders were surprised by the warmth of my greeting for it seemed to me that I had been away a long time.

After lunch I hurried to the library and again checked the outline of my dissertation. It seemed to me nearly completed. There were to be nine chapters and each was outlined in detail. In addition, I had prepared an introduction and extensive bibliography which contained all sources consulted up to the present time. I wished so much that Professor Turner could see this and go over it with me, but it was now September 2nd, and I had to return to Norman within ten days to get located and ready for the opening of the fall semester.

Then an idea came to me. The Turners were at their summer cottage at Hancock Point, Maine, so why not go up there and see them? A hasty look at the map showed that Hancock Point was on the mainland across the channel from Mt. Desert Island on which is situated the famous vacation spot Bar Harbor. The following day I quickly packed a small bag and boarded a train for Mt. Desert Ferry.

This was another example of the "valor of ignorance." Professor Turner was on his vacation and there was no reason for me to think that he would appreciate having a graduate student barge in on him disturbing his rest and interfering with any activities that he had planned for this period of leisure. Such thoughts had never occurred to me so in the classic words of Mark Twain it was "with all the confidence of a Christian with four aces" that I set out on this journey.

The scenery as we ran along sometimes in sight of the sea was beautiful; it was September and the deciduous trees were a blaze of red and gold. When we reached Bangor, I was much interested in the rafts of logs on the river and the huge sawmills near its banks. We reached Mt. Desert Ferry early in the afternoon. The ferry was waiting to take the passengers across to Bar Harbor. There were not many for it was near the end of the season.

206

Hancock Point was about three miles to the west. Some passengers had told me that there were two roads to it; one along the seashore was slightly longer than the one through the woods but was more interesting. My decision was to take the seaside road. It was a most pleasant walk. To my left was the blue water of the ocean for a mile or so and then the island with a steep, rugged mountain behind the village of Bar Harbor. To the right was the forest, a blaze of color.

Hancock Point consisted of a small summer hotel, a general merchandise store, two or three dwellings, and a few summer cottages scattered along the beach. Most of the hotel guests had gone so there was no difficulty in getting a room on the side next to the sea. I was wearing the same type of clothing as I had in New Hampshire—a flannel shirt, riding breeches, and leather puttees. After cleaning up and replacing the flannel shirt with a soft white one and blue bow tie, I started for the Turner cottage.

The hotel keeper had pointed out the way and said it was the last cottage near the beach and only a little over a quarter of a mile so there was no trouble finding it. Surprised as they were, both Professor and Mrs. Turner seemed pleased to see me. Their daughter Dorothy had married several months before and was living in Wisconsin. The Turners had been all alone in the cottage, except for the maid, all summer and seemed a bit lonely. Perhaps the quiet life of fishing and walking in the woods or along the beach had begun to pall for them, so that even an unexpected and unbidden guest was welcome. At any rate, they received me most cordially.

After a brief period of visiting, I produced the outline of my dissertation, and Turner and I betook ourselves to the front porch. Here we went over it almost line by line and talked about sources of information, the planning of each chapter, and every phase of the entire study.

"I like it," Turner said at last. "I believe you are going to have a good piece of work." He invited me to come back for dinner the next day and I left for the hotel in high spirits.

The next evening when I appeared at the cottage, Turner was most cordial but quite apologetic. He had been fishing and had some flounders in the ice box which he had planned to have for dinner but had forgotten that it was the maid's afternoon off. Such being the case, they would have to take me to the hotel for dinner. This prompted me to make a suggestion. I said, "Professor Turner, almost the first lesson that a cowboy learns is that he had two choices: he can cook or starve. I have always preferred to cook, so if you would like to have flounders this evening just show me the way to the kitchen and it will be a pleasure to fry the flounders and prepare dinner."

Turner's face brightened. "Let's do it," he said. "I think it would be fun." Mrs. Turner led me to the kitchen, provided an apron, and I proceded to make a pan of biscuits, praying that my hand had not lost its cunning, and to fry the flounders. They were ready for cooking and required only to be salted a bit, rolled in flour, and dropped into a skillet of sizzling hot fat. Good fortune was with me for the biscuits came out of the oven light and flaky and their rich brown color matched that of the fried flounders. I had also made a pot of coffee and set the table, putting on butter, crabapple jelly, and pickles from the ice box, and we sat down to a real feast. When Mrs. Turner expressed regret that it was Mary Ann's afternoon out and the guest had to cook his own supper, Turner exclaimed, "I'm glad she's gone. Mary Ann in her palmiest days never fried flounders or made biscuits like these."

I stayed at Hancock Point for a week and saw Turner every day but one when I crossed over the island to see Bar Harbor and climb the mountain back of it. He had a canoe with swelling sides which he called "The Mumps" and in this we paddled about and fished for flounders. It was not much sport for all one had to do was bait a hook with a clam and dangle it over the side on a line long enough to reach nearly to the bottom and pull up the fish when you felt a tug at the line. He also taught me to paddle a canoe.

We usually fished in the forenoon and after catching a dozen or more we dressed them, built a fire of driftwood, and Turner then brought down the cooking utensils, and made coffee and fried the flounders. Mrs. Turner brought bread, butter, plates, cups, etc., and the three of us would have a delicious "shore dinner." On some days we would dig a bucket of clams and start the meal with steamed clams dipped in melted butter. After we had eaten and washed the dishes, Mrs. Turner would go back to the cabin for a nap while her husband and I would lie on the sand or the sunny side of a huge rock and talk, sometimes for hours.

He seemed deeply interested in my experiences on the frontier as a hunter, cowboy, clerk in a frontier trading post, claim holder, deputy sheriff, and rural school teacher. This prompted me to relate many yarns of humorous or tragic incidents which I had witnessed, and he told me some of his own. He inquired eagerly about the relationships of the ranchmen with the homesteaders who came to displace them. He also expressed considerable interest in the Indians of Oklahoma and seemed surprised to learn that the Kiowa and Comanche Indians would never break their own horses if they could hire a white man to do this for them.

I expressed some surprise that he was not swimming every day for the clear water looked very inviting.

He remarked that they seldom swam, but if I would like it, we would take a plunge to celebrate my coming. I detected a twinkle in his eyes and felt that he was challenging my hardihood. This made me determined to take a dip in the ocean even if it were necessary to break the ice to do it. We accordingly put on bathing suits, walked down to the sea, and from the top of a half-submerged rock, plunged into the crystal-clear water. Cold? Never in my life had I dreamed that water could be so cold and not freeze. It simply took my breath away. We swam about for a few minutes before Turner suggested that we go ashore and no second invitation was needed. I had learned that the sea on the upper part of the Maine coast in early September is no place to take a swim.

The day I took the ferry for Mt. Desert Island was an interesting one. Many of the so-called cottages at Bar Harbor owned by New York millionaires were only somewhat smaller than our administration building at the University of Oklahoma! After looking over the little town, which did not take long, I started up the Gorge Trail which leads to the top of the mountain behind the village. It was steep and rough going. About half way up I found a sweater lying in the path. I picked it up and continued to climb hoping to meet the owner coming down the trail or find him at the top.

Apparently there was no one but myself on the mountain that day, however, for I met no one and there was no one on the mountain top. The view from here, however, was magnificent. The little villages along the coast and ships or boats of various kinds were most picturesque. After resting for an hour and admiring the scenery, I began the descent by the same trail. I was hoping to meet the owner of the sweater coming back to look for his property but saw no one. My first impulse was to take it to the police station, but seemed probable that this would only mean providing some Bar Harbor police officer with a good sweater. So instead I went by the newspaper office and paid for inserting an item in the Lost and Found column, giving my Oklahoma address.

Time was running out for me so the following day I called to say good-bye to the Turners and to thank them for all their hospitality and kindness. They seemed genuinely sorry to see me go and said that the past week had been the most enjoyable of their summer there. I told Professor Turner that unless I could get a commission as a line officer in the army he would see me back at Harvard in the autumn of 1919.

Returning to the hotel I packed my bag, said good-bye to my host, and set out on the three-mile walk to the ferry. My train for Boston left, as I recall it, at eight o'clock and reached Boston about five in the morning. Turner had warned me that it would be wise to get a reservation, but there were few passengers and I got a lower berth without difficulty.

After a bit of breakfast in Boston, I took the subway to Cambridge and hurried down to my room to begin packing for the long journey by train to Oklahoma. It did not take long for I had learned not to carry a typewriter all the way from Oklahoma when a far better one could be rented at Cambridge for about three dollars a month. I called on Merk to say goodbye. His parents had not yet arrived but were expected within a week.

Chapter XIII

And So
They Were Married . . .

The University was to open soon after my arrival in Oklahoma and I had little time to look after my personal affairs. Two or three days were spent in southwestern Oklahoma visiting my brother and other relatives. I then returned to Norman to get settled in my room, find a boarding house, and make up a list of the books to be put on library reserve for my classes.

My most important personal interest was the brown-eyed girl, Rosalie Gilkey, who had been my French teacher. She had refused the offer to teach a second year at the town some twenty-five miles south of Norman and had accepted a job at Chickasha, a small city of 12,000 people about forty miles southwest of Norman. This was a much better position and the salary was considerably higher than her former position.

While I had written her several times during the summer, her replies had usually been delayed for some time, and as a rule, were quite brief notes. They were always friendly but I searched in vain for evidence that she had any sentimental interest in me.

She seemed glad to see me which was encouraging, but there was scant time for visiting. The school at Chickasha opened, taking her away from Norman. Also, recruits for the Student Army Training Corps (S.A.T.C.), created by the United States government, hit the University campus like a swarm of locusts. All male students of the University less than twenty-one years of age and physically fit were required to join.

It took time for the physical examination. While waiting, the boys from Blair asked me to help them enlist in S.A.T.C. Obviously, there was nothing I could do to hurry the army officers in getting them processed. I did encourge them as much as possible and urged them to be patient. So far as I know all the lads from Blair were accepted.

Twenty-five commissioned officers including First Lieutenant Philip F. LaFollette, later governor of Wisconsin, processed more than 1,000 students including a navy reserve unit of 80. The men were lodged in newly constructed barracks or fraternity houses. Large mess halls, a bath house, infirmary, and guardhouse were erected and by the first of October, O.U. resembled a military camp.

The army officers taught military tactics and courtesy, drilled the men and did all in their power to make soldiers of them. The recruits were also enrolled in mathematics, geography, government, and special classes called "war issues." I taught one such special class and a class in American government for S.A.T.C. students. My other classes were in history and were about as large as usual. However, except for a few men whose physical status barred them from military service, my students were girls.

S.A.T.C. training was pretty hard on some of these raw country lads who were grossly ignorant of everything military. Lieutenant Liesendahl was a hard-boiled Prussian who rode them hard. For a few of these, who had been in my classes the previous year, I felt little sympathy. At five a.m. I would be awakened by the sound of marching feet and a voice barking, "Close up ranks there! Column Right—March!" It was a real pleasure to roll out of bed, go to the window, and in the dim light see three or four of my old loafers from whom I had never been able to get a tap of work out on a little pre-breakfast march of six or seven miles.

As the weeks went by I continued to hope that there would be another examination for officers' training camp. About the middle of October these hopes were realized. An announcement was issued that candidates for officers' training at Camp Zachary Taylor might take an examination in Oklahoma City, given by a colonel and an army doctor. My weight was up a pound or two so I got by the medico, and Colonel Shirk, after checking my education, voice, etc., certified that my examination was satisfactory. I was told that when this was approved by higher authority, the local draft board at Norman would be ordered to induct me into the army and provide transportation to Camp Zachary Taylor.

Needless to say I hurried back to Norman delighted that at long last my ambition to become a line officer might be realized. There was always the chance that the "men upstairs" might refuse to approve my appointment. My worry was brief. Within a few days came the notice that I had been appointed to receive training at Camp Zachary Taylor for a commission as an officer in the Field Artillery. The notice added that "competent orders" would be sent the local draft board at Norman to enlist me as a soldier and supply my transportation to the camp.

Professor Buchanan had already made plans to take care of my courses, and my brother George from Mountain Park and Rosalie from Chickasha both came up to bid me goodbye which pleased me a great deal. I had expected my brother but had not been at all sure that my former French teacher would come. When I met my last class, it was necessary to tell the students that at the next meeting they would have a new teacher.

"As for me," I asserted jauntily, "the next time you see me, maybe I'll be wearing eagles on my shoulders!"

This was only an attempt to brighten the atmosphere because several of the girls were crying and the others were looking a bit doleful. They knew as well as I that my chance of ever wearing eagles on my shoulders was about equal to that of my eloping with the daughter of the Empress of Japan.

The following day the chairman of the local draft board telephoned me to come to the courthouse as he had received orders to induct me into the armed forces. This ceremony was brief and I was ordered to return the next afternoon at two o'clock for transportation to Camp Zachary Taylor. My train left at four and, as my instructions were to take only hand baggage, packing was easy.

214

It was a thrill to find myself at last a soldier, but this was lost in the screaming headlines of every newspaper announcing the signing of the armistice. Just before two p.m. the next day, the chairman of the local draft board called to tell me that he had just received telegraphed orders from Washington to stop inductees who had not yet started to camp. Thus I was a soldier until discharged but in the meantime I was free to return to teaching.

There was public rejoicing that the war was over and most troops were eager to get home as soon as possible. It took time, however, to discharge the vast number of men in the armed forces in November, 1918. As for the 1,000 men in S.A.T.C. on the O.U. campus, they were impatient to return to their homes. All of the lads from Southwestern Oklahoma who had implored me to tell them when they would get *into* S.A.T.C. now missed no opportunity to ask me if I had an idea when they would get *out* of S.A.T.C. Of course I did not know but at long last they were discharged on December 21, 1918.

With the coming of peace, a determined effort was made by the War Department to return those troops from overseas for Christmas. These included several O.U. professors and former students. Most of the faculty members resumed their duties the second semester. Others whose discharge came later would be back for the 1919-20 school year, and I was determined to return to Harvard for that year to finish work for the Ph.D.

When my request for sabbatical leave for 1919-20 was presented to President Brooks he was surprisingly coopera- tive. By September, 1919, I would have been with the University of Oklahoma only five years and during 1916-17 I had been on leave of absence. President Brooks knew this, of course, but said, "If a man had one year out of seven off with half pay, it *should* be the *first* of the seven-year period instead of the last, then the University would get the benefit of his year of study and research. I'll be glad, Dale, to approve your request for sabbatical leave."

Naturally, this pleased me a great deal. My salary had been increased to a point that half-pay for nine months would be $1250. I had not applied for an Austin Teachers' scholarship for I had already received two and doubted if Harvard would give me a third. Also, I knew that a scholarship granted to a bachelor would be canceled by his marriage, and Rosalie's coming to say goodbye when it seemed that I was going into the army had been encouraging.

She often came to her home in Norman for the weekend so we were together a great deal, but she was shy and would almost never go with me to a picture show and never to any University function. Always she would make some excuse to stay home. Sometimes it was to bake the bread or take care of some other chore if her mother was working in the evening or visiting a neighbor. Perhaps she wished to avoid unmerciful teasing by her girl friends for I was forty years old the eighth of February, 1919, while she was about twenty-three. So my role was often that of "fireside companion."

Needless to say by this time I was deeply in love and it was hard to think of leaving her for an entire school year at Harvard. Yet, it seemed doubtful that she cared enough for me to entrust her future life to my care and go to Cambridge with me as my wife. She had never been outside of Oklahoma except for a few weeks to visit with relatives in Missouri. She was as innocent as a little child and it would require a great deal of love and trust to give her the courage to leave everything that she had always held most dear to go with me to far-off Massachusetts. Did she love and trust me that much? Frankly, it seemed doubtful.

At our boarding house there was an attractive girl from Vinita, Oklahoma. She was one-eighth or possibly one-fourth Cherokee. She borrowed one of my books and returned it with a note inside thanking me for giving her the privilege of reading it. She did not room at the boarding house, as most of the other girls who ate there did, but resided five blocks down the street running parallel with University Boulevard on which my room was located. As a result, I sometimes walked home with her.

Florence was a nice girl who seemed to like being with me so as the warm days of spring came, our walks were sometimes extended to town for a cold drink, the early picture show, and a dish of ice cream afterward. While Mrs. Williams, who operated the boarding house, served fairly good meals, a change was always welcome so on a couple of occasions, I took Florence to Oklahoma City for dinner and a movie.

Then came the closing of the public schools late in May, and Rosalie came home just before University commencement. The summer session opened in a day or so after commencement. I had been working on my dissertation most of my spare time all the year, but there were several places where information was lacking which it was my hope might be found in the Kansas Historical Society at Topeka.

Florence was enrolled in the summer session and we were both still boarding at Mrs. Williams's so I saw her three times a day. I had told her something of Rosalie and, that while we were not engaged, it was my hope that she would become my wife. As for Florence herself, I am sure that she never had any serious romantic feeling toward me. Perhaps she was a bit flattered by receiving some attention from an older man and did not object to a little mild summer flirtation, but that was all.

She said she would like to meet Rosalie so one Sunday afternoon I made an appointment and we walked over to the Gilkey home. Rosalie was wearing a white dress and had never looked lovelier. The three of us sat on the front porch and chatted for half an hour or so. Then I took Florence back to her rooming place.

An evening or so later I called on Rosalie and instantly sensed a change in her attitude toward me. During the past year she had seemed to have grown increasingly fond of me but never had she seemed to care enough to warrant my feeling that she would, without hesitation, trust her entire future life to me. That evening was different. For the first time her eyes revealed that she would gladly leave her home, parents, relatives, and friends and go with me to the ends of the earth.

It made me feel very humble. Never did I have any doubt but that she would make me very happy. My only question was could I make *her* happy? Would an old bachelor of forty be so set in his ways that he could not adjust them enough that a twenty-three-year-old girl might find in living with him all the happiness of her youthful dreams? That was my responsibility.

At any rate, the time had come to ask the momentous question that had so long been in my mind. For years I had been proud of my ability in the use of words, but in this instance it left me completely and I blurted out my question like a schoolboy, "Will you go to Harvard with me as my wife?" The reply came back without a moment's hesitation, "I certainly will." She was sitting in a rocking chair and I on the sofa. I asked her to come and sit beside me and brought out the little box containing the diamond ring which had been burning my pocket for a month or more. I slipped it on the third finger of her left hand as I breathed softly a wish: "May I put another on your hand soon and may neither ever bring you anything but happiness." At long last we were engaged and within a few weeks would be married.

I walked back to my room that evening probably looking like I had "swallowed a sunset!" At the same time there was a feeling of great responsibility. Up to that time it had never seemed necessary to take out life insurance or to save money for anything except to complete work for my Ph.D. at Harvard. Consequently, like most cowhands, my money had been spent with a lavish hand.

Much as I wanted to get back to the Harvard Library as early as possible, there remained a few gaps in my dissertation where the information to fill them would much more likely be found in Wichita or Topeka, Kansas, than in any library in New England. Clearly the materials in these two cities must be gone over carefully before leaving for Cambridge.

In addition, I had a "promise to keep" made to a good friend a week or so before school closed, Professor Henry Hubbard Foster of the O.U. Law School. He had told me that at the end of the school year and after all of his papers had been graded, he was always so tired and nervous that he could not sleep. I told him a little about my New England hiking trips and jokingly remarked that he should take a similar trip with me in the Ozark Mountains of northwest Arkansas as soon as school closed.

To my surprise he had jumped at the suggestion and we had made plans to put on walking garb and take a train to some point in Missouri near its southwest boundary. From there we would walk south on the country roads for three or four days always keeping fairly near the Kansas City Southern Railroad.

The next evening when I called to see Rosalie, I told her of this promise and asked if she would go with me to see my brother George and his wife Anna for a couple of days upon my return from this trip with Foster. She assured me that she would be glad to go for as yet she had not met any of my relatives.

By this time we were both down to earth a little more than when we had parted the evening before. There were still stars in Rosalie's eyes and my feet were touching the ground a little on the high spots instead of nothing but the air. Even so we were both sane enough to realize that we must make some plans as to when and where we should be married. She promised to think this over a bit while I was gone.

The next day Professor Foster and I donned our hiking clothes and boarded the train for our trip. I was wearing a flannel shirt, riding breeches, and puttees and had my old army mess kit with salt, sugar, and coffee. Foster was wearing walking clothes and each of us had a small pack containing our pajamas, extra socks, handkerchiefs, and a soft white shirt and bow tie. We knew that it might be cool in the evening so we each wore a light tweed jacket.

We left the train at Neosho, Missouri, where we spent the night in a "bowl'n pitcher" hotel. The following morning after a good breakfast we started south by west until we reached the railroad. We then turned nearly due south and followed the country roads paralleling the railway. There were few automobiles on these roads. When one going in our direction came along, we always declined the driver's invitation to ride except when we were passing across a prairie area where there was little of interest to see.

We continued our journey for three days. The weather was perfect and it was a joy to travel with Foster. To him this was an entirely new experience, and it was a delight to see how much he was enjoying it. The scenery was lovely. There were many wild flowers blooming beside the road and more than once we came to a patch of blackberries and stopped to pick and eat the luscious fruit.

We crossed many crystal-clear brooks and beside one of these or at some clear, cold spring we almost always stopped for lunch or supper for we ate no meal except breakfast at the little hotels where we slept at night. Since Foster's knowledge of cooking was close to absolute zero, I prepared all the meals and tried to make them first class. The stores in the little town usually provided all we needed, but sometimes I could buy fresh eggs, sweet corn, butter, or strawberries from a farmer near the road.

We would often have country-cured ham and eggs and sweet corn roasted in the husk, toast, plenty of butter, and for dessert, strawberries or peaches and cream. One evening two boys stopped as we were eating supper by a brook only a quarter of a mile from a small village. They refused to eat supper with us but each accepted an orange and a couple of doughnuts. They said that they lived about four miles back in the hills and had been sent to town for a jug of syrup. They insisted on pouring some of it on our plates, and it was quite good.

Foster seemed to be having such a good time that he would probably have insisted on continuing our trip a day or so longer, but he developed a blister on one foot by the afternoon of the third day. I had forgotten to warn him not to wear mended or darned socks. As a result, he had put on a pair that had been roughly darned and by late afternoon had a blister that made it necessary to stop walking.

Fortunately, this was near a town where a short line of railroad from Oklahoma joined the Kansas City Southern, and we were able to get a train that took us to a small Oklahoma town on the main line of railway running to Oklahoma City. Foster was getting tired so we spent the night at a "bowl'n pitcher hotel" in this Oklahoma village.

Soon after breakfast we boarded a train for Oklahoma City from which it was less than an hour's run by the interurban to Norman.

It had been a grand trip for both of us. To Professor Foster, it was an entirely new experience. To me it was a joy to see his reactions. Educated at Cornell and the Harvard Law School, he had apparently never been farther west than Buffalo until he came to teach law at the University of Oklahoma.

He was very eager to please these Ozark hill people, however, and when two or three of them in a battered old T-model Ford would insist on giving us a ride for a few miles, he would talk to them in what he thought was their own language. This was eastside New York! They would look at him and then at me in puzzled fashion when he called them "Bo" and used similar terms which he had heard in the eastside New York slums. Apparently they wondered where I had picked up this strange traveling companion.

Rosalie seemed glad to see me when we returned from this little jaunt and a couple of days later we were ready for the trip to southwestern Oklahoma for a weekend with George and Anna. We took the slow Frisco train about nine a.m. and reached Snyder about four p.m. George met us with a wagon and drove us the five miles northwest to the farm. Rosalie had lived on a farm as a child and was delighted with everything she saw.

Anna welcomed us and about six we sat down to an excellent farm supper with fried chicken, cream gravy, hot biscuits, new potatoes, peas, and a dessert of blackberry cobbler. After supper Rosalie helped Anna with the dishes, and I helped George with the milking and other chores. Both Anna and George accepted Rosalie at first sight. Anna played a few pieces for us on the piano and we talked until about ten o'clock.

We stayed two full days with George and Anna and I am sure that they and Rosalie enjoyed the visit as much as I. The first day, Rosalie and I climbed the mountain situated 200 yards northwest of the corner of the 160-acre tract upon which George had filed entry as a homestead early in

August, 1901. The summit must be nearly 700 feet above the level of the plains.

The view was magnificent for it was a clear summer day with almost no wind. Otter Creek valley lay like a map below us. To the northwest the Twin Mountains seemed very near. To the west and southwest we could see the North Fork of Red River which made a turn to the east in a horseshoe bend with the seven peaks of the Navajoe Mountains lying across the open end of this giant horseshoe.

We could, of course, see Mountain Park and Snyder as well as the farms lying about with the fields of corn, cotton, and alfalfa. The dwellings looked like doll houses, the roads like narrow paths. I pointed out the boundaries of the Dale farm and told Rosalie of the agreement that George and I had made that if one of us drew a lucky number and the other did not, we would divide the 160 acres equally when a patent to it had been secured.

Later we had amended this and had agreed that the first one who married should have 100 acres with house, barn, and other buildings, and the other should have 60 acres. Immediately after George's marriage, he had given me a deed to the 60-acre strip on the north side of the 160-acre homestead. I showed Rosalie the approximate boundaries of this 60-acre tract and added that she was not marrying a completely penniless man for this 60 acres was worth $4,000 or $5,000. To this she replied she was not interested in whether I had property which, of course, pleased me a great deal.

On our way down the mountain we came to currant bushes loaded with fully ripe black currants. I had folded a paper bag and put it in my pocket thinking we might find currants for I had often picked them on the Navajoe Mountains when I was a boy. I brought this out, and we picked enough for Anna to make a delicious pie for dinner the next day.

On our last day's visit, I took Rosalie up to see the site of Old Camp Radziminski established by Earl Van Dorn before the Civil War at the mouth of the canyon where Otter Creek flows through a gorge in the mountains.

It was a picturesque spot then, but a dam has since been

built to form a lake which provides water for Snyder. As we were returning it began to rain so we stopped at a neighbor's house a little way down the stream from the mouth of the canyon. It lasted only a little while, but we had just left the house when George met us in his buggy and we rode the rest of the way with him. He said that he was afraid we would not be able to find shelter from the rain.

The next morning George took us to the train and we said goodbye promising to return for a longer visit the following summer. In the meantime, we would send them our address in Cambridge as soon as we found a place to live and would write often.

We reached Norman in the late afternoon, and decided that it would be best for me to pack all that I needed for the year in Cambridge and take it with me when I left Norman for a week or so of work in Wichita and Topeka, Kansas. This would give Rosalie time to do her packing. When my work was about finished in Topeka, I would call her and she would meet me in Kansas City where we would be married and go from there to Cambridge.

Just before I was ready to start for Wichita, Professor Foster invited Rosalie and me for a "cook-out" in his backyard. He added he wanted Mrs. Foster and Rosalie to see how we prepared our meals on our walking trip. We were glad to go, of course, and Foster brought out thick steaks to be broiled over a "campfire" in his backyard. It was a good dinner but not much like those we had eaten on our hiking trip.

A day or so later I said goodbye to Rosalie and friends in Norman and boarded a Santa Fe train for Wichita. Here it was my privilege to meet C. Q. Chandler, a banker who had been in Wichita for many years, and who handled a great deal of "cattle paper." I also met Dave Leahy, an old-time newspaper man, who gave me information on the Cherokee Strip Livestock Association and its members. Johnnie Blair, former secretary of the Association, was out of town and I did not meet him until some years later.

After three days in Wichita I moved on to the Kansas Historical Society in Topeka where I found an enormous amount of material on early Kansas and Oklahoma history, particularly in newspapers. I had been writing Rosalie almost every day and at the end of a week called her to say that my work in Topeka was about finished. She said that she would finish packing the following day and take the evening train which reached Kansas City at eight next morning.

The following day I was up early and made the short run into Kansas City and engaged a room at the Baltimore Hotel registering for Mr. and Mrs. E. E. Dale. I explained to the room clerk that my wife would not arrive until eight o'clock the next morning.

Next, I returned to Union Depot and purchased Pullman tickets for New York. Since the war was over I had no difficulty obtaining a section near the middle of the car. Naturally, I would have been glad to get a compartment or drawing room, but since we would be away for a year, it seemed that we could not be extravagant at the very beginning of the year.

I had bought the wedding ring before leaving Norman but it occurred to me that perhaps I should arrange for a minister and a church. However, I decided to wait until Rosalie arrived and see if she had any preference as to the church or minister.

I was up early next morning and after shaving, showering, and getting dressed in my best suit I hurried over to the Union Station. It was only 7:30 so I bought a newspaper and took a seat near the exit for the Santa Fe trains. Probably I looked at my wrist watch a dozen times or so in the next thirty minutes.

At long last it was eight o'clock, and I was on my feet beside the long ramp as the first passengers came in sight. A minute or so later Rosalie appeared followed by a porter carrying her two big suitcases. She looked lovely in her blue suit and smiled happily when she saw me.

I shook hands with Rosalie and asked about breakfast. When she replied that she had not had breakfast, I assured her that neither had I so we had the porter check the grips and we had breakfast. It was a happy meal. Rosalie said

224

that she had slept fairly well in the Pullman and was not tired.

After a leisurely breakfast we retrieved the suitcases and took a cab to the hotel. Here I left Rosalie suggesting that she might like to take a bath and a nap while I made a trip to the courthouse to get the marriage license. The clerk explained that he could not issue me a license unless the bride-to-be or someone representing her was with me.

I had studied the Missouri law enough to know that no physical examination or three-day waiting period was required as was the case in some states, but this was a detail I had overlooked. There was nothing to do but return to the courthouse with Rosalie. She received the information that she must go with me to the courthouse in order to get a marriage license good-naturedly.

She came down in twenty or thirty minutes looking very lovely and we took a cab for the courthouse. The clerk greeted us cordially and looked approvingly at the bride-to-be. After he had issued the license and recorded it on his books, he volunteered the information that there was a retired minister who stayed around the courthouse to marry couples who were strangers in the city. He added that we might meet him as we left the building.

He was quite correct for when we reached the street, a kindly-looking old gentleman greeted us and gave me a card with his name and the words, "specializing in weddings and funerals." I introduced Rosalie and myself and said that we wished to be married in a church as my father had been ordained as a minister and my bride-to-be was a member of the Presbyterian Church. He replied that there was a little church only about three blocks down the street in which he had married many couples.

I looked at Rosalie and she nodded her approval so we followed the minister. The church interior was attractive with stained glass windows and flowers on the altar. The organist, his assistant, and the janitor served as witnesses.

The minister stationed us before the altar and began the ceremony. He had a remarkably good voice. To me it was a most impressive ceremony, for the minister had married so many couples that he knew the words perfectly and so never hesitated in the least. I kept a firm grip on the ring and did not drop it when the time came for the words: "with this ring I thee wed." Then came the final words: "I pronounce you husband and wife. Whom God hath joined together, let no man put asunder."

I kissed my bride and slipped the minister a ten-dollar bill as I shook hands with him. The witnesses shook hands with both of us and the minister gave us a marriage certificate signed by himself and the witnesses. Then the organist began to play a recessional and we walked down the aisle to the open door as husband and wife. It was July 18, 1919.

Edward Everett Dale

Rosalie Gilkey Dale

226

Honeymoon in Cambridge

We were up early the next morning for the train to Chicago which left at eight o'clock. As I recall we had our "wedding breakfast" at a Child's Restaurant which indicates that we were far from stylish. I had sent a night letter to Rosalie's mother the evening before. When we boarded the train for Chicago about five minutes before eight we knew that she would receive it in the next few minutes and be assured that all was well with her younger daughter and that she was now on the train with her husband.

It must be confessed that it seemed strange to think of myself as a "husband." I was reminded of a remark made by George's top hired man, Alex Hash, when seventeen-year-old Sam Ellis married sixteen-year-old Ruthie Webb just before Christmas. I told Alex that Ruthie had been showing me her Christmas gifts and when she came to a beautiful toilet set in an ornate case she said proudly, "My husband gave me this."

"Husband, husband," snorted Alex, "Heluva husband ain't he?"

I told Rosalie of this and we laughed about it a little but to my confession of feeling myself a husband, she admitted that she felt equally strange being a wife.

The run to Chicago was pleasant. We talked, admired the countryside, read a magazine, and both of us took a short nap so it did not seem long until we reached Chicago. Here we took another train for New York. On this lap of our journey there was more of interest to see but soon after we had finished dinner, darkness fell. We retired early and next morning, after a good breakfast, admired the scenery the rest of the way to New York.

I had stayed once at a very nice little hotel quite a distance uptown. I took Rosalie there and after we had eaten lunch I left her there and went downtown to arrange our transportation to Boston. The Cape Cod Canal had been opened a year or so earlier so I had suggested that we might be able to get a cabin on the night boat to Boston.

When I reached the booking office there was a long line of persons waiting to pick up their reservations and I was told that there was no vacancy unless someone canceled a reservation which was most unlikely. Nevertheless, I joined the line but each person paid his money and received his ticket. It seemed that there was not a chance of a cancellation, but the Providence which is said to take care of children and fools seems also to look after newly married couples. The man directly ahead of me asked for a cancellation of his reservations and the return deposit. It was almost uncanny that such good fortune should be mine for his reservation was for a very nice cabin near the middle of the ship.

Much elated by my good fortune I hurried back to the Grand Central Station, arranged for the transfer of our baggage to the *Northland*, and hurried to the hotel to tell Rosalie.

We went aboard the *Northland* about five-thirty which gave us time to freshen up a bit before going to dinner at six-thirty. After dinner we sat in the lounge and talked a little with our fellow-passengers until the ship got underway. The wind was blowing quite a bit and while the ship was not rolling we were conscious of the waves lapping against it. Travel by ship was a new experience for Rosalie and while she seemed to enjoy it, she probably felt at times that she would just as soon be in a Pullman on dry land.

It had been a long, hard day so we retired early and I think we were both sound asleep in two or three minutes and did not wake until we found the *Northland* at a pier in Boston Harbor. Just when we had reached Boston I never knew. I

228

shaved quickly while Rosalie combed her hair and "prettied up" a bit and we dressed, packed our small overnight bags, and went ashore. It took only a few minutes to get the rest of our baggage delivered to a checkstand. We then set out in search of breakfast.

Once more a Child's Restaurant furnished it and we then faced the problem of finding a place to live for the next ten months. Obviously, it must be in Cambridge and as near the University as possible so we walked over to the Park Street Under Subway Station and took the train for Harvard Square. The trains are underground all the way except in crossing the Charles River.

To Rosalie everything was new and strange and she was delighted to see the many places which I had described to her. The University did not open for several weeks but the library was open all day and that was where my work would be done. At the moment the most important thing was to find quarters while looking for an apartment. Staying at a hotel in Boston would be very expensive but a room in Cambridge should be relatively cheap.

Naturally, the first place to look would be the Elders at 76 Hammond Street where I had stayed both my first and second year at Harvard. We accordingly entered Harvard Yard through the south gate with the inscription above it, "Enter and Grow in Wisdom." It was only a ten-minute walk across the Yard and through the north gate and on past Peabody Museum and Divinity Hall to Hammond Street and the Elder home.

Mrs. Elder and her daughter seemed very glad to see me and looked admiringly at Rosalie. When they learned that we were seeking a room for a week or more while looking for an apartment, they seemed genuinely sorry that all of their rooms were occupied. They suggested Mrs. Nickerson, an elderly woman like themselves from Maine and who lived only four houses down the street. The daughter added that she would telephone Mrs. Nickerson and find out the situation.

Apparently Miss Elder recommended us highly for Mrs. Nickerson seemed delighted to let us have a room. She showed us a nice room on the first floor with old-fashioned furniture. It had no bath but there was a bathroom only a short distance down the hall. We were the only roomers she had or would have for three or four weeks when Harvard students would be coming in. The price for a week's stay was no more than a good Boston Hotel would charge for a day.

We had our baggage sent over and began the search for a furnished apartment. The real estate people told us that there were none and that we should find a furnished room and get our meals at the various eating places around Harvard Square. To this my response was that I had eaten at boarding houses and restaurants for many years and now that I had a wife I intended to find a place where she could cook and keep house. To this the real estate men replied that they wished me luck but my quest was hopeless.

They did not know of my discovery that the same kind Providence which looks after children and fools also takes care of newlyweds. Just who it was that mentioned 37 Concord Avenue as a possible place to inquire about an apartment I cannot recall. At any rate we called there and found that two elderly sisters who occupied one of the six apartments in William Dean Howell's former home wanted to rent it.

We learned later that after Howell left this home, it was occupied by Hellen Keller for some years. After she left, the purchaser had transformed the big three-story residence into six small apartments, three on each side of the central hallway. The two sisters occupied the ground floor apartment on the north side. It consisted of a living room with a bay window, a dining room with a woodburning fireplace, a bedroom, kitchen, and bath.

We fell in love with the place at first sight. The furnishings were in good taste and the location was perfect. It was in easy walking distance of Harvard Yard, and there was only one house between this one and the rear entrance to the grounds of the Harvard Observatory. Only a few minutes walk up the street was a little shopping center with a grocery store, drugstore, and one or two other small business houses. Finally, it was very near the home of my friend John Kennedy Lacock.

The two sisters welcomed us courteously and said they had a brother who was a businessman in Boston. They had lived in this apartment for years and were very fond of it, but their brother felt that they should spend the winter months in a residential hotel in the city. There they would be nearer him and would have their meals in the dining room and not have to go out to buy groceries when it was bitterly cold and the ground was covered with sleet and snow. While it would be some months yet until cold weather, their favorite residential hotel could give them a very nice suite *now* but later it would be impossible to find pleasant living quarters anywhere in the city.

I had of course introduced myself as an assistant professor at the University of Oklahoma and assured them that my wife was a good housekeeper, that we would take care of their apartment, and that we would gladly provide references. In spite of this I sensed there was something in the older sister's mind that made her hesitate. Finally it came out when she said, "Mr. and Mrs. Dale, I would prefer to rent the apartment to Protestant people."

This surprised me a little but I hastened to tell her that Rosalie was a member of the Presbyterian Church and that my father had been a devout member of the Old School Baptist Church and fairly late in his life had been licensed to preach and then ordained as a minister. While he had never been pastor of a church, he had often preached to congregations at frontier schoolhouses or churches where the people had no regular pastor. I added that while not a member of any church myself, it had been my practice when teaching public school, to attend church services twice every Sunday, usually the Methodist service in the morning and the Baptist in the evening.

Apparently my words relieved the minds of both sisters and removed any lingering doubts which they may have had. When I gave them the names of half a dozen persons including three or four professors at Harvard, Fred Merk, John K. Lacock, and John Peakes whom they might telephone to ask about me, they assured us that this was not necessary. They added that they were perfectly willing to rent us the apartment for fifty-five dollars a month.

This seemed almost too good to be true, and when they added that they had already packed their clothing and we could move in "tomorrow afternoon abut four," it seemed that truly everything was "coming our way." I wrote them a check for the first month's rent and suggested that they probably had a few supplies in the kitchen as salt, sugar, spices, flour, butter, potatoes, crackers, etc. If so, we would be glad to have them make a list of such things and their value and we would pay for them. They assured me that they would do this so we said goodbye.

Promptly at 4:00 p.m. the next day, we appeared at 37 Concord Avenue in a cab with all our luggage. The two sisters were waiting for us. They had already sent their own baggage to their new quarters in Boston and were only waiting to give us the keys to the apartment and a card with their address to which the monthly rent check should be sent. They also gave us their telephone number in case we needed to call them.

The apartment was spotless and they told us about the janitor who would pick up the garbage if we would set the containers outside the back door each evening. They also told us what time the mail came each day. Then I asked the older sister if she had made me the list of groceries which they were leaving in the kitchen for us.

"Oh, yes," she replied as she handed me a slip of paper, "here it is."

I looked at the ten or twelve items listed beginning with: "Two onions, two cents; three potatoes, three cents; one-fourth pound of butter, thirteen cents; etc." The total amount was seventy-nine cents. Very carefully I counted her out that amount for which she thanked me. They refused my offer to call a cab to take them to the subway station at Harvard Square, saying that they preferred to walk. They said goodbye quite cordially and assured us that they were glad to have us in their apartment.

After they were gone we laughed quite a bit about their list of groceries as an example of New England thrift, so different from what we were accustomed to in Oklahoma. Some ten days later came a sequel to this incident. We had

232

gone for a long walk and upon our return found a large crate of beautiful apples at our back door. I was sure that they must have been sent to the sisters by some friend who had not learned of their removal to Boston.

Certainly there was no one in that part of the country who would be sending *us* half a bushel of choice apples! I accordingly called the sisters and the older one answered. I told her of the apples that must be intended for her and her sister and asked if I should send them to her or would she send someone to pick them up. "Oh, no," she replied, "those apples are for *you*. We have a little farm a few miles out in the country and the apples are unusually nice this year so we thought you and your wife might enjoy a box of them."

I thanked her from the bottom of my heart and left the telephone with a better understanding of "the New England Way" than I ever had before. Charging us seventy-nine cents for a few left over groceries was a matter of business while sending us at least five dollars worth of choice apples was a token of friendship.

As we unpacked, we realized more fully how fortunate we were. There was ample closet space for all our clothing and other belongings, and every inch of the apartment was scrupulously clean. Over the colonial fireplace in the dining room, which had been Howell's study, were small paintings of the four seasons by his daughter. All the furniture was in excellent taste and there were plenty of dishes and cooking utensils as well as table and bed linen.

Within an hour all unpacking and putting away was done and we walked up to the store to get a couple of little steaks, bread, sugar, bacon and eggs, which with the seventy-nine cents worth of groceries, would get us by for supper and breakfast. We promised ourselves that "tomorrow" we would stock up on such staples as flour, breakfast food, shortening, potatoes, fruit, syrup, and anything else which we might need. We found the little grocery well-stocked and that the proprietor would sell his customers any quantity needed no matter how small; i.e., one egg, two slices of bacon, half a cube of butter, or half a pound of hubbard squash.

233

When I called on John Kennedy Lacock, his nephew, who was staying there for a few days, said that John had gone to western Pennsylvania to visit his brother but would be back at the end of the week. We had been so busy getting settled that we decided not to contact Merk for a time.

After we had finished unpacking, I telephoned Merk and the following day went over to see him and his parents. They and Fred were in the house which I had helped him find for them and all three seemed content. While the father was quite German, he spoke English with little accent. The mother's English, however, was very broken and Fred often teased her about her pronunciation of English words. She never seemed to mind this good-natured "ribbing" but would in turn poke fun at some of Fred's habits or expressions.

Within a day or so after we moved into our little apartment, John Kennedy Lacock was back and when I telephoned him, he rushed down to see us. I had never written him of my marriage, but like all of my Cambridge and Boston friends, John was charmed by Rosalie. He insisted on taking us up to his place. Of course, I had been there dozens of times, but he was eager to show Rosalie his home and garden.

He had several kinds of vegetables in this garden including ten or twelve rows of potatoes. He promptly gave Rosalie three rows of potatoes designating the first three rows on the east side of the patch. He had a beautiful crabapple tree loaded with fruit and told us to gather all we could use in making jelly or butter. Within a day or so he had a party for us at which he played old songs on the phonograph illustrating them with colored slides thrown on the screen by a projector.

Once we were settled in the apartment which was to be our home for the next ten months, we planned a budget as best we could. My sabbatical leave pay was about $112 a month. In addition, we hoped to get a little money from the forty acres of cotton on my sixty-acre tract which had been rented every year to one of the neighbors. In the past my share of the crop had seldom been over $75 to $100, but even that much would help. In addition, I had a few hundred dollars in the bank which we were keeping for use in an emergency and to pay for our transportation back to Oklahoma at the end of the school year.

About all we did toward a planned economy was to agree that Rosalie should take fifteen dollars every Monday for weekly household expenses. Whatever was left after buying food for Sunday, we would spend on a show, trip, or other recreation on the weekend. Sometimes it was very little but we might have as much as three or four dollars of what we called "fun money."

Although University enrollment did not begin until shortly after the middle of September, there were always several visiting scholars engaged in research in the library. In addition, many students came early in order to get settled in their living quarters. These, like myself, secured a "stall" or cubicle in the stacks and began work. It must be confessed that I did comparatively little work in August because John insisted on having two or three parties for us and we had him over for dinner once or twice.

With the coming of September, there also came an event of some importance which I witnessed and even played a small part. This was the Boston Police Strike which was to make Governor Calvin Coolidge President of the United States.

The story of the Boston Police Strike is a part of American history which can be read in a number of books, magazine articles, and newspapers of that time. All that seems necessary to give here is a brief account of my own observations and experiences during the hectic few days of disorder early in September.

Before the middle of August, the American Federation of Labor had granted a charter to a police organization of Boston called the Social Club making it the Boston Police Union. Police Commissioner Edwin U. Curtis had earlier announced that no member of the police force could belong to any organization outside the department. He now charged the officers of the new union with insubordination but delayed disciplinary action in order to give them a chance to withdraw from the Federation. The union declared that if these men were punished the police would strike.

We knew this much from the newspapers, but Bostonians did not take the threat of a police strike seriously. They knew that the police were underpaid and some of the stations were old, dirty, and in need of repair, but could not believe that they would strike. Some asserted that even if they did, the people of the large, peaceful city of Boston could get along without a police force for a week or so. President Lowell of Harvard was not so naive. As the situation grew tense, he published a letter to all Harvard men stating that if the police should strike, he trusted that, in the age-old tradition of Harvard, they would volunteer their services to protect life and property.

On September 8, the police voted to strike. They turned in their police box keys and badges to their respective stations and went home. As darkness fell, thieves and other underworld characters came to the surface like the scum in the kettle of boiling liquid. They smashed windows of shops and stores around Scollay Square and along Washington Street, and according to newspaper accounts, stole over $600,000 worth of property. Men were knocked down and robbed and women attacked within 100 feet of the Statehouse.

By morning the staid old city of Boston was in the grip of a reign of terror. As I read the morning paper, I told Rosalie that it was my duty to offer my services as a volunteer police officer to protect the lives and property of the citizens. My experience as deputy sheriff at old Navajoe and other places in Southwest Oklahoma would be very helpful. Rosalie agreed and, after a hasty breakfast, I slipped five cartridges in my old Colt's revolver, strapped it to my right hip under my coat, and started for Harvard Square.

A number of young men had gathered there and just as I arrived, a car came from Boston after delivering four or five young men to police headquarters. Two other cars appeared to take more men to the headquarters. I climbed into one of these together with four other men. The driver of the car just back from Boston told us to keep away from Scollay Square as it was in possession of a howling mob of 10,000 to 12,000.

Our driver heeded this advice and gave that area a wide berth. After delivering us to police headquarters, he started back to Harvard Square for men while the rest of us entered the building to receive our assignments. Here a clerk took our names so that appointments to the police force might be issued by Commissioner Curtis. Each of us then received a card assigning us to a particular police station where the captain would administer the oath of office and give us instructions.

My assignment was to the East Dedham Street Station in South Boston, regarded as a tough district even in normal times. I promptly started for that station, but to reach it I had to leave the train at the Douglas Street Station and walk about three or four blocks. Along the sidewalks men were operating the old shell game with a large group around each little table eagerly putting up their money. Also there were numerous wheel of fortune men each calling, "Put down your money men. Here she goes. Where she stops the Lord only knows and He won't tell. Choose your number gentlemen. Someone is bound to win!"

This was in Boston, the city which was regarded as the cultural and intellectual center of America! It was hard to realize that it was not one of the wild Western cowtowns or mining camps.

It was with some difficulty that I pushed my way through the gamblers and onlookers and reached the police station. The large room had a counter across one end. Behind this stood Captain Driskill and a desk sergeant. Three other volunteers were ahead of me and the Captain questioned each of them one by one. He asked:

"Where and when were you born?
Have you ever been arrested?
Are you familiar with the use of firearms?"

Two of the men ahead of me said that they were, and each was given a badge, key to police boxes, and a small nickle-plated pistol. It was of the same type as the little revolver which a seventeen-year-old lad, fresh from an Ohio farm, once proudly showed a dozen of us gathered about a chuck wagon waiting for supper. The only comment was from top cowhand, Tex Allen, who remarked, "Kid, if you'd ever shoot me with that thing, and I ever found it out, I'd tie you up and whup you 'till you broke loose."

The third man said he was *not* familiar with the use of firearms so was given a "night stick" instead of a gun.

When my turn came to the question of where and when born, my response was, "Texas, 1879." To the question as to my having ever been arrested, I explained briefly the Duke School incident. Then the Captain did not ask if I was familiar with the use of firearms but pushed across the counter to me the same type of small pistol given the other men. No doubt he assumed that any man born in Texas as early as 1879 must be familiar with the use of firearms which was correct.

I picked up the little nickle-plated gun which, as I recall it, was a .38 caliber Smith and Wesson double-action pistol; not a bad weapon at close range but useless as a club and with little shocking power compared with a .45 caliber. "Captain Driskill," said I with some slight hesitation, "I've never cared too much for these little double-action guns. Of course, it is my hope that in my service as a volunteer policeman I'll never need a gun, but if I *do* need one, it will be needed 'mighty bad.' Now here is one that I've owned for nearly twenty years and know what it will do. If not contrary to regulations, it would please me very much to take it with me instead of the police revolver." With this I drew my old .45 Colt's and laid it on the counter.

The Captain's eyes widened as he looked at big blue .45 beside the shiny little .38 which I had returned to the counter. Then he swallowed a couple of times and replied, "Certainly, Mr. Dale, take your own gun if you wish, but I would like for you to take the police revolver, too. We want every police officer to have a pistol issued by the Department so if someone is shot we can tell whether or not it was with one of our guns."

As a result when I went to walk my beat, it was with the little police issue gun on my left hip and my own on the right. Fortunately, there was no need to use either of them for Governor Coolidge ordered out the National Guard. The soldiers killed a man on Boston Common and another in my district and wounded two or three more who were looting a store.

The volunteer police stayed on for a few days after the guard was ordered out. My shift began at two p.m. The next day after my joining the force, a group of us was sitting in the station waiting for two o'clock when one of the group remarked that such a crisis as this brings together men of various vocations. "Probably there are no two of us here in the same type of work," he continued. "I'm a lawyer, what is your work?" The man next to him said, "Insurance," the next, "Carpenter," then came "Painter," "Advertising," etc. When my time to reply came, my answer was, of course, "University Professor at the University of Oklahoma."

Captain Driskill came in just then and heard my answer with the result that when a reporter came down later looking for news or a story, the Captain said, "I've got a college professor among my volunteer members of the force. He's from Oklahoma, and he's a two-gun man. He came in the first day and when I gave him a badge, key, and pistol, he pulled out a huge blue .45 Colt's and asked if he could take that along. I told him to take 'em both. He probably shoots equally well with either hand."

I knew nothing of this, but the reporter evidently thought he had found a good story. At any rate, the next morning about ten when Rosalie and I returned from a walk, we found two men sitting on the fence in front of the house waiting for us. One said he was a reporter for the *Boston Globe* and had been sent out to interview us and get a picture. He asked each of us a few questions and had us pose for the picture. When the story appeared the next morning, my picture had been retouched to make me look about three axe handles high, and my face was that of a stern, determined individual ready to tackle at least three or four lions and a couple of tigers at a moment's notice.

When I returned to the police station early the next afternoon, it was readily apparent that the story in the morning paper had "got around." The desk sergeant, lieutenant, two or three police privates that had had not walked out with the others, and even the Captain looked at me with increased respect. The situation in the city seemed almost normal except for the presence of soldiers and volunteer police everywhere.

An election was being held in this precinct and Captain Driskill ordered me to accompany one of his loyal men in uniform as the law provided that two police officers must be present at all places of voting in every election. The election was held in a vacant school building as public schools were not yet in session.

We did nothing except stand around for no trouble came, but after the polls were closed, my police companion led me farther back in the building where we could not be seen. Here he asked, "Would you show me just how you draw a gun?"

I whipped out the .45 and brought it up to the level of my eyes, returned it to the holster, and repeated the action two or three times.

"Don't you ever bring the gun up above your head and then down level with your eyes?"

"Certainly not," I replied. "To bring it up above your head and down level is to waste time, and you have none to waste."

He then asked to see the big gun and examined it carefully. Apparently puzzled because there were only five cartridges in the cylinder, he asked why. I explained that no western peace officer or cowhand ever put but five cartridges in a "six shooter" but left the chamber under the hammer empty to prevent the accidental discharge of the gun if it happened to be dropped or if it were used as a club. Also I told him that one old cowhand had remarked to me that, "If you can't do it in five shots, it's time to get the hell out o' there and hunt a place to hole up!"

When my policeman companion asked if it were true that I could shoot equally well with either hand, my reply was that this was true for I couldn't hit a barn door at a distance of 150 feet twice in sucession with either hand. The officer was not convinced but replied earnestly, "That's what you *say,* but I wouldn't let you take a shot at me two hundred *yards* away for all the money in the biggest bank in Boston!"

This seemed to be the attitude of every police officer who talked with me during the next two or three days. It was useless to protest that any pistol is a poor weapon at best, and that my skill with one left much to be desired. Always they insisted that such modesty was commendable but it was plain that none of them believed me. They were sure that I was one of these soft spoken, blue-eyed western gunslingers of whom they had read in many of the cheaper magazines.

Just before I left the force, one Hearst newspaper sent a reporter to interview me. Here were the elements of a good story: a couple of newlyweds on their honeymoon reaching greater Boston just in time for the police strike. The lady reporter played up the romantic aspects of the story, and the article was published in Hearst newspapers throughout the nation.

Once the National Guard was in full control of the city, the volunteer police were released from duty. This pleased me for although I was away only from about one to seven, that seemed a long time to leave Rosalie alone. Mildred Prescott, the nurse and John Lacock's tenant, was not working that week and she and Rosalie were together some afternoons, and once Rosalie visited Mrs. Merk. Mrs. Merk was delighted to visit with Rosalie for whom she developed a real affection. The Merks had a daughter younger than Fred but she had died in her late 'teens. Mrs. Merk confided to Rosalie that it seemed that her own daughter had come back to her.

The final phase of the Boston Police Strike is a matter of history. When the striking policemen realized that the disorder had turned public opinion against them and wanted to come back to work on the old basis, neither Commissioner Curtis nor Governor Coolidge would have anything to do with them. None of them were taken back but a new police force was recruited consisting largely of former servicemen and the policemen's minimum pay was raised from $1160 to $1400 a year. Coolidge issued his famous statement: "There is no right to strike against the public safety anywhere, any time." This statement elected him Vice-President and upon the death of President Harding, he became President.

The Boston Police Strike taught me a great many things. It revealed clearly how dependent we are upon police protection even in the most quiet and peaceful city. It also revealed how quickly public opinion can be formed. At the beginning of the strike many persons said that the police had real grievances and the city government should compromise with them. Then after three days of disorder and looting of shops and stores, no one except members of the striker's families and relatives would say a word in their defense.

As for my own experience, the newspapers in Oklahoma picked up the story of my work as a volunteer policeman and published it with some embellishments. As a result, I have never been able to live down the "two-gun" episode and even as this is written, elderly persons occasionally refer to me as "two-gun" or "two-gun Dale." As some slight compensation, the Boston Chamber of Commerce sent me, and I presume all other volunteer police, a certificate of thanks for my services. Also when my wife and I were in Washington a few years later working on a problem, we received an invitation to visit President Coolidge at his office in the White House. We found him a genial host quite unlike the "Silent Cal" which he was often called.

Soon after the police strike had been settled the school year for Harvard opened. I enrolled in only one course—*Manuscript Sources of American History.* It was only a half-course throughout the year taught by Worthington Ford. It met once a week for two hours in the building of the Massachusetts Historical Society in Boston. Professor Ford's work was with this society, but his home was in Cambridge. I spent most of my study time working on the dissertation.

With the opening of school it was necessary for me to buckle down to work on my dissertation and this kept me in my "stall" in the Widener Memorial Library all day, as it was too far to go home for lunch. The dissertation was clearly going to be long, probably about 400 double-spaced typed pages, and Rosalie suggested that she learn typing and save us as much as $150 by typing it for me. Of course, I could type a little by the old "Columbus method of discover and land" but a document of 400 pages was quite beyond me.

The suggestion pleased me very much. It was not expensive to rent a good typewriter and a manual to accompany it. So equipped, Rosalie settled down with a ream of white paper to learn touch typing. It must have been a hard job, but she worked at it persistently and by Christmas was an expert typist.

This was a major achievement. Not only did she type the pencil draft of my dissertation but also my first hard cover book, *Tales of the Tepee*, published by D. C. Heath and Company in 1920. Perhaps it should be stated here that for the next twenty years or more she typed every book and most of the articles I wrote.

I worked steadily on my dissertation and Rosalie, in addition to her typing, kept the apartment spotless, did most of the shopping for food, cooked the meals, and did most of the other housework. Yet we seemed to have ample time for recreation, visiting friends, and entertaining.

In order to have some "fun money" for weekend outings, we had good but simple meals. When working in the library, I had lunch at a little restaurant just across the street. For dinner we often had fish, usually fillet of flounder, which was always good and cost less than beef or pork. We discovered that Hubbard squash could be bought by the pound and was delicious baked with butter and sugar. When we had company we often served roast pork with gravy.

We dug the potatoes in the rows John Kennedy Lacock had given to Rosalie and picked quantities of crab apples from which we made jelly and marmalade or "butter" from the pulp. Sugar was a real problem for no grocer would sell a customer more than a quarter of a pound at one time.

John and the Merks often came to dinner. Also, John often had us up to his house for me to cook flapjacks for his friends.

A good Oklahoma friend, Sanford Salyer, who taught English at O.U., was a frequent visitor. He roomed in Grays Hall in Harvard Yard and would often come to the kitchen and sit on top of the refrigerator while Rosalie was cooking dinner. Another Oklahoman who had been a student of mine was Lanson D. Mitchell whom I had urged to come to Harvard that year to work for a master's degree. He and his roommate came to see us from time to time.

Dr. Samuel Silas Curry, who with his wife and a staff of teachers operated the Curry School of Expression, had insisted on appointing me a member of the board of directors of his school. Most Curry School Students were young women. Each must have a sponsor for her recital that she was required to give every term. Rosalie was often called upon to serve as sponsor for one of these girls.

In addition we were invited to all recitals and when the school had a dinner for some notable visitor we were invited. I recall one dinner in particular when the poet Yeats was guest of honor. Dr. Curry was seated by him but after half an hour or so came and asked me to change places with him so I could get acquainted with the distinguished poet. Within fifteen minutes I realized that the good doctor's move was not a disinterested one. Conversation with Yeats was impossible, at least that evening.[1]

Dr. Curry had some months earlier brought a group of his students to the Charlestown Prison to entertain the inmates for an evening. When the prisoners gave a minstrel show, they reciprocated by inviting the entire Curry School, including faculty, students, and directors. Of course, Rosalie and I went along and it proved to be one of the greatest such shows we ever saw.

On weekends we often attended plays in Boston. Most of the plays and players are now largely forgotten. Helen Hayes, when we saw her in *Bab*, was only about sixteen. We also saw Jane Cowl in *Within the Law*, Forbes Robertson and Gertrude Eliot in *Hamlet*, and Southern and Marlow in

---

[1] William Butler Yeats, Irish poet, dramatist, and essayist.

Hamlet. In addition we attended several shows at the Castle Square Theater, owned and operated by John Craig and his wife Mary Young and their stock company. They gave several Shakespearean plays as well as some clever modern comedies.

We were entertained at dinner by several friends whom I had met during my second year at Harvard. Among them were Reverend George L. Perin, a Unitarian minister who was also a trustee of the Curry School and who built the Franklin Square House as a home for working girls. We had Thanksgiving dinner with Mr. and Mrs. Murray. He was a businessman and he and his wife had five or six children. Just where I first met Mr. Murray it is impossible for me to recall. The dinner was a typical New England feast with roast turkey, two or three vegetables and apple, mince, and pumpkin pies.

Christmas eve we had dinner with John Kennedy Lacock and Christmas day with the Turners in their home. They had only one other couple as guests and I recall that this was the first time that Rosalie had seen the plum pudding brought in wrapped in blue flames from the lighted brandy poured over it. I recall too that when we awoke Christmas morning it was to find our world wrapped in a soft, clinging snow. It was so beautiful that as soon as breakfast was over we took a walk through the grounds of the Harvard Observatory. This was the first snow of the year and we loved it. Yet the time came when the snow plow cleared the streetcar tracks of Concord Avenue and the snow banks in front of our apartment were so high that we could see only the top of a tall man's hat if he were walking along the sidewalk across the street.

Before we had been in Cambridge a month Rosalie realized that some of her dresses brought from Oklahoma were not suitable for wear in Cambridge. Clearly she needed a new dress or two but the family budget would not permit buying them. It was nearly cotton picking time in Oklahoma, and my acres usually yielded enough to give me about $100 rent. I accordingly promised Rosalie one half of my cotton money.

This was a grave error. A week later I received a cotton check for $125. At the end of the next week one for $250 came. This continued until I had received nearly $1,000. As a result, at the end of the year she had more money than I had which forced me to borrow from her to help pay for our transportation back to Oklahoma. That year forty acres of my farm land produced a bale per acre and the price was about $200 a bale.

The year slipped by amazingly fast. John Kennedy Lacock continued to have us to flapjack parties and often had dinner with us. Nat Fowler had died in November, 1918, and Bill Macy was secretary of the Puddingstone Club. He was very clever and the meetings were always fun but I did not go often. We were invited to attend a meeting or two of the Twentieth Century Club now called the "Twentieth Century Association." Later it was my privilege to speak to this group sharing time with Harold J. Laski. The Boston Authors Club also invited me to read some of my verses to its members. A little later in the year I was elected to membership in both of these clubs and have paid my dues as a non-resident member.[2]

There was little time for making speeches but I had the privilege of speaking to the Brighthelmstone Woman's Club of which Mrs. Stratton D. Brooks had been a member. The subject was ranching and cowboy life and I had some lantern slides made and showed some pictures of cattle, cow camps, roping, and a trail herd. The club treasurer gave me a check for twenty-five dollars for this talk. I recall other talks made, including one to the students of a girl's school in Boston, one to the Presbyterian ministers of Greater Boston, and one to the Daughters of Maine Club.

In this one all my jokes or funny stories fell flat as a lead nickel. Again and again my efforts to get a laugh or even a smile were in vain. At last I gave up in despair and closed my talk as soon as possible. The applause was good which seemed surprising until a severe looking lady who had been sitting on the front row came up, shook my hand quite

---

[2] Harold J. Laski, English political scientist.

warmly, and said, "Mr. Dale that was the funniest speech I ever heard in my life. There were five or six times that I could hardly keep from laughing right in your face!"

On my birthday John gave me a party. He brought in a number of interesting people and he, Rosalie, Mildred Prescott, and Miss Gardiner each gave me one of Denis McCarthy's four books of poems each eloquently inscribed to me. Later John conspired with Rosalie to have her type most of my verses on suitable paper and John had them bound with the title stamped on the cover in gold letters. This was not too long after the appearance of the afore-mentioned, *Tales of the Tepee.*

In spite of these outside activities I worked hard on writing my dissertation, usually going to my stall in the library at nine every morning and writing steadily with pencils until five with only a half-hour break at noon. At five I headed for home, knowing that as I approached the house I would see my wife sitting in the cushioned bay window seat watching for my return. Sometimes she had typed half a chapter of my pencil draft of the dissertation that day, but always there were the makings of a good hot dinner in the kitchen ready to be cooked and served. It made me feel very humble when I realized that regardless of the bitter cold and deep snow, she had walked up the hill to the grocery store to get something for dinner that I liked.

One day each week it was necessary for me to go to Boston for the course with Professor Ford. In addition I read German with Mr. Merk two or three times a week, but I tried to arrange these for the late afternoon and Saturday. Eventually I felt that my German had improved enough to enable me to pass an examination. Once more Professor Ferguson tested my ability to read German. My knowledge of the German language this time was far from being "as deep as a well or as wide as a church door" but it was enough. At least it served to make it possible for Professor Ferguson to report to Dean Haskins that I had a reading knowledge of German.

Meeting with Professor Turner for an hour or so every week to go over a chapter of the dissertation was a pleasure.

Under his direction a finished draft steadily grew but as spring approached it became evident that it would not be possible to complete it in time to take my final oral examination for the doctor's degree before the close of the spring term.

In addition to meeting with Professor Turner for consultation on the dissertation we also had a number of social contacts with him. A few weeks after Christmas Mrs. Turner left Cambridge for Madison, Wisconsin, to be with their daughter Dorothy who was expecting a baby. Knowing that Professor Turner was alone in their cottage, we asked him to dinner one evening assuring him that we would excuse him immediately after we had eaten if he had work to do.

He seemed to enjoy the dinner a great deal and after it was over we adjourned to the living room. He was smoking a cigarette and I my pipe when we heard a hand organ in the street. Rosalie ran to the window as she said: "That surely brings out my childhood instincts." Professor Turner rose quickly and said "Lets go to the Pops Concert." In vain did we assure him that we did not want to take him away from work he might need to do. He declared that he was not busy and wanted to go to Pops Concert. So to Pops Concert we went and sat at a little table and drank lemonade while we listened to that part of the Boston Symphony Orchestra which gave popular concerts. Not long after this Professor Turner took us to dinner at the Brattle Inn. Then we went with him to his cottage where we spent a very pleasant evening. He came to see us at least a couple times for a supper of country sausage and flapjacks which he seemed to enjoy a great deal. On one occasion when my wife had gone to the Curry School to act as sponsor for one of the girls' recitals, I remained at home to entertain a Cheyenne Indian named Griffice, an ordained Presbyterian minister, who was coming to see me. He was an interesting person who had come to Boston with his fifteen year-old daughter to give lectures on the lifeways of the Plains Indians to public school children. He told an amazing story of being captured by Indians when very small. He was freed by

Custer's troopers at the Battle of the Washita and sent to live with a white family in Texas. His mother was a Cheyenne woman and his father a white man, possibly California Joe.[3]

His Indian nature made him dislike life with white people, so after a few weeks he ran away from the white family, stole a good horse, and made his way back to the Indian country where Chief Big Bow of the Kiowa tribe took him into his family and became his foster-father. When 18 or 19 years of age he became a scout and guide for the army. While an army scout he killed a man and was tried for murder and sentenced to death. He escaped from the Fort Sill guardhouse and fled to Canada. There the Salvation Army took him in and sent him to school. Later he was sent to college and to seminary and became pastor of a Presbyterian Church in Buffalo, New York, while still under a death sentence. Eventually he was pardoned by President Theodore Roosevelt. His Indian name was "Tahan," and he had written a book with that title.

When he came in it was raining but it occurred to me that Professor Turner was alone in his cottage and might like to talk with Griffice. When I telephoned him telling him just a little about my guest he came over at once and the three of us smoked and talked. Tahan told us his life story in detail and while it seemed incredible, neither Turner nor I could find anything in it that our knowledge of history made impossible.

On the 19th of April John, Mildred Prescott, two or three other friends, Rosalie, and I went to Lexington and Concord to attend the annual celebration. We saw Paul Revere in colonial costume ride in and enjoyed watching the foot races, broad jumps, funny "sack races," "three legged races," and other contests. We then went on to Concord to see "Orchard House," Emerson's home, "Wayside," the

---

[3] California Joe, army scout assigned to Fort Supply; led Custer's 7th Cavalry to Cheyenne Chief Black Kettle's village in the upper Washita valley, November 27, 1868.

Concord School of Philosophy, where Bronson Alcott taught, Sleepy Hollow Cemetery, and "the rude bridge" with the monument at one end and the statue of the "minute man" at the other. We ate baked beans and brown bread for lunch at a tiny restaurant, saw "the Old Manse" of Hawthorne and the original Concord grapevine. We were all tired when we returned to Cambridge but John insisted that we all stop at his house for supper of flapjacks, crisp bacon, and coffee with me flipping the flapjacks!

That was a memorable day but there were others. On one we went to Salem to see the House of Seven Gables and from there to Marblehead where we had a shore dinner, which the small daughter of a couple with us persistently referred to as a "shore 'nuf dinner." Asked how she liked it she replied that it was "wunderful" but what she liked best were the potato chips and ice cream!

I recall also a lovely evening party at the home of Amy Bridgeman in one of the Newtons. She was an interesting member of the Boston Authors Club and her half dozen or so other guests were mostly members. Miss Bridgeman was a lovely person, and her little book of poems *Song Flame*, we read with much pleasure.

Spring seemed long in coming as is always true in New England, but when it finally arrives one feels it well worth waiting for. No doubt the "long and dreary winter," as Longfellow called it, makes Spring in New England seem unusually attractive but even a visitor from the Deep South reaching New England in May must be impressed by the loveliness of the countryside.

It was my privilege in May to be invited to a bachelor Sunday dinner by Ralph Davol, a well-known writer of pageants who lived near Dighton. There were half a dozen or more other guests including John Kennedy Lacock who took me in his little car. We all stopped to see Dighton Rock and a retired college professor who lived near it. He had given a great deal of time to a study of the inscriptions carved on it and was sure that they were the work of Indians rather than Norsemen as some persons claimed.

Daval's dinner is still vivid in my memory fifty years

later. Beside each plate was a single strawberry the size of a large egg. I had heard of Dighton strawberries but these were the largest I have ever seen. The main course was grilled Kennebec salmon steaks and green peas. Altogether it was a delicious dinner and the fellowship of the group of congenial friends was delightful. The drive down there and back was also very pleasant, for the wild flowers beside the road formed a colorful pattern.

Rosalie and I were forced to decline an invitation to spend a weekend at Hyannis to pick mayflowers. The dissertation had been finished but I yet had checking, polishing, and a bit of rewriting to do. This also prevented our making a trip to Plymouth with John, Mildred Prescott, and a few other friends which was a great disappointment.

Professor Turner had approved the dissertation subject to a few slight changes in the last chapter. These had been made and I walked over to the Turner home to deliver the manuscript the morning we were to start for Plymouth, happy that my work on it was at long last done. To my consternation Turner looked over my handiwork and suggested the revision of half a dozen more pages. If he had only known what a disappointment he was giving both Rosalie and me, I am sure that his kind and generous heart would have prompted him to accept it as it was!

There was nothing for me to do, however, but carry it back and tell Rosalie and telephone John that we could not go with him and his party to Plymouth. Moreover, we could not go later for within the next two or three days we must leave for Oklahoma as I was scheduled to teach in the O. U. summer school. Our packing was quickly finished and the goodbye's said to the many dear friends. Most of them I hoped to see within a little more than a year upon my return for my final examination for the Ph.D. degree. It had been a grand year yet we were glad to be going home. However, I am sure that we both felt we were leaving a bit of our hearts in New England.

Mother, Home and Harvard

It must be confessed that I worried a little about the long journey home. Rosalie was slightly over six months pregnant but she did not show and only Mrs. Merk, Mildred, and John had been told. Of course I did my best to make the trip as easy for her as possible. At any rate she seemed to be quite comfortable and we reached Norman safely to be met at the station by her father and mother.

We spent a couple of days with them while I looked for a furnished house to rent for the two months of summer school. Fortunately for us a young chemistry teacher and his wife were to teach in another university summer school and rented us their neat little bungalow home for two months at forty dollars a month. As they were leaving at once we promptly moved in and I set to work helping enroll students for the summer school.

My classes, made up largely of school teachers, were large, so during June and July I was quite busy. With the close of the summer school, about the first of August, we moved to another furnished house at the corner of Main Street and University Boulevard. Here our son was born August 18, 1920.

For some strange reason, or no reason at all, we were expecting a daughter. We had decided to name her "Dorothy," not for anyone we knew but because "Dorothy Dale" seemed a neat sounding name. Now that we had a lusty seven-pound son his mother, who had always been a bit partial to boys, would consider only "Edward Everett" as a name for him.

Edward Everett Dale, Jr.

There was no hospital in Norman until some years later and, although we had a good doctor and a practical nurse with long experience, Rosalie had quite a rough time in bringing the young offspring into the world. Once she was free of pain, however, she was radiantly happy. We kept the nurse for three weeks, however, and both of us saw her leave with considerable regret, for we felt inadequate to take care of a baby. This feeling was gone in a few days, and in two or three weeks we were quite competent to deal with the newcomer although it must be confessed that my clumsy hands were never able to put a diaper on correctly.

We had missed wedding presents, of course, but our friends in Oklahoma generously sent numerous small gifts to our baby son. This was to be expected but we were surprised and delighted by the reaction of our friends in Boston. Not only did we receive many lovely letters congratulating us on the safe arrival of our son, but the Puddingstone Club sent its greetings in verse by the Secretary.

Hail Hail, little Dale
We're certainly glad you came.
Hallelujah, here's to you
And we surely like your name.
From us unanimous
Welcome to the Puddingstone.
Your daddy, little laddie,
We love as one of our own.
So boy, here's joy
May the world be good to you.
Much gladness, little sadness,
Luck a-plenty, troubles few.
'Nuf sed, Little Ed
To our circle you we bid.
God bless you, we address you
As our Oklahoma Puddingstone Kid.

Members of the Boston Authors Club and Puddingstone Club sent personal greetings in verses to our infant son.

Among them were Nathan Haskell Dole, Carl Dreyfus, and John K. Allen. Also Nixon Waterman wrote this brief toast.

Here's to Edward Everett Dale number two.
It's the Puddingstoners' wish for you
That you grow to be a laddie
Charming as your clever daddy
And as good and sane and sound clear through.

Denis McCarthy wrote as follows:

Here's to Oklahoma Dale
And the missus and the boy
May the fairies never fail
To give them every joy.
But be careful Dale, old chap,
With that new boy come to town
Or you'll let him fall mayhap
"Butter side down."

Although I was deeply touched and much flattered by these verses and letters from friends in Cambridge and Boston, the newcomer who inspired them seemed to have no interest in anything but eating and sleeping and occasionally exercising his lungs, apparently just for the hell of it. Normally, however, he was a good baby and a great joy to us both.

Rosalie was by nature a fundamentalist and nothing could have pleased her more than to be able to feed her small son "in the good old-fashioned way," to quote the words of a familiar hymn of that time. From the first, however, it was clear that this was impossible so a formula was quickly found upon which he grew amazingly fast. Rosalie was a wonderful mother and for a full year she was up every night to warm a bottle and feed the young sprout. Of course, I tried in blundering man-fashion to help care for him but I fear that I was not too successful. Yet when Rosalie was not feeling well I did the cooking.

My classes for the school year, 1920-21, were large and interesting. They included *History of Spain,* another in

Spain in North America, and *The French Revolution and Napoleon,* also *The West, American Colonies,* and *Oklahoma History.* In addition to these there was a *Seminar in American History* and a course in *Historiography.* Obviously, these were my courses for the entire year, about half of them being given each semester although a *Seminar in American History* was given both semesters.

Living in a rented house was distasteful to me. While the forty dollars a month was reasonable rent, neither of us liked the furniture nor the general arrangement of the interior. And we felt that if we owned the place we could in time make it an attractive and comfortable home.

I accordingly called upon the owner of the property, Mr. T. E. Smith, and suggested that we would like to buy the place if we could agree upon the price and terms. He said that he wanted $5,000 for the house and seventy-five foot lot on which it stood. He added that he did not need the money but would expect a down payment large enough to be sure that he would not have to take the property back if the buyer was unable to make payments.

Obviously, I had no money but owned sixty acres of land in Kiowa County free of debt. Mr. Smith agreed to sell me the place, taking my note for $2,000 payable in six years and secured by a mortgage on my little farm. The remaining $3,000 was to be paid in six annual installments of $500 each. For these payments I gave six $500 notes and the Norman property was the collateral. The interest on all notes was 8 percent.

We were glad to be living in our home but the heavy debt meant that I must earn some money in addition to my regular salary. Fortunately, the University Extension Division needed faculty members to give evening courses in Oklahoma City to public school teachers. The classes usually met from 7:00 p.m. to 8:30 p.m. and from 8:30 p.m. to 10:00 p.m. By teaching two extension courses I was able to add a few hundred dollars to our income.

It was sorely needed for when he sold us the house Mr. Smith, of course, removed all his furniture. The situation was not too bad, however. Rosalie's mother was able to contribute a few things which we gratefully received. It was my young wife, however, who, in this emergency, proved herself not only a true helpmate but a real heroine.

Down the street only a short distance from us was a secondhand store which not only had used furniture but junk of all kinds. Rosalie visited this place and bought "for a song" chests of drawers, cabinets, chairs, tables, etc. She had them sent to our place, bought white paint and brushes, and set to work on them. Within a few days she had transformed them into attractive pieces of furniture.

In addition she painted the floors, bought cheap but attractive cloth, made curtains for the windows, and painted the floor of the screened front porch where we spent leisure time in warm weather. Also she painted the floors of the living room, dining room, and bedrooms.

The months slipped by as if on wings. With a "little anchor" in the house we had only limited social life. Yet our friends visited us frequently and we attended Wabunaki and Newcomers' Club fairly often and went to a picture show once in a while. Rosalie's mother and father always seemed glad to "baby sit" but we tried not to impose on them. We occasionally had one of my girl students come in as baby sitter; she usually charged only twenty-five cents an hour.

With the coming of spring we planted flowers, set out some fruit trees, and made a little kitchen garden with onions, radishes, beans, and a few rows of potatoes. We also put the baby in a little wagon and took long walks after supper, sometimes going a mile out in the country.

Summer school began immediately after the June commencement. I was glad to teach in the eight weeks' session, for at its close I planned to return to Harvard to prepare for the final examination for the Ph.D. degree. Since enrollment at Harvard did not begin until around September 20 it would not be possible for me to get the examination until the work was well under way, but Dean Haskins and Professor Turner had both assured me that they would arrange for me to have the examination as soon as possible. Professor Buchanan and President Brooks had both told me that they would get someone to meet my classes at the University the first two weeks and longer if necessary.

Accordingly, as soon as summer school was over, final exams given, the papers read, and grades turned in, I boarded a train for Boston. It was hard to leave Rosalie and our small son, who was beginning to walk.

The trip to Boston seemed restful after several days of final examinations and grading papers. It was also much cooler in Cambridge than in Norman, but most of my friends in Boston were away on vacation. John Kennedy Lacock was at home and so were Mr. and Mrs. Merk but Fred was in London. The Elders and Mrs. Nickerson were somewhere in Maine, the Turners at Hancock Point, and the other Harvard professors at various seaside or mountain resorts or summer cottages.

I had no difficulty in finding a room, for a woman living not far from the Merks was in charge of a big three-story house belonging to a Harvard professor who was in Europe. She agreed to rent one of the rooms to me.

Being all alone in a big house seemed strange and a little ghostly at first. My footfalls echoed from the walls when I walked down the corridor to my room on the second floor. This served to emphasize my loneliness but in a few days this feeling disappeared and I did not mind at all living alone in this big house.

The problem of finding a good place to eat was major. The little restaurants on Massachusetts Avenue near Harvard were fairly good for a single meal but to eat three meals a day, even at the best of them, seemed to me just about impossible.

When I appealed to my landlady she told me of a woman living only a couple of blocks away who gave room and board to three or four young women who were attending summer school at Harvard and supplied meals to at least one man who roomed nearby. I hastened to call on this woman and she seemed pleased to have another boarder for a couple of months. My fellow boarders, as I recall them, were one elderly woman, a very young man, and two teachers in one of the Pittsburgh, Pennsylvania, high schools. These were Helen St. Peter, who taught German, and Grace Knox, an English teacher, both pleasant young women.

With a pleasant room and an excellent place to eat I buckled down to work determined to learn enough in my special field during the next two months not only to pass my examination but to make, if possible, so brilliant a showing that Professor Turner and Dean Haskins would be proud of my knowledge in American history in the nineteenth century. I knew only too well that my showing in the general examination had not been impressive. While Turner was on leave in 1916-17 and not on my general committee, he frankly told me this, but I already knew it.

By trial and error methods I soon learned how many hours a day I could work without becoming so worn out as to be unfit for work the following day. Within a week I had discovered that twelve hours was about my limit. Ordinarily I was up at six, shaved, showered, and ate breakfast. Then came the short walk to the library to read and take notes until lunch. At one p.m. I was back in the library to read and take notes until five. From five to six came a long walk. Usually this was along the Charles River. After dinner, which was at six or a little after, I returned to my room to work until eleven.

This was a hard day's work but occasionally John would ask me to come to his place for a flapjack party or some other friend would have me in for dinner so some weeks I had only five evenings to work and I seldom worked on Sunday.

My examination was to be on American history from 1815 to 1900 but it seemed to me that it would be well to review carefully the period from 1800 to 1815 because some events or movements immediately after 1815 were vitally affected by events in the decade and a half prior to that date. Just how to fix in mind the details of American history during the nineteenth century was a problem but it seemed to me that it might be well to try doing it by presidential administrations.

I accordingly bought a number of cardboard sheets about three feet square. On the first I wrote at the top in large letters Thomas Jefferson—1801-1809. Below it I wrote in letters large enough to be read from the chair at my desk the names of the members of his cabinet and the vice president. Then followed in chronological order the events and movements of his administration including dates and names of those associated with them. All were written large enough to be read from my chair. The sheet was then attached to the wall.

Once I had complete notes this was done for every president, except if one died in office only one sheet was used for him and his successor. This method of preparing for a final doctoral examination may seem childish but for me it was excellent. While reading at my desk or merely sitting there thinking, I needed only to look at the wall to see the details of any presidential administration as yet studied in detail.

Soon after the close of the summer school Harvard professors and students for the 1921-22 academic year began to pour into Cambridge to get settled in rooms and apartments before registration. Among this throng of students was Morris L. Wardell, an old friend and former student of mine at the University of Oklahoma.

I first met Wardell in the summer of 1917 upon my return from my second year at Harvard. He was attending summer school working for a degree in history after graduating from Northwest Normal School at Alva, Oklahoma. I got a room not far from the place where he was boarding and we ate at the same table for a couple of weeks. Toward the close of the summer school he was drafted and served in the Army Air Corps at Kelly Field near San Antonio.

When the war ended Wardell returned to O.U. and completed the work for a bachelor of arts degree. We roomed at the same place on University Boulevard. He had a course or two with me and we became close friends. Soon after completing work for his degree, he married Jessie Barden, a Texas girl who had taught school for a year or two in that state. The young couple settled at Pawhuska, Oklahoma, where Wardell was principal of the high school.

He was eager to take a master's degree in history and at

Edward Everett Dale and colleague, Morris L. Wardell. (Courtesy Western History Collections, University of Oklahoma Library)

my suggestion decided to come to Harvard in September, 1921. I was able to assist the Wardells in getting settled at Cambridge.

By this time a sheet for every presidential administration had been made up and tacked to the walls of my large room but some of the later ones still lacked details. I had talked with Dean Haskins and Professor Turner and they assured me that my final examination would be scheduled at a date as early as possible after classwork had begun. My cardboard sheets for the presidential administrations gave the facts and my notes recorded in greater detail their effects and significance. Also each cardboard sheet had a short list of books and other materials on each administration. The items, like everything else on the sheet, were written large enough to read from the desk and chair near the center of the room.

Only a few days after classwork had begun, Dean Haskins sent me a note stating that my examination would be held in his office at four p.m. October fourth. I happened to meet him in crossing the yard the day before the fourth. He greeted me cordially, spoke of my examination, and told me not to "study any tomorrow."

Whether I could have followed his instruction is a bit doubtful but I had no chance to find out. I was just finishing breakfast the next morning when my landlady called me to the telephone and I heard John's familiar voice saying, "Dale, I've got to drive down to Quincy to get some grapes to make grape juice and I want you to go with me. I'll pick you up at your room in about thirty minutes."

"John," I protested, "My examination is at four o'clock this afternoon and I'd better stick around home. Just suppose we had car trouble and I couldn't get back?"

"Don't worry," said John, "We're not going to have any car trouble, and I'll get you back in time for you to have a long rest before you have to go to your exam. The drive will do you good. I'll be by your place for you in about half an hour." With that he hung up giving me no time for further protests.

John reached the street in front of the big house in which I roomed in thirty minutes just as he had promised and found me waiting for him. It was a lovely day. The sky was a turquoise blue, the air cool and bracing, and the trees presented a glorious picture in red and gold. I forgot my worries and felt deeply grateful to John for taking me with him although it was plain that going for grapes was only an excuse for getting me away from my room and the Library.

The expedition was for me a happy experience. John pointed out the homes of both John Adams and his son, John Quincy Adams. We found a vineyard and John bought two large cartons of grapes. Then he said that he had a friend living in Quincy he wanted me to meet.

The friend proved to be a major in the U.S. Medical Corps. He and his wife and her attractive younger sister greeted us cordially and insisted that we stay for lunch as it was then eleven o'clock. John explained that I had an examination coming at four p.m. but the hostess still urged us to stay, saying that she would serve lunch early and would excuse us immediately after we had eaten.

Although I was beginning to feel a little nervous, John assured me that he would get me back to my room by two p.m. Reassured, I thoroughly enjoyed the luncheon which was served about a quarter to twelve.

True to his promise, John left me at my room a few minutes after 1:30 p.m. We shook hands, he wished me luck and made me promise to have dinner with him at the City Club in Boston after the examination. I assured him that he could expect a telephone call from me within a few minutes after six p.m. when the examination was scheduled to end.

I climbed the stairs to my room, took a shower, laid out my best suit, a clean white shirt, and my favorite tie, for, like Caesar, I was determined to "die with decency." My little alarm clock was set for 3:15 which would give me ample time to dress and walk up to University Hall. I then lay down for a nap and surprisingly went to sleep immediately and slept until awakened by my faithful little alarm clock.

It took only a few minutes to dress and walk leisurely up to University Hall, so I crossed the street to the little restaurant for a cup of coffee and was at University Hall and Dean

Haskins's office about ten minutes to four. The Dean asked me to take a seat in the hall just outside his office where a chair had been placed for me. In a few minutes the other members of the committee including Professors Hart, McIlwain, Merriman, and Turner came in. They all greeted me cordially and Professor Turner, who came last, shook hands, giving me a grip which cheered me considerably.

A minute or two after four I was called in and seated at the end of a long table on which lay the bound copy of my dissertation, "The Range Cattle Industry in Oklahoma." Turner, as chairman, asked the first question. Frankly, I cannot recall a single question asked me. About all I can remember is that for two hours the members of the committee plied me with questions on the history of the United States from 1815 to 1900 and that I snapped back the answers without the slightest hesitation. The details of every presidential administration were so firmly fixed in my mind that dates, names of cabinet members, leaders in war, and in peace, the significance of events, and movements enabled me to answer every question instantly.

The two hours slipped by so fast that it surprised me when the chairman stated that it was six o'clock and unless someone had further questions the examination should be closed. Apparently no one had, so Turner asked me to step outside while the committee conferred. I went out and sat down though I did not feel tired. It seemed to me that I had done all right but whether or not the committee thought so was a problem which grew more acute as the minutes passed and the door remained closed.

At long last it opened and Dean Haskins followed by Turner and the rest of the committee came out. The Dean shook my hand cordially as he said, "Congratulations doctor, we all think that you did remarkably well." Some days before I had given Professor Turner four or five small pictures of myself in cowboy costume. As he came through the door, I saw him putting them back in his wallet and realized that he had been passing them around to other members of the committee while I was almost sweating blood out in the hall thinking that they must be debating whether or not I had passed the examination!

Everyone shook my hand and offered their congratulations on passing the examination in what they declared was excellent fashion. Turner asked me to go home with him and make some flapjacks and he would stir up a welsh rarebit and Professor Hart asked me to have dinner with him at the Harvard Club as I had done once before in my second year at Harvard. Both of these invitations had to be declined as I explained, because of my promise to my old bachelor friend, John Kennedy Lacock, to have dinner with him at the City Club if I was still alive at seven o'clock that evening. So we all said goodnight.

My first thought was to send a telegram to Rosalie, so I hurried across the street to the Western Union Telegraph Office and wrote my message. The young woman at the counter took it and said the charge would be a dollar and ten cents.

I gave her two one dollar bills and she gave me ninety cents in small coins including one quarter and the rest in dimes and nickles. There was a Salvation Army box on the wall at the end of the counter so I stepped over to it and dropped in the quarter, followed by the smaller coins one by one. The young woman looked at me wild-eyed but as the last coin was dropped in I said:

"Don't be alarmed, young lady. I'm neither crazy nor drunk but have just passed my final examination for the Ph.D. degree and am making a little Thanksgiving offering."

When I telephoned John telling him that all was well, he drove down to Harvard Square, picked me up, and took me to the City Club, of which he was a member, and we had an excellent dinner. I was fairly tired so he took me back to my room and I retired early but lay awake for hours, savoring my great happiness. My work at Harvard was done. I had a Ph.D. degree from the oldest, and, to me, the greatest University in the United States and tomorrow would see me on the train going home to my young wife and little son. Could any man wish for more? It is not surprising that my happiness kept me awake for hours.

In spite of my wakeful hours in the early part of the night,

I awoke at the usual time the next morning, which was Sunday. Soon after breakfast I took the subway to South Station to arrange for transportation to Norman. Early in October travel was lighter than in the summer so there was no difficulty in getting a lower berth all the way to Oklahoma City. Packing was a small job but it was hard to be forced to leave my big cardboard sheets on which so much time and effort had been spent but it had to be done.

As I recall it the Merks had asked me to have Sunday dinner with them at 12:30, and John had insisted on taking me to my train which left at 9:00 p.m., but he wanted me to come to his house to make flapjacks, adding that he would have the Wardells down to eat with us and we would have time for at least a brief visit before he took me to the train.

It was a delightful day. Mrs. Merk served a delicious dinner and we had a long and most pleasant visit before the goodbyes were said. I returned to my room and waited until John drove over to pick up my bags and me. The flapjack party was a huge success. The only participants, besides John and myself, were the Wardells and Mildred Prescott. A little after eight I told the Wardells goodbye and John drove me to the station. Here, with some emotion, I said farewell to one of the finest men and closest friends I ever knew. Yet as I mounted the steps of the car and found the way to my Pullman seat, my heart was full of joy. I was going home! Home to my wife who had worked so hard to help me, and to my son. He was still too small to understand, but to her I could say proudly, "Mission Accomplished!"

O.U. and the Department of Agriculture

Class work had been going on for over two weeks when I reached Norman to receive a warm welcome from Rosalie and her parents. My small son seemed to have forgotten me but within an hour or so he accepted me as a good friend and sat on my lap and played with the toys I had brought him.

Dean Buchanan and Professor Gittinger both appeared delighted to see me. They had taken charge of my classes with the help of two of our graduate students for which I was deeply grateful. Dean Buchanan, sometimes called "Uncle Buck," was often in our home. His wife, who had been a semi-invalid for some years, had died and he was quite lonely.

My classes in the school year 1921-22 were quite large because with the close of World War I former servicemen flocked to colleges and universities in large numbers. This continued for the next three or four years making it necessary to add more teachers and to erect more buildings. President Brooks was a builder and in September, 1921, the Women's Building was completed adding one more to the some half a dozen that President Brooks had already built.

In 1922 I received by mail my Ph.D. diploma for although I had been addressed as "doctor" by Dean Haskins at the close of my final doctoral examination, Harvard did not issue diplomas except at the June commencement. The diploma, however, is only formal proof that one had completed all requirements for the doctor's degree. I was listed as having received the Ph.D. in 1922.

While my salary had been increased in 1919, my rank as assistant professor remained the same until 1922 when it was raised to associate professor. In fact, 1922 was a memorable year for me and for many others at O.U. for it was a state election year. The Democrats nominated John C. Walton, commonly called Jack Walton, for governor while the Republicans nominated John Fields. The campaign was a bitter one. Walton toured the state with a jazz band and was elected by a huge majority.

I attended the huge barbecue with which Governor Walton celebrated his inauguration. His friends had shipped in carloads of cattle, sheep, and hogs. Long trenches were dug at the State Fair Grounds and three coffee pots, each holding 8,000 gallons, were constructed and connected by iron pipes with spigots two or three feet apart. Thousands of tin cups were stacked in boxes near-by. It was a great show for it was estimated that over 75,000 people came to partake of the barbecue and to watch dances by a large group of Indians.

Governor Walton immediately set to work to place his personal friends in office. For some reason he apparently did not like President Brooks who was quite popular with the faculty, students, and people of the state.

At any rate Walton began to dismiss members of the Board of Regents and replace them with his friends. When he had dismissed five of the Regents, President Brooks saw clearly that the Governor meant to control the University and other state colleges. He accordingly resigned, effective July 1, 1923, and accepted the Presidency of the University of Missouri which he had declined when it had been offered him several weeks earlier. If President Brooks had not resigned, he could probably have remained indefinitely as President of O.U., but no one could foresee that Governor Walton would be impeached and removed from office in less than a year.

The Board of Regents appointed James S. Buchanan, Dean of the College of Arts and Sciences and head of the Department of History, acting President until a younger man could be found to replace President Brooks. The appointment of Buchanan as acting president pleased me a great deal for he had not only been my major professor in my undergraduate days, but also my close friend for over ten years. Looking back over a period of years, I feel that I owe more to him than to any other man, with the exception of my own father, and possibly Professor Frederick Jackson Turner of Harvard.

At a meeting of the Board of Regents in March, 1922, I had been promoted to the rank of associate professor. Naturally, I was delighted, for it seemed that my rank as assistant professor had lasted far too long. As a matter of fact, it had lasted only six years and two of these had been spent as a student at Harvard.

In 1922, Dean Buchanan had brought Dr. A. K. Christian to the University as an associate professor of history. He was born in the Deep South and held B.A. and M.A. degrees from the University of Texas and a Ph.D. degree from the University of Pennsylvania.

Dean Buchanan had been teaching classes each semester but had no time for this after becoming acting president. He accordingly asked that I be promoted to the rank of Professor of History and at the next meeting of the Board of Regents he came to our house for a short visit. Almost his first words were, "Well Dale, I fixed you up for life. I had you appointed head of the Department of History." If I had served a long time as assistant professor, when promotions came, they came with a bang!

The years of Buchanan's administration, from July 1, 1923, to July 30, 1925, were busy ones for me and all other O.U. faculty. Classes were large and the teaching load was usually sixteen hours for those with no administrative duties. In April, 1924, I attended the annual meeting of the Mississippi Valley Historical Association held, as I recall, in Omaha, Nebraska. The previous year, this association had met at Oklahoma City and Norman, and I had read a paper on the subject, "The Spirit of Sooner Land," which had attracted some attention.

At the 1924 meeting I was approached by Dr. O. C. Stine, who was head of the Historical and Statistical Division in the Bureau of Agricultural Economics of the Department of Agriculture. Dr. Stine said that he had heard my paper the previous year and was impressed with the style of writing. He added that since my doctoral dissertation at Harvard had been on "The Range Cattle Industry in Oklahoma," he wondered if he could interest me in coming to Washington for about six months to write a history of the range cattle industry on the Prairie Plains.

The suggestion appealed to me so I promised to talk the matter over with President Buchanan when I returned to Norman. Stine said that he would discuss the matter with his bureau chief and write to me. President Buchanan seemed pleased that the Department of Agriculture should want a man from O.U. to do this scholarly study for it, so by correspondence an agreement was quickly made.

Dr. Stine wanted me to start work on this project as soon as possible but I was committed to teach in the summer school beginning about the first of June and ending around the first of August. Moreover, I knew that six months was hardly long enough to do the job even though work on my doctoral dissertation had given me a fair knowledge of the literature of ranching in the Trans-Mississippi West.

It was therefore agreed that I should go to Washington as soon as the O.U. summer school ended and spend the month of August locating the material available in the libraries there and in making an outline of the study. This would give me an understanding of the project before returning to O.U. about the first of September for fall semester enrollment.

During the first semester, Dr. Stine's division would carry me on its rolls as a dollar-a-year man. This would make it possible for me to travel and employ secretarial help at the expense of the federal government during the first semester at O.U. Then I planned to take a leave of absence and return to Washington for five months to finish the study. My salary was to be $400 a month which was the same as that at the University and Stine's division would pay my transportation.

Just why I took Rosalie and our young son to Washington with me when we were to be there only a month it is difficult to say. Added to the fact that we disliked being separated, it is probable that as Rosalie had never been to Washington, I thought a month there would be a little vacation for her and give her an opportunity to see the historic spots in and around the capital city.

The eight weeks of summer school slipped by quickly and as soon as my last paper had been graded, we boarded the train for Washington. Young Ed proved to be a good traveler so the trip was a pleasant one. Rosalie was quite thrilled by her first sight of the Capitol and the Washington Monument. We found a pleasant room at the Virginia House just off Thomas Circle, a place where you can get killed by traffic from more directions at once than any I had ever seen. Here I left Rosalie and young Ed while I went down to the Bieber Building where Stine's division was located.

Dr. Stine seemed pleased to see me. He introduced me to his secretary who gave me a list of apartments in easy walking distance. Stine then showed me the office which I was to occupy, and I returned to our room. The next morning we started apartment hunting.

There were plenty of apartments because in August many people were on vacation, but the prices were shocking. Finally we chose one on K Street N. W. which seemed a trifle less dirty than others, and the woman in charge agreed to have the living room rug cleaned.

The month went by quickly. I went over the material in the library of the Department of Agriculture and as far as possible in the Library of Congress. I also looked into the narrative reports of all the Indian agents of the large reservations in the West occupied by Indians for whom the United States government bought millions of pounds of beef on the hoof from so-called "beef contractors." In addition, I made a list of all materials found and prepared a rough outline of the study.

The high rent and prices of food forced us to live simply. We ate fish more often than beef or pork, spent very little on entertainment, and our recreation was largely confined to short trips made on Saturday afternoons and Sundays. As Rosalie had never been in Washington, we visited Mount

Vernon, Arlington Cemetery, the Library of Congress, the White House, Rock Creek Park, and a few other places including the Capitol. Except for the weekends, the days must have proved a little boring for Rosalie and my son, for they were alone all day in a small apartment while I was at work in my office or in the Library of Congress, but she never complained. She and the son took short walks at times and entertained themselves in the apartment as best they could. Before the month was over, we met a number of pleasant people whom we came to know better when we returned to Washington.

The days slipped by quickly and in early September we left Washington for Norman. It was truly good to be back in our own home again. Our small son was especially happy to be in "our brown house," as he called it. We reached Norman in time to help enroll students and my classes were larger than they had been the preceding year.

In addition to teaching, I gave considerable attention to my study of the range cattle industry. As I was head of the history department, my secretary was kept busy with departmental matters. This made it necessary to employ a part-time student stenographer and typist to deal with the correspondence with ranchmen, librarians, superintendents of forests reserves, large Indian reservations, and heads of stockyards or livestock commission companies, and others who dealt with cattle or "cattle paper."

In my files are letters from Murdo MacKenzie of the Matador, John Clay, Swanson Brothers of the S.M.S. Ranch, Robert Kleberg of the King Ranch, Ike Pryor, Charles Goodnight, and many other well-known ranchmen or former ranchmen. These letters were in response to my inquiries as to what they might have in the way of records of ranching operations including photographs, diaries, letters, etc., that would be useful to me in preparing a history of the range cattle industry in the Prairie West since the close of the Civil War. The replies were courteous and often invited me to visit ranches. Murdo MacKenzie was quite insistent that I come to the Matador at any time, adding that he would go with me himself over both the Matador and Los Alamositos ranches.

Obviously it was not possible to make long trips while teaching except during the Thanksgiving and Christmas holidays, but some short ones were made on weekends when the weather permitted. One was to the Wichita Mountain Forest Reserve, now the Wichita Mountain Wildlife Refuge.

We had bought a new Ford car so I drove down there one Friday afternoon in response to an invitation from Superintendent Tom Shanklin of the some 65,000-acre reserve. He met me quite cordially when I entered his office which was some distance from his home. After shaking hands, he stepped to the door and called loudly to his wife, "Put another dipperful of water in the soup. Mr. Dale is here!"

After an excellent dinner we talked until bedtime about the number of cattle on the reserve, the price per head, the need for fire guards and for destroying predatory animals, etc. I saw that Superintendent Shanklin knew very little about ranching in this part of the country at least and that I could help him a great deal. At the Thanksgiving holiday break it was possible for me to go to Wichita, Kansas. Here I met Dave Leahy, an elderly newspaper man, C. Q. Chandler of the First National Bank, which made loans to cattlemen and which much later republished my article on "The Cherokee Strip Live Stock Association." To the original article the bank added the charter and by-laws of the Cherokee Strip Live Stock Association adopted at the meeting held early in March, 1883.

In addition to these two sources of information, I had a long talk with John A. Blair who had been secretary of that Association from the time of its formation in 1883 until 1893 when it ceased to exist. Unfortunately, Mr. Blair was leaving Wichita the day following the interview for the state of Washington to make his home with his daughter.

During the Christmas vacation of about two weeks, I spent over half of the time in Texas, the cradle of the range cattle industry, on the great stretch of prairie plains between the Mississippi River and the Rocky Mountains. In Fort Worth I talked with officials of the Texas and Southwestern Cattle Raisers Association, including E. B. Spiller, Ted Moses, and several field inspectors who looked after the interests of the association by checking trail herds to be sure that they contained no cattle belonging to persons other than their legitimate owners. They also watched for cattle thieves who were all too numerous in some parts of the cow country.

Then they showed me the minutes of the annual meetings of the association for some twenty years after its formation in 1873. I expressed a wish for time to go over these and make notes, and Mr. Moses suggested that I take them home with me and have a copy made.

From Fort Worth, I went to Austin for a couple of days in the University of Texas Library and then on to San Antonio where I took a room at the famous Menger Hotel. It was my first visit to this historic city so I had to take a little time off to visit the Alamo, the collection of the Buckhorn Curio Shop, formerly the Buckhorn Saloon, and one or two other historic places.

Upon calling Ike Pryor for an interview, he promptly invited me to have lunch with him at his civic club. At the luncheon he introduced me to several elderly cattlemen who had retired from active work on the range but still had financial interests in ranching.

After the luncheon we returned to the Menger and talked for over two hours about cattle and the cattle business. Knowing that he had probably driven or sent more cattle north over the Chisholm Trail and Western Trail than any other man, I asked him to tell me something of his experiences in trail driving. He responded that while trail driving was impossible now, it had been in earlier years the most economical means of moving cattle from Texas to ranges in Wyoming, Montana, and the Dakotas.

He added that in the 1880s he could drive a herd of 2,500 steers from Texas to Dakota for less than a dollar a head. Moreover, the animals would gain weight if the herd was properly driven by an experienced foreman and crew of cowboys. It was a rare experience to visit for two hours or more with Colonel Ike Pryor and listen to his discussion of every phase of ranching.

After three days in San Antonio and talking with a

number of old time ranchmen, I returned home because the Christmas vacation was about over.

Once back in Oklahoma, I began to make final preparations to leave for Washington for the second semester. Morris L. Wardell had returned to Oklahoma in June, 1922, with his M. A. degree from Harvard and had accepted a position in the Tulsa High School. However, I had brought him to the University to teach in the summer school and liked his work so much that I asked him to come to the University the second semester of 1924-25 and teach my classes during my absence in Washington. I added that he could rent our house.

Exams began late in January, and on the first of February we started for Washington by train. Friends had given a dinner for us just before we left, which pleased us very much. The journey by train to Washington was a pleasant one.

My work progressed and following the outline which I had made on my first trip to Washington, I wrote the first chapter, "Texas at the Close of the Civil War." It was heavily documented using such manuscripts as D. E. McArthur's "The History of the Cattle Industry in Texas," James Westfall Thompson's manuscript, and volumes titled *Six Year's Residence*, and *Texas, the Australia of America*. Of course, various other sources were used. The chapter also included two maps, one showing the zones of rainfall in America and another the vegetation of the great plains region. By the time I had completed the first chapter, I had become accustomed to the work with the result that the second chapter, "The Central and Northern Plains" of about seventeen pages and four maps, was more easily done.

This brought me to the third chapter called "The Northern Drive," where my work in Texas and the former cow towns of Kansas and my correspondence and interviews with Ike Pryor and other informants began to pay dividends.

I thoroughly enjoyed research in the Library of Congress and in the libraries of the Department of Agriculture, as well as those of the Interior, especially Office of Indian Affairs and General Land Office. The establishment of the National

Archives lay several years in the future, so it was necessary to go to the various departmental files for historical material now in the National Archives Building.

Of course, it was not necessary for me to punch any time clock, as my research often had to be done outside my office and in various libraries, especially the Library of Congress. My writing, however, was all done in my office. I had no personal secretary, but when I needed secretarial assistance for typing letters, pencil drafts of outline chapters, or a chapter written in pencil, I called "the pool" for a secretary. She weighed about 180 pounds and seemed to come down on the typewriter keys with every pound because both the original and several carbon copies were perfect.

Although we had little social life, the Daughters of the American Revolution held their Annual Constitutional Convention in Washington in April which brought us a very welcome house guest from Oklahoma. This was Mrs. Mallie Glenn, who lived across the street from us in Norman. She was probably eighty years of age, but spry as a cricket and a real joy to have with us for a few days.

Rosalie had been named as the "Page" from Oklahoma, which forced me to buy her a white dress and to find a baby sitter for the small son, but after a couple of days of "paging" which consisted largely of carrying notes from one member to another, she was so worn out that she skipped the last session and swore never again to take on such a job.

The Farmhand's Club asked me to one or two of its meetings, which were quite interesting and widened my acquaintance among persons in the Bureau. Also we staged a picnic when Spring came. Nearly all of the staff of the Division came, as well as Nils Olsen, the new chief of the Bureau. None of us knew him well, but he proved to be a charming young man who added much to the pleasure of the outing.

Some weeks before this, Olsen and Stine had called a meeting of half a dozen or more of the older men of the Division to consider forming an agricultural history society which would be nationwide in scope and would publish a journal.

A couple of weeks later a second meeting was called and the Agricultural Historical Society was formed with adoption of a constitution and by-laws and election of officers. Stine was elected secretary, and I was elected president and instructed to prepare a "Presidential Address" to be given at a third meeting about a month later to which all persons in the Department were urged to attend. Other persons in the city interested in agriculture were also invited.

Obviously, I had no time to prepare an address, but decided to read a paper which I had given at a meeting of the Wabunaki Club. It was called "Those Kansas Jayhawkers," a study in sectionalism which dealt with the feud between Texas drovers and Kansas farmers. When herds of Texas cattle reached the southern line of Kansas farmers, fearing the Texas cattle would bring disease to their animals, attempted to halt the cow columns.

The weeks slipped by and by the latter part of May my study of the range cattle industry was completed. Dr. Stine had read each chapter as soon as it was written and seemed pleased with my work, so about June first we said goodbye to friends in Washington, put our possessions in our car, and headed for home. There was need for haste because the preceding December, when the program for the 1925 summer school had been made, I had put myself down as one of the teachers. As commencement came early in June and enrollment in the summer session of eight weeks began immediately afterward, it was important for me to reach home as soon as possible.

Wardell wrote me that he had rented a house near the campus and would move into it a day or two before we reached Norman. Upon my recommendation, President Buchanan had appointed him to the history staff with the rank of assistant professor, an action which the University regents approved.

The drive was uneventful except that we burned out the Model T coupe's brake bands crossing the Appalachian Mountains which delayed us a few hours. Our son had seen me put a rock behind one of the rear wheels so often when we stopped on a grade in the mountains that when we reached

William Bennett Bizzell, President of the University of Oklahoma from 1927 to 1941. (Courtesy Western History Collections, University of Oklahoma Library)

the prairies of Ohio, he would look around for a rock every time we stopped, even if the land was as flat as a table. Also, any time we reached a fork of the road he would earnestly inquire, "Does this road lead back to our brown house?" Only when assured that it did was he content to sit back and view the scenery.

On the fifth day, we reached Norman to find that the Wardells had left "our brown house" spotlessly clean, the lawn freshly mowed, and Rosalie's father and mother were waiting to welcome us with a chicken dinner.

President Buchanan and his wife also came to see us later in the evening. Two days before Christmas he had married Katherine Osterhaus, a woman much younger than himself. They had been on their honeymoon when I was in Fort Worth, Austin, and San Antonio.

His marriage had pleased Rosalie and me very much for after the death of his first wife several years before, he had been a lonely man. An elderly woman came each day to cook the meals for him and his two boys and clean house. Miss Osterhaus had been in some of my classes and I knew her to be a lovely person. We were delighted to see them both and pleased that they should come to see us.

Registration for the summer school was to begin the next day so neither Rosalie nor I had time to rest from the journey. She set to work getting our soiled clothing washed and ironed, and I to enrolling students for the summer session. As for the small son, he could do nothing but almost pathetically enjoy living again in "our brown house" with the big back yard in which were planted fruit trees, flowers, and even a small kitchen garden planted for us by the Wardells.

Dr. Buchanan had also brought us the news that the Regents had at long last found a man for President. They had chosen William Bennett Bizzell, a Texan, forty-nine years of age, who, after graduating from Baylor University at Waco, had taught for some ten years in a Texas public school, four years at a woman's college at Denton, Texas, and, when elected President of O.U., had served for fourteen years as President of Texas Agricultural and Mechanical College at College Station.

Dr. Bizzell was to take over the Presidency on July first so the Buchanans were making plans to move their possessions out of the President's home. The Board of Regents had granted him a year's leave of absence with salary. At the end of his leave, he would return as Vice-President of the University.

We had a large number of teachers in the summer school, many of them older persons who were in the Graduate College working for master's degrees, so as department chairman I was kept quite busy helping each find a subject for a thesis and search for materials on which to base the thesis.

The new President, Dr. Bizzell, and his family arrived in Norman the first of July. Dr. Bizzell was a gentle, kindly man, and a scholar. Yet he was an excellent administrator who could be as firm as the Rock of Gibraltar when necessity demanded it. My relations with him during his entire administration of sixteen years were very close and I never made a request that he did not grant.

September and the opening of school came all too soon. The number of students registered showed a considerable increase in 1925-26 over the preceeding year which kept all of us in the Department of History busy. In addition to teaching and administrative duties, I delivered several speeches during the first semester to various groups in Norman including the Buchanan Club of History Students, Kiwanis Club, and one or two women's clubs.

In December, I accepted an invitation to teach in the University of Texas summer session. Unlike O.U. which had a summer session of only eight weeks, the summer session of Texas University consisted of two six-week terms. We were seldom able to use the entire staff of the History Department in the summer so my teaching in the summer school of Texas left a position open for one of the younger men of the department.

It must be confessed, however, that my delight in accepting this invitation was due to the fact that I sorely needed to earn more money that summer! The job in Washington from a financial standpoint had been little short of disastrous.

The high cost of living there, buying a used car, some unexpected dental bills, and the payment of 8 percent interest on my debts plus $500 on the principal had reduced my bank account close to the vanishing point!

Each six-week term of the summer school at Texas paid about as much as the eight weeks term at O.U. so my earnings in the 1926 summer would be virtually doubled by going to Austin. Moreover, Professor Eugene Barker had written me that we might occupy his home on San Gabriel Street in easy walking distance of the University at a price which seemed ridiculously low compared to what we had paid in Washington.

The second semester at O.U. was no more eventful than the first. Perhaps there were a few more invitations for speeches as at this time the chief feature of every high school and college commencement was an "inspirational" address to the graduating class by some fairly well-known person. I made five or six of these, usually receiving a check for from twenty-five to fifty dollars for expenses. The high school commencements were sometime in May while the O.U. commencement was soon after the first of June.

At the annual meeting of the Mississippi Valley Historical Association, I visited with Professor Eugene Barker of Texas University whose home we were to occupy during the summer session. He told us a little about his two-story house.

He added that there was a large back yard with several peach and fig trees. He had been told that the fruit was very good but could not speak from experience as he and his wife had spent every summer in Colorado since the trees were planted, leaving long before either the figs or peaches were ripe. He hoped that we would enjoy the fruit and added that an old Negro called Uncle Rufus would come every week to mow the lawn and do anything else required to keep the yard in order.

As soon as final examinations were over and the papers graded, we loaded the little car and headed to Texas. We had rented our home to a superintendent of schools from a small Oklahoma town. And Dr. Christian was to serve as head of the History Department as he had done during our months in Washington.

We felt that our journey was too much for a single day so we spent our first night out at a small hotel in an equally small town and reached Dr. Barker's house in Austin about the middle of the next day. We found the Barker home just as he had described it except that he had failed to mention the fact that the back yard was enclosed by a high hedge fence, which gave us complete privacy but also effectively shut out the gulf breeze as well as the breeze from any other direction. In addition, Barker's study, while small, had many attractive books which I promised myself to read.

The University of Texas had not yet started its building program but still utilized a large number of small wooden buildings constructed during World War I. I was given one of these as an office and found it very comfortable. Of course, air conditioning lay far in the future, but the office had large windows and we usually had a cool breeze from the south.

I had met most members of the Department of History at meetings of historical associations and Professor Walter Prescott Webb was my good friend as was J. Frank Dobie of the English Department, who had formerly been head of the English Department of the Oklahoma A. & M. College and had visited us in Norman. These men greeted us cordially.

I was glad to meet another visiting professor, Thomas Maitland Marshall of Washington University in St. Louis, who taught five summers at the University. Another visitor to the campus was John G. Neihardt, a poet who I recall remained for only a week or two to present some lectures.[1]

We had very little social life because the weather was too hot for much entertaining. I played golf quite a bit with three of my students. They were all interesting men and their golfing was about like mine, mediocre, but we enjoyed it and the opportunity it gave us for visiting.

---

[1] John Gniesenau Neihardt, author and poet, lived among the Omaha Indians at their reservation near Bancroft, Nebraska, and wrote lyrics and stories about them. His books include *Black Elk Speaks*, the autobiography of an Indian medicine man as told to Neihardt.

Rosalie enjoyed driving out to Barton Springs, a beautiful spring-fed swimming pool, but the water was so cold that we did not swim very much preferring the more temperate water of Deep Eddy, another pool only a short distance from town. Our small son had no playmates, but when Uncle Rufus came to mow the lawn, the youngster trailed him until the work was finished, asking questions about every other step. Uncle Rufus did not seem to mind too much although I once heard him say, "Boy, you talks too much!"

Young Ed greatly enjoyed picnics, so we often drove out in the country, built a fire, cooked bacon and eggs, or whatever we liked, made coffee, and lingered after we had eaten supper to toast marshmallows and talk or tell stories.

Once Frank Dobie asked me to go with him to a beautiful spot about thirty miles away for a swim in the crystal clear water of a stream and a "cookout." We were going in Frank's elderly Ford and seven or eight miles from town had a flat tire. We put on the spare and continued but five miles farther and had another flat. This meant taking the tire off and patching the tube. If my memory is not at fault we had three flats going and two on the return for a total of five flats. Yet we had a glorious swim, a delicious dinner, and a wonderfully good time.

At the end of the first month, the bills for groceries and the various utilities came in. I had closed my bank account at Norman and bought traveler's checks so I made the rounds of the grocery store, telephone office, and the offices of other kinds and then walked over to the Bursar's office to pick up my pay check for the month. Here to my horror I learned that in summer school checks were given not at the end of the month but at the end of each six weeks term!

I had cashed my last traveler's check in paying the grocery bill so I hurried home to ask Rosalie how much money she had. It was only a little silver, about sixty-five cents, and I had a dollar and seventy-five cents. That was our total cash and it would be two weeks before my check came. Of course, our bills were all paid, but how about a haircut, the beauty shop, gas for the car (the credit card had not yet appeared), and other calls for cash?

Of course, we could call the bank at Norman and borrow any reasonable amount of money. Or my brother George would send me what I needed. Perhaps a bank in Austin would make me a small loan or my watch or gun should be good for a small loan at a pawn shop. We discussed all of these and rejected them. Grimly, we decided that we would live for two weeks without money.

That good angel, however, who had guided us to a lovely little apartment in Cambridge when everyone we asked had said there were none, and in many other instances had looked after us, was nearby. Only a few blocks from where we lived was a small finishing school for girls. It specialized in music, speech, dancing, social graces, and physical training.

On the next day after our decision, the lady at the head of this school called to see me. She said that their school year ended that week on Friday evening. They had planned a little program with the girls giving two or three brief numbers, but she wanted to bring them something fine and inspiring that they would always remember. She wondered if I would consider giving them a thirty- or forty-minute graduation address. She added that she could not make any adequate payment for this but would gladly give me a little token offering of twenty-five dollars to show their appreciation. It was difficult for me to restrain myself enough to say calmly that I would be very glad to speak to her students and that twenty-five dollars, under the circumstances, would be all right.

The time was short to prepare a speech, but I dug out my notes from three or four old commencement speeches and tried to embody the best things from all of them in my notes for this address. Just what title I gave to that particular address I do not remember but when the fateful evening came, we both dressed in our Sunday best and drove over to the little school where we were given a warm welcome by the principal and her staff. The student body consisted of about forty or fifty attractive girls, and when I rose to speak it was with the determination to give them and their teachers the best I had.

It must have been enough because for some forty minutes everyone in my little audience leaned forward to drink in my words. When I sat down, they gave me a standing ovation. There were some tears in the principal's eyes as she came forward to wring my hand and pass me a check for twenty-five dollars. The girls and their teachers all came up to shake hands and tell me that they would never forget my speech. Even Rosalie said later that I seemed inspired and had given the best speech she had ever heard me make.

We now had ample funds to last us to the end of the first term, slightly less than two weeks away. Examinations were then given to those students who had registered for only the first term, but most of mine had enrolled in both terms so there were not many new students in my classes.

The second term was little different from the first. The peaches and figs in the back yard were ripening even before the first term had ended. All of us liked peaches and figs, but there were far more than we could eat so Rosalie found some glass jars in the cupboard and began to make fig and peach preserves and to can some of the peaches. When she inquired of some of the neighbors as to where she could buy some more figs, the word got around and for nearly two weeks my afternoon nap was often broken by some Negro woman with a water bucket full of large purple figs appearing at our doors saying that she had a few figs she'd "like to expose of."

The second term of the summer session closed late in August and, as soon as final examinations were over, the papers graded, and grades sent to the registrar, we packed our car and started for home. In spite of the heat, Rosalie had worked hard to preserve figs and peaches from the back yard. Exactly one-half of the fruit from this source, she had put into Mrs. Barker's glass jars and stored away in her cupboard in order that the Barkers might at last eat some fruit from their own trees. The other half, and all the figs which we had bought, we put into cartons and placed them in the trunk of our car. My wife had worked so hard at preserving and canning that there was scant space left for the rest of our stuff, but by careful planning and utilizing every inch, we at last got everything in the car.

It was so heavily loaded, however, that we did not reach home until in the early afternoon of the third day. It was good to be home. Our tenants had left the house in perfect order. The lawn was smooth and green and the flowers were lovely. Rosalie and I had thoroughly enjoyed the summer at Austin. We had made new friends and renewed contacts with old ones. Yet, we agreed that nearly five months in Washington and three months in Austin in fairly close sequence had kept us away from home too much. I assured her that my travels were over for some years at least.

Little did I realize that within two months I would be leaving our Norman home for the greatest adventure of my life, on a project that would take me to the most remote spots in our country and make it impossible for me to see my home and family, except on two or three brief visits, for an entire year.

Trailing the Indians

We reached home about the first of September to help with enrollment for the first semester of the 1926-1927 school year. As expected, there was a considerable increase in the number of students.

School was barely under way, however, when I received a letter from Washington, D.C. It was written on the letterhead of the Institute for Government Research and was signed by Lewis Meriam.

His letter stated that at the request of the Secretary of the Interior, Herbert Work, the Institute had agreed to make a comprehensive survey of the conditions of the American Indians and the Indian Service. This agreement was contingent upon the Institute staff being able to secure funds for such a survey, and while it would supply the director, he would have to employ professionals from the outside because Institute staff were on other assignments.

Meriam then added that the funds had been secured and that W. F. Willoughby, Director of the Institute, had asked him to head the project. He had agreed to do so and was now seeking to recruit a group of eight or nine persons, each of whom might be considered an expert in one of the fields which must be investigated.

He closed his letter by stating that I had been recommended to him as a person qualified to deal with problems facing American Indians. This had prompted him to write me. The survey was to be completed in a year of which eight or nine months would be spent in the field visiting as many

Indian reservations and schools as possible. If the assignment appealed to me, he would like to interview me and would either come to Oklahoma or pay my expenses to Washington. While the fact that work at the University had already begun made it difficult for me to consider leaving for a year, I replied promptly by air mail that I was interested.

My workshop at that time was a small room in the yard which the former owner of the property had probably used for storage. We had cleaned it up, put in gas and electric lines to supply heat and light, and moved my desk and a couple of chairs out there. It made an excellent office and for some three or fours years all of my "home work" was done there.

On the Sunday morning a few days after replying to Meriam I was working at my desk when Rosalie called me to the telephone. Meriam was at a hotel in Oklahoma City. He said that he left Washington soon after receiving my letter and had reached Oklahoma City about 10:00 p.m. Saturday evening. He apologized for calling me on Sunday and said that if I preferred not to see him until Monday, he would wait to come to Norman then.

I assured him that I would be glad to see him as soon as possible and urged that he take the next interurban for Norman and have Sunday dinner with us, adding that I would meet him at the station, only a short distance from our house.

I liked Meriam at first sight. He was probably in his middle forties of medium height and of a quiet and unassuming manner. After I had introduced him to Rosalie and our son, we went to my study for it was still over an hour until dinner time. He told me a little about himself and the projected survey of the condition of the American Indians. He said that he was born in Salem, Massachusetts, had a bachelor's and master's degree from Harvard, and his special fields had been statistics and government administration. He added that his knowledge of Indians was very slight and that as director of the survey he was not taking any special field for himself.

He then listed the fields in which he was seeking a specialist. It was obvious that the Commission must have a physician to study health conditions of the Indians, including hospitals, field doctors, and nurses. Another "must" was an experienced educator to study and report on the government boarding and day Indian schools, schools operated by missionaries, and public schools in which Indian pupils were enrolled.

In addition there must be a lawyer to study legal problems of the Indians, a woman, preferrably trained in sociology and social work, to study the problems of women and children, a sociologist with knowledge of statistics, an agricultural specialist to work with the agency or school farmer, and an educated Indian who could help the members of the Commission understand Indian customs and manners. Finally, he wanted a person to deal with economic conditions among Indians, their sources of income, and what could be done to help them earn more money and thereby improve their standard of living. This was the phase of the Commission's work in which he thought I could be of greatest value, but no doubt I could also contribute to the study of education and agriculture.

About 3:00 p.m. he left for Oklahoma City after saying goodbye to Rosalie and thanking her for an excellent dinner. I walked with him to the interurban station and he said that he was eager to get his staff chosen and promised to wire or write me an air mail letter within a day or two after he reached Washington.

It must be confessed that the thought of traveling all over the West visiting Indian reservations and schools was most attractive. It would be of enormous educational value and at the same time an interesting experience. Also the income might help solve our financial problems. True, it would take me away from home and family, but Rosalie agreed if the position should be offered she would cheerfully accept my decision.

Meriam was as good as his word. Five days after our Norman visit I received a telegram from him saying that my appointment as a member of his Indian survey staff had been approved by Dr. Willoughby at a salary of $7,500 a year plus expenses. He added that he earnestly hoped to have my acceptance by telegraph and a statement as to how soon I could reach Washington.

Seven thousand five hundred dollars a year was approximately twice my salary at O.U., at that time $3,800 a year. Of course, this salary at O.U. was for only nine months and that offered was apparently for twelve months, but even so, "all expenses" would mean that my income as a member of the Indian Survey Commission would be more than twice as much as it would be by remaining at O.U. in my present position.

Rosalie and I talked it over and agreed that it could not be refused so I called upon President Bizzell and told him of the offer which would require a year's leave of absence. Dr. Bizzell was a sociologist and apparently knew more about the Institute than I. At any rate, his reaction was immediate. "Dr. Dale," he said earnestly, "I think it is a great compliment to this University that you have been asked to share in the work of such an important commission. Moreover, if you feel financially unable to accept it, the University will make it possible for you to accept this position."

Breaking away from my work at O.U. was surprisingly easy. I wired Meriam my acceptance and told him that I would start for Washington within twenty-four hours. Dr. Buchanan was back after a year's leave and agreed to take over the work of acting head of the history department for a year. Wardell, who had completed Turner's History of the West, took my class in that field, and a mature graduate student was given a class or two of freshmen history.

It was hard to leave Rosalie and Ed, but the grandparents lived only a block away and my son was now a husky lad of six about ready for school. If I could have forseen that before the winter was over he would have most of the diseases that childish flesh is heir to, no doubt my worries would have made me unfit for work.

When I reached Washington Meriam was still busy recruiting his staff. So far he had only Dr. Fayette A. McKenzie at work in Washington although he had recruited several others.

I found McKenzie at work in the census files, but he said that what he was doing was a one-man job and he needed no help so I returned to Meriam's office and asked if he could give me an approximate itinerary of our field work until Christmas. He had made out a plan of the reservations and schools we were to visit before we returned home for a Christmas vacation and he gave me a copy of it.

I looked it over and saw that we were to start at Haskell Institute, near Lawrence, Kansas, and from there to Mayetta, near Topeka, Kansas, to visit the Potawatomi Indian reservation. We would then go south to Wichita, Kansas, to visit the little school established by Henry Roe Cloud who had been chosen as a member of the staff. Cloud was a full blood Winnebago, and his wife was a half-blood Chippewa whose father was of German ancestry. From there we were to visit the University of Oklahoma and the Cheyenne and the Arapaho Agency at Concho and the Kiowa-Comanche and Wichita-Caddo Agency at Anadarko. We would then travel to reservations in Arizona and New Mexico.

With this information I went to the Bureau of Indian Affairs library. In my work in Washington for the Department of Agriculture I had used the reports of the Commissioner of Indian Affairs which included the annual reports of the various Indian agents of the United States. Each Indian superintendent or agent, as he was often called, sent in an annual narrative report. I had worked with these reports while with the Department of Agriculture because the Indian reservations were often leased to cattlemen and also the United States purchased beef cattle to feed Indians on most of the western reservations. As a result, I was already fairly familiar with information which would be valuable when we reached any reservation.

It seemed to me that we should not visit any Indian reservation or large independent school without first getting as much information as possible before leaving Washington. There were good reasons for this. In the first place, we had to know something of the size of the reservation, who was superintendent, whether there was one or more boarding schools or day schools there, the approximate number of Indians and, of course, the type of reservation or school.

While I was engaged in this work, Meriam was completing the commission. To study legal problems he chose Ray A. Brown, a member of the law faculty of the University of Wisconsin. Dr. Herbert R. Edwards, one of the field secretaries of the American Tuberculosis Association, was secured as physician. Dr. W. Carson Ryan, Jr., head of the Education Department of Swarthmore College, was appointed to study Indian schools. The most difficult position to fill, from Meriam's standpoint at least, was a woman to study Indian women and children. She could go, of course, where the men could not, and the Indian women would likely feel freer to talk with her than a man. The choice which he made was Mary Louise Mark, Professor of Sociology at Ohio State University. Miss Mark, or Mary Louise as we always called her, was an excellent traveler who put up with the hardships and difficulties of life on the road and was consistently cheerful and agreeable. Meriam chose Dr. William J. Spillman, with the Department of Agriculture, as the Commission's expert on agriculture. Dr. Spillman was the oldest member of the staff and in poor health, so it was agreed that his wife might accompany the expedition for at least part of the time to look after him.

Dr. Fayette Avery McKenzie had already been appointed. He was Professor of Sociology at Juniata College in Huntington, Pennsylvania, and upon his recommendation, the registrar of that college, Robert Stambaugh, was chosen as field secretary. Some weeks later a social worker, Miss Emma Duke, was chosen to deal with what we called "migrated Indians," meaning those who had left the reservations and were living in cities such as Los Angeles, San Francisco, New York, and Chicago. She did not travel with us, and most of us knew her only slightly.[1]

With one or two exceptions this was a group of quite

---

[1] This reference to "migrated Indian" is an interesting antecedent to the government's policy of "relocation" during the 1950s and 1960s, in which federal agents sought to colonize Indian families from their reservations to the cities.

remarkable persons. The only Commission member who had any contact with Indians, except myself and Henry Roe Cloud, was McKenzie who had taught for a year or so in an Indian school on the Wind River Reservation in Wyoming when he was quite young. He later became president of Fisk University, a Negro university in Nashville, Tennessee. Some of Meriam's advisors thought that this experience with people of a different race and color would be helpful. However, both Meriam and I agreed that it probably would do more harm than good because of the great difference between Indians and Negroes.

During the three weeks in Washington, I was busy recording facts as to the agencies and large non-reservation schools which we expected to visit before Christmas. Yet, there was time for breaks in this work. One was to accept the invitation to attend a meeting of the Board of Indian Commissioners. This was a body of ten persons created by Congress in 1869 appointed by the President to serve without pay, except travel expenses, had no jurisdiction over Indians, but served in an advisory capacity to the Commissioner of Indian Affairs. The Board maintained a secretary and an office in Washington. The holder of this position was Malcolm McDowell. We found the meeting of this Board interesting, and from time to time we visited with Secretary McDowell at his office.

I also came to know John D. Rockefeller Jr.'s personal representative, Kenneth Chorley, who was in charge of one phase of Rockefeller's grants.

About a week before we left Washington for the West, Meriam asked how I planned to dress in the field. I replied that I would wear a flannel shirt, riding breeches, and leather puttees because I knew that we would be around Indian camps and homes and there were always a great many dogs, and I had no intention of letting one take a lunch out of my leg. The chief agreed with me and, in fact, most of the other members of our group followed suit. Only McKenzie refused to make any concession to the fact that we would be traveling and stuck to a blue serge suit with white shirt and collar throughout our travels. Stambaugh, who was McKenzie's prote'ge', also made little change in his clothing.

I had reached Washington on October 17, and on Friday, November 12, we left Washington at three p.m. on the Baltimore and Ohio Railroad bound for Lawrence, Kansas. There were only four of us in Washington at that time— Meriam, Edwards, Stambaugh, and myself. Each of us had a lower berth and enough baggage it seemed to me to sink a good sized ship. McKenzie, for some reason, had gone to Chicago, probably to visit a relative. We reached Chicago at nine o'clock, where we were joined by McKenzie and our law representative, Ray Brown. From Chicago we went to Lawrence by way of Kansas City and took rooms at the Hotel Eldridge.

We were tired and went to bed immediately, but I was up at seven the next morning. Soon after breakfast Meriam called Superintendent Clyde M. Blair of the Haskell Indian School, situated two miles south of Lawrence. Blair came in at once and insisted that we stay at the school as he had ample room for us.

Blair was a tall, handsome man, and Mrs. Blair and their twelve year-old daughter, Jane, gave us a very kind welcome and turned over the top floor of their home to us.

Haskell had a beautiful campus and an enrollment of over 1,000 students coming from reservations all over the United States. Its plant was attractive, although most of the buildings were forty years old, and required expensive maintenance. We were there until Friday afternoon and enjoyed our stay.

On the whole Haskell was rated as the best Indian school in the government system. All large non-reservation schools followed its pattern of operation.

Henry Roe Cloud joined us at Haskell early Sunday morning. He had been in Washington. We spent all day Monday and Tuesday until noon visiting the farm, dairy, hospital, and the various shops where the boys worked, as well as the sewing room, laundry, kitchen, and dining room, and had eaten two meals with the students and found the food well prepared.

Next, we traveled to the Potawatomi Superintendency, located about twenty miles north of Topeka. I had made notes on this agency while in Washington, so we did not think it would take long to inspect it.

In the agreement between the Institute for Government Research and the Commissioner of Indian Affairs, it had been specified that the various agencies should open their files to us and that the superintendent should arrange to meet us at the nearest railroad or bus station, to take us to the reservation, and to furnish us with transportation to visit any and all parts of the reservation which we wished to see. He should also provide us with sleeping quarters when hotels or tourist courts were not available near the big western reservations in Arizona, New Mexico, and other Western states. We would usually eat at the employees' mess if meals were not available at a restaurant or hotel.

The employees' mess was something like a dinner club where the unmarried and in some cases married staff ate. The food of both employees and students at Haskell had proved to be excellent, but we found that this was far from true on many reservations, especially students' food.

Superintendent Blair offered to take us to Topeka, which was thirty or forty miles from Lawrence, so we traveled in two agency cars with a small pickup truck transporting our baggage. And upon reaching Topeka, Blair insisted on taking us on to the Potawatomi Agency at Mayetta, about twenty miles north of Topeka. When we reached Mayetta we met Superintendent A. R. Snyder, but because it was too late to tour the reservation, we agreed to begin the next morning. The agency had no sleeping quarters for us so we proceeded to Holton, about ten miles north of the agency, where we took rooms at the City Hotel. When the others arrived, Superintendent Snyder was with them. He described the condition of the Potawatomis and other Indians under his jurisdiction.

We left this agency with a feeling of disappointment for while a few Indians were fairly prosperous, most were poor, and children did not attend school regularly, although those who did attend seemed to be bright and eager to learn.

We remained at the Potawatomi Agency through Friday in order to visit as many homes as possible, then early

Saturday morning agency employees drove us to Topeka. From there we were to travel by train to Wichita to visit Cloud's school which he had named the Institute for the North American Indians. It had an enrollment of forty students.

Thereupon we proceeded on the Santa Fe train to Norman and on arrival I stayed at home while the other commission members put up at the local hotel. The next morning at ten o'clock Dr. Bizzell called an assembly for us at which all students of the Indian Club of the University attended, and I introduced the members of the Commission. Meriam made a short talk, and Cloud made a somewhat longer talk. He told of his life in an Indian school where he remained for two years, and he explained how lonely he was. He recalled the experiences of his trip to school. He had been warned by his people not to speak to any white person, but there were four or five Japanese on the train and he thought they were Indians so he shook hands very warmly with each of them. He added that he had put his shoes down beside his berth and a porter had given them a nice shine, so in the morning Cloud did not recognize his own shoes. He complained to the porter that these were not his at all, but finally became convinced that they were. Cloud said that when his father came to take him home, he had forgotten the Winnebago language and could not talk to his own father until after two or three days of practice.

We spent the day talking with members of the Indian Club, explaining to them what we were doing, and Rosalie had us to dinner that evening. We left early next morning for the Cheyenne and Arapaho Agency at Concho, Oklahoma. This reservation had been liquidated by allotment and opened to settlement in 1892, but the Bureau of Indian Affairs maintained a boarding school which we inspected. Also we visited several Indian homes. We planned to resume the Cheyenne-Arapaho inspection later. However, we had been urged by the Commissioner of Indian Affairs, McDowell, and other officials to spend considerable time with the Superintendent of the Kiowa Agency in Anadarko. This agency had jurisdiction over the Kiowas, Comanches, and the Wichita-Caddo tribes. These reservations had been opened to settlement in 1901 and officials of the Indian office seemed proud of the progress the Indians were making under the direction of Superintendent John Buntin.

I had lived for many years near the border of this reservation, had taken part in the opening, and my brother George and I owned 160 acres of land on what had been the Kiowa-Comanche reservation. There were not many Indians, however, who lived on the western part of this former reservation, and I knew very little about the former Wichita-Caddo reservation, which lay north of the Washita River and had been occupied by the Wichita and Caddo tribes together with a few Delawares and one or two families of the nearly extinct Tawakoni tribe. The agency was situated at Anadarko and maintained a reservation boarding school near there as well as one at Fort Sill. In addition the Catholic Church operated St. Patrick's School near Anadarko. It had been subsidized by grants from the Bureau of Indian Affairs. This superintendency in 1925 served over 5,000 Indians.

We completed our work at the Kiowa-Comanche Agency by November 27, and Buntin and another member of his staff drove us to Weatherford where we boarded the Rock Island for El Paso, Texas. From there we would take a train to Sacaton on the San Carlos Reservation. When we reached El Paso, Dr. Edwards's mother-in-law, a resident of that town, invited us to tea. We were dressed in field garb, and Dr. Edwards telephoned his mother-in-law saying that we would be glad to accept on condition that we not be required to dress for tea. Mrs. Edwards urged us to come "as we are," as it would be difficult to change and then change back when our train left that evening for San Carlos around 7:30 p.m. We were free until 5:00 p.m. so we crossed over to Juarez to get a little glimpse of Old Mexico. It was Sunday and bullfight day. McKenzie and Stambaugh attended the spectacle while the other commission members explored the city. At that time Juarez had both a positive and negative atmosphere. In certain sections it was dirty and sordid, in others every evidence of wealth and culture.

After wandering about the city for two hours and buying souvenirs, we crossed back to the American side, and a little later McKenzie and Stambaugh joined us. We made our way by taxi to the home of Dr. Edwards's mother-in-law. Her husband was pastor of the large and imposing Episcopal Church. Mrs. Edwards was an attractive woman, perhaps forty-five years of age, who looked the part of the wife of a minister or a D.A.R. regent. After grace our hostess leaned over and said in a whisper to Henry Roe Cloud, "That little fork is for your cocktail." Cloud immediately whispered back as he picked up the salad fork, "And what is this fork for?" "That is your salad fork," she whispered. Cloud then displaced his napkins and whispered, "And what is this piece of cloth for?" "That is your napkin," replied our hostess. Dr. Edwards, who knew that Cloud held a bachelor's degree and a master's degree from Yale and was an ordained Presbyterian minister, was turning all colors of the rainbow in trying to catch our hostess' attention, but in vain. Personally, I felt that Cloud was a bit cruel. His hostess, on the other hand, although well meaning, should not have assumed that Henry was an illiterate Indian. I have often wondered what our hostess felt like when her son-in-law revealed to her that Cloud was a highly educated man who knew as much of table manners as she or her husband.

At about 7:30 we boarded the train for the San Carlos Agency in Arizona and arrived at the railway station on the reservation at 7:00 a.m. the next morning. The station was situated about a mile north of Rice Indian School; the principal of the school and one of his helpers met us with two cars at the station. We were lodged in the employees' building in comfortable rooms.

We remained at San Carlos Reservation from November 28 to December 4. On the second day we called a general council to meet on the desert near the agency. A table was brought out and fifty or more Indians sat on the ground in a semicircle, while our party sat behind the table. Meriam opened the proceedings at 2:00 p.m. with a statement making it clear that we were not government employees but a group

298

entirely independent of the Bureau of Indian Affairs. When Meriam sat down, an Indian arose, walked up, and shook hands with all of us, and then stepped back and made a short speech. He then returned to his place, and council members reflected on his words. A second Indian came up, shook hands with all of us, and made a short speech. The Indians spoke in Apache and two interpreters rendered their orations in English. This continued hour after hour. Each commissioner wrote notes on each speaker's comments.

The following day Superintendent Kitch and I. E. Chippman prepared to go to Ash Flat some forty miles back in the mountains. This was a valley where the tribal herd of around 2,000 head of cattle was located. We immediately asked to go with them, but Kitch explained that it would be a very hard trip for us. We insisted, however, and the next morning very early we started in two cars, moving slowly and dangerously over dim mountain trails. Kitch had brought a shotgun and he bagged ten blue quail. Eventually we reached Ash Flat, a long valley high up in the mountains, perhaps ten miles in length and six or seven miles wide, where there was no cactus but excellent grass.

We stopped at the camp where the white cowhand lived in a rather crude shanty, but he was not there. He had an Indian helper who lived in a wickiup a short distance away with his wife and little girl, but they could speak no English. So we went in, built a fire in the cowhand's little wood stove, cut some steaks from a quarter of beef hanging in a shed, and I proceeded to fry the quail and beefsteak and make a couple of big pans of biscuits while Cloud made a pot of coffee. We sat down to the most excellent meal and before we finished, the cowhand came in to eat with us.

We drove down to see the cattle. There was a steel tank and a pool of water brought down from a spring in the mountains. The cattle seemed to be doing very well. After making notes on the tribal herd, we returned to Rice.

We left Rice Indian School on December 3 for Globe, Arizona, where we spent the night and continued by bus to Phoenix to visit the Nonreservation Indian School, arriving in the late afternoon of December 4. By this time we were beginning to feel like veteran troopers.

We were met at the bus station in Phoenix by agency staff and spent the first night at a hotel. The following day, we transferred to the employees' building at the school.

Our next stop was the Pima Agency, located at Sacaton, some thirty miles southwest of Phoenix. I did not see too much of the Pima Reservation because Meriam asked me if I would go to Papago, seventy miles southwest of Tucson on an independent mission. By this time, we had talked about Indians and Indian problems so much that each of us knew fairly well what the person in every branch represented on the Commission would check. I readily agreed and an agency employee drove me over to Florence where I took a bus for Tucson.

It was late when I reached Tucson so I went to bed immediately, for I had to catch a bus at Phoenix about eight o'clock the next morning. I reached Phoenix fairly early in the afternoon, and found my party waiting at the hotel. They had spent their time at Pima, which was one of the oldest and most important agencies in the West, set aside for the Pimas in February, 1859.

From Phoenix we were able to get a train for Laguna, New Mexico, on December 11 about 6:10 in the evening; Stambaugh had made Pullman reservations for all of us. We reached Laguna, one of the largest of the Pueblos, about 11:30 the next day. We stopped at the Hotel Acoma and after lunch rented cars to take us out to Acoma, about fifteen miles south of Laguna, often called the "Sky City," because it stands on top of a lofty rock some 300 to 400 feet high. We climbed up on the north side part way by steps cut in the side of the cliff and in one place by a ladder. There is a very large church on top with huge beams fifteen or twenty feet long supporting the roof. These had been carried on the backs of men for ten or twelve miles. Here we met the Catholic father who had charge of this huge church. Behind the church was a little garden made from soil carried up the steep trail by men or on the backs of donkeys.

After three days at Laguna, we moved to Isleta, some ten

or fifteen miles south of Albuquerque. The name would suggest an island just as Laguna would suggest a lake, but there is no island any more at Isleta than there is a lake or lagoon at Laguna. Isleta had at the time we visited it about 1,000 people living on a reservation of over 175,000 acres, though only 3,000 acres were under irrigation.

From Isleta we moved up to Albuquerque, where the agency for the Southern Superintendency is located. We spent several days there, and some of us visited the pueblos. From Albuquerque we continued to Santa Fe, situated near nine pueblos. The superintendent in 1927 was Colonel C. J. Crandall, who had been head of this superintendency since April, 1923; he had previously been in charge of all the pueblos for ten or eleven years.

Our entire party visited Taos. As we were getting ready to leave the La Fonda Hotel for Taos, the last and perhaps best-known Pueblo, it was only about three days until Christmas. Dr. McKenzie had bought a sheep-lined vest in Albuquerque, which did not go too well with his blue suit, but of which he was very proud. There were a number of persons in the lobby, and when McKenzie found that he was to ride with Mr. Faris in a closed car, he meant to hand his sheep-lined vest to Stambaugh to take care of it. Later when he asked Stambaugh for it, Stambaugh said he did not have it and McKenzie had to admit that he had handed it to some perfect stranger with the remark, "You take this. I won't need it. I am going in a closed car." Evidently, the stranger thought that Christmas was coming early, for that was the last time we ever saw that sheep-lined vest.

The drive up the Rio Grande Canyon to Taos was over an unpaved road, and there were two or three inches of snow on the ground. It looked dangerous to me, but we made it through and spent one night in Taos at a beautiful hotel.

Taos Pueblo is about three miles northwest of the town. The Indians did a certain amount of farming but discovered that it was easier to pose for artists at so much an hour than it was to raise corn and chilis.

The two large "apartment houses" making up the pueblo were five stories high with a little porch before each entrance to the apartment house. As we drove away from the village after holding a fairly long council, we looked back to find that the children had kindled little fires on the porches in order that Santa Claus might be sure to know that they were expecting him and to be sure to come. Stambaugh remarked to me as he saw the brilliant lights that, "Now I have a subject for my next Sunday School lesson."

It was the 22nd of December and from Santa Fe a bus took us to the railway station. We boarded the train which would get all of us home for a week or more to spend with our families.

More Indian Trails

I reached Norman and home the day before Christmas. The trip had been pleasant and I had learned a great deal. To me, Santa Fe seemed the most interesting city in the United States and I still think so. We had visited reservations and non-reservation schools, and I felt that everything had been satisfactory in this first lap of what was to be a long journey. It was wonderful, however, to be at home and to see Rosalie and my son again and old friends, though a good many of them were out of town over Christmas.

The vacation was all too short. December 28 I boarded the train for Washington. While there was little time at home, I realized that we had even less time left to prepare for the next trip, and it promised to be a long and fairly difficult one. I knew that we had a long way to go to visit all the Indian reservations and non-reservation schools, and clearly we would have to divide because we could not visit the many remaining agencies and nonreservation schools as an entire commission.

I worked all day Sunday in my office at 26 Jackson Place, which was the headquarters for the Institute for Government Research. Meriam gave me an itinerary, and I set to work making a brief sketch of the many agencies and schools to be visited in the next three months. It seemed wise to keep a diary so I purchased a little book in which to record the events of every day until the first of April.

On Friday, January 15, the Commission members, together with Thomas Jesse Jones, head of Phelps-Stokes Foundation, and Kenneth Chorley, John D. Rockefeller's

Photographs taken by Edward Everett Dale illustrating the itinerary of the Meriam Survey. (Courtesy Western History Collections, University of Oklahoma Library)

(top left) A Cheyenne woman. (top center) Pima Indian homes near Casa Blanca, Arizona. (bottom left) Santa Clara Pueblo. (center) Miss Mark at Santo Domingo Pueblo. (bottom right) Lewis Meriam (in hat) at Santo Domingo Pueblo. (Courtesy Western History Collections, University of Oklahoma Library)

personal agent, had lunch with the Board of Indian Commissioners. We lingered after lunch for a couple of hours talking over Indian problems, and I felt that it was not only very interesting but a very worthwhile meeting.

Two days later Meriam and I boarded the train for Chicago, where we picked up some of the others. Miss Emma Duke, the professional social worker, visited us in Washington. She did not travel with us, but did her work independently in various cities. After a short layover in Chicago, we continued to Pocatello, Idaho, which is about twelve miles south of the Fort Hall Agency for the Shoshone and Bannock Reservation. Here we registered at the Pocatello Hotel and Meriam telephoned Agent Stephen Janus, who came down to see us about ten o'clock. After lunch we caught a bus for Fort Hall and continued on to Blackfoot to visit with agency staff. The following day, Thursday, January 20, we caught the bus for Fort Hall.

On the second day of our stay Meriam, Dr. Edwards, and I decided to visit the community on Bannock Creek, some forty miles from the agency. The superintendent had told us that Garfield Pocatello, an elderly Indian, lived there and could tell us more than any other Indian on the reservation. The other members of the group, Miss Mark, Dr. McKenzie, and Stambaugh decided to stay at the agency office studying files and reports.

Our driver, who was also our interpreter, was a full blood who had gone to school a good deal and spoke perfect English. It was considerably lower than twenty degrees below zero, so I had put on my warmest clothes and the others apparently did the same. The car was an open touring car with side curtains, and we really did not feel the cold very much.

A while after noon the driver stopped the car at an Indian house where he said we were to have dinner. The owner and his wife welcomed us and we sat down to a meal consisting of beans boiled with salt pork, fried bread, and coffee.

We drove on after dinner about five miles to Garfield Pocatello's home, but we ran into a fence and had to walk about three-fourths of a mile through deep snow. We were all wearing four-buckle arctic overshoes with heavy woolen socks, so we did not feel the cold very much. When we came to a large tent, we saw an elderly Indian outside chopping wood. He greeted us cordially enough, and then the interpreter told him a little about who we were. Meriam said, "Interpreter, tell Mr. Pocatello that we would like to talk with him at a good council, and ask him to tell us about conditions and what we might be able to do to improve them." The interpreter spoke to him in a Bannock tongue, and the old Indian replied through the interpreter, "He says do you mean that you want to sit down out here in the snow and hold council?" Meriam replied, "Interpreter, tell him that we have come a long way to see him. If he wants to sit down out here in the snow and hold council, we will be glad to do that. If he would rather invite us into his home where it is a little warmer, we would be glad to do that. Tell him it is for him to say." The interpreter translated it, and the old man nodded and went inside. Apparently, he stopped a gambling game of the women, his wife and her sister, the interpreter said, for I saw the gambling sticks in a basket that had been pushed aside.

There was a fire in the middle of the tent and a very old man lying on a blanket beside it. He looked up, nodded to us, and said, "Washington, politician." He held out his hand with the index finger, moving it in a crooked line, the sign of the snake. I said, "Oh no sir. Interpreter, tell him we are not politicians and we are not from Washington." The old man nodded and seemed to feel a little bit better about our visit.

Our next stop would be Pendleton, Oregon. We decided to stay one more day at Pocatello since it seemed certain that because of the weather we would not be able to reach the Umatilla Reservation near Pendleton. We spent the day visiting with the family of the superintendent. He showed us his pictures, carvings, and Indian work, and we attended a session of the Tribal Court of Indian Offenses. Then we returned to the hotel, packed up our gear, and got ready to leave early the next morning for Pendleton.

We registered at the Pendleton Hotel, and spent all day visiting several places including the Pendleton Woolen

Mills. Here we were introduced to the superintendent of the mills, and spent most of the morning buying blankets. I bought three, two plain ones, and one which they called the Harding Robe because the pattern had been designed especially for President Warren G. Harding when he visited there. Later we inspected a public school near the agency which had two teachers and several Indian children. After dinner we had a final conference with the superintendent.

We left Pendleton on Wednesday, January 26, and after a long and tiresome journey by train and motor car reached Buena, a few miles from the agency at Toppenish. Superintendent Estep, and three other employees met us at the train to take us out to the agency.

We were up at 6:30 the next morning, having planned to go to White Swan, a small village, and from there to Fort Simcoe. There was a school at White Swan with about eighty Indian students. There was also a mission school headed by a Mr. Francis. We then continued to Fort Simcoe, and after looking over the old fort, returned to Toppenish.

At the council with the Yakima Indians it was disclosed that a large part of the reservation had been allotted and the Indians had water for irrigation. One man who was wearing a business suit and looked like he was not more than a half-blood, though he spoke in the Yakima language for the sake of those Indians who did not know English, attracted my attention. When the council broke up, I was shaking hands with various Indians and walked up to this man to shake hands with him. I said, "Mr. Olney, you are not a full blood of course." "No," he replied. "I'm a half-blood. My mother was a full blood Yakima woman. My father was a white man. You may have heard of my father's brother. He was Richard Olney." Richard Olney had been Grover Cleveland's Secretary of State, and this man was his nephew!

Meriam and I had talked over the Yakima assignment and he had decided that the time had come when we would have to divide our forces. There were a number of small reservations under one agency near the coast, and he directed that I should take McKenzie with me and go to

Spokane where I would meet Dr. Edwards, who had already left to visit a large sanitarium for Indians at Fort Lapwai. We would travel north to visit the huge Colville Reservation. McKenzie and I caught the train about seven o'clock in the morning for Spokane.

Our next destination was Nespelem on the Colville Reservation, a small town a little difficult to reach, especially in the winter. We traveled by train part of the way, then by a little bus to Almira, and last by stage. Here I called Superintendent Harvey K. Meyer, who had been in charge of the Colville Reservation for some years.

The driver of the stage had his wife with him, and they occupied the front seat, while Edwards, McKenzie, and I sat back among the mailbags and express packages. The snow was more than a foot deep, and the road ran along the bank of the Columbia River. It was thirty-five difficult miles and the stage became stuck three times in the deep snow, but we continued, the driver shoveling snow on one mishap, and twice we were pulled a short distance by horses borrowed from a farmer. About half-way to our destination we were running very close to the bank where the drop into the Columbia River was 400 or 500 feet. The driver stepped on the brake a little too hard, and we skidded to the very edge before he was able to stop. As we continued our journey, his wife shivered a little, and I asked if she were cold. She answered that she was not cold because of the condition of the weather, but she shivered at the thought of how close we had come to going over the steep bank.

Our next stop was Coeur d'Alene, Idaho. It had snowed more Monday night so there must have been at least eighteen inches of snow on the ground. We reached the river without difficulty and crossed on the ferry, but a mile or so beyond we became stuck in the snow. From then on we were continually getting stuck. Finally, the driver said, "It is no use. We can't shovel ten or fifteen miles." So he got out, walked up to a farmhouse, and after an hour came back with two men, a team of horses, and a bobsled. We hitched up the team to the car and seemed to be getting along all right, so we decided that one man could take the bobsled back and the other could drive the horses.

In spite of this, we eventually got stuck again, and the driver again visited a farmhouse and got another farmer and a team of mules. Finally, we came to a fairly good road only about five miles from Almira and reached there about six in the evening.

We hurried to the nearest restaurant and gave our order, and the waiter looked out the front window to see how many more were coming, but we assured him that this was all. The next morning we caught the 7:30 bus for Spokane. Dr. Edwards had visited the sanitarium at Fort Lapwai so he did not want to go again. We all had lunch at the hotel as McKenzie and I had yet to visit both Coeur d'Alene and Fort Lapwai.

We boarded the bus for Tekoa which was about ten miles from our destination, the Coeur d'Alene Agency. When we arrived the superintendent said he would drive in for us the next morning. It was a snowy, icy drive of nearly ten miles.

The agency was in a lovely spot, and we met the superintendent's wife and employees. We talked with the superintendent, and McKenzie worked until about five o'clock in the agency files. I went with the agency farmer to his home for dinner and also to the home of the chief forester who showed me a good many pictures of scenes about the reservation.

Several days later, on Saturday, February 12, we were up at 5:30 because Meriam had decided we would take the day off and drive up to the lake where two Indians had agreed to take us in their canoes from the lake down the river to Tahola. It was about a forty-mile drive to Lake Quiniealt where there was a fish hatchery and a tiny hotel where we had breakfast. We also had a lunch packed to take with us on the trip down the river.

Meriam, Stambaugh, and I were in one canoe with an Indian, and Cloud, Edwards, and another Indian were in the other. We had looked forward to this trip with a great deal of pleasure, but it proved to be most disappointing. The canoes were long and very narrow, and one almost felt that he should part his hair in the middle and keep his chewing gum or tobacco in the center of his mouth or the thing might overturn. We had expected to find some rapids to run but there were none. One had to sit very still so we were a bit cold. There was nothing much to see except the forest flanking the river. At several log jams we had to carry the canoes. At one of them we built a fire, made coffee, and had lunch.

At long last, we reached Tahola at the mouth of the river, stiff and cold from sitting in one position for so long. Here we met the driver with the car to return us to Hoquiam. We had been told by Agent Sams that he did not know exactly how much the Indians would charge us but felt it would not be more than ten dollars. However, when Meriam offered them each a ten-dollar bill, they refused and said that they would not take less than thirty-five dollars. A search of our pockets revealed that all of us together did not have seventy dollars but the keeper of the store agreed to cash a check for us. We paid up for there was nothing else to do.

As we started back to Hoquiam, everyone was feeling blue until I remarked that if a boatman on the Sea of Galilee had charged prices like that, it was no wonder that Christ walked on the water. This brought a laugh from everyone, and we agreed that in the future we would have a clear understanding of what we were to pay before we made another trip.

We left Hoquiam early Sunday morning, February 13, and took the bus to Portland, Oregon, a long and tiresome ride. We reached Portland at 3:00 p.m., boarded a train, and spent the night in Eugene. Here we met some other members of our group. We were up early the next morning, and after breakfast we left for the little town of Chiloquin, where the agency for the Klamath Indian Reservation is located.

Soon after we reached the reservation we called a council to learn the Indians' needs. The leaders demanded that a stenographer be present to record all that was said. There were the usual complaints about the work of the agency staff. When the council closed that afternoon our group started for the next agency which was at Sacramento, California.

We were all up early when our train reached Davis, just

outside Sacramento, at 6:30 the next morning. We had gone from winter into spring for the acacia trees were blooming and everything was green. It was thirteen miles from Davis to Sacramento where we registered at the hotel and took a bus for the office of the agent. For some reason the letter of our field secretary had not reached the agent and he was greatly surprised when we appeared at his office.

The next morning we decided to go to Ione, a little town several miles east of Sacramento. Dr. McKenzie and Stambaugh remained to study the office records.

We stopped at a little Methodist mission school operated by Mr. and Mrs. Fish. They had only thirteen Indian students and the place had the appearance of poverty. We visited three or four other Indian families. Clearly there was little need to spend much time at the Sacramento Agency for the agent told us that the Indians who nominally belonged to that agency were scattered over the country west of Sacramento and his control over them was minimal. They did come to him, however, when they were in trouble and he did his best to help them.

So on Sunday, February 20, we left for San Francisco. Our chief object in going there was to talk with John Collier who was the leading member of the Indian Defense Association. Collier was somewhere in the East, probably New York, and there seemed little reason for staying any longer in San Francisco so on Wednesday, February 23, we started for Reno, Nevada.[1]

At Reno we found a social worker who lived near the Reno-Sparks Colony. Her name was Mildred Ring and if there was ever a saint on earth, she deserved the title. An Indian girl named Josephine was her helper. They went into the worst part of Reno to places where most men would have hesitated to go at night. They did not hesitate to pick up a drunken girl, load her into the car, take her home, put her to bed, and give her black coffee and tomato juice to bring her out of her drunken stupor.

---

[1] John Collier, social reformer, and Commissioner of Indian Affairs beginning in 1933, largely responsible for the Indian Reorganization Act, called the Indian Magna Charta, adopted in 1934.

The following day we packed our baggage and, except for a small handbag each, shipped it to Los Angeles, and proceeded to Bishop, California. It was a wonderful drive along Walker Lake. We had lunch and then drove over Montgomery Pass, stopped to walk a little when we reached the summit, and then drove into the valley. We reached Bishop about 9:30. At the Grammer's School we observed fifteen Indian children attending with thirty white youngsters. Indians in this valley lived on small tracts of land. We visited in the homes there.

We then drove on to Independence where we spent the night. The next morning we continued the journey visiting homes of Indians and the small reservation of 360 acres. One home on this reservation belonged to a Mrs. Cleveland. Her grandson played the violin for us exceptionally well. She said that he performed in concert in Los Angeles. It seemed to me quite wonderful when he played a melody in F, *Humoresque*, and one or two other bits of classical music.

At five o'clock we took the train for Los Angeles, arriving at 7:00 a.m. There we met Dr. Spillman, Brown, and Miss Duke who reported on her contacts with Indians who had left reservation life for jobs in the city. This was on Sunday, March 6.

Monday morning we visited with members of the Indian Defense Association or the Indian Rights Association. Then the next morning we headed to Riverside Indian School, about an hour's drive east of Los Angeles. From Riverside it was only a short distance to Sherman Institute, which is one of the largest non-reservation schools in the U.S. It is often referred to as Riverside because this was the nearest town. We met various other employees and were housed in the employees' dormitory. After supper we attended an employees' meeting where Meriam made a brief speech. The next morning we went to classes in various departments. We were impressed with the school and found that the children were reasonably well fed for we ate lunch with them. We told the superintendent just before lunch was served that we wanted to eat with the children and he urged us to wait till the next day, but we insisted that we eat with them *that* day. While the lunch was fairly good, I think that the cook and the dining room matron must have added one extra dish.

On March 10, we started for mission country jurisdiction in Southern California, a series of very small reservations extending south to the border of Mexico. The Mission Agency is located at Riverside but it dealt with approximately twenty-eight small reservations set aside for Indians of various stocks and tribes.

Most of these reservations, of course, had Spanish names for there were many persons of Spanish background in this area. Some of the larger tracts of land were Morengo, Los Coyotes, Capitan Grande, Manzanita, and Campo which was on the border of Mexico. At Campo, Cloud and I found the Indians making acorn porridge from the live-oak acorns.

The acorns were roasted much as we roast peanuts or chestnuts, pounded to remove the hulls, and the kernels beaten to a powder in a stone or wooden mortar. The resulting powdered acorn kernels were placed in a bag, and the bitter taste removed by pouring warm water through the bag leaving a brown paste much like peanut butter. Cloud, who never hesitated to ask favors, told one elderly Indian that we would like very much to eat some acorn porridge, and the Indian took us to his home and asked his wife to prepare some. Cooked as almost any other cereal and served with sugar and milk, it was very tasty and in my opinion better than any breakfast food I have ever eaten. At Campo we saw a very old Indian coming out of a tiny shack not much larger than a pup tent. The other Indians called our attention to him saying that he was 140 years old.

We visited a number of day schools including Volcan, Mesa Grande, and Rincon. On March 12, we drove to San Diego, then north to Riverside School. It must have been several hundred miles and we were stopped from time to time by border patrol officers who inspected the cars for Mexican immigrants.

The Indian Trail Ends

By March, 1927, the members of the Commission assessed our progress to that point. We had now been in the field nearly four and a half months—approximately two months before Christmas and two and a half since Christmas. During this time we had visited most of the reservations in the Pacific Northwest, California, Southern Arizona, and the Rio Grande Pueblos, but we yet had to visit the Navajo and Hopi reservations, the Utes in Colorado, and several Apache groups including the Jicarillas, as well as the northern reservations and schools from Colville to North Dakota and the Oklahoma Indian facilities except the Cheyenne-Arapaho and the Kiowa. In addition we needed to visit the Indian reservations and schools in Minnesota and Wisconsin, the eastern Cherokees in North Carolina, and someone had to visit the Wind River tribes in central Wyoming and the Seminoles of Florida.

During our travels we had talked of Indians on the bus, on trains, in hotel rooms, and in the long travels from reservation to reservation the members of the staff had traded experiences with the result that each of us knew fairly well what the others wanted to know about each jurisdiction. The fact that I had grown up on the Oklahoma frontier made it a little easier for me than for some other members of the staff to get a fairly clear picture of conditions, for I had known a good many Indians of the Kiowa-Comanche reservation. I also had known a full blood Choctaw lad or two living in the home of my wife's mother, since my wife's sister had married Charles Turnbull, a three-quarter

(top from left) Edward Everett Dale, Henry Roe Cloud, Lewis Meriam, and Herbert Edwards with agency engineer at site of Coolidge Dam. (bottom) Boarding canoes on the Quinault River. (Courtesy Western History Collections, University of Oklahoma Library)

(top) Students at the Riverside School parade for inspection. (bottom) Miss Mary Louise Mark at the Missouri River. (Courtesy Western History Collections, University of Oklahoma Library)

Choctaw. Because we were scheduled to finish field work by the middle of June, it was clear that only one or two persons would be able to visit every jurisdiction.

It was also clear that the author must give less detail for by this time we had visited most of the various types of Indians. For example, there were the sedentary tribes who depended mostly on agriculture for a living. These were the Rio Grande Pueblos, the Pimas, and of course the Five Civilized Tribes of Oklahoma. Some others were the prairie tribes who had formerly depended on buffalo, the fish eaters of the Northwest Coast, and the Indians that lived in the forest who depended largely on the sale of trees to the lumber companies, such as the Klamaths.

Our legal expert Brown and, as I recall, Dr. and Mrs. Spillman left us at Riverside. When we reached Needles, California, Meriam, Miss Mark, and McKenzie left the train since this was close to the Mojave jurisdiction.

I left the train at Kingman, Arizona, to make a survey of the Walapai. I especially wanted to see this reservation because it had a tribal herd of 350 young cattle. I went with the superintendent in an agency car to see these cattle while Ryan and Cloud visited the school and studied the problems which the chief clerk explained to them. The main problem was that the reservation had been set aside on land where every other section had been granted to a railroad but the railway people had so far not objected to the cattle pasturing the land and using water from Peach Springs.

When I returned we had a council with the Indians and dinner served by several attractive Indian girls. We then returned to the train and reached Flagstaff. The Navajo country was divided into nearly half a dozen jurisdictions at this time and the agency headquarters for the western jurisdiction was at Tuba, sometimes called Tuba City, about eighty miles to the north. Just south of Tuba reservation is a village of Hopi Indians called Moencopi. We stopped there and visited with some families. They were a very friendly people and one woman insisted on giving me some sticks of piki bread which tastes something like cornflakes.

We found Tuba Agency a very attractive place with trees

and shrubs which seemed an oasis because we had been traveling over a barren desert. We were given lodging in the employees' building and walked about to see the school and had supper at the employees' mess.

We had a short visit with some of the employees and the next morning after breakfast we drove out to see the water supply, a group of springs that also supplied water to the Hopi village. We visited homes and found them neat and clean. The floors were of dirt, hardbeaten and carefully swept. Indians showed us large ears of corn of different colors and permitted us to go down into the kiva which was somewhat like those we had seen at the Rio Grande Pueblos.

The kiva, which we found in every village of the Pueblo Indians, is an underground room which is used for ceremonies. The young men coming in late slept there and the old men wove a bride's wedding dress there. It is something like a temple, a council house, and a storage for masks and costumes worn in the dances. It is regarded in most cases as a sacred place.

We also visited the little Hopi school. It had a dairy with an employee in charge and we were told that the herd produced nearly seventy gallons of milk a day. We drove home for supper at the agency and felt that we had a pretty fair understanding of the conditions at this agency.

The following morning we started for Flagstaff which we reached about 12:30. After lunch we drove to the Leupp agency and reached it about supper time. It seemed to us a rather dreary place but they found quarters for us. McKenzie and I were put in the men's dorm, and Henry and Miss Mark in the employees' building which were fairly good quarters.

The following day we drove out to visit the reservation. We saw a good-sized herd of milk goats, the tribal herd of sheep, visited a traders store, and the hogans of five or six people. We also visited Canyon Diablo and parts of the school. I found the other agencies for the Navajos very much like this one. We did find an epidemic of measles among the children at Leupp and no doctor was available.

On Sunday, March 20, we were up early and drove to Winslow on the railroad where we had lunch. Thence we drove to the Hopi Reservation at Keams Canyon. Several commission members went to Crown Point Agency and from there to Fort Defiance, a central Navajo jurisdiction. A water development man, a federal employee, had been assigned to the Hopi. It was his business to visit nearly 100 wells scattered about over the Hopi Reservation and to develop springs at locations where it seemed there was a little water to dig out a seep. He also was to line these with cement since water was of primary importance to the Hopi people.

At Keams Canyon we met Superintendent Edgar Miller and his wife. He had been there for some years. When we went to his home I was a bit surprised to see a pamphlet on the living-room table next to the family Bible. Upon looking at it, I saw that it was something that Dr. McKenzie had written when he was teaching an Indian school at Wind River Reservation in Wyoming.

The agency had a school for young children and I saw the little girls lined up to go to lunch. All were wearing little red sweaters except one and I said to her, "Daughter, why aren't you wearing your sweater, it is cold today!" She said, "Nothing." The matron said, "Oh, don't say 'nothing'. You can speak better English than that. Tell Dr. Dale that you don't have a sweater." And she obediently replied in that curious little Indian dialect, "I don't have a sweater." I asked the matron why she had no sweater and the matron said that the girl had lost it on a picnic and that to punish her they weren't giving her a new one. I expressed my disbelief in that form of punishment and said that if Uncle Sam was too poor to buy her a sweater then I would. The matron said that they would get the girl another sweater.

A school employee drove me over to the first mesa which was perhaps a couple of miles from the agency. There was a little mission and trading post there, the latter operated by an educated Hopi, Tom Pavatea. Cloud suggested that we have a council that night which would leave us free all the next day, and I agreed to it.

Cloud left to visit the mission station and apparently had supper there but I went in Tom Pavatea's store and asked for a can of salmon and a large can of peaches. The clerk brought out two bowls, opened the cans for me, and put a good sized pile of crackers on the counter. I had done this so often as a cowhand that I did not mind having such a supper, but when I had eaten about half the can of salmon and somewhat less than half of the can of peaches I thought it good manners to ask the three or four young men sitting on the counter to finish up the two half-filled bowls. I turned to the clerk and said, "I seem to have ordered a good deal too much. That's all I can eat." He said, "We'll let the boys finish that up." The words were hardly spoken when each young Hopi reached for a cracker and scooped up salmon with one hand and peaches with the other. I felt assured that I had not made any mistake in expecting these young men to take the leavings of my supper.

Cloud appeared a few minutes later and said he had eaten with the missionaries. Our driver said he would drive to his home at the foot of the second mesa and come back later for us after the council was over. There was a road to the top of the mesa and I felt that I would just as soon have walked, especially when we later ran within a foot or two from the edge of the roadway. The driver pointed out the remains of a car half way down the side of the mesa where he said a tourist had gone too far to the left three or four years before. The driver and all his family except one small son had been killed. However, we reached the flat top of the mesa safely.

The village crier had been calling the Hopi equivalent of "Oyez, oyez, oyez, the honorable commissioners are asking for all to meet them for a council in the home of," and he called an unpronounceable name. "All come as quickly as possible." Three or four of the head men of the village cordially shook hands with us and steered us over to the home where we were to meet. In a few minutes the council began.

I asked Cloud to speak first, but he only rose and introduced me as assistant to our chief who would himself come later. I rose and gave the usual introduction, stating that we were not from Washington nor were we connected with the Indian Service, but were a group of men and one woman who were having our expenses paid by a wealthy American. I said that we were to travel among the Indians, discover their needs and wants, and then to transmit our findings to the Secretary of the Interior, the Indian Department, and the President. I then asked them to speak freely.

After they had spoken, I assured them that we would take their words to our chief and he would tell the President what they had said. I assured them also that our chief and other members of the party would be with them in the next few days. With this the council broke up and I shook hands with the head men. Tom Pavatea drove us back to the agency.

The following day we went to the second mesa, a few miles west of Walpi. Here we found that they had a huge cistern to catch rain water but the water problem was about the same as at the other mesas.

The council had been held the evening of March 21, and the following day had been largely spent at the second mesa. We returned first to Polacca and from there to the agency to find Miss Mark and some other members of our party including Meriam. The following afternoon we started for Holbrook.

Our next stop, on March 24, was at Fort Defiance which was another of the some half-dozen Navajo agencies. It had a large school and we watched the children eat dinner, did some more visiting, inspected a mission, then proceeded to Gallup to spend the night.

The following day Meriam asked me to take Cloud and go to the northern unit of the Navajo country at Shiprock. He added that they would make some further study at Fort Defiance as Superintendent F. M. Lobdell was eager to show them the entire plant and the school of over 250 youngsters and would also visit Crown Point. The Shiprock Agency was so called because of a huge rock several hundred feet high which looks exactly like a full rigged ship as you sight it coming in from the south.

From there Cloud and I went east on the narrow gauge railroad to Ignacio in the Ute Reservation. Before we reached Shiprock we stopped at a trader's store at a tiny village called Drollet. Here I bought a silver belt for my wife and visited the little mission school of the Christian Reformed Church.

We reached Shiprock about dinnertime and ate with the superintendent and the judge of the Court of Indian Offenses. We talked with the old judge until about 9:30 p.m. He was very wise, but unable to speak English. He communicated with us through an interpreter. There had been talk of petroleum discoveries on the Navajo reservation and we asked the judge if he thought the Indians would stop making rugs and blankets if they became rich from oil wells. He said he thought not, that Indian women loved to make rugs just as white women loved fancy work, and said that his wife made rugs though she did not need the money for them. After he had answered many of our questions he arose and shook hands with us. Cloud remarked, "Interpreter, tell the judge that he has read the story of three wise men in the Bible and we think we have found a fourth wise man here this evening, yourself." The interpreter smiled and said goodnight as he left us.

Cloud and I were up early on March 26, and took a walk before breakfast to see the barns, dairy cows, and a little of the agency farm. We also saw a large orchard. We returned for breakfast and later drove out to see the farms. All the farms and gardens were under irrigation and we saw a number of men at work on the ditch. We found that there were two schools at the Shiprock Agency, one called the camp school and the other the usual type of Indian school. At the camp school we met Miss Lupe Speor, apparently a full blood Pima, and another young woman from Moencopi.

We found Superintendent J. T. Kneale most cooperative. When I called a council the Indians had nothing but praise for him. He had us for dinner Sunday, March 27, and after dinner we held a council at which many good speeches were made. It closed about 4:30 p.m. and we rode with Superintendent and Mrs. Kneale over the reservation. The roads were good and we stopped about 7:30 p.m. at a small village where we had an excellent dinner. The next morning Cloud and I took the train for Ignacio, on the Colorado Utes reservation.

Cloud went on to Dulce, which is on the Jicarilla Apache Reservation, while I rode out to the agency. The agency farmer took me to the Indian school near Ignacio and to the various parts of the reservation. We visited several homes but got back to the school in time for supper.

After a couple of days at Dulce I said goodbye to the superintendent and took the train for Antonito and Santa Fe. Here I found most of the rest of our group. They had visited Zuni and Hotevilla, the third Hopi mesa which I had not seen, and they had also visited two Navajo agencies, Fort Wingate and Crown Point. The following day we took the train for Oklahoma City.

From Oklahoma City the nearest Indian agency was Shawnee. I had lived in Oklahoma for so long and had visited most of the tribes in the state so there seemed little reason for giving details as to the condition of the Indian people there. Some years later Miss Muriel H. Wright wrote a book, *A Guide to the Indian Tribes of Oklahoma*, and at this time I had written and had published my first history of Oklahoma which gives in detail the condition of the Oklahoma Indians.[1]

At this time there were five Indian agencies in western Oklahoma. These were the Kiowa-Comanche, Caddo, and Wichita Agency at Anadarko, the Cheyenne-Arapaho Agency at Concho, near El Reno, the Ponca, Otoe-Missouri, Pawnee, and Tonkawa, under the agency near Pawnee, the Osage and Kaw, sometimes called Kansa, with the agency at Pawhuska, and Sac-Fox, Kickapoo, and Iowa Agency near Stroud. The two agencies on the east side of old Indian Territory were the Five Civilized Tribes, the Cherokee, Choctaw, Chickasaw, Creek, and Seminole, with the agency at Muskogee, and a group of small tribes, each on its own land in the extreme northeast corner of Oklahoma, the

---

[1] See Muriel H. Wright, *Guide to the Indian Tribes of Oklahoma* (Norman: University of Oklahoma Press, 1951).

Quapaw, Peoria, Ottawa, Shawnee, Wyandot, Seneca, and Modoc, under the Quapaw Agency at Miami.

From Shawnee we went north to the Pawnee Agency where we found a people far more progressive than any place we had yet visited. From there we moved to the Poncas of Siouan stock and as a rule tall in stature. They were by no means as well-to-do as the Pawnees. They had been buffalo hunters while the Pawnees were agricultural. Ponca headmen had some complaints about ranchers to whom they leased their allotments. Each time we arrived at their council house they were playing a game something like "find the thimble."

Next we visited the Otoes who were largely mixed-bloods, some of them being really blonde. Like the Pawnees they were farm people. They numbered hardly more than 100 persons.

On April 12, we visited Chilocco. This is by far the largest Indian school in Oklahoma. In 1927 it had about 800 students. It was a non-reservation school which meant that it was not under the jurisdiction of any agency but was independent, reporting directly to the commissioner of Indian Affairs.

We spent a couple of days at this school and then moved on to the Osage Superintendency at Pawhuska on April 14. This was a particularly important superintendency because the Osages were at this time probably the richest people in the world. The reason for this was of course the huge oil fields on Osage lands. Although the land had been allotted in severalty before statehood, the sub-surface rights were held by the Osage people as a whole. Here the members of our staff who had never visited an oil-rich people found large and expensive homes sometimes with a brush or hay arbor in the backyard or a small wooden structure which they called a summer house. Here too were found a number of worthless men and women which the officers of the agency usually referred to as "pot lickers." They were, in most cases, worthless whites who had flocked to the Osage country in spite of the best efforts of the superintendent.

From the Osage country we crossed over to the Cherokee

country on April 18. Here we visited Sequoyah School which had been the Cherokee Orphanage before statehood but after statehood was taken over by the federal government as a non-reservation school. The superintendent was John Brown who was of Cherokee descent. The school had about 300 students and was operated as other government schools. It owned about 180 acres of land and had a dairy herd of twenty cows which provided some sixty gallons of milk per day. About seventy acres were in cultivation, planted in feed for the dairy herd.

There were eight teachers for grades fourth to the ninth, and a few children were in the third grade. The children seemed to be happy and well fed. They had a huge garden and orchard. From the school we drove over to Tahlequah, only seven miles away, and met a number of businessmen including Ed Hicks, W. W. Hastings, who was a member of Congress, O. H. P. Brewer, and Lawrence Wyly, a banker, all of Cherokee blood.

On the 19th of April we visited the teachers' college which was formerly the Cherokee Girls' Seminary. Congressman Hastings was a graduate of the Cherokee Male Seminary, but the building had been burned before statehood and had never been rebuilt. We visited the orphanage and found that most of the children were of Cherokee descent.[2] Out of a population of 6,390 in the county, 1,590 were Indian which did not include the population at the public school or the Indians away at schools such as Chilocco and Haskell.

On April 20, we went to Muskogee, the site of the agency for the Five Civilized Tribes. Here we met a great many people of Indian blood, including lawyers, bankers, and businessmen. From Muskogee we drove to Durant and visited Choctaw and Chickasaw settlements.

Next day we visited the large and attractive Chickasaw school called Bloomfield. The school had been a Chickasaw tribal school but there were a few students who were from other tribes. It was strictly a girls' school at this time and

---

[2] Presently Northeastern Oklahoma State University.

326

was very clean and neat and seemed to be quite efficiently operated.

This completed our Oklahoma circuit, although we all agreed that we should return and check conditions there more thoroughly. There still remained Indians in the north and northwest to be visited. Accordingly, Meriam asked me if I would take Cloud and go to the northwest while he took the rest of the commission to Nebraska and South Dakota to visit the large Sioux and Northern Cheyenne reservations. Cloud and I were to join the rest of the party at Cass Lake, Minnesota. We knew that by this time the field work would be completed and we would go to Washington about June 15 to make a first draft of our report.

Cloud and I started about April 30. I had checked on the Fort Duchesne Reservation before we left Washington and had made up a brief report on it. My secretary made several carbons so we all knew something about the reservation and the Indians there.

Cloud and I proceeded to Green River and on May 2nd found that the superintendent had sent a car to bring us to the agency, a distance of a little more than 100 miles. It was a pleasant drive but very cool in spots and other places intensely hot. I called for a council which we had the second day.

Cloud and I spent three days at the Uintah reservation and then an agency driver took us to Price, Utah, over the so-called Indian Pass. Here we caught a train for Salt Lake City where we spent the night and the following morning took a train to a point near Dixon, Montana, to visit the Flathead Reservation.

We had passed by that reservation some weeks earlier but had not stopped. It was beautiful country and Flathead Lake was one of the loveliest I had ever seen. The superintendent was Charles Coe.

We enjoyed our stay on the Flathead Reservation and met some interesting characters among the mixed-bloods. These included two brothers, Malcolm and Duncan McDonald. They were sons of a Hudson's Bay employee and a full blood Uintah woman. They spoke English with a pronounced

Scottish accent. Duncan McDonald said to me, "I want you to go with me down to me hoose for I want you to see my father's books." I promptly agreed and found that his was a one-room frame house about fourteen by sixteen feet, with one entire wall lined with bookshelves. Here I saw many English classics such as Shakespeare, Dickens, Scott, and a certain number of American volumes. The shelves must have held several hundred volumes, some of them beautifully bound. Duncan looked at them lovingly as he said, "These were my father's books. My father was barn in Scotland and was a well-educated man. He wanted me to go to the univaresity and sent me. I was there for three yares but that was over fifty yares ago. For more than fifty yares I have not seen a univaresity. For more than fifty yares these glens and cairns have been my univaresity. I love them and they have taught me much." Needless to say I was astonished to find such a library on the Flathead Indian Reservation and to find men like that as members of an Indian tribe.

We stayed on the Flathead Reservation where we had two councils and visited a good many homes and the two schools. After our experience with the White River Utes, the Flathead Reservation seemed most attractive but we looked forward to visiting the Blackfeet Agency, administering a large reservation situated at Fort Browning. The Blackfeet were so named, of course, by early explorers or trappers. They did not call themselves Blackfeet. Their Indian name was Piegan. They were situated near the Canadian border and most of them spoke good English. Superintendent James Campbell had been in charge of the reservation for some years.

The next morning at the agency I found Cloud had already packed so I hastily did the same then went to say my goodbyes. We caught the eastbound train of the Great Northern to our next stop, Fort Belknap.

Cloud and I had spent four days at the Blackfeet agency. They had been most interesting but it must be confessed that loss of sleep had left me half dead on my feet. Cloud had found an old friend with whom he had spent a night or two and so had missed that last council.

We traveled a great deal at night, so we were still two days ahead of our schedule. I had planned on using the extra days visiting a reservation across the border in Canada. These Indians were related to the Blackfeet, but since they were under Canadian control it seemed to me that it would be interesting to compare the conditions of these Indians with those of related tribes in the United States living in virtually the same environment. Unfortunately, we found that all roads leading north were blocked by snow, so I proposed to Cloud that we use the two-days' time to visit the Rocky Boy Reservation, located about fifty miles south of Havre, Montana.

We reached the Rocky Boy Agency in a stage carrying the mail to the agency and to the neighboring town. The Indians occupying the reservation numbered only slightly over 100 families at this time. They had fled from Canada to the United States to avoid punishment for their part in a rebellion of Canadian Indians under the leadership of Louis Riel. Once across the border they were safe from the Canadian government. They camped around the town of Havre working at odd jobs, eating from garbage cans, and being chased off vacant lots by whites until the United States government established a little reservation of about three townships of mountainous land for them.[3]

I had written Agent Luman W. Shotwell before we left Washington. Since there were no hotel facilities and very few buildings, Shotwell insisted that we be guests for a couple of days in his home. I called a council soon after we reached the agency for the afternoon, and most of the men and some of the women came. I asked Cloud to take the lead at this meeting, but again he introduced me. I explained why we were there, and that we would be glad to hear of their needs and wants and how the government of the United States could help them.

---

[3] Riel Rebellion from two insurrections (also called Red River Insurrections) in western Canada (1869-1870 and 1885). Metis and mixed-blood factions with some full blood Indians revolted against harsh treatment by Canadian government and because of hardships and starvation, caused by intruding white settlers who exterminated the game and seized tribal leaders. Louis Riel led both outbreaks.

After visiting homes and talking with tribal members, we visited Fort Belknap and Fort Peck. Thence, we traveled to Fort Berthold, North Dakota, an agency for three tribes, the Gros Ventres, the Mandans, and the Aricaras. The superintendent was L. W. Page. The weather outside was damp and chilly, and the roads were muddy with patches of snow in various places even this late in May. We left the train at a small station called Stanley where we expected the agent or an employee to meet us with a car to take us to the agency which was at Elbowoods, several miles from Stanley and near the Missouri River.

Superintendent T. A. Page met us and greeted us cordially. He was a fairly young man, and our association with him convinced us he would go far in the Indian Service if he continued in that work. We were lodged in his home and he and his wife made us feel welcome. After dinner he introduced us to various members of his staff. He had another guest, a full blood Gros Ventre Indian, Joe Packeneau. This was one of the few times when I found a superintendent entertaining a full blood Indian in his own home.

The following morning was still cold and a bit misty, but I wanted very much to go to an Indian village a few miles down the river. Fortunately an Indian was kind enough to lend me a sheep-lined coat, and we took a boat with a steering wheel propeller driven by an automobile engine and ran for a few miles down the river to an Indian settlement where there was a school and a store.

Word had been sent of our coming, saying that we would like to council with these people, so when we arrived we had a group meet us at the landing to escort us to the schoolhouse. When I explained our position, Cloud made a brief talk. We then asked for speeches from our audience. Half a dozen men made brief talks. On the whole they seemed satisfied. They spoke kindly of Superintendent Page and no one offered any special complaints.

Cloud told a little Indian story about magic moccasins which seemed to please them, for they had just given him a pair of beaded moccasins. They gave me a handsome beaded belt for which I made a little speech and told of my experience with Indians.

They then took us to the nearby council house where they had a long table. We were served a good meal of barbecued beef, fried bread, and coffee, and then brief talks were given. We shook hands with everyone, thanked them for their hospitality, and boarded the boat.

We talked late that night with Superintendent Page and his wife. The following day Page took us back to the railroad, and we boarded the train for Cass Lake to meet the rest of our party.

We reached our destination on May 19. They were all there except Brown and Emma Duke. I found that they had covered the agencies in South Dakota including Rosebud, Pine Ridge, Lower Brule, Cheyenne River, and Turtle Mountain Reservation and School. Meriam had gone to Crow and Wind River in Wyoming, and one or two other schools. They had also checked with the Cass Lake Reservation and one or two others in Minnesota.

There remained only to visit the Keshena agency in Wisconsin, a rather important reservation of which William Donner was superintendent with jurisdiction over the Menominee reservation. We were given quarters at the employees' building, but there was not room enough for all. Three or four were sent to Neopit, a lumber center on the reservation a few miles northwest of the agency. On the day after our arrival Superintendent Donner, Meriam, Miss Mark, and I took a car to visit the power site on Wolf River. Here there were swift rapids in the river and two falls, one of over ten feet, which it was estimated would develop 3,000 horsepower electricity. There were three or four other power sites on the reservation with a maximum possible development of 24,000 horsepower. There was a large boarding school with several dormitories at Keshena which we visited as soon as we returned from our visit to the water-falls.

Agent Donner felt that the beauty of the reservation would attract a great deal of tourists, and planned to establish tourist camps with comfortable cabins and opportunities for fishing and boating on the lakes.

I visited the lumber center of Neopit where some of the people were lodged and saw something of the lumbering operations. It also had quarters for the workers in the sawmill. We visited a great many homes and so did not leave Menominee until the 30th of May when the entire party started for Oklahoma.

We reached Muskogee, Oklahoma, on June 1, at 5:40 in the morning and went straight to Tahlequah by bus. Cloud had been delayed but came in on June 2.

It was my task to serve as guide to the commission during the resumption of our inspection of Indian facilities in Oklahoma. At Tahlequah we visited the old Cherokee capitol building which had been made the county courthouse. I introduced the members of the commission to Cherokees who were county officers, bankers, attorneys, and one member of Congress. We also visited the full bloods who lived in the hills on small farms. Some of these lived in log cabins and grew a little corn and vegetables, raised a few pigs, and perhaps a few cattle, but for the most part they were very poor. Among the homes we visited was that of George Wilson, a full blood minister.

We also visited some of the one-room rural schools where the majority of the students were full blood Cherokees. In Tahlequah itself we found fashionably dressed women and well-dressed men who had studied Latin, science, and higher mathematics in the Cherokee seminaries.

In the Creek Nation we visited the capital at Okmulgee which had been made into a museum. We also found a community of full blood Creeks who were quite poor and lived as subsistence farmers. They spoke little or no English. It was the same story in the Choctaw and Chickasaw area where the former schools administered by the Choctaw and Chickasaw Nations had become government schools. In some cases the full bloods living in the hills clung to the old manners and customs, while the mixed-bloods were ranchers, farmers, bankers, managers, lawyers, or physicians. The same was true in the Seminole country. I had to explain many of these things to some members of our group.

The Seminole capital had been Wewoka, but the biggest town at that time was Seminole, situated in the center of a huge oil field. The streets were muddy and difficult to get from building to building. We saw many underworld figures, the kind that always flock to towns where there is easy money to be had.

The largest town in the Chickasaw country was Ardmore, where there were comparatively few full blood Chickasaws. I also insisted that we should visit the remaining schools in Oklahoma, including Carter Seminary, near Ardmore, and Seneca School at Wyandotte in the extreme northeast corner of the state. Among the Choctaws there were Goodland, Wheelock, a girls school, and Jones Academy, a boys school. Creek schools were situated at Eufaula and Bacone, just east of Muskogee, which gave college credit. In western Oklahoma there were Fort Sill boarding school near Lawton, Riverside near Anadarko, and Concho near El Reno. There were public schools all over Oklahoma which had a large attendance of Indian children, especially in the old Caddo-Wichita reservation where in some cases the public schools had a majority of children of Indian blood.

It was pleasant for me to be again in Oklahoma, for when we came to Oklahoma City I had the opportunity to see Rosalie and my son. Rosalie had the entire group to dinner one evening. After ten days most of the group including Meriam left for their homes for a day or two, and then on to Washington. Meriam insisted that I remain at home for three or four days.

As a result I did not reach Washington until June 22. Here I found that Meriam had rented a house at 1728 Eye Street. Ryan, Brown, and Spillman already were on the job, and Miss Mark and Cloud came in later in the day. Edwards had gone to New York for a day or two. I saw Meriam for only a brief visit, but he returned the following day. When all the commission members were assembled, we got down to work.

The house which was to be our address for the summer was a large two-story dwelling. The living room had been fitted up as a conference room with a long table and chairs, while the bedrooms had been turned into offices. Meriam would live at home in Kensington, Maryland. Cloud rented an apartment and brought his family to Washington for the summer. Stambaugh took a room just north of the capitol. Brown rented an apartment, brought his wife with him and commuted. Dr. Spillman lived in Washington, and McKenzie secured a room in the area near our headquarters. Ryan had rented a room, but he planned to bring his family a little later to an apartment he had rented on R Street, only a couple of blocks from our headquarters. I found a room within a couple of blocks of the house. Miss Mark lived at Westerville, but decided it was too far to commute so she got a room temporarily near headquarters.

In less than a week we were all pretty well located and the work of writing the report was well under way. Cloud and I officed together in a large room. We were given a secretary, Mrs. Hynson, a widow of uncertain age and none too attractive in appearance, but said to be an excellent stenographer and typist.

The house which we occupied was close to the Brooking School. I had brought my field notes and quite a number of books for reference, which I put up in a case near my desk. Cloud was out for two or three days doing some work at the Library of Congress when a young woman from Brooking School entered my office. She said that she was writing a paper on Indians, and asked to use the books in my bookcase since it was so far to the Library of Congress. She assured me that she would not disturb me, but added that it would be a great favor if she could use my books until the paper was finished. I told her she would be perfectly welcome.

She was sitting in our office reading when Cloud came in one day. I had told him of our arrangement, and he assured me that he did not mind. When he came in the girl looked up and saw this full blood who asked her, "Good morning, young lady. What are you reading?"

She replied, "This is a book on an-thro-pol-o-gy. Does that sound like a pretty hard word to you?"

"Well, it is not an easy word to spell." Cloud replied. "Is that what you study in school here?" Cloud asked. She said that it was and Cloud said, "I wish I could go to that school."

"Oh," the young lady said, "You have to have an A.B. degree to study at the Brooking's Institute."

Cloud replied rather apologetically, "Well, I have an A.B. degree."

The girl looked at him again and said, "You really should have a masters degree. Most of the students do but I have only a bachelor's degree and I am working on my masters."

"It must be very interesting," said Cloud. "I have a masters degree."

The girl was positively incredulous but said, "You mean you have a masters degree! Where did you take your masters?" Cloud responded, "At Yale," and she asked, "What subject did you take your masters in?"

With a straight face he responded, "Anthropology."

I was out of the office and did not witness this. I did not see the young woman again for a couple of days, but when she did return her face was still red as she said, "Dr. Dale, Mr. Cloud made a complete fool of me the other day." Cloud had told me gleefully about the incident so I could only reply, "Mr. Cloud didn't really make a fool of you, young lady. You must admit you certainly gave him a lot of help." This was only another instance of Cloud's Indian sense of humor which he had displayed so well, and perhaps cruelly, to our hostess in El Paso.

There seems little reason to tell of our work during the next two months and a half. Each member of the staff worked on his particular field, and once a week we met in the conference room. One member of the staff read what he had written, and we discussed it, offering suggestions.

By early September my section of the report was completed, as was that of all the others. Some members of the staff had to leave for brief periods. Ryan attended a meeting in Switzerland, but he returned almost before we missed him. Cloud and Edwards also were called away for two or three days on matters of business, but I cannot recall that I ever missed a single day of hard work.

I was in close touch with Rosalie, and early in September I said goodbye to Meriam and the others who had not already left. My part in the Indian survey was over for the moment. Meriam retained a secretary and read every section of the report. It made the rounds of the entire staff with such additions, deletions, and slight changes as Meriam suggested. For this work each of us was paid $2.50 an hour, which in my case was a very welcome addition to my salary. Looking back, I feel that the year spent in this survey was one of the most interesting and profitable of my life.

(below) The University of Oklahoma campus in 1924. (right) Edward Everett Dale as chairman of O.U.'s Department of History. (Courtesy Western History Collections, University of Oklahoma Library)

337

Department Chief

I had been head of the History Department of the University of Oklahoma since 1924 and had been away from the job for three semesters and one summer term. I felt it was high time for me to resume the teaching of university students, doing my best to build an outstanding department of history in the institution I loved so much and was so proud to call my *alma mater*.

The Department of History had grown quite a bit during the year. I had brought Morris L. Wardell to the department in 1924, and while Dean Buchanan was acting as head of the department in 1927 he had added Dr. A. B. Thomas.

It would not be productive for me to list the names of all those who served for a time at least as members of the History Department during the nineteen years that I was its chief. Some were with us only for a year or during the summer session. Others remained throughout my years as chairman and continued with my successors until they reached retirement.

Low salaries caused us to lose men, and President Bizzell once remarked to me, "Your department has been a training school for young scholars who, after two or three years, have proved to be so good that some richer University or college takes them away from us by an offer of more money than we can pay."

My relations with President Bizzell were always cordial, just as they had been with President Brooks. While the student body steadily increased year after year, it was never

338

too large that any important departmental matter, at least in the College of Arts and Sciences, could not be taken directly to the President.

This meant that if a man resigned or if the enrollment in history courses became so large that it was imperative to add another teacher to the staff, I secured an appointment with the President, explained the situation, and asked how much salary could be paid.

Never did he offer a suggestion about the person to be employed. When, with the help of other members of the history staff, a decision had been reached on an appropriate candidate, I took credentials, academic history, photograph, etc., to President Bizzell. He looked them over briefly, and his comment was always the same, "Dr. Dale, if you can get this man for the salary suggested, I feel that you will have made a contribution to this University."

In my administration of the department, we had no fixed time of meetings, but usually met only when some matter affecting the department needed to be discussed. Minor problems were usually handled over a cup of coffee in the Student Union or at a nearby coffee shop at what was known as "Varsity Corner."

My relations with students were cordial. Someone has quoted me saying, "I will do anything in the world for one of my students except give him a grade he has not earned." Since any departmental head was advisor to all students majoring in that department, it was my business to approve the enrollment of history majors and changes made later by dropping or adding courses. This applied to graduate as well as undergraduate students.

Every graduate major had to write a thesis for which four hours credit was given. Since my special fields were Western, American, and Oklahoma history, several wished to write their masters theses with me. Later, when the History Department had been approved to grant the Ph.D. degree, I usually had two or three candidates for the doctor's degree writing a dissertation under my direction.

Eventually, it became clear that more library facilities were sorely needed for graduate work in history, but the

University did not have the money to increase the annual appropriations to the History Department for this purpose. In desperation the idea came to me to try to find an "angel" who would be willing to pledge a sum of money each year for several years to establish a collection of books, pamphlets, and manuscripts in Western American and Oklahoma history. These were the fields in which many graduates wished to do their research.

It seemed to me that the money pledged should be a definite amount each year for several years, rather than a lump sum paid all at once. In this way the donor would be able to take the annual payment as a tax deduction. Also our department would have an additional amount to spend every year and would be able to look for bargains and choose the material purchased more wisely.

Obviously, a wealthy oil man seemed the most logical person to approach, but none that I knew seemed a likely prospect. At last it occurred to me that Patrick Jay Hurley might be sympathetic to an appeal for funds to establish a special collection of material on Oklahoma and Western American history.

He was not an oil magnate but a Tulsa lawyer who had made a comfortable fortune in real estate. He had won high honors as an army officer in World War I. His younger sister, Alice, was a favorite student of mine and a good friend of Rosalie and myself. Of course, his distinguished career as Secretary of War, Major General in World War II, Minister to New Zealand, Special Envoy to Russia, and Ambassador to China lay in the future.

When I called on Hurley at his office in Tulsa he greeted me as an old friend and listened patiently to my story of our need for funds to provide a special collection of material for graduate student research. "How much do you need to start this special library, Eddie?" he asked. Pat Hurley and my brother George were the only people who called me "Eddie."

"Well, if I could get a pledge of $10,000 to be paid in five payments of $2,000 a year for five years it surely would help," I replied. Today this amount seems small but in the mid-1920s $10,000 seemed a large sum, especially to a college teacher.

Pat was thoughtful for a moment before he replied, "Well Eddie I'm trying to do so much with what little I have to do with that I don't feel that I can give you that much, but I'll get it for you. Just go home and leave it to me and you'll be hearing from me in a few days." I thanked him and said goodbye with considerable hope but a little doubt that any man could get a pledge of $10,000 in such easy fashion.

I did not know Pat Hurley, however, as well as I came to know him later. Within a week I had his letter instructing me to write a brief note to Frank Phillips at Bartlesville stating that I would like to see him at his convenience to discuss a business matter which our mutual friend, Patrick Jay Hurley, had mentioned to him recently. Pat had added that he had talked my request over with Mr. Phillips and believed that he would give the amount suggested. As a postscript Pat stated that if Phillips would give only half of the $10,000 he would give the other half but not to tell Frank so, for he was worth at least $30 million and could well afford to give the entire amount.

Mr. Phillips promptly answered my letter inviting me to meet him the next weekend at his country place, Woolaroc Lodge near Bartlesville. I had never met Frank Phillips nor visited Woolaroc, which was said to be a fabulous place on which Phillips was reputed to have spent $1.5 million.

Mr. Phillips proved to be a most courteous and genial host, and the huge Woolaroc ranch with its African antelope and other wild animals was impressive. How many rooms the lodge, built of logs, had I never learned, but I knew there were enough bedrooms and baths for a dozen or more guests.

Mr. Phillips showed me his collection of Western books which contained perhaps 200 or 300 or more volumes. He was quite proud of it and said that he was adding to it all the time and hoped eventually to have a fairly extensive library about ranching and Indians.

Later, when I brought up the subject of my sore need for funds to establish a special collection of Western history for my graduate students, he asked me whether or not I was proposing to do what he was doing there at the lodge. To this my only reply was that this might be true, but his collection at Woolaroc would not be available to my students at the University of Oklahoma.

I must have made a fairly eloquent statement of our need for more and better library facilities for our advanced students of history, because Mr. Phillips agreed that he would give the University of Oklahoma $10,000 by sending us a deposit slip on his bank in Bartlesville every year for five years.

It took time to get a contract prepared by Grant Foreman of Muskogee, a retired lawyer and distinguished historian specializing in the history of the Five Civilized Tribes, to finalize the agreement. It provided that the Phillips Collection should be placed under the control of three trustees consisting of the President of the University, the head of the Department of History, and a third trustee named by Mr. Phillips. He named Patrick Jay Hurley as the third member, and I became the Director.

Very soon after the details of the contract had been worked out came my appointment as a member of the Meriam Commission, so little was done until my return to the University early in September, 1927. Once the school year of 1927-1928 was under way, I began making purchases of material in the fields of Oklahoma, Indian, and Western frontier life. With only $2,000 a year to spend, no rare and expensive items could be bought, but it was my good fortune to find some collections of rare manuscripts, pictures, pamphlets, etc., that could be had at a very reasonable price.

Students were most helpful in telling me of rare material which they had seen. On one occasion I was teaching a class in Oklahoma history and when we reached the period of the Civil War in Oklahoma, some mention was made of General Stand Watie. When the class was over a young man stopped at my desk and told me that a woman living near his hometown of Grove in northeastern Oklahoma had a great many letters of General Stand Watie and members of his family. I could hardly believe this, but he insisted that it was true. He said that he had visited in her home and had seen a trunk full of such letters. He added that her name was Mrs. Jeff Jordan.

342

Edward Everett Dale in the Phillips Collection library. (Courtesy Western History Collections, University of Oklahoma Library)

I at once wrote a letter to Mrs. Jordan, and within a week she replied stating that she did have a great many letters of Stand Watie and his family. She enclosed samples to see if they included anything of interest to me. I looked at the enclosures and nearly collapsed to see that one was Stand Watie's commission as Brigadier General signed by the Confederate Secretary of War, and the other was a letter to Stand Watie from General S. B. Maxey of the Confederate Army stating that, "I am enclosing herewith your commission as Brigadier General, etc., etc."

To ask me if I would be interested in this material was like asking if a duck could swim! The first Saturday after receiving the news saw me on a train to Grove. Here I was able to hire a car and drive to the home of Mrs. Jordan who lived about three or four miles from town.

Mrs. Jordan was a widow living with her son. They received me courteously and proudly showed me three trunks almost full of letters of the Watie, Boudinot, Ridge, and Bell families and other Cherokees who were their close friends. No seeker of buried treasure was ever more thrilled by the discovery of doubloons and pieces-of-eight buried by their Spanish owners than I was by finding these letters in a humble farmhouse in what was once the Cherokee Nation.

To my delight Mrs. Jordan and her son agreed to place these letters in the custody of the University. I assured them that they would be kept in a fire proof brick building. I then drove back to town for wooden boxes into which the letters were emptied and sent by express to the University. Here my secretary, the graduate student in charge of the Phillips Collection, and I set to work to put the letters in usable form. The letters of each person were placed in separate files and arranged chronologically.

They numbered nearly 3,000, extending over the period from 1824 to around 1900. The most important letters were those of Stand Watie and his family, the Boudinot and Ridge families, and the Bell family. There were scores of other letters, however, from various other persons, especially in the years of war from 1861 to 1865 and for some years thereafter. The letters, plus copies of a few others secured from the University of Texas Library and the private collection of Professor T. L. Ballenger of Northeastern State College at Tahlequah, were eventually placed in large scrapbooks to make them easier to use by those engaged in research.

Housing for the Phillips Collection soon became a problem. At first the books, pamphlets, etc, were put in two tall cases in my office in the basement of the Law Building. They were soon transferred to a larger room next door to my office. When a new library was constructed and another classroom and office building completed, I was given an office in this building, called Buchanan Hall, and the Phillips Collection was transferred to a long room at the east end of the new Bizzell Library Building.

The Phillips Collection was not a circulating library, and while visitors were always welcome, permission to work there was limited to holders of a card signed by the director. Most card holders were graduate students or visiting scholars, although no one who needed to use material in the collection in writing an article or term paper was refused admission.

The Phillips Collection was at first operated on funds allocated to the History Department, but was soon given a separate budget which included provisions for a small monthly salary for the custodian, usually a graduate student in history, and for stationery, postage, library cards, material for binding, and photographic prints from a large collection of glass negatives.

When the first $10,000 had been spent at the end of five years, Mr. Phillips gave a second grant of $10,000. I remained director of the collection until my retirement in June, 1952.

I have always been proud of the Frank Phillips Collection and of my part in securing funds to establish it. This would not have been possible, however, without my close friendship with General Hurley. To him, more than to me, the University is indebted for the creation of this excellent collection of material on the Western American Frontier.

Once money had been made available, however, it became

my responsibility to use it as wisely as possible in the purchase of books, pamphlets, pictures, manuscripts, government documents, etc., dealing with life on the American Frontier. The collection grew in importance until it became fairly well-known outside Oklahoma. Many visiting scholars have worked in the collection. Of course, it was largely used by our own graduate students in the field of history, but graduate students or upperclassmen in Government, Sociology, Anthropology, and English also often found material there for theses or term papers.

A year or two before retiring I checked the number of masters' theses, doctoral dissertations, etc., which had been written largely from material in the Phillips Collection. To my surprise I found that 135 masters' theses, four doctoral dissertations, and three books had been written from information obtained from the Phillips Collection.

Phillips's gift to the University came at a time when it was most needed. The period of the Depression was a hard time for the University of Oklahoma and for most other colleges and universities in the country. All state institutions of higher education were largely dependent upon funds appropriated by the state legislature. That body was elected by the voters who demanded economy in government. This meant a reduction in the pay of all persons on the state payroll, including teachers and other employees of state educational institutions.

My own salary as head of the History Department was reduced from $4,500 to $3,800 a year. Other teachers and administrators suffered similar reductions.

When Franklin D. Roosevelt became President he set to work to provide jobs for unemployed persons by projects sponsored by the federal government under W.P.A. and P.W.A. While it was comparatively easy to provide employment for laborers, it was more difficult to find useful work for so-called "white collar workers."

It seemed to me, as head of the History Department and a director of the Oklahoma Historical Society, that the two organizations might combine to set up a W.P.A. project to increase the material for use by students of Oklahoma history and also to foster a greater interest by all the citizens of Oklahoma in the history of their state. This of course was not my idea alone, but I was one of the first to suggest it, and it became my responsibility to administer the History Department's share in it.

We organized a W.P.A. project in which the Historical Society and the Department of History placed a "white collar worker" in virtually every county in the state. Their role was to call upon early settlers and get the story of the migration to Oklahoma and their early life here. In the case of Indians, whites, or Negroes born in Oklahoma, the interviewer was to get the account of the "old timer's" story.

Grant Foreman of Muskogee, the director of the project, was assigned a staff of typists. The accounts collected by field workers were sent to him for typing. The final result was 132 thick volumes of memoirs called the Indian-Pioneer Papers, one set given to the Phillips Collection, the other to the Historical Society Library.

The discovery and eventual acquisition of the Cherokee letters and papers had given me the idea that there must be a great deal more material of historical value in Oklahoma, especially in the eastern half of the state. This area had been occupied by the Five Civilized Tribes beginning about 1820. It seemed logical to assume that there might also be material in the region occupied by the Choctaw, Chickasaw, Creek, and Seminole nations. I had no doubt that letters, journals, pictures, documents, etc., were stored away by families in trunks, or boxes in attics, closets, or garages. These documents would come to light if someone could obtain funds to support travel for a month or two in eastern Oklahoma to search for such material.

I accordingly applied to the Rockefeller Foundation for a grant of $1,500. Unfortunately there were some delays and I was invited to teach in the 1934 summer school of the University of Nebraska, so I could not start on the search for historical material in eastern Oklahoma until after the 1st of August. I asked Dr. Morris L. Wardell and C. C. Bush, both of the History Department, to go with me. Bush was a young man who had written a master's thesis with me on the anti-draft troubles in Oklahoma in World War I. His interest was primarily in military history and later he served for a time as Dean of Men. His chief duties with us were to drive the car and service it, and to keep a "log" of each day's work including the distance traveled, the names of the persons we met, and any "leads" given us as to where collections of historical material might be found.

Wardell, mentioned in an earlier chapter, taught Oklahoma history and several other courses in American history. He had been a soldier in World War I and was one of my students in his undergraduate work at O.U. where he received his bachelor's degree. He attended Harvard for a year and was awarded his masters degree, and later took his Ph.D. at the University of Chicago.

The story of our five-week survey of historical material in eastern Oklahoma would make several chapters, but only a brief statement need be given here. The complete log of ninety-eight pages of text, plus two maps giving in detail the area covered, may be found in the Dale Collection of the University of Oklahoma Library. Perhaps it is enough to say that we started our work on August 6, 1934, and ended our travels on September 12, after driving a total of 2,738 miles, and to give a few of the more important incidents that occurred and discoveries that were made.

Mr. Bush was able to check out an elderly University car for our use on this project. The speedometer showed some 63,000 miles, and it ran fairly well once on the road, but was quite tempermental about starting.

We spent the first two days visiting the Oklahoma Historical Society in Oklahoma City compiling information on materials in its library. The party then left Norman on August 9, 1934 for Okmulgee. Chief point of interest there was the Indian museum in the old Creek Capitol building in Okmulgee.

Our next stop was at Muskogee, arriving a little after six o'clock. We called on Mr. and Mrs. Grant Foreman and spent some time in conference with them. The Foremans were deeply interested in the history of Indian Territory, and Mr. Foreman had written a great deal on the Five

Civilized Tribes. Mr. Foreman went with us to the Federal Building which housed the offices of superintendent of the agency for the Five Civilized Tribes. There was no time to go through the files of the agency, but we did get some idea of what they contained.

We left Muskogee shortly after four o'clock and drove to Tahlequah which I have always thought was the most interesting town in Oklahoma. This was the site of North-eastern State College, the main building of which had been the Cherokee Female Seminary. I had many friends there, including the president of the college and several members of the faculty.

While at Tahlequah we visited the Sequoyah Orphan's Training School which had originally been the orphanage of the Cherokee Nation. We found the records of the school quite interesting, but the very early ones had been destroyed by fire. The college library, however, had a great many Cherokee documents, including letters and manuscripts of *Home Sweet Home.* The public library of Tahlequah also had a great many bound files of the *Cherokee Advocate* and the various editions of the laws of both the Choctaw and the Cherokee nations. While in the Tahlequah area we visited the National Cemetery in Fort Gibson.

Our next stop was at Eufaula, a very old town. We visited the Eufaula Boarding School but found that they had no records prior to 1920. The old ones had been burned.

I then visited Mr. Walter Grayson and his sister, Mrs. Eloise C. Smock, and Colonel Wash Grayson. Mrs. Walter Grayson showed me the books of her husband's late father, Captain G. W. Grayson, former chief of the Creek Nation and a soldier in the Civil War. She seemed to be very proud of an encyclopedia and other handsomely bound books in her living room.

I then asked her where Chief Grayson's other books were. She said that there was a number of old volumes out in a storeroom. We assured her that we would like to see them but she was reluctant, saying it would be so hot in there that we could not stand it. We assured her we were accustomed to the heat, so she took us to the little building in the yard. There we found the usual tools, a couple of old trunks, and some boxes, but when she opened the trunks and boxes we found several volumes of the laws of the Creek Nation and various other old documents that she apparently thought were worthless. There also was one very rare volume of Creek laws which was worth at least $50. We urged her to move the books into the house and later send the letters and documents to a bank vault or a school that was fireproof.

My happiest discovery was the autobiography of Chief Grayson he had given his daughter, Mrs. Smock. We found it very interesting, and Mrs. Smock agreed to let me take it and make a copy. I did this and later tried to find a publisher for an edited version.

I was especially eager to find some material giving a bit of history of the eight Indian tribes in northeastern Oklahoma. This agency, first called the Neosho Agency, and later the Quapaw Agency, was old. It included the Quapaw Reservation as well as the remnants of the Ottawas, Miamis, Wyandots, Senecas, Peorias, and Modocs. The latter were brought to Oklahoma from northern California after an outbreak in which Captain Jack of the tribe had killed General E. R. S. Canby and two or three other officers. The agency was situated at Miami.

When we reached Miami on August 27, the superintendent told us that he had no records of that agency for more than ten or fifteen years back. When we asked what had happened to them he said he was not sure, but the agency had formerly been at Wyandotte and when the time came to move the agency to Miami, he understood that the agent had a bonfire and burned all the records. We accordingly left Miami and drove down to Wyandotte. Joe Kagey was the principal of a large Indian boarding school there. An employee informed us that there were some boxes in the attic of one of the buildings there, but she did not know what was in them. We then asked Mr. Kagey to show us the attic, and let us take a look at them. To the surprise of everyone, we found that six boxes contained the early files of the Quapaw Indian Agency going back to before the Civil War.

This was a great discovery. The Secretary of the Interior

had authorized the superintendents of all the Indian agencies and schools in Oklahoma to transfer materials not required for current purposes to the Oklahoma Historical Society. We therefore wrote to the president of the Oklahoma Historical Society and a truck was sent to Wyandotte to transport the files to Oklahoma City.

We visited every important town in eastern Oklahoma and all the Indian agencies of the former Indian Territory, finding many old letters and documents at most places visited. At Bacone College, just outside Muskogee, we found a large collection of diaries, letters, and documents called the J. S. Murrow Collection. Murrow had been a missionary in Oklahoma. The materials found here and in other schools and agencies are all listed in the bound log of the survey which is in the University of Oklahoma Library. It was a little surprising to us that we discovered many valuable books, manuscripts, journals, etc., at every Indian agency and many of the schools visited, and in some cases in libraries of small towns where the librarian had no idea of the value of some things on the library shelves or stored away in boxes. Consequently, our Oklahoma survey proved to be successful in discovering material of historical value.

Throughout my tenure as Department head, my relations with students were most cordial. I shall always remember that three or four of my graduate students would come almost every afternoon and ask if I were going to have a cup of coffee. When I said yes, they asked if they might go with me. Over the coffee we discussed history or current affairs. Almost every semester my wife would have one of my classes of graduate students to dinner in our home. It was usually a one-dish meal of baked beans or spaghetti with meat sauce or some other easily prepared dish with coffee and dessert. If the class was large, some students sat on the floor on cushions. After the meal they sang songs and had a very pleasant evening. There were some people who asserted that a professor should not become too intimate with students; rather, one should hold himself aloof. I never found this to be true. On the contrary, when I went out for coffee with three or four students they would insist on holding my chair, helping me with my coat, and making me feel 100 years old. I came to feel that close relations with students made me a better teacher and gave me a greater influence with these young people.

While I asked President Bizzell not to appoint me to any more University committees than absolutely necessary, there were some committees on which I served during most of the later years when I was head of the Department of History. One of these was the unofficial committee headed by Dean Edgar Meacham of the College of Arts and Sciences. This committee consisted of only three men. One was from Humanities including the English Department, one from the Sciences, and the third from the Social Sciences, to which I was appointed. We met once a week in the Dean's office to talk over matters concerning the work in these divisions of the University. This was purely an informal meeting in which we discussed various aspects of University work. No records were kept.

Another committee on which I served for three years handled a fund of $25,000 given to the University by the Rockefeller Foundation. The purpose of the grant was to subsidize the writing of books by authors dealing with the Southwest. Our task was to choose persons who were to receive such grants, each award amounting to $2,000. The president agreed to give anyone receiving such a grant a sabbatical leave with half salary which usually brought the total to about the same amount as the chosen person's salary. To our surprise, however, we could not always secure applicants for such grants from the faculty of the University of Oklahoma. For example, one grant was given to an English professor at the Texas School of Mines at El Paso, a school which later became a branch of the University of Texas. Another grant was given to Dr. Angie Debo for a book called *Oklahoma Foot Loose and Fancy Free*, a study of the people of Oklahoma. Debo was not a member of the faculty at Oklahoma University. In addition to these two committees, I served on committees of a temporary nature from time to time. I also was a member of the graduate council for some years. This was a group of seven who assisted the Dean of the Graduate School.

352

Dr. Homer L. Dodge came to the University as a professor of physics in September, 1919, and seven years later became Dean of the Graduate School. A few years later Dean Dodge was granted a leave of absence to spend a year in Europe and asked me to serve as acting dean during his absence. I could not well refuse, and I really learned a great deal during that year because I met graduate students from all departments.

Fortunately, Dean Dodge left me his secretary, Miss Whitaker, who knew the details quite well, and I depended upon her to keep me informed as to many matters of the position. Evidently I did not always deal with individuals in exactly the same way as had the former dean, for one day Miss Whitaker said to me, "Dr. Dale, you don't talk to people like Dean Dodge does. If he talked to them like you do, they would get awfully mad at him but nobody ever seems to get mad at you."

I tried to recall what prompted her remark, and then remembered a young woman who had been in my own classes in history. She had come in complaining that Professor Stuart Tompkins had given her a "C" in Russian History. While she was a fairly good student in my classes, always making at least a "B," her spelling left a great deal to be desired. I told her that I knew nothing of Russian history and that there was nothing I could do for her. She was still furious and said, "I think I deserved a higher grade. I have a good friend on the Board of Regents, and I am going to write to him about this." To this I replied, "Why by all means, write your friend on the Board of Regents. If you like, I will sit right by you and help with the spelling." She smiled and said, "Oh, well, I guess I won't write my friend. I know it wouldn't do any good." While I seemed to get along very well as acting Graduate Dean, I was truly glad when Dr. Dodge returned, for during the year of his absence, I had nearly worn a trail from my office to the Phillips Collection and back to my own office, and I had not been able to get much writing done.

During the years, I did a great deal of public speaking. Every high school had commencement exercises which included a speaker from some college or university. I was called upon to give many commencement speeches throughout the state because of my status with the University. I did not mind this, for it gave me an opportunity to get acquainted with public school superintendents and teachers. Moreover, I had quite a bit of training in public speaking for I had attended two of the summer schools of T. E. Jones and had also been appointed a member of the Board of Directors of the Curry School of Speech by its president, Dr. S. C. Curry. He had offered to give private lessons to members of the board of directors so I took advantage of this. It seemed a great opportunity, for normally he got ten dollars an hour for teaching oratory to individuals, and I could never have taken them at that price.

It was also my privilege to give lectures every summer at Oklahoma A&M College, now Oklahoma State University. Its president during the years when I was head of the History Department was Dr. Henry G. Bennett. I had known him when he was superintendent of schools at Hugo in southeastern Oklahoma. He had spent a year at O.U. taking a masters degree in education with a minor in history. Later he took a Ph.D. and became president of Southeastern State College.

Two or three years after he had been elected President of Oklahoma A&M at Stillwater he told me that sooner or later he was going to add me to the faculty at A&M or make me refuse a very good offer of position there. To this I only replied that I never refused anything before it was offered me, but I really had no thought of going to A&M as a member of its faculty.

A year or so later, however, Bennett telephoned me asking if I could meet him at the Huckins Hotel in Oklahoma City about four o'clock the next afternoon. At this meeting he reminded me of what he had said about my coming to the A&M College. He asked me if I would consider coming the next year as Dean of the College of Arts and Sciences. He offered a salary far larger than I was getting at O.U. and assured me that he would do everything possible to give me time for writing, that I could bring my own secretary, and finally added, "You need not feel that you are leaving your friends; the state of Oklahoma is your campus. You have students and friends all over the state, and we will do everything possible to make your life with us a happy one." It was a very tempting offer, but I did not want to be a dean and so had to decline. He then said that if I ever changed my mind to be sure to let him know and that there would be a position for me at a higher salary than I was drawing at the University of Oklahoma.

Dr. Bizzell's administration of University affairs ended at the close of the summer session of 1941. During the sixteen years of his service as president, the University had grown amazingly. From 1925 to 1941 the University library holdings had been increased from 65,000 volumes to over 225,000, in addition to 120,000 pamphlets and 8,000 uncatalogued government documents. The College of Law Library had grown proportionately. Enrollment had increased from slightly more than 5,500 in 1924-1925 to over 8,500 in 1940-1941, and enrollment in the graduate school had risen from 325 to over 1,500 in this period. President Bizzell conferred over 18,000 degrees during his sixteen years as president of O.U., while all presidents before him had conferred slightly over 5,200.

President Bizzell was very popular with both faculty and students, and before retirement he was presented a beautiful desk purchased from donations by faculty and all employees of the University. It was my privilege to give the presentation speech in which I pointed out that virtually every person employed by the University, including secretaries, janitors, and workmen on the buildings and grounds, had made a freewill offering without solicitation once they learned that a gift was to be presented to Dr. Bizzell.

Though Dr. Bizzell was only sixty-five years of age when he gave up the presidency of O.U., his health was not good, and most of the University regents felt that he should be replaced by a younger man. Some asserted that the new president should be a graduate of the University. They declared that the University of Oklahoma had been established fifty years, and if it had not produced a man capable

(top) Joseph August Brandt, President of the University of Oklahoma 1941-1943. (below) The Bizzell Memorial Library, a fitting tribute to William Bennett Bizzell's tenure as president of the University. (Courtesy Western History Collections, University of Oklahoma Library)

of managing its affairs in half a century, it had better close its doors to students and let them seek an education elsewhere.

This sounded logical but did not give consideration to the fact that O.U. might have graduated scores of men quite capable of managing its affairs as president but who had achieved so much success in business, law, engineering, or some other field that they would not consider leaving their present vocation for the presidency of a University.

The man chosen to succeed President Bizzell was Joseph August Brandt who seemed to have the qualifications demanded by anyone. Although born in Indiana in 1899, he had spent his boyhood and youth in Oklahoma, had graduated with the class of 1921, and had gone to Oxford as a Rhodes Scholar. He returned to Oklahoma where he worked for a time as a journalist, serving as city editor of newspapers in Sapulpa, Ponca City, and Tulsa. He had come to the University in 1928 as Director of the University Press. He had served in that position for ten years, but in 1938 resigned to accept the directorship of the Princeton University Press.

Dr. Bizzell was named President Emeritus and Professor of Sociology but taught very little because his health remained bad. He bought a home on a street facing the campus. His health continued to decline and he died in May, 1944. He had been a great president of the University of Oklahoma, and his death was mourned by thousands of persons throughout the state. His statue by Professor Joe Taylor stands near the north end of the South Oval facing the library to which he added so much and which bears his name.

The new president arrived in Norman during September, 1941. A tall, handsome man of forty-two with a wife and two children, his manner was gracious, and everyone on the faculty welcomed him and hoped that he would have a long and successful tenure as president. It soon became evident that Brandt expected to make some sweeping changes in the administration of university affairs. Even before he reached Norman he had written me giving me the names of two men he would like to me to consider if we had a vacancy in the History Department. Since Dr. Bizzell had never offered such a suggestion I began to wonder if Brandt might not overstep what to me seemed the proper functions of a university president.

The new president's first change was to insist that all students entering the university as freshmen go through a formal matriculation ceremony. In this the student wore a gown and a beret-like cap with the top divided into triangular segments of different colors. This was not difficult, although it created something of a problem for students enrolling late. It seemed a bit paradoxical, however, for a president who urged everyone to call him "Joe" to introduce this bit of old world pageantry to a prairie university only fifty years of age.

President Brandt clearly felt that the University had been too conservative in administration. It must be confessed that there was some reason for his thinking so. Up to this time the Department of History had as its chief only two men, Dean Buchanan and myself, although there were brief periods when both of us were away for the summer or on a temporary assignment when some other member of the department served as acting head. In most other departments the situation was the same, and most of the deans were middle-aged and had served for several years in those positions.

The president also believed that all students entering the University for the first time should take approximately the same courses in order that those planning to be engineers, geologists, pharmacists, anthropologists, etc., might have a better knowledge of language, history, and other disciplines at graduation. He, therefore, established the University College composed of freshmen and sophomores. As dean of the new college he appointed a young teacher of English who, although an excellent English teacher, lacked experience in administration.

The preliminary work of planning the program for 1940-41 had progressed so much by the time the new president arrived that he was unable to put his plans into operation.

He worked so hard at formulating them, however, that he could not keep up with his correspondence and complained bitterly that there were letters on his desk that should have been answered a week or two before.

A feeling of dissatisfaction and apprehension began to pervade the campus. When you saw three or four faculty talking earnestly over coffee at the Union you could safely bet that they were not discussing politics or religion but this "university college" and the situation at O.U.

I remember a conversation I had with the dean of the University College soon after the close of the summer school in early August, 1942. I told him that I did not see how the History Department could take over all freshmen, for we had only eleven teachers at that time and the University had enrolled over 1,400 freshmen the previous year. The dean replied that if each man would take two sections of U.S. History he believed it could be done. After that we could see about getting some additional help in the department but he doubted if we would have over 1,000 freshmen that year. I protested that I would like to have assurance from the president that we would have some additional help, but the dean said that we should wait until school opened and see what the situation was.

Dean Meacham of the College of Arts and Sciences asked me to his office. He was one of my closest friends, having been at Harvard together for one year, and he and his wife had often gone with us to spend a weekend at our log cabin near Turner Falls. I hurried over to his office and he said, "Dale, you will read in the paper tomorrow morning that the president has secured the approval of the Board of Regents to abolish all departmental heads in the University and substitute departmental chairmen each to serve for a four-year term. I told the president that I would not wait for the departmental heads in the College of Arts and Sciences to read this in the paper but would tell them one by one this afternoon. He has asked me to recommend a departmental chairman in each department, and I have selected Dr. C. C. Rister because I believe he is the one that you yourself would have chosen."

As a matter of fact, I would not have selected Rister because he had no interest in administration and knew almost nothing about what was required for a degree with a major in history. His interest was primarily in writing. There was nothing for me to do, however, but to accept something already done. I thanked him for letting me know in advance. The morning papers, of course, carried the story in detail and Rister came to see me immediately, expressing some consternation because of the new responsibility that had been thrust upon him and to ask my help which I assured him would be cheerfully given. I told him that I would, of course, turn over the history office to him since it contained all the files and records. I also assured him that I would ask Alberta McCann, my secretary for fourteen years, to remain secretary to the head of the department. I assured him that she knew all the details of administering the department and he would have no difficulty in his work as chairman as long as she remained in that position.

As a matter of fact, I had no objection to turning the administration of the department over to another of its members, for it relieved me of considerable work and also a great deal of responsibility. So far as I know, there was no change in Rister's salary and none in mine, but Rister was relieved of a little part of his teaching in order to give time for his work in administration.

I talked with Miss McCann and, while she was quite unhappy about the situation, she somewhat reluctantly agreed that she would remain as secretary to Dr. Rister for the coming year. I asked for an appointment with the president, however, as soon as possible, for I was leaving Norman for a week or ten days to give a couple of lectures and at the same time secure some material for a book which I was writing. The president greeted me cordially enough, and I told him that since I had a personal file or two in the history office as well as a case of books and some pictures, I would like for him to have the proper person to secure an office for me and also a part-time secretary. He said office space was scarce and secretarial help difficult to find, but he would see what he could do and I left on my trip. Immediately after my return I again called on the president and asked if he had found a space for me to remove my personal property, books, files, and other things from the History Department. He said he had been so busy with other things that he had not had time to do this.

School was to open within two weeks and apparently there was no place for me to go. By this time I was feeling pretty well disgusted with the situation and recalled that Dr. Bennett of Oklahoma A&M had told me that if I ever considered coming to that institution, there would be a position there for me. So I wrote him a brief letter saying that I would like to come to see him as soon as it would be convenient. Nearly a week passed and Dr. Bennett called. He explained, "I have been out of town for a week and returned only last night to find a letter from you saying that you would like to see me. I will be in my office all this week, Dr. Dale, and will be glad to see you at any time you can come to Stillwater. And if it is not convenient for you to come to Stillwater to see me, I will be glad to come to Norman to see you."

The following day my wife and I drove to Stillwater. I explained to Dr. Bennett that the situation at O.U. was not a happy one, not only for me but for many others, and reminded him of what he had said to me some years before. He seemed delighted to see us, and after talking a little while he called in Dean Scroggs, a former student of mine who had accepted the position of Dean which I had refused. President Bennett said that he would like for me to come to the A&M College in a new position as Director of Graduate Studies in Social Sciences. In this position I could teach a class or two if I wished and would serve as advisor to all teachers of the social sciences. He said that he had fixed a salary at $5,000 a year, that I could bring my own secretary, and that they would do their best to make me happy in my new position. This seemed to me a most attractive offer but I asked to have two or three days to consider the matter. He assured me that he hoped that I would accept it and reminded me that, as he put it, the state of Oklahoma was my campus and that I need not feel that I was leaving my friends when I left O.U.

With that we parted and my wife and I looked about for a house to buy or rent.

Neither of us, I am afraid, felt quite happy, for we talked about it as we drove home, each feeling no particular elation at the prospect of leaving our home in Norman. We agreed, however, that President Bennett's offer was too good to refuse. The next morning I dictated a brief note to Miss McCann as follows:

Dear President Brandt:

It has been said that brevity is the soul of wit. Sometimes I think it is the essence of wisdom also. I hereby tender my resignation of my position as professor of history at the University of Oklahoma, effective immediately.

Sincerely yours,

E. E. Dale

I called the president for an appointment and he said to come over. He received me cordially. I handed him my note thinking he would be glad to see me go. To my surprise, he seemed almost horrified. He said, "No, no, no! We can't do this." He tore the note up and tossed it in the waste basket and said, "What can we do?"

I said nothing except to let me slip out quietly with no publicity. "You have a rule that is not worth the paper it is written on that says no faculty member can resign after the first of August but one can always quit. You have certain policies with respect to the administration of the University of Oklahoma which you of course believe in, and you have a right to carry out your policies with men and women who agree with you that they are correct. As long as I am a member of the faculty of the University of Oklahoma I will try my best to carry out the policies of the president, but you can hardly succeed unless you have men on the faculty who believe in what you are doing. You may be perfectly right. Just let me go and put someone in my place who believes as you do."

President Brandt said, "Come back this afternoon. We can't let this happen. Come in about two o'clock, and I will *(top) The University of Oklahoma Department of History faculty, 1959. (below) Five historians from the University of Oklahoma at the opening of the Western History Collections Suite. (Courtesy Western History Collections, University of Oklahoma Library)*

363

have Dean Meacham here." I returned to find Meacham in the president's office, and President Brandt said, "I would like to make you Dean of the Faculty at a dean's salary."

I asked what would be my duties. He said they would be to sit in his outer office and to meet faculty members who had come to see him, find out what they want, and help all I could in answering their questions and advising them. I said, "No, Joe. I don't want to get that close to the administration." Dean Meacham said he rather expected that would be my answer.

Then the president said, "Well, would you be willing to accept a special professorship? The University of Texas has them. They are called distinguished professorships, pay a dean's salary, require a man to teach a half a load and devote the rest of the time to writing and research and to help others with their writings and research."

My reply was that this sounded like an ideal sort of position but that I did not want to be called a distinguished service professor because I did not feel that I had rendered such service. I asked if he couldn't call it something else. He decided to call it a graduate professorship. He told me I would have an office to myself and the same salary as a dean. I replied that I did not want to leave O.U. and would be glad to accept such a position.

The next day an office had been set aside for me and my personal property was moved to my own office in the Business Administration Building. I was instructed to look for a fulltime secretary. My work as head of the History Department was over. The next year my title was changed to Research Professor of History and professors from three other departments were added to the list of research professors. I telephoned both Dr. Bennett and Dean Scroggs that I deeply appreciated their offer, but the situation at O.U. had changed so I had decided it was best to remain with the University of Oklahoma.

Our Indian Daughter

I have said little about our son, Edward Everett Dale, Jr., except the fact that he seemed to acquire almost every type of illness common to children during my year with the Indian Survey. By the time I returned home early in September, 1927, he was in excellent health again, and for the remainder of his childhood was seldom ill. Except that he had traveled a bit more than most children his age, he grew up a perfectly normal boy—adverse to hard work, the use of soap and water, and dressing up. He was fond of picture shows, especially "Westerns" with plenty of action, but he hated what he called "love shows."

In good weather he and his playmates were fond of playing "cops and robbers" and engaging in "rubber gun wars." In rainy weather when it was not possible to be out of doors he was always busy making toy airplanes or carving chains from soft wood, even the kitchen type of matches, usually filling the entire house with the smell of banana oil and mucilage. At such times, however, he sometimes voiced a wish that we had another "kid" or that he had someone to play with, although he read quite a bit in the more exciting books for children to entertain himself.

We had a large fenced backyard, for the money earned during the Indian Survey, added to some good crops on the farm, and royalties from one or two of my books, had enabled us not only to pay all of our debts but also to make some improvements on our home. We had added another large bedroom and a basement where we installed a coal-burning furnace, and we built a study for me on the east side of what had been our diningroom.

My salary had been advanced to $4,500 a year before the Great Depression struck. We had bought a lot on a mountainside near Turner Falls with a medium large log cabin as a place to go on weekends for rest and recreation.

In June, 1932, Miss Flora Malloy, who was a teacher at Chilocco Indian School, visited us bringing with her a young mixed-blood Indian girl named Pearl Garen. She left Pearl in the car and came to tell us that she had brought down a girl who had just graduated from Chilocco and wanted very much to find a place for her to work for her room and board while she attended the University. She said that the girl was one of the best students that had ever studied at Chilocco and had won the George Washington Medal for scholarship her senior year.

We had known Miss Malloy and her sister for a long time, and she knew that I had been on the survey of conditions of the Indians. She had come to us hoping that we might be willing to take the young woman into our home to help in the housework while she attended the University.

We were a bit surprised because we had no room suitable for a student, but Miss Malloy insisted that she would like to bring Pearl in and let us talk with her. She was about seventeen years old and quite an attractive young woman; a bit shy, of course, but she sat down and crossed her ankles primly as she had been taught to do by the matron at Chilocco School who had told her that a lady must never cross her knees.

We were impressed by her appearance but we explained that we had no room suitable for her and suggested that she look about among other faculty homes and see if she could find a place that had a bit larger house than ours where the family would be willing to give her room and board for the help she could render in household work.

We told her that if she did not find such a place to come back and I would pay for a room at the home of Mrs. Glenn, an elderly lady, who kept a few roomers and lived almost directly across the street from us. I was sure that Mrs. Glenn would be glad to give her a room, and I would pay for it. She could take her meals with us and help Rosalie a little in the household work.

Miss Malloy said that she would take her around to some other faculty homes and they left us with the promise that if she could find no suitable place they would return. Some three days later she wrote us a brief letter saying that she had found a family who would give her room and board for help in the household work, but she knew that she would have many adjustments to make and felt that she could make them easier in our home than anywhere else.

A day or so later Rosalie had a hard fall from her car, and the doctor put her to bed for a few days. I took over the housework with a little help from Rosalie's mother who lived only a block away. Rosalie's mother kept roomers and had her own work to do. So after three or four days I called Pearl and asked if she could come down and help us out for a week or so, and perhaps during that time we could work out a plan by which she could live with us. She came down immediately and after a few days, we decided that we could make an additional room by moving a smaller building which stood in our back yard up to my study and adding a few feet to it. I had used this little building as a study by having it wired for electricity and putting in a gas stove. I had moved my desk and a bookcase out there, and for two or three years had done my work there away from the house. Later, after a study had been built for me, I moved from this little building to the new study. Ed and his friends had used it at first for what they called a "liberry" where they brought their books, and they later used it as a "labatory" when they began to do childish chemistry work.

I accordingly contacted the lumber yard people and had this little building moved up and connected with my study and a couple of feet added to it making a very nice bedroom about twelve by ten feet. Electricity and gas were already there so it was only necessary to put in a bed, chairs, desk, and rugs, and we very gladly turned this room over to Pearl.

In addition to other improvements I purchased the seventy-five foot lot just east of the lot on which our house stood. The owner had permitted it to grow up in weeds, making an unsightly spot. When he offered to sell it for $1,500 I borrowed the money at the bank and bought it. I then had the weeds cut, the ground plowed and leveled, and planted in bermuda grass. We then extended the yard fence around the entire tract and put out a number of fruit trees, giving us 150 feet in our property, all enclosed in steel fence except for the front yard. This gave Ed a large backyard to play in.

Pearl seemed happy with her room and furnishings and while she was shy at first, she became less so. Ed was delighted to have another person added to the household, for while Pearl was five years older than he, they were soon comrades. We found that she loved to read and had already read a great deal, including some great books as well as some more or less trashy ones. She sometimes pronounced her words in weird fashion if she had never heard them but only picked them up in her reading.

As she became accustomed to her new life she told us how shy she had been at first. She said once, "I was especially afraid to meet your mother—I thought she might be a regular old dough-wagger!" Rosalie looked blank but I knew instantly that she meant dowager. As for me, I thought she had coined a rather apt description of some dowagers I had seen, if by dough one means money.

It was hard to remain shy in our household, so within a few weeks our new member of the family began to tell us some things about her family. Her father was a full blood Mohawk, the grandfather having come to Oklahoma from Canada. She was very fond of her grandfather who died within a few weeks after she came to us. Her father had married a full blood Caddo widow with a son by her former marriage to a full blood Caddo man. Of course, this son was not at all related to Pearl, but she referred to him as "my brother—Indian way." Apparently he was a worthless individual.

I once expressed a desire to see him. To this Pearl replied, "Why it would not be difficult to see him if you wish. Just drive to Anadarko some Saturday to the jail and if he's not there just wait a while and an officer will bring him in!"

She told us a good many things about the "brother—Indian way" whose name was Harrison. She said that Harrison and his wife owned 320 acres of good land with a wickiup or arbor in the yard beside the house. Near the arbor was a well with pulley and buckets, and in the summer Harrison had the habit of sitting out under the arbor and watching for tourists coming along the road. The tourists would frequently stop and ask for a drink of water and of course, engaged Harrison in conversation saying, "This is a beautiful farm you have here." To this Harrison would reply, "Yes, it's a pretty place but I would like to sell it." "How much would you want?" the tourist would ask. "Well I'd want some money down but I'd take about $1,000 for the 320 acres."

Easily the farm was worth at least ten times that amount and the tourist would say, "Well, I believe I'd give $1,000 for it." "Well, I'm willing but I need some money down right now because a man is coming to collect for a horse he sold me and I need about $50."

The tourist would open his wallet, hand out $50, and say, "Give me the legal description of the land and I will go up and bring back the papers for you to sign. I will pay the balance in cash by having that amount telegraphed to me from New York."

The purchaser would drive up to Anadarko, go into a lawyer's office, present the numbers of the land, and say, "I bought this farm from an Indian here. I'd like to have you fix up a deed and the necessary papers."

"What Indian!?" "Harrison." "Harrison! Why he's a full blood Indian and he can't sell his land or mortgage it! I hope you didn't pay him any money!!" "Well, not much." the tourist would reply.

The tourist would then jump in his car and fairly burn up the road getting back to Harrison's home only to find him gone to Lawton having as much celebration as fifty dollars would buy. The tourist had no recourse and could only get in his car and continue his journey, a sadder but wiser man.

I never saw Harrison but Pearl told me a good many other

stories of his methods of acquiring money, most of which went for whiskey.

The full blood Caddo wife bore Mr. Garen two children, Joe and Effie. The Caddo wife died a few years after Effie was born, and Mr. Garen married an Irish widow with one son from her white husband. She became the mother of Pearl and her brother Claude, who were, of course, half-bloods. Facetiously Pearl remarked to me, "My father was a full blood Mohawk and my mother a full blood Irish woman. I don't have a drop of white blood in my veins."

As the weeks went by she began to feel quite at home with us, and we began to feel for her a real affection. She told us quite a bit of her childhood days which must not have been too happy, although her keen sense of humor no doubt helped her to endure a certain amount of hardship.

Her mother had died when Pearl was only six or seven years of age and her brother Claude was only a toddler. She always felt that she must take the place of her mother and assumed all the responsibility for the welfare of her little brother. Her father had considerable knowledge of mechanics and could get a fairly good job, but the care of the two children was a real problem for him. Soon after her mother's death he removed to a town in New Mexico and opened a barber shop. He found a family to take charge of the little boy and sent Pearl to live with an Apache family on a ranch not too far from town.

The family had a small boy about six years old and she and "Bill," as she called him, became playmates. They were each given a pony and rode about over the ranch. Bill could not speak English so they could not talk to each other very much except by signs, but they had a good deal of fun playing together.

There was a missionary who lived not far from this Apache home who was a frequent caller. When Bill was sent to bring the visitor a dipper of water from the spring near the house, he filled the dipper with water, spit in it two or three times, and carried it in and handed it to the missionary whom he apparently cordially disliked! As the missionary drank, Bill lay down on the floor and rolled over and over laughing which puzzled the mother a great deal as she could not see anything funny to cause his laughter.

Pearl's father then sent her to a Mexican ranch also not far from town. The family there sent Pearl to herd the goats—not that they needed herding, for they were in a pasture, but in order to get her away from the Mexican children because they quarreled and fought so much.

Eventually, Mr. Garen brought the children back to Oklahoma and established a home in Oklahoma City. He hired a housekeeper, a white woman, and sent Pearl to a white school, but then decided that she was old enough to go to Chilocco which Joe and Effie had attended.

The decision to send Pearl to Chilocco may have been a trifle early because of the difficulty of finding a housekeeper and keeping her for any length of time. At least Pearl told us that until she went to Chilocco no white woman had ever been kind to her. She told us of one housekeeper that stayed only two days. Mr. Garen had gone to work early, before the children awoke. When the new housekeeper discovered that three-year old Claude had wet his bed, she picked up a leather strap and said she was going to whip him for it. Pearl must have been about ten or eleven years old at that time and she told the housekeeper that she would not let her whip the little boy, and that she should wait until the father was home, tell him, and let him punish Claude if he felt that the child needed to be punished.

The woman insisted that she would not have Pearl as her boss but only Mr. Garen, and that she was going to whip the little boy regardless of what Pearl thought. When she caught the boy by the shoulder and lifted the strap, Pearl picked up a huge butcher knife and started toward the woman and frightened her so that she bolted toward the open door and did not stop running until she was a block away.

She did not return but met Mr. Garen as he was coming home from work and demanded payment for the two days that she had worked, saying that she would send someone after her clothes but would not enter that house again for any amount of money! Pearl told us that she did not know what she would have done, but hardly thought she really would have stabbed the woman.

The matrons at Chilocco were kind to Pearl, but for days after she reached the huge Indian school with more than 1,000 students she was very lonely. She did not know any of the students and would sit in her little room and cry, sometimes from sheer loneliness. She felt that the kindness of the white matrons was only temporary. After all, they were white, and sooner or later they would come out in their true colors and be unkind, for she firmly believed that was the way white women were.

After some weeks, however, when they continued to treat her kindly, she at long last decided that some white women could be kind to children. Long before her first year was up she became quite happy, for she was treated kindly by the teachers and matrons and made many warm friends. During the Indian survey we had visited Chilocco in 1927 and were well impressed with the school and felt that the children were fairly well fed. We did find, however, that it was operated on the same military basis as was the first big Indian school at Carlisle, Pennsylvania, which was established by General Pratt. The students there were divided into companies with a captain and a couple of lieutenants. Each company rose with the bell, dressed and fell into line by the bell, marched to breakfast, and stood beside the table and all said grace as follows:

"God is great and God is good
And we thank him for this food.
By his hand are all men fed.
Give us, Lord, our daily bread."

Chilocco owned a large tract of land for growing corn and vegetables and kept a considerable herd of cattle. The students worked one-half day and attended classes the other half. The work was supposed to be part of their education, but in many cases it was not teaching the children much after the first few weeks, but became merely the drudgery of operating the school. For instance, the girls who worked in the laundry feeding sheets, towels, and pillow cases through a machine did not learn much after the first week.

372

When Pearl had been with us for a few weeks and had recovered from her shyness, we discovered that she had a very keen sense of humor, and she began to tell us stories of her life in school. Since Meriam Commission members stayed at any school only three or four days, it was not possible for us to get much information from the students.

But Pearl delighted in telling us about her life at Chilocco. The matrons continued to be kind to her and she became quite happy, though the rules were strict. Even when we visited the school in 1927 the dormitories where the children slept still had barred gates across the stairways. They also had a "lock up" which was pointed out to me by one of the matrons. This was a long narrow room with only a small window over the door, and the matron assured us that it was fairly easy for a student, either girl or boy, to get put in the "lock up" for some misdemeanor. Demerits were also given for bad behavior such as using bad language, dancing Indian dances, singing Indian songs, or refusal to obey faculty or supervisors of work.

She told us a good many stories of the resident missionary who held long services every Sunday and was known to the students as "Brother Ether." It seems that Brother Ether always held a revival meeting sometime in May before the school was dismissed and most of the children went home for vacation. He brought a professional evangelist who tried earnestly to get as many children as possible to profess Christianity and be baptized, evidently in the hope that they would not backslide during the summer vacation at home.

Students with excessive demerits were denied certain privileges, such as going to Arkansas City with the matron on Saturday afternoon where they could walk along the streets, window shop, buy candy, or even go to the picture show if they had the money. Students with excessive demerits were "campused," not permitted to go to town. Pearl said that there was one full blood Creek girl called Mandy who was always "campused" because she had so many demerits that she was never permitted to go to town or to leave the campus at any time. She was often in the "lock up" for a day or so and was denied any special privileges.

When the evangelist came for the revival meeting which lasted several days, Mandy conceived the brilliant idea to profess religion and ask to be taken to Arkansas City to be baptized, since there was no suitable place for baptism on the campus. Apparently she was an orphan who remained at the school during the summer, but after her baptism she speedily backslid and continued to use bad language, break rules, occasionally get in fights with other girls, and end up in the "lock up."

The next spring, however, she would again attend the revival services which were, of course, compulsory, confess again, and demand that she be taken to Arkansas City for baptism. After this had been repeated several times, Pearl said that they again took Mandy along with a good many others to the Arkansas River to be baptized and when the preacher led Mandy into the water and baptized her, Pearl, who was sitting some distance away, saw Mandy's lips move and the matron standing on the bank look horrified. When they all returned to the school Mandy was given seventy-five demerits!

Pearl, at the first opportunity, said, "Mandy, why did they give you seventy-five demerits? What did you do at the baptism?!" "I didn't do nothin'." "Well, what did you say? Did you say something to the preacher?" "No." "Well, you must have done something or they wouldn't have given you seventy-five demerits!" "Well, when the preacher lifted me up I just said to myself that it seems like the damn water gets colder every year! I wasn't saying it to anybody in particular, but they gave me seventy-five demerits just the same."

This little story is just an example of many more which Pearl told of life at Chilocco school. There were, of course, pleasures too. There were occasional picnics, the food was fairly good, and the work, while often tedious, was not too hard. Even so, there were many children who ran away but they were usually stopped and brought back to school before they had gone far. This was especially true on rainy days and nights or dark misty types of weather where a dozen or

374

more boys or girls would run away, but they were usually caught.

I helped Pearl enroll in the University and paid her tuition, fees, and books. Her studies consisted of the ordinary freshman courses and she made fairly good grades. For laboratory science she took a class in chemistry, but by the end of the year she had given up the idea of taking a degree in medicine. As the months lengthened into years she decided at one point to enter the law school, but after one semester she gave it up. She found she could use her courses in law as electives for a master of arts degree. She liked the study of law but for some reason disliked the Law School.

To my great surprise, she never liked to go for weekends to our cabin at Turner Falls. She would go with us but did not enjoy the trips. This was probably due to the fact that we usually had another couple with us and while she loved to read, she did not play cards and probably felt that she was a sort of fifth wheel. On the other hand, she thoroughly enjoyed weekend visits to my brother George and his wife, Anna, on their farm.

Gradually it seemed to me that she gave up some of her Indian nature, though she never entirely lost it. For example, she remarked to me one day, "Do you know that I am getting so that all white people smell just alike to me." When I asked if different white persons smelled differently to her when she first came, she replied, "Oh yes, each one had a different smell then, but now it is getting so they all smell just alike."

She loved bright colors too, so when Rosalie and I went on a trip to New Mexico, leaving her with Rosalie's mother, Rosalie bought some red calico at a trader's store. When we were back home, she made Pearl two red calico dresses. I shall never forget how proud she was of those and how she hung them up in her room so she could see them first thing when she woke up in the morning.

Her father died about two years after she came to us and Effie, who was a nurse, had no time to come to see her while Joe, who rented his land and worked as a carpenter and a mechanic, had no time either. Her only full brother, Claude, attended either Chilocco or Haskell Indian school. Gradually she drifted away from contacts with her Indian relatives and accepted our friends and relatives as her own. She and our son Ed became almost like brother and sister, and she became as close to us as though she were our own daughter. We bought her clothing, paid for her schooling, and made no difference between her and our own son, Ed.

Her grades were good, and she at long last decided to major in government and take a minor in history. Although she was usually quite gay and talkative, every few weeks she would get a quiet spell which puzzled us at first until we found that she had done this all of her life. Before she left us, however, she had stopped having such little moody spells which had never lasted more than a day or two.

In the summer of 1935 I taught at Ohio State University in Columbus. Pearl stayed at home with two other girls. Rosalie's mother lived only a block away, so she looked after them a bit while they attended the eight-week summer school. Later I wrote Pearl to close the house and come by train to Columbus to be with us for the last four weeks. I promised her that we would take her to Washington as soon as the second six weeks of work at Ohio State closed.

We met her at the train and were delighted to see her because this was the first time that the four of us had not been together since she had come to live with us. She seemed pleased to be with us again, and told us with great glee of her experience of talking with an Indian woman she had met on the train. At some town in Oklahoma she said an Indian couple, apparently full bloods, boarded the train and sat down across the aisle from her. Very soon the husband got up and went to the smoking compartment and the wife sat down next to Pearl.

She said, "Child, I see that you are Indian—I am too." "Yes, I thought so. I am pretty quick that way." The woman continued, "That is my husband. We have not been married very long but we are so happy. He is such a fine man. We had both been married before to white persons. His wife was so mean that nobody could get along with her! It keeps us about half broke paying alimony now for he got a divorce only a little over a year after they were married. Now that wasn't true of my white husband. He was a good man. The only thing wrong with our marriage was that we just didn't seem to understand one another. Why you know, when the Indian dances would start up in the spring and I wanted to go, he said we had to stay at home and work the crops. Why, we did not worry about working the crops at our home before I was married. When the Indian dances started we just let the crops go. Of course, they grew up in weeds a bit, but you got to put first things first, and we did not let anything interfere with our dances, but my husband just up and kept me at home. When we would go to town to do a little shopping there I would see something that I wanted and he would say, 'Don't you think that is pretty high? Maybe we could find one that you would like just as well at some other store that would not cost as much.' It was not any pleasure to shop with him at all. Now this husband isn't like that. If I see something I want he would say, 'Sure! Let's buy it' It is some fun to shop with a man like that. But the worst thing about that white husband of mine was that when he would see two or three carloads of my folks drive up to visit us— he'd just act like he wasn't glad to see them! Well, I could not live with a man like that so we finally got a divorce. This husband isn't like that at all."

Pearl said that she thought this woman gave a real understanding of the differences between Indians and white people.

School closed in Columbus about the first of September, and we packed up and started for Washington. My friend, Patrick J. Hurley, was living in Leesburg, a short distance across the river from Washington. He urged us to come by and spend a day or so with him, assuring me that I could drive from Columbus to Leesburg in a day. Maybe Pat could, but I could not, and we spent the first night at a tiny motel with a small restaurant and a little general merchandise store as the only public buildings other than the few cabins for tourists.

Meriam had earnestly urged us to spend our time in Washington with him and his family at Kensington, Maryland, where Miss Mark and I had stayed during part of the time we had been in Washington while working on our report on the Indian Survey. We reached this place in ample time for a remarkably good dinner, and I spent the following day showing Pearl something of Washington including the capitol, the Library of Congress, various other buildings, and the White House. At 6:30 that evening Meriam had us to a special dinner at the dining room of the Institute for Government Research. It was an excellent meal, and he placed Pearl at his left so he could visit with her during the dinner. The next morning we began our trip home to Oklahoma.

School was just beginning when we reached Norman. Pearl finished her bachelor's degree that year and entered the graduate school. The following year she lacked only one summer before securing her master's degree and decided that she would teach that year and finish her degree the following summer.

Our friend Dan Baker and his wife were at Pryor, Oklahoma, and he offered Pearl a teaching job at a good salary. On Saturday before school opened the next year we took her up to Pryor, where she spent the night at the home of Dan and his wife about three miles out in the country. They asked her to stay with them, but she insisted that she would rather take a room in town where she would be closer to the school and could get acquainted with the parents of the children and would be free to visit people and fit into the community.

She was home for the summer, finished her master's degree, and went back to Pryor for a second year. She apparently found that she liked teaching more than she had expected and next taught at Sulphur, Oklahoma. This was closer to home and only ten miles from our log cabin at Turner Falls, so we were with her much more than we had been when she was at Pryor. Her last teaching was at Pampa, Texas.

When Pearl Harbor came on December 7, 1941, she was eager to get into the WACs in hope of being sent abroad, but there was no recruiting station for women anywhere near. Navy officers, however, were recruiting Waves at Amarillo, only a short drive from Pampa. Apparently fearful that the war might be over before she could have a share in it, she tendered her resignation at Pampa and joined the Waves.

When naval officials found that she had a master's degree, they sent her to Smith College for training. She graduated and was commissioned an ensign.

She spent a short time at Corpus Christi and was then sent to a naval air base near Clinton, Oklahoma. Soon after the war closed, she married Lieutenant Commander Gordon Fechter. They established a home in Santa Clara, California, and they had a son and daughter. She visited us every summer—usually with Gordon. She remained our Indian daughter whom we loved as much as if she were our own.

Adventures in Authorship

As a small child I was very fond of reading. Something interesting to read, however, was very scarce in our Cross Timbers home. My father was not by any means an educated man and read very little except the *Bible* and his religious paper, *The Signs of the Times*, published by Gilbert Beebee in New York state. This magazine was the official publication of the Primitive Baptist Church, sometimes called "Hard-Shell" Baptist.

Both my brother George and myself must have had a good deal more imagination than most of our playmates, who seemed to care little about reading. It is true that what I read I did not understand too well in some cases. Someone gave us a copy of *Pilgrim's Progress* which I read at a very early age. I took the story literally, The Giant Despair to me was a real giant just as were Pope and Pagan. Doubting Castle in which Christian was confined was a real castle and the key called Promise, was a real key. Not until I was considerably older did my young mind begin to understand the allegory.

In the tedious farm work of thinning corn and chopping or picking cotton George and I began to tell stories "made up in our own heads" in which we had some stirring adventures hunting in Africa, getting shipwrecked on a desert island (after we had read *Robinson Crusoe* or *The Swiss Family Robinson*), or some western tales of trouble with the Indians on our way to California.

Eventually I began to write verses and occasionally made an attempt at writing a short story. I did not attend school

Edward Everett Dale at work on a new book in his home study. (Courtesy Western History Collections, University of Oklahoma Library)

until I was eight years old, for the laws of Texas at that time provided free school only to children of eight to sixteen years of age. The stories and poems in George's school books I read with much interest, and I soon began to memorize the poems in *McGuffey's Reader*. I thrilled over the story of William Tell and various other legends, and started to school in the fourth reader class. Within a few weeks I was transferred to the fifth reader class which was taught by the principal of the school. His sister, who was the assistant teacher, taught the students from the primer through the fourth grade. They were in what was called the "little room," while fifth reader pupils were in what was called the "big room." I soon began to tell stories which I made up for children younger than myself.

When we removed to the Prairie West we worked in the field with my older brother John, the youngest of the five brothers by my father's first wife. When we suggested to John that he tell us some of the stories which he had read, he said that he would rather tell us an original story, so we had some lurid yarns by both John and George.

When I entered the college at Edmond I roomed and boarded in the home of a Mrs. Barlow. She had two daughters, the youngest being Georgia, about six or seven years of age, whose bosom friend was Alma Comstock, about the same age. When these two youngsters asked me to tell them stories, I spent hours entertaining them with a prose version of one of Scott's novels or some other book which I had read and liked. Also at Edmond I took a course in English with Professor Jameson which required the writing of themes from time to time, and when I entered the University of Oklahoma I took a course in English which required daily themes and short stories every month or so. Sometimes the instructor gave us the characters in the story and a brief statement of what happened and told us to compose a brief story.

When I entered the University of Oklahoma I received sixty-four hours of transfer credit from the college at Edmond. I had started my education late, so I worked very hard taking as many hours of academic work as was permitted. I had one two-hour course in history with Professor Buchanan called "Territorial Acquisitions of the United States." I took the papers written in this course and prepared a booklet with an introduction and a bibliography. There were no footnotes, and the statements with regard to the acquisition of Oregon and the work of Marcus Whitman as given in my little booklet have been proven wrong. I was teaching at Blair, Oklahoma, and could not read proof on the manuscript or choose the binding or the type used, so the little book has a number of typographical errors, but it does give considerable information to the average reader.

The following year when I applied for a scholarship at Harvard I accompanied my application with letters of recommendation from all the professors at O.U. who had studied at Harvard and included a copy of "Territorial Acquisitions of the United States." I wonder now if this helped or not, but it probably did for I was given the scholarship. Since then I have thought that the Harvard professors who chose the applicants for scholarships may have felt that here was one who wanted to write. At the time I did not think too much about why they had awarded me the scholarship. I only knew that I was deeply grateful and that the following year I would be at Harvard.

It must have been in the school year of 1915-16 that I talked with Professor Buchanan and some other professors including some in the English department about the formation of a folklore association. I had picked up a good many Indian stories and had talked with some students of Indian descent including Ruth Muskrat, a Cherokee, and during a summer session we decided to call interested people to a folklore meeting. We advertised it rather widely and during the meeting, which lasted a couple of days, we had an interesting program of Indian tales, cowboy songs, and old stories and songs from pioneer farmers. At the close of the meeting we formed what was known as the Oklahoma Folklore Association and elected ourselves to the various offices. I was elected president and as I recall Miss Muskrat was made secretary, and the son of a missionary to the Comanches was made treasurer.

I had to teach the next year but during the month of August I felt that I should do something to justify the fact that I had been made president of this association. I traveled about in my second-hand Model-T Ford, visiting Indian homes. I can still remember how a little girl almost as shy as a bird would stand in front of me with downcast eyes telling me two or three Indian legends which her grandfather had told her.

I had been made custodian of the little Indian museum where we had various Indian artifacts such as bows and arrows, bead necklaces, beaded moccasins, and head-dresses. Also, I had secured a considerable number of Indian pictures made by the wife of an Indian Service doctor at the Kiowa-Comanche agency at Anadarko.

I was at Harvard during 1916-17, and dropped into the offices of the publishers D. C. Heath and Company. By this time I had written up the Indian stories and showed the Heath people the manuscript and the photographs which I proposed to use. It so happened that the president of the company, Mr. Pulsifer, was there, and I showed him the work, which seemed to interest him a great deal.

There were delays, of course, but eventually the manuscript was published by Heath and Company early in 1920. The little book consisted of fourteen stories and a glossary. It had 110 pages and ten illustrations and became quite popular in the schools, not only in Oklahoma but in other states as well.

I have never inquired as to exactly how many copies the book sold, but it must have been between 20,000 and 30,000 for I found a copy in virtually every Indian school we visited on the Meriam Commission and in public schools in all parts of the United States. I recall that a teacher in California wrote me a letter saying that the children in her room had been given as part of their work the reading of the little book and stated which story each one liked best. The teacher said she did not expect me to answer every letter, but I did write a letter to the class and asked the teacher to read it to them. This little book plus the name Edward Everett were probably responsible for my being invited to join the Boston Author's Club.

Writing a history of Oklahoma had long been one of my ambitions even while I was teaching in the public schools. I started for Harvard in August, 1913, and decided to stop off in Washington for a few weeks and do some work in the Office of Indian Affairs and other departments of the federal government to collect material on the history of Oklahoma. I called the office of Claude Weaver, an old friend who had given my commencement address at Blair, Oklahoma, and who was now a member of Congress. He greeted me fairly cordially, and I sensed that he had been called on by a good many Oklahomans seeking an appointment to office.

When I told him that I was on my way to Harvard and that I would like to have a note of introduction to the Commissioner of Indian Affairs, he shook hands with me again and assured me that he would give me a note immediately. He added that if I needed books from the Library of Congress, he would have them sent over to his office. He invited me to use his office as my headquarters. I thanked him, of course, and he gave me letters of introduction to the Commissioner of Indian Affairs and to one or two other departments, so I stayed in Washington for nearly a month. I visited not only the Commissioner of Indian Affairs but also the State Department where I was well received and told that staff would furnish me photographic copies of the early Indian treaties and maps of the Indian country at various times.

When I reached Harvard I had not only Professor Turner's "History of the West" but also his "History 20K" which was individual research. I chose to work on the Indians of Oklahoma and on the settlement of Oklahoma.

When I returned to Oklahoma as an instructor in the History Department I was delighted when Professor Buchanan proposed that he and I do a history of Oklahoma for the ninth grade. We talked it over and made an outline of the proposed book, and I started to work on it. Unfortunately President Brooks resigned to accept the presidency of the University of Missouri, and Buchanan was named acting president of the University so he had no time, of course, to work on a history of Oklahoma.

At this time Oklahoma history was a required subject for a teacher's certificate. There was, however, no text that we thought was suitable. Scott Glenn, representative of Row, Peterson, and Company, was eager to have me complete the history of Oklahoma and assured me that his company would publish it. He was certain that we could get it adopted by the State Textbook Commission for use in the ninth grade public schools.

I knew that there were others who were working on a history of Oklahoma, but Dr. Buchanan was sure that our book would be adopted. When the date of the meeting of the Textbook Commission was announced, he drove by our house and picked me up to go to the capitol. As we left the house Dean Buchanan said, "Well, we'll go up there and get our book adopted now." Rosalie replied, "There will be other books offered. Aren't you counting your chickens before they are hatched?" "Oh, no," replied Uncle Buck as we always called him, "you don't realize what big men we are!"

When the Textbook Commission adjourned after going through all the school books and making the adoptions, a good friend, Jim Hatcher, and a former student, Mr. Montgomery, came out. Jim said, "Well Ed, we beat you out. Our book was adopted." When we reached home Dean Buchanan said as he let me out, "I won't go in and see Mrs. Dale. I'm too humiliated." The next time she saw him she said, "Well, Dean, we found out what big men you are!"

Five years later when the Textbook Commission met again our book was adopted, and the commission wrote us a letter thanking us for writing this book and making it available for the children of Oklahoma to use. For the next twenty-one years it was the sole text for the ninth grade and brought royalties of over $16,000, of which Buchanan or his widow received one-third.

In 1924 I decided that we should have an outline and references for Oklahoma history, and Professor Wardell and I published with the Peerless Printing Company a fifty-eight page booklet called *Outline and References of Oklahoma History*.

The next book in which I had a part was *The Problem of*

Indian Administration which described the work of the Meriam Commission. My contribution was devoted to the economic condition of the Indian and how it could be improved. However, I helped with most of the other chapters also just as the other members of the staff helped me. The book of 872 pages of which I wrote 116 was published by Johns Hopkins Press in 1928.

I have stated that Herbert Jenkins, chief editor of Little, Brown and Company, was a member of the Puddingstone Club. Jenkins asked me if I would get all my poems together and send them to him, for he would like to consider publishing them in a small book. After final examinations at Harvard I stayed in Boston a couple of weeks longer and worked on adding a few so-called poems, writing the introduction and so forth, and sent the manuscript to Little, Brown and Company. I am sure that Jenkins gave this manuscript careful consideration, but in a few days returned it with the observation that the company had decided not to publish it. He felt that interesting as some of the poems were, they were better when I recited them myself. I was disappointed, of course, but when I returned home I sent the manuscript to the Cooperative Publishing Company, Guthrie, Oklahoma, and it was published in 1929 under the title *The Prairie Schooner and Other Poems*. It contained eighty-five pages with preface and introduction and the book had about fifty poems including some Western and some children's rhymes.

In an earlier chapter an account of my work in Washington on a manuscript called the *Range Cattle Industry* has been given. I had expected that this would be published by the Department of Agriculture as a bulletin or in its publications of the Division of Agricultural Economics, but apparently the chief decided to make a few typed copies to be sent to officials in Washington, especially those in the Bureau of Animal Industry, but not in book form for general distribution. In 1930 it was released to the University of Oklahoma Press which published it that same year. It was a historical study of the range cattle industry and had eight illustrations and seventeen maps. The small first edition was soon out of print, but a second edition was published in 1960 with a new preface, eleven illustrations, and 207 pages.

Another small book published by an Oklahoma press was entitled *Lafayette Letters*. A classmate of mine at Edmond wrote me in 1924 that an elderly man living in his town in eastern Oklahoma, John D. Rinehart, had a number of letters of Marquis Lafayette and his son, George Washington Lafayette. Of course, I was deeply interested and wrote to Rinehart.

He came to see me in Norman. He was in his mid-nineties, and he brought the letters with him. I told him that I thought I could get them published in a small book, so he left them with me. I prepared a small volume. There were fifteen letters by Lafayette and his family, addressed to Captain Francis Allyn, commander of the ship *Cadmus* in which Lafayette and his son came to the states in 1824. With the help of my wife I translated the letters which were written in French. The little book of sixty-four pages was published by the Harlow Publishing Company of Oklahoma City in 1925.

A banner year for me with respect to book publication was 1930. In addition to the *Range Cattle Industry*, I also prepared with the help of O.U. Librarian Jesse Lee Rader a volume of readings in Oklahoma history. Rader helped find the material though the writing is mine. It made a book of 865 pages giving information outside the textbook on the history of Oklahoma from the time of the early Spanish exploration to the year 1930.

The third volume I published in 1930 was the autobiography of Frank Canton. It was a matter of editing, but I put in as much time and effort on it as on some of the books I have written. Frank Canton was a professional peace officer. He had lived on the wrong side of the law for some years as a young man, but later became a U.S. deputy marshal, sheriff of a county in Wyoming, an employee of various livestock companies, a U.S marshal in Alaska, and was general of the Oklahoma National Guard for more than twelve years. Soon after his death his widow placed his papers with me in the Phillips Collection for safekeeping. Among them I found five thick pencil tablets on which he had written his life story. My wife and I read these and found that the pencil copy was fairly legible and told a remarkable story of his active and adventurous life.

When my wife typed the manuscript, I divided it into various chapters, found titles for them, wrote an introduction and an afterword, and found pictures. The manuscript was sent to Houghton-Mifflin. It had excellent reviews, and a literary agent in California wrote me that he believed he could sell the book to one of the moving picture companies. I sent him a copy immediately, but after a few months he returned it saying that the Great Depression had curtailed purchases by the movie companies. The book was soon out of print, but the University of Oklahoma Press republished it in its Western Frontier Library Series in 1960. Frederick Jackson Turner wrote me a brief letter saying that he and his wife read the book with much pleasure.

In 1936 I edited and had published by Houghton-Mifflin the autobiography of another westerner. The book was *A Rider of the Cherokee Strip* written by Evan G. Barnard, a young brother of George Grey Barnard, a famous American sculptor. The Barnard brothers' father was a minister. They left home at fairly early ages. George Grey Barnard went to Europe to study sculpture and painting, and Evan G. to the West to work as a cowhand. He worked with various ranching firms in Texas and the Cherokee Outlet. As he grew older and the Cherokee Outlet was opened to settlement and the days of most of the large ranch operators came to an end, he married and settled down on a homestead. It was then that he decided to write his life story, but was inexperienced at writing for publication. His manuscript was sent to publisher after publisher, but he was unable to get a contract. Evidently someone told him of me, for he appeared at our home in Norman late one afternoon, told me something of his experiences, and asked my help. He brought with him only the manuscript and baggage for an overnight stay as I had often done myself as a cowhand. He spent the night with us and I asked him to leave the manuscript and I would see what I could do with it. The manuscript was in type, but it was easy to see why he could not find a publisher for it was clearly not in publishable form. It was not divided into chapters but was written as a continuous narrative. Yet I felt it was a good story.

I went over it very carefully and wrote him to come to see me again. On his second visit I showed him the revised manuscript and explained why it was necessary to divide it into chapters, get some illustrations, and prepare a preface and introduction. He approved what I had done or rather what my wife had done with some direction. The manuscript was sent to Houghton-Mifflin, but it must be confessed that I had little hope of getting a contract.

The success of the Canton book, however, probably was one factor in a speedy acceptance, although his relationship to George Grey Barnard probably had some weight too. At any rate I received a contract within two weeks. The volume did not have the sale, by any means, of the Canton *Frontier Trails*, but for three years sold fairly well. It was not too long, though, until the book was out of print.

The next book and, in my opinion, one of considerable importance, was entitled *Cherokee Cavaliers*. It was done with the assistance of one of my former students, Gaston Litton, and consisted of 200 letters from the Stand Watie collection referred to in an earlier chapter. The subtitle of the book was *Forty Years of Cherokee History as Told in the Correspondence of the Ridge-Watie-Boudinot Family*. The forty years covered were from 1832 to 1872. It was a difficult task because in some cases we had too many letters, and in others not quite enough to make a complete story. When necessary we added explanatory footnotes.

The book was published in 1939 by the University of Oklahoma Press and had 319 pages divided into seven periods. There was a calendar of letters, an index, and a genealogical table of relationships of various persons mentioned. It was a beautiful example of printing and binding, and gave much information difficult to find elsewhere.

Perhaps my favorite of all the books I have written or edited is *Cow Country*. It was also published by the University of Oklahoma Press in 1942. It contains 265 pages with preface and index. Five of the chapters had been previously published in a historical journal. In *Cow Country* each chapter is preceded by a brief bit of verse. It includes something of my own experiences and has such chapters as "The Humor of the Cowboy," "Cow Country in Transition," and "Ranching on the Cheyenne-Apapaho Reservation." Each chapter has a line drawing by Richard G. Underwood. The first printing in 1942 was quickly sold out, and a second edition was published in 1943 and a third in 1945. It then remained out of print until 1965 when the University of Oklahoma republished it in the Western Frontier Library Series.

While the Buchanan and Dale *History of Oklahoma* was fairly adequate for the public schools, there was no book that seemed adequate for use in college courses in Oklahoma history. College teachers in Oklahoma history sometimes used *Readings in Oklahoma History* as a text, or at least as a supplement by putting several copies in the library, but it seemed to me that there should be a text for use primarily in college classrooms.

I accordingly secured a contract with Prentice-Hall Inc. and proceeded to produce one. I had written seventeen chapters when World War II began and the book lacked some seven chapters being completed. Prentice-Hall wrote me that they could not get material or labor, and asked me to defer further work on the manuscript until the war ended. I put the manuscript aside, but when the war closed Prentice-Hall asked me to complete the manuscript as quickly as possible.

I had been urged for a year or more to prepare a new ninth grade history of Oklahoma to replace the Buchanan and Dale book which had been in use for twenty years. I had completed the manuscript of such a book and mailed it to the Row-Peterson Company with illustrations. Before they could get started on its publication, however, the Textbook Commission met and froze the present edition of all school books for six years or until the end of the war. Naturally Row-Peterson, like Prentice-Hall, could not get either labor or material to produce the book during the war, so placed it aside and we continued to use the Buchanan-Dale book.

A year before the outbreak of World War II, I had received a grant from the Henry Huntington Library in San Marino, California, to write a book on the Indians of the Southwest. The Southwest was defined by the Treaty of Guadalupe Hidalgo in 1848, ending the Mexican War, and included California, Arizona, New Mexico, Nevada, Utah, and part of Colorado. When the treaty was signed this vast Mexican cession became part of the United States. Of very considerable importance was the fact that it contained many Indian tribes that had been the responsibility of the government of Mexico but were now the responsibility of the government of the United States. My assignment was to explain how the United States dealt with these Indian peoples for the next 100 years.

My grant from the Henry Huntington Library was from funds that the library had received in a grant of some $75,000 from the Rockefeller Foundation to pay for studies of the Southwest. One scholar was given a grant to deal with the Mormon migration and occupation of the Southwest. Another dealt with a study of gold mining in California. Others received grants to study the history of fruit growing. The grants were of varied amounts but were sufficient to pay travel and living expenses.

My grant from the Huntington Library to do a book on the Indians of the Mexican Cession was not for a specific amount, but provided only for transportation from Oklahoma to the library and back and living expenses while there. It was expected, however, that the study could be completed in three summers, 1944, 1945, and 1946.

I had looked forward to it with much pleasure, for although I had never visited the library it was one of the most famous in the world. The director was Dr. Leslie Bliss who had a staff of a dozen or more persons. We were still at war, however, and travel was difficult. Pullman reservations had to be applied for some time in advance, and it was my luck to be placed with some woman with a badly spoiled child.

The library had more readers in the field of literature than

392

in history, although it was very rich in both. Readers or researchers lived at the Athenaeum on the grounds of the California Institute of Technology and Mount Wilson Observatory.

The food was good and the rooms quite comfortable, but it was half a mile or more from the library. The director of the buildings and grounds, however, unlocked the back gate for half an hour every morning which shortened the walk quite a bit. If you overslept, however, it was necessary to go around to the main gate which lengthened the walk to about a mile. I thoroughly enjoyed my work at the Huntington Library except that I could not bring my wife with me because her mother was living with us. I was separated from my family both the first and second summers.

I worked hard and made considerable progress. My work with the Meriam Commission gave me remarkably good background. I had an excellent secretary in the office at O.U., Miss Josephine Bond, who had been with me for three or four years, so I wrote each chapter in longhand and mailed it to her. She put it in type and returned it for my proofreading. She also, of course, gave me any news from home.

A rather interesting incident occurred while I was at the library. I think it pleased Dr. Bliss and other officials. I received a call from a young man named Arthur Evans who told me that he was the son of the second president of the University of Oklahoma. He said his wife, Carmelita, had a rare journal and letters that she would like for me to see. It was the journal of an officer of Napoleon Bonaparte's army during the invasion of Spain. After Napoleon pulled out of Spain the officer remained in Spain, and after a while crossed over to Mexico and to California where he received a grant of land. In addition to the journal there were letters from a number of Napoleon's marshals. I persuaded Carmelita to let me show the journal to Dr. Bliss. Eventually she agreed that if the library would give her an exact copy of the book and letters beautifully bound, she would leave the original in the library. I was sure that Dr. Bliss would be delighted to have this valuable item.

Edward Everett Dale with a copy of The Indians of the Southwest, *published in 1948. (Courtesy Western History Collections, University of Oklahoma Library)*

The second summer was not particularly interesting except that I met a large number of distinguished people, some from England, and made some friends, especially in the field of English literature. I also did some work in the Southwest Museum where I worked with Frederick Webb Hodge and his wife. I also became a member of the Zamorano Club of Los Angeles and still retain absentee membership in that remarkable group of book lovers.

The war ended while I was still at the Huntington Library, and our son returned from the Phillipines in the late spring of 1946. He enrolled in the graduate school to finish work on his master's degree which he had left half done when called into service. He and his wife lived in our home and looked after Rosalie's mother, so Rosalie went with me for my third summer's work at Huntington.

For three or four months I had had a pain in my side and eventually discovered that I had gall stones. My Oklahoma doctor insisted, however, that while my condition should not prevent me from going to California, I should not have surgery at my age for it would be a bad risk. For approximately a month after reaching California I got along very well and then had a bad attack. My doctor nephew, Phillip Dale, urged that I go to the hospital for surgery. I did, but complications developed which brought me to the very brink of death before the doctors finally pulled me through. After three weeks in the hospital, I recovered my strength enough to work a little in the library. By September the doctors agreed I could return to work in the classroom.

The book was nearly finished and the University of Oklahoma Press and the Huntington Library published it in September, 1949. The first edition sold out very quickly and a second printing was made in March, 1951.[1]

The Dale-Wardell Oklahoma history still lacked six or seven chapters, and the public school text, *The Story of a State*, replacing the Buchanan-Dale book, was still in the

---

[1] See Edward Everett Dale, *The Indians of the Southwest: A Century of Development Under the United States* (Norman: University of Oklahoma Press, 1949).

files of Row-Peterson, and Company, complete with pictures and maps, but two or three additional chapters had to be added to update it. *The Story of a State* was published in 1949. It is still in print and is used in many schools in Oklahoma. It was updated in 1955 and again in 1963. The Dale-Wardell book was first printed in June, 1949. It was reprinted without revision every few years until December, 1964. It went out of print after the '64 edition was printed.[2]

I shared in the production of only one other book before my retirement in June, 1952. My friend Dwight Dumond of the University of Michigan where I had taught one summer proposed that we write a high school history of the United States together on a new plan of presentation for the history of the country. His idea was that instead of following a chronological pattern, we should divide the history of the United States into seven epochs of five chapters.

Dumond felt that this would not only present the history of the United States in thirty-five chapters, but would be of enormous value to students preparing for an examination with its sections on economic history, political history, building a government, and foreign affairs. The idea seemed of value to me, but we felt we should have a third man who was well known in the field of education to prepare what is technically known as the "apparatus" at the end of each chapter giving details for study, discussion questions, suggested activities, outside readings, and general references. For preparing these educational helps Edgar B. Wesley, head of the Education Department of the University of Minnesota, was engaged. The contract was secured with D. C. Heath and Company.

The work was tedious but we met from time to time, especially at historical meetings, and completed the book of 847 pages, including the index with an enormous number of maps and illustrations. Dumond wrote a large part of the text while I wrote the final draft from his first draft. Wesley prepared the questions and suggestions at the end of each

---

[2] See Edward Everett Dale and Morris L. Wardell, *Oklahoma: The Story of a State* (Englewood Cliffs, New Jersey: Prentice Hall Company, 1949).

chapter, and Dumond and I chose the illustrations and maps.

The book was published in 1948. Dumond was very enthusiastic and insisted that he would not take less than $50,000 for his share of the royalities. It must be confessed that I had some hope that it might be well received by teachers of American History, but would have sold my future receipts for only a fraction of Dumond's evaluation of his share.[3]

My own misgivings proved only too true. Schools in two or three states adopted the book for high school use, and we received a few hundred dollars for a year or so, but the amount grew less and less and finally disappeared. The publishers had high school texts by other authors, so eventually ceased publishing our book in favor of the others. I still feel that the volume deserved a better fate and that every high school library should have a few copies on its shelves for use as a reference.

The fact that this was my last book before retirement in 1954 does not mean that I did not write thereafter, because between 1948 and 1954 I produced a number of articles for historical journals and an article or so for encyclopedias. After retirement in 1954 I published three books: *Pioneer Judge: The Life of Robert Lee Williams*, with Dean James Morrison of Southeastern State College, *Frontier Ways*, which consisted almost entirely of previously printed articles, and *The Cross Timbers: Memories of a North Texas Boyhood*.[4]

---

[3] See Edward Everett Dale and Dwight Dumond, *A History of the United States* (Lexington, Massachusetts: D. C. Heath Company, 1948).

[4] See Edward Everett Dale and James Morrison, *Pioneer Judge: The Life of Robert Lee Williams* (Cedar Rapids, Iowa: Torch Press, 1958). Also, Edward Everett Dale, *The Cross Timbers: Memories of a North Texas Boyhood* (Austin: University of Texas Press, 1966).

Visiting Professor

I have related my teaching at the University of Texas. This was by no means the only experience I had in teaching at other universities and colleges. There were several reasons why I preferred to teach at some other university or college than Oklahoma during the summer session. Obviously I needed to work somewhere during the summer, because few teachers can afford to go from their last check in June during the second semester to the first check in October of the fall semester. This was not the reason, however, for my preferring to teach elsewhere than the University of Oklahoma during the summer months, for by the time I paid transportation for myself and family, rented a house or apartment, and paid living expenses, we probably ended the summer with less money than if we had stayed at home.

Normally in the nineteen years that I was head of the O.U. History Department, we had eleven men in that department including myself. In the summer session of eight weeks, the director of the summer school usually had to bring in visitors to the school of education, while all other departments were given only about half as many teachers as in the regular year. This of course meant that if I taught in some other institution, there was one place open for one of the younger men who sometimes could not get a job teaching at another university or college.

It must be confessed though that I preferred to teach summers in some other institution, because I made new friends, and in many cases, it was cooler at the host place than Oklahoma. Getting acquainted with people in other departments of history also made it possible for me to place my graduate students after they completed their doctorates.

One of my most pleasant assignments was at the College of William and Mary at Williamsburg, Virginia; in fact I taught two summers there, the first in the summer of 1929 when the so-called "Restoration" was just getting under way, and the second time some years later when it was almost completed so far as the major buildings were concerned.

We left Norman as soon as I had turned in my grades after the first of June, 1929, and headed east for Williamsburg. My class was large, and the work pleasant. We had never been in that part of Virginia and were delighted with the housing facilities.

It was really warm in Williamsburg which is only a few feet above sea level. Yet, to me it was a real joy to live for several weeks in a place which had so much history in a small village and the surrounding country. It was only seven miles to Jamestown and not more than ten or twelve to Yorktown, so we visited both of these historic spots several times. Bruton Parish is one of the oldest churches in the United States. The pews of eminent men who worshipped there were marked, and include Patrick Henry, President James Madison, and Justice John Marshall. The surrender field where General O'Hara gave his sword to Washington is only a short distance from the village of Yorktown.

I found the students good, but I was a bit surprised to find virtually no graduate students. I remember giving a talk at Phi Beta Kappa Hall and the Christopher Wren Building, which to me is one of the most beautiful buildings in America. My second summer school assignment at William and Mary College was in 1940. It was little different from my experience there in 1929, except for an excursion to the Virginia Indian reservations. These were the Mattaponis and Pamunkeys, two groups of Indians that I never dreamed of seeing. They were unlike any other Indians in America, since by this time they were so mixed with whites.

The only other university where I taught for two summers

was at the University of Nebraska, Lincoln, during 1934 and 1938. While in Nebraska, I saw no Indians although the Omahas lived not far away. The first summer at the University of Nebraska we lived in the home of an English professor, Sherlock Gass. It was a little brown house with the study and library mostly underground where it was quite cool, for at this time there was no air-conditioning, and the summers in Nebraska are usually pretty hot. The owners were taking a summer off to go to a cooler climate, and before the summer was over we were almost wishing we had done the same.

The head of the department was Charles Henry Oldfather whom I had met before at historical meetings, and I knew several other members of the faculty. I also had a number of relatives in Nebraska. Some of them lived on farms or in villages in the vicinity of Lincoln. They included the descendants of my father's second son and my sister Fannie's two children, Laura and Alfred, and Fannie herself for she was a widow having lost her husband a few years before.

In addition there were the widow and children of my brother Frank. He had died in his late fifties and had left a family of seven sons and two daughters. The older daughter, Sadie, was married to John Polk, who was municipal judge of the city of Lincoln and later district judge. John and Sadie had one small son four or five years of age.

There is little to tell about this first summer at Nebraska. I had one very large class in American History and a couple more classes. I found the students there much like those at Oklahoma, although there were many second generation students from Europe with names that were almost impossible to pronounce. In fact, the day after the first meeting of my large class I commented to a fellow professor about calling the roll. When I happened to sneeze, three students on the back row answered "here." The summer session at the University of Nebraska ended about the first of August. In the meantime, I had received the grant of $1,200 from the Rockefeller Foundation to collect Western material in Oklahoma which I related earlier.

Before I returned to the University of Nebraska campus in 1938, I taught in the summer sessions at Ohio State University at Columbus, and University of Missouri in Columbia. The summer school at the University of Missouri closed in early August, and we packed as quickly as possible and returned to Norman.

President Bizzell had asked me if I would be willing to make a trip to California to interview David Ross Boyd, the first president of the University of Oklahoma, who had served as President from September, 1892, until the spring of 1908. Dr. Boyd was born in Ohio on a farm on July 31, 1858. The oldest of a family of ten children, he had attended school in Ohio, taught in that state, and had a distinguished career as an educator and superintendent of various schools. At the time of his appointment to President of the University of Oklahoma he was superintendent of the Arkansas City, Kansas, schools. He came to Norman, a small town on the prairie with hardly a tree in sight, on August 6, 1892. He had never been in Norman but he took a room at the Agnes Hotel, and in early September he was joined by his wife and daughter Alice. They lived in rooms rented on East Comanche Street, but soon started building a home of their own. He had employed three men as his faculty and had rented an old stone building on West Main Street for twenty dollars a month. It was in the shade of this building that they had their first faculty meeting while eating a watermelon.

The school opened with some fifty students, most of them in the preparatory department, but the institution continued to grow until after statehood when Boyd and some twenty members of the faculty were discharged by the first governor of the state of Oklahoma, who removed them to make room for his friends. Boyd served as a missionary in a Presbyterian church after leaving the University of Oklahoma, but in a few years was appointed President of the University of New Mexico. Seven years later he retired due to age.

His daughter Alice secured a teaching position in Los Angeles, and the Boyds purchased a cottage in Glendale, a surburb. He was quite old and his health was not good.

(top) David Ross Boyd, first president of the University of Oklahoma, 1891-1907. (bottom) George Lynn Cross, president of the University of Oklahoma, 1943-1968. (Courtesy Western History Collections, University of Oklahoma Library)

President Bizzell felt we should get Dr. Boyd's life story, so he set aside $500 to send my wife and me to California where we rented a small apartment not far from the Boyd's home. I came to see him every morning at 10:00 except on Sundays, and we worked together until 12:00 getting details of his life from early childhood. He was pleased, apparently, to have the chance to give some of the interesting details of his family, especially of his father, James Boyd, whose home was a station of the Underground Railroad. By the first of September, we had the story complete, for my wife and I both took careful notes which she typed in the afternoons or evenings. It was a pleasant experience, and the Boyds were most cooperative. Mrs. Boyd brought out old letters, diaries, and papers to verify dates and details.[1]

Dr. Boyd, who seemed quite feeble when we first started on this work, seemed to grow stronger and assured me that he expected to visit Norman the next summer. We said goodbye to them soon after the first of September, feeling that we had material for his life story. We had been very careful not to tire Dr. Boyd and had every hope of seeing him again the following summer. We had acquired some 116 pages of notes and 24 photographs which we felt comprised his life story. Our notes lacked little in tracing his life from cradle to the grave, because he died on November 17, 1936, less than three months after we left his home in Glendale. We had secured his story just in time. I had hoped to publish it in a small book, but the O.U. Press was short of funds. It was not published until 1964 as the lead article in an issue of *The Chronicles of Oklahoma*. It comprised some thirty-five pages with several illustrations.[2]

My last off-campus summer school appointment was in 1942 at Duke University. Contracts for summer school faculty are usually made before Thanksgiving, and Duke

---

[1] Underground Railroad, the abolitionist path from the South to freedom in the North and into Canada, including established secret stops along the way for runaway slaves to hide and rest in the course of the flight to freedom.

[2] Edward Everett Dale, "David Ross Boyd," *The Chronicles of Oklahoma*, XLII (Summer, 1964), pp. 2-36.

officials had contracted for two, George Howe from the University of Cincinnati and me. The Japanese attacked Pearl Harbor on December 7, 1941, but the officials of Duke had no thought of asking us to cancel our contract. When we reached the campus, however, we found less than a dozen students for both of us. The dean, however, asked us to give our best efforts to the few we had, and not to worry about lack of students, for our salaries would be paid according to contract.

The summer was pleasant, fairly warm of course, but we each had an excellent opportunity to show what we could do in the way of teaching when we had only a handful of students.

The summer passed quickly, and in early August we said goodbye to friends and returned home. My students seemed to enjoy working with me, and at the close of school gave me an attractive tie as a small token of appreciation for what they felt I had done for them.

When I saw my seventieth birthday coming up, I wrote President George L. Cross a note explaining that I would reach that anniversary on February 8, and supposed that he would expect me to retire June first. To this I added that I was director of the Phillips Collection and trustee of a small fund given by Mary Laing of New York state to support education of Indians students.

In my note to the President, I said that I would like to have an appointment with him at his convenience to talk over who should succeed me as trustee of the Phillips Collection and the Mary Laing fund. When I reached my office the following morning President Cross called me and said that I could come to see him at anytime to visit, but he did not want me to retire yet. I was at that time Research Professor of History and continued in that capacity for three more years, retiring on June 1, 1954 at seventy-three years of age.

President George Lynn Cross and Professor Edward Everett Dale at Dr. Dale's retirement, 1954. (Courtesy Western History Collections, University of Oklahoma Library)

The Closing Years

As the conclusion of my professional career approached I seemed to become ever busier with public appearances. In addition to occasional summer school appointments as mentioned, I continued writing on historical subjects. But increasingly I became involved as a public speaker and visiting professor, both in the United States and abroad. My enlarging career as a public speaker consisted of addresses before civic groups in the region, high school and college commencement speeches, and extended lecture tours across the nation, schedules for which Rosalie and I worked out well in advance. Often a speaking itinerary would keep us on the road over two months, with travel in excess of 5,000 miles, sometimes nearly 8,000 miles.

One circuit began at Stillwater on the Oklahoma State University campus, to Kansas State University, Manhattan, on to the University of Nebraska in Lincoln, the universities of North and South Dakota, then to the University of Minnesota, into Wisconsin for appearances at the State College at Superior and the University at Madison, south to the University of Missouri at Columbia, and ending the tour at the University of Arkansas, Fayetteville, with a return to Norman. Other intineraries took us to the Pacific Northwest for appearances in Washington and Oregon, thence to the University of California at Berkeley and nearby Stanford University, and on to other Golden State institutions before returning home.

On several campuses I presented what amounted to a short course with ten to twelve lectures. The favorite with audiences seemed to be "Ranching—the Romance of the Cowboy," "Cow Country in Transition," "Pioneer Settlers," "Speech of the Pioneers," "The Indian and His Problems," and "Our Frontier Heritage." As a general rule I was surprised and pleased by the crowds that turned out and the warm reception and interest my addresses stirred. I remember a woman in a Wisconsin audience commenting: "As a child I read a story about a girl who could take a straw and spin it into gold. Dr. Dale reminds me of that because he can take the straw of history and really spin it into gold."

In 1953 at the University of Oklahoma commencement I received the Distinguished Service Citation award, the highest recognition the University can bestow (the state constitution prohibits state institutions from awarding honorary degrees). In my brief acceptance speech I announced my retirement from the University. About the same time I received a Fulbright award which assigned me to lecture at several Australian colleges and universities.

Rosalie and I sailed from Vancouver March 12, 1954. After stops in Hawaii, Suva, and New Zealand, we docked at Sydney to conclude a pleasant voyage. My first teaching assignment was at the University of Melbourne. Teaching there was leisurely and pleasant. Students seemed interested in American history as I interpreted it through my lectures, and they made interesting comparisons with Australia's evolution from wilderness to modern nation not unlike that of the United States.

I purchased an English Ford, and Rosalie and I toured much of Australia. We found Canberra a particularly interesting place. Other Australian cities of interest were Brisbane, Geelong, Camden, and Tancutta.

We returned to Norman by way of Ceylon, Bombay, through Suez into the Mediterranean, a stop at Marseilles, and on to London for three weeks. Rosalie and I returned to New York on the *Queen Mary*. We reached Norman and home, after a year's absence, in late 1955.

After a rest in Norman I undertook an extended lecture tour of the North and East, appearing on campuses in

Illinois, Michigan, and Missouri. Thereafter, I planned to cease traveling and remain in Norman to complete several writing projects I had promised editors I would do. However, friends at Rice University recommended me to the dean at the nearby University of Houston for a temporary professorship in American history. With some hesitation I accepted, planning to teach there for only one year but, to my surprise, the faculty urged me to return the second year, and even for a third. Thus, it was 1959 before I was able to resettle in Norman and seriously resume my writing, striving to complete several manuscripts including this *Autobiography*.

Looking Back

As I look back over three quarters of a century the thing most apparent is that I have surprisingly few regrets. Certainly my life has been much shaped by chance. The study of law, or the acceptance of a position as assistant county treasurer, would almost certainly have steered my course into far different channels than those I have followed. How far my life has been useful and productive of good results is not for me to say. That privilege belongs to the men and women who have sat in my classrooms. My own opinion is that it has been more useful and productive and more happy than it would have been if I had pursued any other calling. Perhaps after all "There is a Divinity that shapes our ends rough hew them as we may."

Every man has his pet fear. Mine has been that I might become local or provincial. With all due respect to the Rotarians and presidents of chambers of commerce, I have ever sought, and I think found, a vision wider than theirs, and have looked for far horizons beyond the ken of many, even of my closest friends. With this end in view, I have traveled in many strange places and have formed many strange friendships. My conception of history has been to see beyond the facts to causes and interpretations, to secure not only knowledge but understanding. "Wisdom is the principal thing, therefore get wisdom and with all the getting get understanding," is my favorite text. This has led me to have the comradeship of young people and of the very old. The young have their dreams, the old their memories.

All too often the middle aged have lost the one and have not yet acquired too much of the other.

I have sought to avoid too exclusive associations with my own profession and my own class. To travel round and round in a circle always meeting the same people, the same type, wears down a rut, and Elbert Hubbard has said the "only difference between a rut and a grave is the depth." To mix and mingle only with those of your own kind may be the way to material success, but it is not, I am persuaded, the way to an understanding of the world and the people who inhabit it. Rather one must go down into the slums and meet those who dwell there upon a common level; he must meet and talk with the sailors who go down to the sea in ships, and the miners who go down into the earth; he must talk to cowboys and blanket Indians, and tenant farmers, and dwellers in remote deserts and mountains. He must also know men of large affairs, captains of industry and artists and soldiers, and scholars and social leaders. Then when he has learned to see into the hearts of all these people and to understand their hopes and dreams and ambitions, perhaps then when he is old and about ready to die, he may have achieved wisdom and understanding.

Index

Hilltop School, 101
History of Oklahoma, Buchanan & Dale, 391
History of the United States, A, Dale & Dumond, 397
Hobart, 74, 87, 89, 151
Hodge, Frederick Webb, 395
Holbrook, Arizona, 322
Holton, Kansas, 295
Homestead Act, 99
Hopi Indians, 315, 318, 319, 321, 324
Hopi Reservation, 320
Hoquiam, Idaho, 311
Horse Creek, 83
Hotevilla, Arizona, 324
Houghton-Mifflin Company, 389, 390
Howe, George, 404
Howell, William Dean, 166, 230
Hudson River, 129
Hunt, G. W., 47, 50, 51
Hurley, Patrick Jay, 340, 341, 345, 377

— I —

Ignacio, Colorado, 322, 324
Illinois, 408
Illinois Central Railroad, 141, 142
Independence Hall, Philadelphia, 128
Indian Defense Association, 312, 313
Indian Survey Commission (also Meriam Commission), 289, 290, 293, 300, 303, 315, 327, 336, 342, 365, 373, 378, 387, 393
Indian Territory, 6, 30, 93, 113, 187, 348, 351
Indian-Pioneer Papers, 347
Indiana University, 189
Indians of the Southwest, Dale, 395
Institute for Government Research, 287, 295, 303, 378
Institute for the North American Indians, 296
Ione, California, 312
Isleta, New Mexico, 300, 301

— J —

James Russell Lowell House, Boston, 173
Jamestown, Virginia, 399
Janis, Elsie, 135
Janus, Stephen, 306
Jenkins, Herbert F., 179, 180, 387
Johns Hopkins Press, 387
Johnson, Robert Matteson, 186

Jones, T. E., 34, 35, 36, 43, 44, 55, 64, 354
Jones, Thomas Jesse, 303
Jones Academy, 333
Jordan, Mrs. Jeff, 342, 344
Juarez, Mexico, 297
Juniata College, Huntington, Pennsylvania, 292

— K —

Kagey, Joe, 350
Kansas, 6, 60, 123, 224, 275, 277
Kansas City, Missouri, 41, 57, 60, 61, 64, 65, 223, 224, 294; Union Depot, 224
Kansas City Southern Railroad, 219, 220
Kansas Historical Society, 217, 223
Kansas State University, 406
Keams Canyon, Arizona, 320
Keller, Helen, 230
Keller, Texas, 34
Kelly Field, Texas, 260
Kendig, Richard, 167
Kensington, 377
Kensington, Maryland, 334
Kentucky, 3, 4
Keshena Agency, 331
Key West, Florida, 142
Kingman, Arizona, 318
Kiowa Agency, 296
Kiowa County, 74, 256
Kiowa Indians, 249, 296, 315
Kiowa-Comanche-Apache Agency, 291, 297, 324, 384
Kiowa-Comanche-Apache Reservation, 15, 70, 71, 73, 128, 297, 315
Klamath Indian Reservation, 311
Kleberg, Robert, 272
Klein, Julius, 156
Kneale, J. T., 323
Knights of Pythias, 116
Knox, Grace, 259

— L —

Lacock, John Kennedy, 164, 170, 181, 188, 230, 231, 234, 235, 241, 243, 245, 246, 247, 250, 251, 252, 258, 262, 263, 265, 266
Laconia, New Hampshire, 202
Lafayette, George Washington, 388
Lafayette, Marquis de, 388
Lafayette Letters, Dale, ed., 388
LaFollette, Lt. Phillip F., 213

Morgan, Julius Spench, 133
Morrison, Dean James, 397
Morton, Richard Lee, 158, 167
Moses, Ted, 273, 274
Mount Vernon, Virginia, 128, 271-272
Mount Wilson Observatory, California, 393
Mountain Park, 89, 96, 98, 145, 222
Muleshoe Cattle Company, 15
Munsterburg, Hugo, 136
Murray, William H., 127
Murrow, J. S., 351
Muskogee, 326, 332, 333, 342, 347, 348, 349, 351
Muskrat, Ruth, 383

— N —

Nashville, Tennessee, 293
National Archives, 275-276
National Hotel, Washington, 126
Navajo Indians, 315
Navajo Reservation, 318, 322, 323
Navajoe, 11, 12, 26, 32, 34, 35, 38, 40, 42, 43, 44, 51, 58, 63, 67, 68, 69, 70, 72, 73, 76, 77, 79, 82, 87, 96, 133, 236
Navajoe Mountains, 222; photo of, 10
Nebraska, 5, 6, 7, 31, 53, 123, 125, 327, 400
Needles, California, 318
Neihardt, John G., 282
Neopit, Minnesota, 332
Neosho, Missouri, 219
Neosho Agency, 350
Nespelem, Washington, 309
Nevada, 392
New England, 123, 173, 174, 176, 218, 232, 233, 250, 251
New Hampshire, 188, 190, 192, 195, 202
New Mexico, 184, 291, 295, 370, 375, 392
New Orleans, Louisiana, 3, 4, 141, 142
New York, New York, 124, 128, 129, 141, 156, 176, 227, 228, 292, 312, 333, 407
Newcomers' Club, OU, 152, 153, 186, 257
Nonreservation Indian School, Phoenix, 299
Norfolk, Virginia, 141, 155, 156, 181
Norman, 143, 145, 154, 182, 183, 187, 212, 214, 221, 223, 224, 252, 256, 266, 267, 272, 276, 277, 279, 280, 282, 283, 284, 286, 288, 289, 296, 303, 348, 357, 362, 378, 388, 389, 401, 407, 408; Kiwanis Club, 280

North Carolina, 315
North Dakota, 315
North End House, Boston, 169
North Meredith, New Hampshire, 196
Northeastern State College, Tahlequah, 345, 349
Northern Cheyenne Indians, 327
Northwest Missouri, 5
Northwestern Normal School, 260

— O —

Ocean Grove, Maine, 188
Ohio, 125, 237, 279, 401
Ohio River, 3
Ohio State University, 292, 376, 401
Okemah, 183
Oklahoma, 58, 111, 123, 130, 133, 141, 184, 187, 188, 189, 198, 210, 211, 212, 220, 224, 232, 235, 242, 245, 246, 251, 254, 275, 276, 288, 315, 318, 324, 325, 327, 332, 333, 357, 368, 371, 399
Oklahoma A & M College, 282, 354, 361
Oklahoma Board of Education, 113
Oklahoma City, 58, 59, 60, 61, 96, 123, 143, 145, 181, 213, 217, 220, 221, 256, 266, 288, 289, 324, 333, 348, 351, 354, 371, 388; Belle Isle Lake, 123
Oklahoma Folklore Association, 383
Oklahoma Historical Society, 346, 347, 348, 351
Oklahoma National Guard, 388
Oklahoma Panhandle, 187
Oklahoma State Fair Grounds, 268
Oklahoma State University, 354, 406
Oklahoma Territorial A & M College, 45
Oklahoma Territorial Board of Education, 45, 50
Oklahoma Territorial Normal School, 45
Oklahoma Territorial University, 45
Oklahoma Territory, 31, 33, 46, 74, 93, 100, 109
Oklahoma Textbook Commission, 386, 391
Okmulgee, 332, 348
Old-School Baptist Church, 18, 25, 231, 380
Oldfather, Charles Henry, 400
Olney, Richard, 308
Olsen, Nils, 276
Olustee, 104
Omaha Indians, 400
Orcutt, William Dana, 166
Oregon, 406

418

Orth, John, 164
Osage & Kaw Agency, 324
Osage Agency, 325
Osage Indians, 325
Osterhaus, Katherine, 279; marries James Shannon Buchanan, 279
Otoe Indians, 325
Otter Creek, 78, 82, 86, 96, 98, 100, 107, 114, 222
Outline and References of Oklahoma History, Dale & Wardell, 386
Owen, Sen. Robert L., 128
Oxford University, 357
Ozark Mountains, 219

— P —

Packeneau, Joe, 330
Page, L. W., 330
Page, T. A., 330, 331
Pampa, Texas, 378, 379
Pamunkey Indians, 399
Panama, 4
Papago Reservation, 300
Pavatea, Tom, 320, 322
Pawhuska, 260, 324, 325
Pawnee, 324
Pawnee Agency, 325
Pawnee Indians, 325
Peabody Museum, Harvard, 130, 229
Peach Springs, in Arizona, 318
Peakes, John Edwin, 156, 158, 172, 176, 180, 231
Peerless Printing Company, 386
Pendleton, Oregon, 307, 308
Pendleton Woolen Mills, 307-308
Pennsylvania, 176, 234
Perin, Rev. George L., 165, 245
Phelps-Stokes Foundation, 303
Philadelphia, Pennsylvania, 124, 128
Phillips, Frank, 341, 342, 345, 346
Phillips Brooks House, Harvard, 130, 135, 137, 158, 172
Phillips Collection, 342, 344, 345, 346, 347, 352, 388, 404
Phoenix, Arizona, 299, 300
Piegan Indians, 328
Pier, Arthur Stanwood, 166
Pima Agency, 300
Pima Indian home, photo of, 304-305
Pima Indians, 318, 323
Pima Reservation, 300
Pine Ridge Reservation, 331
Pioneer Judge, Dale & Morrison, 397
Pittsburgh, Pennsylvania, 125, 258
Plymouth, Massachusetts, 138, 190, 251

Plymouth Cordage Company, 191
Pocatello, Garfield, 306, 307
Pocatello, Idaho, 306, 307
Polacca, Arizona, 322
Polk, John, 400
Polk, Sadie Dale, 400
Ponca, Otoe-Missouri, Pawnee, & Tonkawa Agency, 324
Ponca City, 357
Ponca Indians, 325
Porter, Eleanor H., 166
Portland, Oregon, 311
Portsmouth, New Hampshire, 189
Potawatomi Agency, 295
Potawatomi Indian reservation, 291, 294
Potomac River, 126
Prairie Schooner and Other Poems, The, Dale, 387
Prentice-Hall, Inc., 391
Prescott, Mildred, 171, 241, 247, 249, 251, 252, 266
Price, Utah, 327
Problem of Indian Administration, The, Meriam, etal, 386-387
Pryor, 378
Pryor, Ike, 272, 274, 275
Public Works Administration (PWA), 346
Puddingstone Club, 159, 160, 163, 164, 165, 166, 170, 171, 179, 246, 254, 387

— Q —

Quanah, Texas, 96
Quantrill, William, 5
Quapaw, Peoria, Ottawa, Shawnee, Wyandot, Seneca & Modoc Agency, 325
Quapaw Agency, 325, 350
Quincy, Massachusetts, 263

— R —

Radcliffe College, 136
Rader, Jesse Lee, 388
Rail-W Ranch, 30
Range Cattle Industry, The, Dale, 388
Ray County, Missouri, 4
Readings in Oklahoma History, Dale, ed., 391
Red River, 25; North Fork, 14, 82, 133, 222; South Fork, 11, 30
Reno, Nevada, 312
Reno-Sparks Colony, 312
Revere Beach, Boston, 173, 175
Rice Indian School, 298, 299

St. Patrick's School, 297
St. Peter, Helen, 259
Stambaugh, Robert, 292, 293, 294, 297, 298, 300, 301, 302, 306, 310, 312, 334
Stanford University, 406
Stanley, North Dakota, 330
Stevenson, Adlai, 59
Stillwater, 354, 361, 406
Stine, O. C., 269, 270, 271, 276, 277
Story of a State, The, Dale & Wardell, 395, 396
Street, Joy, 164
Stroud, 324
Student Army Training Corps (SATC), 212, 213, 215
Sulphur, 378
Superior, Wisconsin, 406
Swanson Brothers, 272
Swarthmore College, 292
Sydney, Australia, 407

— T —

Tahlequah, 326, 332, 345, 349
Tahola, Idaho, 310, 311
Tancutta, Australia, 407
Taos, New Mexico, 301
Taos Pueblo, New Mexico, 301
Tarrant County, Texas, 7, 9
Tawakoni Indians, 297
Taylor, Joe, 357
Tekoa, Idaho, 310
Texas, 6, 7, 24, 30, 31, 33, 67, 81, 93, 123, 238, 249, 273, 277, 281, 389
Texas Agricultural and Mechanical College, 279
Texas Cross Timbers, 9, 19, 21, 24, 380
Texas Panhandle, 17
Texas Rangers, 26
Texas School of Mines, El Paso, 352
The Weirs, New Hampshire, 193, 200, 205
Thomas, A. B., 338
Thompson, G. D., 100, 101
Thompson, James Westfall, 275
Thompson, Jesse, 146, 151
Ticknor, Caroline, 166
Tompkins, Stuart, 352
Topeka, Kansas, 217, 218, 223, 224, 291, 294, 295, 296
Toppenish Agency, 308
Trail Crossing, on North Fork of Red River, 17
Trail Elk Creek, 55
Tuba Agency, 318
Tuba City, Arizona, 318

Tucson, Arizona, 300
Tufts, Nate, 156, 158, 172, 176
Tulsa, 340, 357
Tulsa High School, 275
Turnbull, Charles, 315
Turner, Dorothy, 136, 173, 207, 248
Turner, Frederick Jackson, 132, 133, 138, 148, 156, 187, 188, 206, 207, 208, 209, 210, 245, 247, 248, 249, 251, 257, 259, 262, 264, 265, 269, 290, 385, 389; photo of, 131
Turner Falls, 359, 366, 375, 378
Turtle Mountain Reservation and School, 331
Twentieth Century Association, 164, 165, 166, 171, 246
Twin Mountains, 222

— U —

U.S.S. Constitution, 139
Uintah Reservation, 327
Umatilla Reservation, 307
Underwood, Richard G, 391
Union Agency, Muskogee, 324
United States Board of Indian Commissioners, 293, 306
United States Bureau of Indian Affairs, 126, 127, 275, 287, 291, 296, 299, 322, 330, 385
United States Commissioner of Indian Affairs, 126
United States Department of Agriculture, 271, 275, 277, 291; Bureau of Agricultural Economics, 276, 387; Historical and Statistical Division, 269-270, 276
United States Department of the Interior, 275, 322
United States General Land Office, 275
United States Land Office, in Mangum, 31
United States State Department, 126, 127
United States Supreme Court, 30
United States Tribal Court of Indian Offenses, 307, 323
United States v Texas, 30
United States War Department, 215
University Hall, 263
University of Arkansas, 406
University of California, Berkeley, 151, 406
University of Chicago, 133, 348
University of Cincinnati, 404

University of Houston, 408
University of Melbourne, 407
University of Michigan, 396
University of Minnesota, 396, 406
University of Missouri, 268, 385, 401, 406
University of Nebraska, 7, 53, 347, 400, 401, 406
University of New Mexico, 183, 401
University of North Dakota, 406
University of Oklahoma, 116, 117, 122, 123, 130, 132, 140, 145, 148, 149, 151, 152, 153, 158, 166, 183, 184, 187, 209, 212, 213, 215, 215, 216, 221, 231, 239, 244, 251, 260, 268, 270, 275, 281, 290, 291, 296, 338, 340, 342, 344, 346, 347, 348, 352, 354, 355, 357, 358, 359, 361, 362, 364, 366, 375, 382, 383, 393, 398, 401, 407; Bizzell Memorial Library, 345; photo of, 356; Board of Regents, 145, 268, 269, 279, 280, 352, 355; Buchanan Club of History Students, 280; Distinguished Service Citation awarded to E. E. Dale, 407; Graduate College, 280; historians, photo of, 363; History Faculty in 1959, photo of, 363; Indian Club, 296; Law Building, 184, 345; Law School, 121, 122, 184, 375; Library, 187, 351; Press, 357, 387, 389, 390, 391, 395, 403; Women's Building, 267; photo of campus in 1909, 115; photo of campus in 1924, 336-337
University of Pennsylvania, 269
University of South Dakota, 406
University of Texas, 269, 280, 281, 282, 364, 398; Library, 274, 345; Press, 9
University of Wisconsin, 188, 292, 406
Utah, 392
Ute Indians, 315
Ute Reservation, 322
Utes, 324

— V —

Van Dorn, Earl, 222
Vancouver, British Columbia, 407
Vernon, Texas, 9, 20, 23, 25, 40, 53, 54, 63, 84, 96
Vinita, 216
Virginia, 7, 93, 100, 399
Virginia Beach, Virginia, 155
Volcan Reservation, 314

— W —

Wabunaki Club, OU, 152, 186, 257, 277
Waco, Texas, 279
Walapai Indians, 318
Walker Lake, California, 313
Walpi, Arizona, 322
Walton, John C., 268
Wardell, Morris L., 260, 262, 266, 275, 277, 290, 338, 347, 348, 386, 395, 396; photo of, 261
Warren, Helen, 173, 174, 175, 182, 188
Washington, Booker T., 138
Washington, D.C., 41, 43, 44, 124, 125, 126, 127, 128, 203, 215, 270, 271, 272, 275, 280, 282, 286, 287, 288, 289, 290, 291, 293, 294, 295, 306, 327, 329, 333, 334, 376, 377, 378, 385, 387, 406
Washington University, St. Louis, 282
Washita County, 41, 46, 68, 97; Board of Education, 51
Washita River, 59, 297
Waterman, Nixon, 164, 166
Watie, 390
Watie, Gen. Stand, 342, 344
Weatherford, 297
Weaver, Claude, 126, 127, 385
Webb, Ruthie, 227
Webb, Walter Prescott, 282
Weightman, Red Buck, 29, 30
Wesley, Edgar B., 396
West Indies, 3
Western Cattle Trail, 14, 274
Westerville, Maryland, 334
Wewoka, 333
Wheelock Academy, 333
White River Utes, 328
White Swan, Oregon, 308
Wichita, Kansas, 121, 218, 223, 273, 291, 296
Wichita Indians, 297
Wichita Mountains Forest Preserve, 273
Wichita-Caddo Agency, 291, 297
Wichita-Caddo Reservation, 73, 297
Widener Memorial Library, Harvard, 130, 156, 158, 187, 242, 263
William & Mary College, 399
Williamsburg, Virginia, 399
Willoughby, W. F., 287, 290
Wilson, Woodrow, 126, 128
Wind River Reservation, 293, 315, 331
Winslow, Arizona, 319